Saigon at War

CW0081634?

During South Vietnam's brief life as a natic
democracy through citizen activism and a dynamic press. South Vietnamese activists, intellectuals, students, and professionals had multiple
visions for Vietnam's future as an independent nation. Some were anticommunists, while others supported the National Liberation Front and
Hanoi. In the midst of war, South Vietnam represented the hope and
chaos of decolonization and nation building during the Cold War. US
Embassy officers, State Department observers, and military advisers
sought to cultivate a base of support for the Saigon government among
local intellectuals and youth, but government arrests and imprisonment
of political dissidents, along with continued war, made it difficult for
some South Vietnamese activists to trust the Saigon regime. Meanwhile,
South Vietnamese diplomats, including anticommunist students and
young people who defected from North Vietnam, traveled throughout
the world in efforts to drum up international support for South Vietnam. Drawing largely on Vietnamese language sources, Heather Stur
demonstrates that the conflict in Vietnam was really three wars: the
political war in Saigon, the military war, and the war for international
public opinion.

HEATHER MARIE STUR is Professor of History at the University of
Southern Mississippi and the author of *The U.S. Military and Civil
Rights Since World War II* (2019) and *Beyond Combat: Women and
Gender in the Vietnam War Era* (2011).

Cambridge Studies in US Foreign Relations

Edited by

Paul Thomas Chamberlin, *Columbia University*
Lien-Hang T. Nguyen, *Columbia University*

This series showcases cutting-edge scholarship in US foreign relations that employs dynamic new methodological approaches and archives from the colonial era to the present. The series will be guided by the ethos of transnationalism, focusing on the history of American foreign relations in a global context rather than privileging the US as the dominant actor on the world stage.

Also in the Series

Sarah Steinbock-Pratt, *Educating the Empire: American Teachers and Contested Colonization in the Philippines*

Walter L. Hixson, *Israel's Armor: The Israel Lobby and the First Generation of the Palestine Conflict*

Aurélie Basha i Novosejt, *"I Made Mistakes": Robert McNamara's Vietnam War Policy, 1960–1968*

Greg Whitesides, *Science and American Foreign Relations since World War II*

Jasper M. Trautsch, *The Genesis of America: US Foreign Policy and the Formation of National Identity, 1793–1815*

Hideaki Kami, *Diplomacy Meets Migration: US Relations with Cuba during the Cold War*

Shaul Mitelpunkt, *Israel in the American Mind: The Cultural Politics of US-Israeli Relations, 1958–1988*

Pierre Asselin, *Vietnam's American War: A History*

Lloyd E. Ambrosius, *Woodrow Wilson and American Internationalism*

Geoffrey C. Stewart, *Vietnam's Lost Revolution: Ngô Đình Diih D Failure to Build an Independent Nation, 1955–1963*

Michael E. Neagle, *America's Forgotten Colony: Cuba's Isle of Pines*

Elisabeth Leake, *The Defiant Border: The Afghan-Pakistan Borderlands in the Era of Decolonization, 1936–1965*

Tuong Vu, *Vietnam's Communist Revolution: The Power and Limits of Ideology*

Renata Keller, *Mexico's Cold War: Cuba, the United States, and the Legacy of the Mexican Revolution*

Saigon at War

South Vietnam and the Global Sixties

HEATHER MARIE STUR

University of Southern Mississippi

CAMBRIDGE
UNIVERSITY PRESS

CAMBRIDGE
UNIVERSITY PRESS

University Printing House, Cambridge CB2 8BS, United Kingdom

One Liberty Plaza, 20th Floor, New York, NY 10006, USA

477 Williamstown Road, Port Melbourne, VIC 3207, Australia

314–321, 3rd Floor, Plot 3, Splendor Forum, Jasola District Centre,
New Delhi – 110025, India

79 Anson Road, #06–04/06, Singapore 079906

Cambridge University Press is part of the University of Cambridge.

It furthers the University's mission by disseminating knowledge in the pursuit of
education, learning, and research at the highest international levels of excellence.

www.cambridge.org
Information on this title: www.cambridge.org/9781107161924
DOI: 10.1017/9781316676752

© Heather Marie Stur 2020

First published 2020

Printed in the United Kingdom by TJ International Ltd. Padstow Cornwall

A catalogue record for this publication is available from the British Library.

Library of Congress Cataloging-in-Publication Data
NAMES: Stur, Heather Marie, 1975– author.
TITLE: Saigon at war : South Vietnam and the global sixties / Heather Marie Stur,
University of Southern Mississippi.
OTHER TITLES: South Vietnam and the global sixties
DESCRIPTION: Cambridge, United Kingdom ; New York, NY : Cambridge
University Press, 2020. | Series: Cambridge studies in us foreign relations |
Includes bibliographical references and index.
IDENTIFIERS: LCCN 2019056226 (print) | LCCN 2019056227 (ebook) | ISBN 9781107161924
(hardback) | ISBN 9781316614112 (paperback) | ISBN 9781316676752 (epub)
SUBJECTS: LCSH: Ho Chi Minh City (Vietnam)–History–20th century. | Vietnam–Politics
and government–1945-1975. | Vietnam (Republic)–Politics and government. |
Postcolonialism–Vietnam (Republic)–History–20th century.
CLASSIFICATION: LCC DS559.93.S2 S78 2020 (print) | LCC DS559.93.S2 (ebook) |
DDC 959.704/31095977–DC23
LC record available at https://lccn.loc.gov/2019056226
LC ebook record available at https://lccn.loc.gov/2019056227

ISBN 978-1-107-16192-4 Hardback
ISBN 978-1-316-61411-2 Paperback

To Hoang Cam Thanh, Le Nguyen Anh Thu,
and Nickie Tran

Contents

Figures

Acknowledgments

I got in trouble in Vietnam's National Archives II in Ho Chi Minh City while I was doing research for this book. It wasn't because I tried to obtain classified documents or expose Vietnamese wrongdoing. My research assistant, Le Nguyen Anh Thu, and I got in trouble for laughing and talking a bit too loudly one day while working through a pile of folders on our table. It was bound to happen; through our daily meetings at the archives, we had cultivated a friendship grounded in our common age and shared experiences of marriage and motherhood, and our conversations enlivened the often monotonous and lonely act of conducting archival research. But my friendships with Anh Thu and my other research assistant, Hoang Cam Thanh, were so much more than pleasant diversions from the tedium of research. Anh Thu and Thanh taught me about the Republic of Vietnam, the American war, and the consequences of US military action in Vietnam, and they brought the deep complexities of the human experience of war to bear on the documents we read and on what I thought I knew about the conflict. Much of what is good about this book is because of Le Nguyen Anh Thu and Hoang Cam Thanh and the insights – at times deeply personal and painful – they shared with me.

I am grateful for the support of the faculty, administrators, and students at the University of Southern Mississippi, my professional home since 2008. Financial assistance in the forms of the General Buford "Buff" Blount Professorship in Military History and the Aubrey Keith Lucas and Ella Ginn Lucas Endowment for Faculty Excellence Award was crucial to the research and writing of this book. I thank USM School of Humanities director Matthew Casey for his support and for our conversations about liberation theology. I am especially indebted to the Dale Center for the

Study of War & Society, starting with our primary benefactor, Dr. Beverly Dale. Dr. Dale's unwavering support of Dale Center faculty is behind the books we publish and the programming we sponsor, and I continue to be amazed by her generosity, her commitment to education, and her activist spirit. My colleagues in the Dale Center are some of the most exceptional minds in military history, and they're also some of the kindest and coolest people I've ever met. Conversations with Allison Abra about decolonization and with Susannah Ural about soldiers' families in civil wars helped me understand processes at work in Vietnam. Kyle Zelner, in his former role as History Department chair and current role as Dale Center co-director, offered key assistance in obtaining funding and buying out time to write *Saigon at War*. Andy Wiest is not only a model Vietnam War scholar but also one of my best friends. Andy, his wife, Jill, and their children made Hattiesburg feel like home from the minute I arrived here. When I started at Southern Miss as a newly minted Ph.D., Andy, who at that time was already an award-winning historian, welcomed me as a peer, and he has been one of my greatest professional advocates ever since. His work on the Army of the Republic of Vietnam (ARVN) got me thinking about the possibilities of South Vietnam's nationhood, and conversations with him in our offices and on our front porches formed the heart of *Saigon at War*.

As the ideas coalesced into a book, the inimitable Debbie Gershenowitz, my editor at Cambridge University Press, had a vision for the project even before I did. Herself a brilliant historian, Debbie understood early on that my book wasn't just about Vietnam but about international networks and political processes in the Cold War. She challenged me, through close reading of drafts and conversations over drinks and meals, to realize her vision in my pages. It was a privilege to work with Debbie, and *Saigon at War* is infinitely better because of her. At Cambridge, I also thank series editor Lien-Hang T. Nguyen, content manager Thomas Haynes, editorial assistant Rachel Blaifeder, and the anonymous readers who offered guidance and encouragement in their reports on the proposal and the manuscript.

The year I spent in Vietnam as a Fulbright scholar was critical to the development of *Saigon at War*. Thank you to my colleagues in the Faculty of International Relations at the University of Social Sciences and Humanities in Ho Chi Minh City: Dao Minh Hong, Hoang Cam Thanh, Hoang Minh Thong, Huyen Tran, Khang Tran, Nguyen Tang Nghi, Nguyen Thi To Nga, Nguyen Vinh Hang, Pham Ngoc Minh Trang, and Pham Thuy Tien. I was fortunate to study Vietnamese with the wonderful teachers and staff at Vietnamese Language Studies, and I give special thanks to Vo Thi Thanh Binh and Pham Thi Ngoc Phuc. At the US Embassy in Hanoi, I thank Do Thu Huong for her support throughout my Fulbright year.

Stumbling upon Nickie Tran's restaurant one night in Ho Chi Minh City had to have been fate. Nickie and I became fast friends, and she shared stories of her family, which was divided during the war, as well as her thoughts about Vietnam's history and future. Nickie championed this book when it was still just an idea we discussed over tea in her restaurant and over beer and banh xeo in a tucked-away spot a foreigner would never have found on her own. Nickie is courageously outspoken in a country that does not value free speech, and I admire her activism on behalf of jailed bloggers and other political dissidents who have demanded civil liberties for Vietnamese citizens. Nickie, and young people like her, embody the promise of democratic nationhood for Vietnam.

Colleagues and archivists offered assistance and advice over the years of researching and writing this book. I thank Bill Allison, Christian Appy, Pierre Asselin, Robert Brigham, Jessica Chapman, Greg Daddis, Justin Hart, Kyle Longley, Ron Milam, Edward Miller, Mike Neiberg, Merle Pribbenow, Kara Vuic, Jacqueline Whitt, and Jim Willbanks, as well as archivists at the US National Archives II, Vietnam's National Archives II, the General Sciences Library of Vietnam, and Texas Tech University's Vietnam Archive, especially Sheon Montgomery. I presented portions of *Saigon at War* at the Society for Military History and Society for Historians of American Foreign Relations annual meetings, and I am grateful for the useful feedback I received in those sessions. I also thank Bich Loan for our phone conversations and for sharing the story of the CBC Band, a band that has my vote for induction into the Rock & Roll Hall of Fame.

Academia is only one part of my life, and a fairly small one at that, and I am grateful for the friends and family who constitute the biggest parts of my life. Thank you to my dear friends: Kim and Sarah Crimmins, Lori and Kevin Gibbs, Casey and Kevin Greene, Kati and Uldis Kreslins, Shirley and Patrick McCarthy, Tara and Brian McLelland, Becky and David Rocker, Leslie and Junior Shows, Ken and Lucy Swope, and Chris and Rich Wright and their families. Thank you to my parents and in-laws: Jeff and Mickie Stur, Corinthia Van Orsdol, and Jim and Charlie Van Orsdol. Thank you to my siblings, aunts, uncles, and cousins: Rich and Tina Bronisz, Jonathan Bronisz, Tricia and Kevin Sokolowski; the Burg family; the extended Campbell family; Patti and Eddy Centkowski; the Csernak family; the Eldridge family; Hitomi Kabasawa and Ben Van

Orsdol; Chuck Kennedy and Zoe Van Orsdol; Kathy Nalewski; Tricia Purvis and Jeff Stur; Judith Ann Rutovic; and Eric and Nina Stur. Craig Werner has been a mentor and friend for fifteen years, and his voice remains in my head when I write. In teaching, writing, and how to be a good human, Craig is my model, and I'll spend my entire career hoping to make him proud.

Four people mean the most to me: Jay, Angus, Ignatius, and Stephanie Van Orsdol. Their love sustains me every day, and I am so grateful that I get to share life's journey with them. They are my family – my greatest achievement, my reason, and my reward.

Introduction

It was a tense week in Saigon in October 1974, when a South Vietnamese university student slipped into the office of the city's archbishop to deliver a letter addressed to North Vietnamese youth. Archbishop Nguyen Van Binh was headed to the Vatican for an international meeting of Catholic leaders, and he promised the student he would hand the letter off to his Hanoi counterpart when he saw him at the conference. The letter implored North Vietnamese students to join southern youth in demanding an end to the fighting that the 1973 Paris Peace Agreement was supposed to have halted. Both the archbishop and the student risked arrest for circulating the letter. Authorities had raided the offices and shut down the operations of four newspapers that had published it. That the leader of South Vietnam's Catholics would be involved in clandestine communication between North and South Vietnamese students would have been surprising in the early 1960s, but by the mid-seventies, many Vietnamese Catholics had grown weary enough of the war that they saw peace and reconciliation, even if under Hanoi's control, as the better alternative to endless violence.[1]

Within days of the Saigon newspapers publishing the letter, splashed across the front page of the *Washington Post* was an Associated Press photograph of Madame Ngo Ba Thanh, a prominent anti-government activist, leading Buddhist monks and nuns in a protest against the war

[1] Telegram from Secretary of State to All East Asian and Pacific Diplomatic Posts, Oct. 22, 1974, Record Group (RG) 59: General Records of the Department of State, National Archives and Records Administration (NARA), accessed electronically: http://aad.archives.gov/aad/createpdf?rid=227831&dt=2474&dl=1345.

and President Nguyen Van Thieu. Staff members of one of the seized newspapers believed the *Washington Post* coverage of Ngo Ba Thanh's demonstration was what had led to the government's crackdown on the Saigon press. President Thieu had not yet figured out how to balance freedom of the press with self-preservation, and international media attention to anti-government protests only made him act more authoritarian. Meanwhile, bombs set by the People's Liberation Armed Forces (PLAF), or, as the Americans called it, the Viet Cong, destroyed two spans of bridge just northeast of Saigon, cutting off traffic to a major military installation of the Republic of Vietnam Air Force (VNAF).[2] From a desk in the US Embassy in Saigon, it looked like the type of political chaos that had defined Saigon since the partition of Vietnam, if not before.[3]

Despite various government efforts including imprisonment and torture to repress political dissidents, Saigon, the capital of the Republic of Vietnam, was a politically vibrant city with dozens of newspapers and magazines that promoted political positions ranging from support for the Saigon government to neutrality to peace at any cost. The political dynamism included shifting loyalties that made it difficult to pin a particular group to a particular cause. Unexpected alliances developed, such as that between Catholic leaders and university students. Catholics had been loyal to Ngo Dinh Diem in the 1950s and early 1960s, but by the late 1960s, some Catholics had begun to turn to liberation theology, the Catholic movement throughout Latin America that emphasized social and economic justice alongside political liberation from authoritarian regimes. Vietnamese Catholics interested in this doctrine had moved to the left and joined peace movements, arguing that peace under communism would be better than continued war. University students debated which stance to take regarding the Saigon government and the escalating war in Vietnam. Older social critics worried about the impact of Western culture on Vietnamese traditional values while a younger generation embraced American fashion and music even if they opposed US intervention in Vietnam. These groups worked sometimes in tandem and sometimes alone to assert their views of how democracy should work in Vietnam, what the Republic of Vietnam's[4] (RVN) identity was, and

[2] Ibid.

[3] Telegram from US Embassy Saigon to Secretary of State, Nov. 23, 1974, RG 59: General Records of the Department of State, NARA, accessed electronically: http://aad.archives .gov/aad/createpdf?rid=256715&dt=2474&dl=1345.

[4] Since the division of Vietnam at the seventeenth parallel in 1945, Americans have commonly referred to the Republic of Vietnam as "South Vietnam" and the Democratic

how it related to broader conceptions of postcolonial Vietnamese identity. They were often at odds with the national government.

Saigon, and, by extension, the Republic of Vietnam, had a politically interested and engaged citizenry. Some citizens supported the National Liberation Front (NLF), the Communist movement in the South that Hanoi directed as part of North Vietnam's war effort. It was established in 1960, and it waged political and international relations campaigns as well as fought a military war in alliance with the North Vietnamese forces against South Vietnam and its American allies.[5] Others in the South were vehemently anticommunist. Americans frustrated South Vietnamese across the political spectrum because they seemed indecisive, skeptical of local perspectives, and oblivious to the challenges of nation building. Students, journalists, and politicians traveled the world as diplomats and cultural ambassadors, pleading South Vietnam's case to a dubious international audience. The government and the media worked to construct a national identity with specific roles for men, women, and youth. South Vietnam was born of war and died in war, but in its brief twenty years of life, it contained a chaotic political milieu that reflected what happened when citizens struggle to establish a nation in the midst of a war and under the burden of foreign intervention that was ambiguous in its purpose and goals.

While both contemporary observers and historians and journalists looking back cast South Vietnam as a client of the United States, it actually was an example of democracy lost. The diversity of voices speaking about and acting out what a free South Vietnam might be, illustrated a more complex reality than the image of an American "puppet." Yet it was the very performance of democracy that led to South Vietnam's demise. Its diversity meant that there was not a unified voice to speak for South Vietnam, and both the United States and North Vietnam felt threatened by what often looked to be, and sometimes was, political chaos in South Vietnam. When, as the war carried on without a clear endgame, South Vietnamese activists began to join forces in a strong pledge toward a united Vietnam, the various power brokers who ruled the war continued fighting.

Republic of Vietnam as "North Vietnam." US policymakers often referred to the government of South Vietnam as the "GVN." In this book, I use both the abbreviations "RVN" and "DRV," and the names "South Vietnam" and "North Vietnam." To refer generally to citizens of these states, I use "South Vietnamese" and "North Vietnamese."
[5] An important study of the NLF is Robert K. Brigham's *Guerrilla Diplomacy: The NLF's Foreign Relations and the Viet Nam War* (Ithaca, NY: Cornell University Press, 1999).

A major tension defined Saigon's political scene and South Vietnam's character more broadly. Would any head of state have been able to establish democracy when there was a movement in the country that existed for the sole purpose of destabilizing the Saigon government? The movement employed local actors for both its military and its political wars, and it cultivated sympathy, if not support, from local activists and organizations. Although the NLF was allied with the Hanoi government of North Vietnam, it looked like a southern movement, and so its leaders could claim that they were the true representatives of the southern population. The governmental dysfunction in Saigon inadvertently assisted the NLF. After the assassination of Ngo Dinh Diem in November 1963, a series of coups spun a revolving door that ejected and installed a series of leaders, none of whom were elected or endorsed by the people. From the perspective of Nguyen Van Thieu, the only elected president of South Vietnam since Ngo Dinh Diem, the tension was between cultivating democracy and self-preservation. Thieu and his predecessors were not popular, and the NLF made a compelling case about its right to represent the South. It resonated with those who opposed US intervention in Vietnam and with those who believed that South Vietnam was a puppet nation that would not exist if the elections written into the 1954 Geneva Accords to unite North and South Vietnam had been held. Under these conditions, was it possible to nation-build a democracy in South Vietnam?

Although political action took place throughout South Vietnam, Saigon, as the capital city, was the center of the national government and, therefore, the focus of democratic activism. In 1970, two years after the Tet Offensive failed to topple the Saigon government, NLF leaders decided to try instead to instigate a mass political uprising in the city. In speeches and written communications, NLF representatives asserted Saigon's significance. It was the center of South Vietnam's government, which meant that it carried both symbolic and real weight. Any uprising that occurred in Saigon would attract international attention. Overthrowing the government was the ultimate goal, and NLF leaders believed that drumming up political unrest and chaos in Saigon would precede President Nguyen Van Thieu's ouster and open the gates of the Presidential Palace to the Communists.[6] It would turn out that they would need tanks

---

[6] "VC Plan for Taking Over Saigon through a Large-Scale Mass Uprising," Captured Enemy Document, Aug. 16, 1971. Douglas Pike Collection: Unit 01 – Assessment and Strategy, Box 21, Folder 5, The Vietnam Center and Archive, Texas Tech University.

for that, but in the years between the Tet Offensive and the fall of Saigon in April 1975, the NLF's confidence in Saigon's political war as a primary component of victory illustrated the capital city's unique position in the landscape of the war. With its population concentrated into city blocks and borders, it was easier for activists to build relationships and organize protests than it was in the provinces, where the population was spread out. Villagers wanted the war to end; the political affiliation of the leaders in the capital mattered little as long as they brought peace. This meant that the urban activists held the barometer that reflected South Vietnam's political situation as a whole. It was especially true in Saigon, where the government was, where protests occurred regularly, where diplomats assessed the health of South Vietnam, and where foreign correspondents and other observers talked with each other in cafes, bars, and newsrooms about the war.

In Saigon, an anti-government student leader could hand a pamphlet to a journalist in passing on a sidewalk, and the next day, one of the city's daily newspapers would have published the details of a planned protest. Several hundred demonstrators crammed into a rally in front of the National Assembly building looked more like a mandate in a foreign correspondent's photograph than 300 protesters spread across villages far from the city. Domestic workers, waiters, tailors, pedicab drivers, and small shopkeepers made a living in Saigon serving Americans, but it was a precarious existence that left many wondering what would happen to them once the foreigners left for good. Would Thieu survive and take care of them? Would the Communists? Did giving an American diplomat a ride to the US Embassy or cleaning an independent contractor's villa once a week constitute treason according to the Communists? Did sleeping with an American? Some NLF leaders believed that these urban Vietnamese balancing their lives on the edge of poverty could be fine recruits for the political struggle in Saigon.

Saigon at War examines the complex and chaotic political scene in South Vietnam's capital city by giving voice to Vietnamese urban professionals, students, religious leaders, and diplomats. Much of the existing scholarship on the Vietnam War that looks at politics and diplomacy emphasizes the perspectives of US and North Vietnamese leaders. By focusing on characters who were not high-level decision-makers, *Saigon at War* introduces readers to an ensemble cast responsible for organizing demonstrations, giving speeches, making international connections, and publicizing reports daily about the state of South Vietnam's political development, including government efforts to stifle free speech. Government repression was more effective at bringing down South Vietnam than the NLF's agenda, and local political activists in Saigon were key players in South Vietnam's fate. Representatives of South Vietnam overseas tried to cultivate sympathy for the struggling country, but they competed with anti-government activists who also reached out internationally and shared stories of state-sanctioned political repression and violence.

Huynh Tan Mam was a former president of the Saigon Student Union who was secretly a member of the NLF. He gained international attention not because of his ties to the NLF but because Nguyen Van Thieu's government imprisoned him for speaking out against the government and the war. Ngo Ba Thanh, a lawyer educated in the United States and France, saw her father exiled to North Vietnam after the Saigon government accused him of being an enemy of the state. She developed contacts with the NLF and became an outspoken critic of the Thieu government and US intervention in Vietnam. The foreign press covered her hunger strike while in prison for her political activism. Father Chan Tin and Father Tran Huu Thanh represented the spectrum of Catholic attitudes toward the Vietnam War, US intervention, and the future of Vietnam. Father Tin was closely associated with Huynh Tan Mam and Ngo Ba Thanh, while Father Thanh's anti-corruption movement had the support of young, anticommunist Catholics. Nguyen Huu Thai, another student leader, had contacts in the US Embassy and in the United States, but he, too, like Mam, was a member of the NLF. Vu Van Thai, a consummate diplomat, wrote for *Foreign Affairs* magazine and the RAND Corporation after serving as South Vietnam's ambassador to the United States. He was also a friend of Daniel Ellsberg's, and he was briefly named a co-conspirator in the Pentagon papers case. For all the emphasis Americans placed on winning the hearts and minds of the rural masses, the voices and actions of urban activists garnered the local and international attention that made the difference in the war's outcome.

The relationships between South Vietnam's leaders – presidents and prime ministers – and US advisors are important for understanding the high-level decision-making that shaped the international relations between the United States and South Vietnam. But looking at top-level conversations and policymaking alone does not explain why US nation-building efforts in South Vietnam failed. Studies that position the NLF as the primary voice of South Vietnam beyond the Saigon regimes also do not explain the failure of the southern state.[7] The political activism, the press diversity, and the variety of attitudes about Vietnam's future made for a chaotic yet proto-democratic national culture that the government did not know how to manage. The suppression of dissenting voices and the imprisonment of opposition leaders only enforced the image of the Saigon government as authoritarian and illegitimate that many in the West held. Unable to connect with citizens who operated in a long tradition of Vietnamese political activism dating back to the late nineteenth century, South Vietnam's leaders and their national police forces stifled the development of modern political processes. It was in that context that the NLF could claim moral authority to an international audience.

Anticommunist and communist movements in Vietnam both armed their representatives with the language of freedom and independence and sent them out into the world to connect with global activists, diplomats, and political leaders on the right and on the left. Meanwhile, the governments in Hanoi and Saigon deployed authoritarian tactics to suppress dissent, undermining the ideologies that informed their envoys' rhetoric. The image of the NLF as an indigenous southern movement gave the impression that communism was the will of the people even though the central actors in communist and noncommunist movements were elites. Photographs and newsreel footage of young NLF cadres resonated with the antiestablishment youth culture of the US antiwar movement even though the decision-makers in Hanoi as well as in Saigon were of an older generation. Even though pro-South Vietnam youth connected with conservative student groups such as Young Americans for Freedom, Saigon authorities and their US advisors were never as good at speaking to global youth culture as Hanoi and the NLF were.

Drawing on Vietnamese and US sources, *Saigon at War* examines the interplay between Saigon politics, the war in Vietnam, and international attitudes toward South Vietnam from the assassination of President Ngo Dinh Diem in 1963 through the fall of Saigon in 1975. In the February 21, 1965 edition of the *Malayan Times*, a reporter wrote of South Vietnam:

---

[7] Important works on the National Liberation Front include: Brigham, *Guerrilla Diplomacy*; David Hunt, *Vietnam's Southern Revolution: From Peasant Insurrection to Total War* (Amherst: University of Massachusetts Press, 2008); Sophie Quinn-Judge, *The Third Force in the Vietnam War: The Elusive Search for Peace, 1954–1975* (London: I. B. Taurus, 2017).

"The Americans have more than a tiger by the tail. This tiger has two
tails: the war against Communist Viet Cong and the unending political
war inside South Vietnam itself." The metaphorical tiger actually had a
third tail: international public opinion. Foreign observers paid close
attention to and interacted with Vietnamese who supported the Saigon
government as well as those activists who used the capital city as a
platform from which to critique and call for the removal of various heads
of state. When the whole world was watching, thanks to foreign correspondents and international networks, it did not help the Saigon government's reputation when newspapers published photographs of angry
citizens marching in protest of the imprisonment of student activists or
when former political prisoners testified to an anti-government priest
about how security officers tortured them. The bones of a democratic
structure were there – elections for representatives to the National
Assembly, presidential elections, an active press in Saigon, street demonstrations that occurred with little violence. Yet it was difficult for Vietnamese or observers around the globe to make sense of the democratic
skeleton covered in authoritarian skin.

There were so many divisions in Saigon and in South Vietnam after
the assassination of Diem. Generals controlled the government, which
frustrated civilian activists who wanted representative democracy. The
generals fought for power, and commanders of the various regions of
South Vietnam disagreed about all manner of issues, from who should
lead the government to how much if any negotiation with the NLF they
should consider. The splintered character of South Vietnam frustrated
American advisers and international observers, as though a seamless
transition from colony to independent liberal democracy were possible.
Vietnamese nationalists had begun demanding independence at the turn
of the twentieth century, and under the leadership of Ho Chi Minh, one
faction of activists claimed Vietnam's independence after World War II.
French leaders wanted their colonies in Indochina, though, and, with
US support, France spent nearly a decade fighting a Vietnamese independence movement to regain control. When the delegates at Geneva
divided Vietnam in two, they planted the seed that became the Republic
of Vietnam, a nation born out of postcolonial chaos and war. Establishing stability, including a viable economy and democratic political
institutions, would require time and a careful give-and-take between
Saigon leaders and US advisers. Yet Americans expected to quickly
identify a local leader who fit both American and Vietnamese desires
to implement liberal democracy without a hitch. When it was not

perfect from the start, Americans gave the green light to the coup that killed Diem.[8]

Americans remained impatient after the assassination of Diem, which played well into the revolving door of leaders, military council members, and coups that defined Saigon's political scene in the eighteen months following Diem's death. As General Lam Quang Thi, future head of the Vietnamese National Military Academy in Da Lat, saw it, coups were not uncommon in developing countries as political leaders vied for power. Thi looked to Egypt, where Gamal Abdel Nasser had brought some stability and reform, as a potential model for South Vietnam. Thi had hoped that Khanh would "become the Nasser of Viet Nam and would be able to rally the army to defeat the Communist insurgency."[9] Other South Vietnamese authorities argued that because of factionalism, only a military government had the strength to withstand NLF and North Vietnamese attempts to destroy it. Vietnamese citizens and US advisers had to understand this fact and have faith that eventually South Vietnam would make the transition from military to representative government, officials asserted.[10]

Historian William Duiker has argued that both Western and Asian proponents of democracy were overly optimistic about the ability of local leaders to quickly implement a liberal democratic model of government.[11] Throughout Southeast Asia, newly independent nations experimented with democracy in the years after World War II, but many of those efforts died by the sword of military coups or other authoritarian movements.[12] One of the challenges in South Vietnam was that the noncommunist opposition was disorganized and grounded in factionalism and regional and religious interests that made it difficult to unite a plurality behind a common goal. In North Vietnam, by contrast, the imposition of a

---

[8] The best account of Ngo Dinh Diem's attempts to build a stable South Vietnam, and his contentious relationship with the United States is Edward Miller's *Misalliance: Ngo Dinh Diem, the United States, and the Fate of South Vietnam* (Cambridge, MA: Harvard University Press, 2013).

[9] Lam Quang Thi, *The Twenty-Five Year Century: A South Vietnamese General Remembers the Indochina War to the Fall of Saigon* (Denton, TX: University of North Texas Press, 2001), p. 113.

[10] Viet Nam Cong Hoa Bo Noi Vu Nha Tong Giam Doc Canh Sat Quoc Gia Khoi Canh Sat Dac Biet So Ke Hoach. So 05235, 19–2–1965. Ho so so 15333: Ve tinh hinh an ninh tai Sai Gon Gia Dinh nam 1965.

[11] William J. Duiker, *Vietnam: Revolution in Transition* (Boulder, CO: Westview Press, 1995), p. 80.

[12] Ibid., p. 80.

communist government neutralized the dissent heard in anti-government newspapers, public protests, and opposition assemblymen's speeches. Duiker and others have contended that one of the problems inherent in Saigon politics from Diem to Thieu was that administrations all represented the elites – urban professionals, middle-class merchants, and wealthy landowners – rather than the majority of the population.[13] Yet it was the elites who also led anti-government protests, connected with the NLF, and built international networks in opposition to the government. Much of the rural population, as historian Fredrik Logevall has noted, would have been happy with whatever government put an end to the war.[14]

The chapters in *Saigon at War* explore the attitudes and efforts of groups and individuals who were active in Saigon's political scene in the sixties and seventies. Those with international connections extended the reach of the political action that originated in South Vietnam's capital city to other parts of the world. Given the global attention zeroed in on the Vietnam War, Saigon offered an example of the potential and limits of nation building in the era of decolonization. Chapter 1 sets the scene in Saigon, illustrating how the war played out through urban terrorism as a response to the increasing United States presence in the city and highlighting the political chaos that ensued after the assassination of Ngo Dinh Diem. There is a popular image of youth protest in the sixties, but, as Chapter 2 demonstrates, older activists, some of whom had worked in peace movements in the Diem era, led various anti-government efforts and represented a long tradition of political engagement reaching back to the colonial era. Some were founders and members of the NLF, while others sympathized with the group, seeing it as the best chance for Vietnamese nationalists to decide their future in the face of foreign intervention. In Chapter 3, students who organized to demand a civilian government and democratic freedoms are the central characters. Disagreements over the war limited efforts at student unity, and by the end of the sixties, students increasingly made connections with the NLF and groups demanding peace and reconciliation. All the while, as described in Chapter 4, South Vietnam's government attempted to build a connection between Saigon and the countryside through the state media and cultural programs. Citizens, in turn, looked to their government for assistance, especially for the families of South Vietnam's soldiers and veterans.

[13] Ibid., pp. 95–97.
[14] Fredrik Logevall, *Choosing War: The Lost Chance for Peace and the Escalation of the War in Vietnam* (Berkeley: University of California Press, 2001), p. 89.

Political activism, efforts to establish an independent government, war, and intervention by foreign powers made Vietnam a Cold War hot spot, and Chapter 5 shows how other countries responded to the conflict. Representatives of the Saigon government, as well as activists who opposed the Saigon regime, reached out to international audiences to plead their respective cases about the situation in South Vietnam. After the Tet Offensive failed to ignite a mass uprising in Saigon to dismantle South Vietnam's government, NLF leaders began to implement plans to prioritize the political war in the capital city, which Chapter 6 explores. NLF members asserted in speeches and conversations that their revolution would only work if Saigon was in. President Nguyen Van Thieu tightened his control on the population and allowed less room for political freedom in the years after Tet, but, as Chapter 7 illustrates, Catholics such as Father Chan Tin published testimonies of former political prisoners and met with American politicians who had traveled to South Vietnam to learn more about alleged political prisoners. Conventional wisdom holds that Vietnamese Catholics were vehemently anticommunist, but a closer look reveals that Catholics, like students, sought peace and reconciliation as the sixties drew to a close. In Chapter 8, a new decade brought continued violence as the United States withdrew from South Vietnam, and anti-government self-determination activists, many of whom were members or supporters of the NLF, continued to fight the political war in Saigon, a war that was always linked to what was going on in the provinces.

The tiger's three tails, the war against the NLF, the war within South Vietnam, and the war for public opinion, were entangled in a global war of ideas over which side rightfully represented the future of South Vietnam. Liberals and conservatives throughout the world closely monitored developments in South Vietnam, and Vietnamese political activists, writers, and students worked international connections and foreign media to plead their cases. The rhetorical conflict pitted pro-government South Vietnamese students against antiwar American students; the Asian People's Anti-Communist League against the National Liberation Front; and Ngo Ba Thanh, a French- and American-educated lawyer and self-determination activist, against South Vietnam's President Nguyen Van Thieu. Antiwar Vietnamese Catholics used Latin American liberation theology to explain how they reconciled Catholicism and socialism. Three North Vietnamese students defected through West Germany and embarked on a global speaking tour denouncing Communism. Cadets at South Vietnam's military academies described the honor they felt in training to defend their country. The chaos of so many groups with different ideas and strategies prevented the development of a unified political message among those who supported the Saigon government, or a noncommunist regime in the capital. The lack of cohesion left American military and State Department advisers wary of taking a risk on leaving the Vietnamese to settle their own affairs. By contrast, North Vietnam, because of its lack of political freedom, and thereby a lack of diverse political opinions, was able to present to the world a consistent message about its identity.

Until recently, few historians and writers took South Vietnam seriously. According to the conventional wisdom, South Vietnam was a puppet, a client of the United States, an illegitimate creation.[15] The Vietnam War historiography is highly politicized, which partly explains this pattern. The telling of the conflict's history has been a zero-sum game in which the Vietnam War was a case study amplifying a broader critique of US foreign policy and intervention in the world. This orthodox view of the war emphasizes the actions of American policymakers, military authorities, and troops. Vietnamese actors appear fairly one-dimensional, as corrupt puppets controlled by the US State Department, romanticized revolutionaries, or a faceless mass of peasants caught in the cross fire. The orthodoxy pays little attention to Vietnamese agency, strategy, or worldview, and it does not account for the diversity of opinions in North Vietnam and South Vietnam about what an independent Vietnam should look like.

As Mark Atwood Lawrence has explained, after the partition of Vietnam, many educated professionals, business people, and Catholics from the North fled to South Vietnam out of fear of communism. The DRV lost a million people – most of its middle class – to the southern exodus, and the loss of a skilled citizenry hurt North Vietnam's economy. Educated professionals had clear reasons to leave: Hanoi officials cracked down on dissidents, the press, and intellectuals, and they meted out punishments that included the executions of suspected enemies of the communist government.[16] All the while, Americans saw themselves

---

[15] The "orthodox" school of Vietnam War historiography includes: Marilyn Young, *The Vietnam Wars, 1945–1990* (New York: HarperCollins, 1991); Gabriel Kolko, *Anatomy of a War: Vietnam, the United States, and the Modern Historical Experience* (New York: The New Press, 1994); Guenter Lewy, *America in Vietnam* (New York: Oxford University Press, 1978); Mark Philip Bradley, *Vietnam at War* (New York: Oxford University Press, 2009).

[16] Mark Atwood Lawrence, *The Vietnam War: A Concise International History* (New York: Oxford University Press, 2010), pp. 54–55.

"uniquely qualified" to build "a new anticommunist political order that would command genuine support among the Vietnamese people" in South Vietnam.[17] It would require venturing into the chaotic "wild south" and attempting to help establish a sense of nationalism that would unify the diversity of religions and political perspectives.[18]

Any such effort would be futile, Lawrence argues, because the Hanoi government and the National Liberation Front were the descendants of a nationalist tradition that had existed for much of the twentieth century. This gave North Vietnam and the NLF "a degree of legitimacy enjoyed by no other contender for power in the South."[19] Le Duan, general secretary of North Vietnam's ruling Communist Party, and his like-minded associates believed that they had the moral authority in the Vietnamese conflict, Pierre Asselin notes, and that inspired them to go to war for control of the South. They believed that "history was on their side," and that they would win even if victory only came after a lengthy war.[20] In an era of decolonization, young NLF cadres were more alluring, and were armed with more inspiring rhetoric, than the supporters of a US-backed government, especially for Western intellectuals who saw US intervention in Vietnam as another form of imperialism.

Yet Nu-Anh Tran has asserted that Vietnam was actually a case of "contested nationalism," where Vietnamese above and below the seventeenth parallel battled for the right to claim themselves as the true heirs of Vietnamese nationalism. South Vietnam's brief history from the fifties to the seventies is a story about two groups of Vietnamese, communist and noncommunist, with different ideas about Vietnam's postcolonial future. Their international allies – the United States, China, and the Soviet Union, as well as regional and global opinion, shaped South Vietnam's history, too. Noncommunist governments in Southeast Asia looked to South Vietnam as an example of the region's future political development. International observers, including Americans, assumed that when nation building did not happen quickly, South Vietnam was not and could not be a viable nation.

---

[17] Ibid., p. 53.

[18] On the concept of the "wild south," see Jessica Chapman, *Cauldron of Resistance: Ngo Dinh Diem, the United States, and 1950s Southern Vietnam* (Ithaca, NY: Cornell University Press, 2013).

[19] Lawrence, *The Vietnam War*, p. 109.

[20] Pierre Asselin, *Hanoi's Road to the Vietnam War, 1954–1965* (Berkeley: University of California Press, 2015), p. 268. See also, Asselin, *Vietnam's American War: A History* (New York: Cambridge University Press, 2018).

For much of the past forty years, Americans have written about the war as an American experience. In some cases, the writings were partici- pants' accounts – US military officers, enlisted personnel, diplomats, antiwar activists, and politicians all have written about the war from their perspectives. Because the Vietnam War coincided with major social and cultural transformations on the American home front, some histor- ians have assessed the conflict in the context of US domestic issues, connecting it to the civil rights movement, the counterculture, and the women's movement. Other historians have used the Vietnam War as a case study through which to critique American foreign policy during the Cold War.[21]

All of these ways of thinking about the Vietnam War are valid and important. But they all leave out the perspectives of a major segment of people who participated in the conflict and experienced its consequences – the Vietnamese. Until the past decade or so, Vietnamese voices have largely been absent from the Vietnam War narratives that US historians have written. This is due in part to a lack of Vietnamese language skills and the potential difficulties in accessing Vietnamese archival documents. But it is also because incorporating Vietnamese perspectives, especially those from South Vietnam, can complicate the conventional wisdom about the war. Historians and others have told it as a story of American

---

[21] This is just sample of the voluminous scholarship on the Vietnam War: Marilyn Young, *The Vietnam Wars* (New York: Harper Perennial, 1991); Stanley Karnow, *Vietnam: A History* (New York: Penguin Books, 1997); Francis Fitzgerald, *Fire in the Lake: The Vietnamese and the Americans in Vietnam* (Boston: Back Bay Books, 2002); David Halberstam, *The Best and the Brightest* (New York: Ballantine Books, 1993); Neil Sheehan, *A Bright Shining Lie: John Paul Vann and America in Vietnam* (New York: Vintage, 1989); Fredrik Logevall, *Choosing War: The Lost Chance for Peace and the Escalation of the War in Vietnam* (Berkeley: University of California Press, 2001); George C. Herring, *America's Longest War: The United States and Vietnam, 1950–1975* (New York: McGraw-Hill, 2001); H. R. McMaster, *Dereliction of Duty: Johnson, McNamara, the Joint Chiefs of Staff, and the Lies That Led to Vietnam* (New York: Harper Perennial, 1998); Daniel S. Lucks, *Selma to Saigon: The Civil Rights Movement and the Vietnam War* (Lexington: University Press of Kentucky, 2016); Christian Appy, *American Reckoning: The Vietnam War and Our National Identity* (New York: Penguin Books, 2016); David Kaiser, *American Tragedy: Kennedy, Johnson, and the Origins of the Vietnam War* (Cambridge, MA: Belknap Press, 2002); David Maraniss, *They Marched into Sunlight: War and Peace, Vietnam and America, October 1967* (New York: Simon & Schuster, 2004); Michael Hunt, *Lyndon Johnson's War: America's Cold War Crusade in Vietnam, 1945–1968* (New York: Hill and Wang, 1997); Charles DeBenedetti, *An Ameri- can Ordeal: The Antiwar Movement of the Vietnam Era* (Syracuse, NY: Syracuse Univer- sity Press, 1990); Gabriel Kolko, *Anatomy of a War: Vietnam, the United States, and the Modern Historical Experience* (New York: Pantheon Books, 1986).

imperialists against Vietnamese nationalists without taking into consideration the political divisions among South Vietnamese activists, journalists, politicians, diplomats, students, and religious leaders. Some historians have questioned the legitimacy of South Vietnam as a nation. By taking a closer look at South Vietnamese perspectives, and by placing South Vietnam in regional and international contexts, we can see a picture of the Vietnam War that is less clear but more complete. This is not to justify the US military intervention in Vietnam, but rather to bring Vietnamese and regional Southeast Asian perspectives more fully into the story.

Scholars who have focused specifically on South Vietnam, including Pierre Asselin, Jessica Chapman, Peter Hansen, Van Nguyen-Marshall, Matthew Masur, Edward Miller, Nathalie Huynh Chau Nguyen, Geoffrey Stewart, Nu-Anh Tran, and Andrew Wiest, have challenged the conventional wisdom that casts South Vietnam as a pawn rather than an actor.[22] Especially crucial is scholars' use of Vietnamese sources to move us toward a reckoning of the complexity of Vietnamese attitudes about their country's future. Making the Vietnam War narrative a Vietnamese story as well as an American story offers a more nuanced look at the politics involved, the impact of international opinion on how the conflict played out, and the nature of the violence perpetrated against Vietnamese civilians. The question of who had the right to determine

[22] Important scholarly works on the war from multiple Vietnamese perspectives, including South Vietnamese, are: Asselin, *Vietnam's American War*; Chapman, *Cauldron of Resistance*; Peter Hansen, "Bac Di Cu: Catholic Refugees from the North of Vietnam, and Their Role in the Southern Republic, 1954–1959," *Journal of Vietnamese Studies*, Vol. 4, No. 3 (Fall 2009) 173–211; Van Nguyen-Marshall, "Student Activism in Time of War Youth in the Republic of Vietnam, 1960s–1970s," *Journal of Vietnamese Studies*, Vol. 10, No. 2 (Spring 2015) 43–81; Van Nguyen-Marshall, Lisa B. Welch Drummond, and Danièle Bélanger eds., *The Reinvention of Distinction: Modernity and the Middle Class in Urban Vietnam* (Singapore: Springer, 2012); Van Nguyen-Marshall, "Tools of Empire? Vietnamese Catholics in South Vietnam," *The Journal of the Canadian Historical Association*, Vol. 20, No. 2 (2009) 138–159; Miller, *Misalliance*; Nathalie Huynh Chau Nguyen, *South Vietnamese Soldiers: Memories of the Vietnam War and After* (Santa Barbara, CA: Praeger, 2016); Nu-Anh Tran, "Contested Nationalism: Ethnic Identity and State Power in the Republic of Vietnam, 1954–1963," ISSI Fellows Working Papers, Institute for the Study of Societal Issues, UC Berkeley, Jan. 30, 2012, "South Vietnamese Identity, American Intervention and the Newspaper *Chính Luận* [Political Discussion], 1965–1969." *Journal of Vietnamese Studies*, Vol. 1, No. 1–2 (Feb./Aug. 2006) 169–209, "Contested Identities: Nationalism in the Republic of Vietnam, 1954–1963," Ph.D. diss., University of California, Berkeley, 2013; Geoffrey C. Stewart, *Vietnam's Lost Revolution: Ngo Dinh Diem's Failure to Build an Independent Nation, 1955–1963*, (New York: Cambridge University Press, 2016); Andrew Wiest, *Vietnam's Forgotten Army: Heroism and Betrayal in the ARVN* (New York: New York University Press, 2007).

Vietnam's future was a fundamental part of the broader conflict that involved the governments in Saigon and Hanoi, the NLF, and Vietnamese and foreign citizens across the political spectrum. South Vietnam's neighbors and regional allies monitored the Vietnam War, seeing it as a Southeast Asian issue, not just a Vietnam issue. Southeast Asia was a key example of postcolonial political movements to establish the identities of newly independent nations where communist and noncommunist movements clashed. Leaders and observers throughout Southeast Asia monitored the situation in South Vietnam as an example of how such conflicts might play out.[23] The Vietnam War is a story of decolonization and nation building, a case study exemplifying what was happening all throughout the global South after 1945.

Saigon at War begins after the collapse of the Ngo Dinh Diem regime, picking up where much of the recent scholarship on South Vietnam leaves off. It focuses on the people, issues, and events involved in trying to build a stable national government, including efforts to establish noncommunist government in South Vietnam, efforts to reconcile the conflict between North and South, and opposition to US intervention in Vietnam's affairs. South Vietnam had a working democracy that failed because of political repression at the hands of South Vietnamese government regimes, not because of National Liberation Front actions or a widespread commitment to communism among the RVN population. As a nation that developed under the guidance of the United States, which was committed to democracy building in theory though not in practice, the RVN offered its citizens a taste of liberty only to snatch it away from them via various crackdowns. Saigon's vibrant political scene was exactly what the United States should have wanted if policymakers were serious about building a free nation, but American officials chose to support individual leaders rather than urban activists. Although political action, from voting to protesting, occurred throughout South Vietnam, Saigon, as the capital and largest city, offered a concentrated view of the actors and issues that at times motivated citizens outside the urban centers to make demands of their government and attract global attention. As the seat of the national government, Saigon was the focus of both local and international attention from those interested in Vietnam's political future.

Vietnamese politics featured a nationalist tradition that dated back to the French colonial era. Central to Vietnamese nationalism was the

---

[23] "Decisive Year," *The Straits Times*, Jan. 1, 1965; "Saigon Waits," *The Straits Times*, Jan. 12, 1965.

rejection of foreign intervention in Vietnam's affairs, not a commitment to a particular ideology. Untethered to a political persuasion, Vietnamese nationalism was open to interpretation and molding by groups and individuals who had various and conflicting visions for Vietnam's future. After World War II, as France attempted to reassert control of Indochina, some Vietnamese nationalists who felt trapped between colonialism and communism conceived of the concept of a "third force," an independent political movement that was anticolonial and anticommunist. Prominent among third force proponents in the late 1940s and early 1950s was Ngo Dinh Diem, future president of the Republic of Vietnam. Diem worked across religious and ideological lines to build a coalition of anticommunist nationalists as France waged war against the Viet Minh.[24] His efforts even involved courting the deposed emperor Bao Dai, who some nationalists hoped would serve as a symbol of a noncommunist Vietnamese political tradition. When Bao Dai agreed in 1948 to a French plan to install him as leader of a semi-autonomous "associated state" within the French empire, Diem announced that he would lead a new movement including those who fought against France. By rejecting both Bao Dai's capitulation to colonialism and the Viet Minh's communism, Diem hoped that other nationalists and the general public would accept his vision for an independent Vietnam. However, his attempt to position himself as the leader of a third force that was neither beholden to a colonizer nor communist raised the suspicions of the French and the Viet Minh. Both groups increasingly considered Diem to be untrustworthy and an adversary.[25]

After the First Indochina War ended in 1954 and Vietnam was partitioned at the 17th parallel, Diem focused his attention on consolidating power in the South. He faced a diverse, chaotic political milieu in which politico-religious groups Cao Dai, Hoa Hao, and Binh Xuyen, as well as other nationalists, competed to exert their vision for an independent Vietnam.[26] Once Diem took the presidency of the RVN in 1955, his primary political challenge, historian Jessica Chapman argues, was not communism but rather the politico-religious groups that had gained popularity throughout southern Vietnam.[27] Challenges from these

[24] Miller, *Misalliance*, pp. 32–33. On Diem's attempts to build a viable third force, see also Matthew Masur, "Exhibiting Signs of Resistance: South Vietnam's Struggle for Legitimacy, 1954–1960," *Diplomatic History*, Vol. 33, No. 2 (April 2009) 293–313.

[25] Miller, *Misalliance*, pp. 35–36.   [26] Chapman, *Cauldron of Resistance*, p. 5.

[27] Ibid., p. 6.

organizations were Diem's primary justification for his establishment of authoritarian rule. Chapman argues that US officials accepted Diem's actions without scrutinizing his motives and understanding that Diem's repressive policies were doing more to hurt democracy-building efforts than help them, pushing noncommunist nationalists into the communist camp. Opposition to Diem's authoritarianism provided North Vietnam the impetus to create the National Liberation Front, its representative in the South.[28] "[B]y combining moral and nationalistic appeals ... with a program of brutality and repression directed at those who dared to oppose them," Chapman contends, the Ngo brothers "served to inspire ever greater resentment and hostility toward their administration."[29] As historian Edward Miller notes, attempts to build a third force always "foundered on the ideological and political fissures which divided Vietnam's myriad noncommunist parties, sects, and factions."[30]

In the years after Diem was assassinated to the fall of Saigon in 1975, the National Liberation Front used the idea of a third force as it established political groups that were to appear independent. Organizations such as the Movement for Self-Determination and the Alliance of National, Democratic, and Peace Forces attempted to consolidate anti-government movements and activists and assert that opposition to the Saigon government and US intervention was not necessarily communist. For some members of the NLF who were not members of Hanoi's communist party, these "third force" groups offered a means through which southern nationalists could have a voice in the Hanoi-dominated NLF.[31] Absent Party membership, leaders and representatives of self-determination and peace groups could deny communist affiliation in the face of accusations by Saigon authorities and US Embassy officers. By the end of the sixties, international journalists used the label "third force" to describe anti-Thieu and pro-national reconciliation movements. Thieu, in turn, labeled all third force groups and individuals communists and instructed his administration and supporters to quell third force activism.[32] The concept of a third force remained part

---

[28] Ibid., pp. 7–8.   [29] Ibid., p. 8.

[30] Edward Miller, "Vision, Power, and Agency: The Ascent of Ngo Dinh Diem, 1945–1954," *Making Sense of the Vietnam Wars: Local, National, and Transnational Perspectives*, Mark Philip Bradley and Marilyn B. Young, eds. (New York: Oxford University Press, 2008)137.

[31] Truong Nhu Tang, *A Viet Cong Memoir: An Inside Account of the Vietnam War and Its Aftermath* (New York: Vintage Books, 1986), p. 131.

[32] Spencer C. Tucker ed. *The Encyclopedia of the Vietnam War: A Political, Social, and Military History* (ABC-CLIO, 2011), p. 877; see also Ngo Vinh Long, "Legacies Foretold:

of the political milieu and was codified in the Paris Peace Accords of 1973, which called for a neutral "third force" to assist the RVN government and the communist Provisional Revolutionary Government in holding elections to determine a new government in South Vietnam as a step toward reunification of the two Vietnams.[33]

US Embassy officers spent much of their time in South Vietnam seeking individuals and groups in Saigon they could cultivate into bases of government support. It was a difficult task because the NLF was a chameleon that blended into the city's political landscape. Given the widespread desire for freedom and independence, the US presence was an irreconcilable contradiction, and no promise of eventual withdrawal once Saigon featured a stable national government could convince the most committed of the self-determination advocates that foreign intervention was useful. After Nguyen Van Thieu took control of South Vietnam in 1965 as part of a military junta, and was then elected president in 1967, the image of a developing democracy lost its vibrancy in the shadow of the arrests and imprisonment of political opponents. Thieu was paranoid about his power because the NLF existed to destroy it. His authoritarian responses gave his opponents evidence for their assertions that he was a dictator.

Historians, journalists, and other writers have spilled much ink on the Vietnam War in the past forty years, but South Vietnamese voices outside of the National Liberation Front or Viet Cong remain largely absent from the narratives. What we have from South Vietnamese perspectives comes mainly from the memoirs of RVN government and military leaders.[34] Within the past decade, historians interested in America's relationship with the RVN have begun writing books grounded in South Vietnamese sources, giving voice to perspectives that had been missing from the voluminous scholarship on the Vietnam War. Robert K. Brigham and Andrew Wiest wrote two of the first works that examined the Army of the Republic of Vietnam (ARVN), giving readers glimpses into a military that

Excavating the Roots of Postwar Viet Nam," *Four Decades On: Vietnam, the United States, and the Legacies of the Second Indochina War*, Scott Laderman and Edwin A. Martini, eds. (Durham, NC: Duke University Press, 2013) 19.

[33] Long, *Four Decades On*, pp. 19–20.

[34] Lien-Hang T. Nguyen, "Cold War Contradictions: Toward an International History of the Second Indochina War, 1969–1973, *Making Sense of the Vietnam Wars: Local, National, and Transnational Perspectives*, Mark Philip Bradley and Marilyn B. Young, eds. (New York: Oxford University Press, 2008) 225.

previous scholars, including military historians, had ignored or dismissed.[35] *Saigon at War* builds upon the recent work of Edward Miller and Jessica Chapman, as well as earlier work by Philip Catton, who have written important studies about Ngo Dinh Diem's presidency and the Saigon political world in the 1950s and early 1960s.[36] This book picks up where Miller, Chapman, and Catton leave off, starting in the political chaos of the early post-Diem period and continuing through the fall of Saigon.

It also draws on the work of historian Nu-Anh Tran, who discusses the concept of "contested nationalism" in her analysis of the RVN's national identity. Examining the period from 1954 to 1963, Tran challenges the notion that the DRV had a lock on "authentic" Vietnamese nationalism and that noncommunist nationalism in the South was "weak or inauthentic." In a partitioned state like Vietnam, where a common ethnicity was linked with state power, nationalism was contested as both the DRV and the RVN sought to claim an overarching Vietnamese nationalism.[37] Robert Topmiller emphasizes the role of Buddhists in the third force, but his argument ignores the diversity of the third force and, by extension, the diversity of Vietnamese nationalism. Buddhists, as Topmiller notes, claimed that they represented Vietnamese tradition in opposition to a US-backed Saigon government, but other elements within the third force also demonstrated nationalism and asserted ownership of Vietnamese history and political culture.[38]

Neil Jamieson's pioneering study of South Vietnam, based on his experiences in Saigon and its environs during the war as a USAID worker established the foundation for this book.[39] *Saigon at War* also takes cues from the work of Pierre Asselin and Lien-Hang Nguyen, who have emphasized the agency of Vietnamese actors in shaping the course of the Vietnam War and have pushed the narrative into the early 1970s

---

[35] Robert K. Brigham, *ARVN: Life and Death in the South Vietnamese Army* (Lawrence: University Press of Kansas, 2006); Wiest, *Vietnam's Forgotten Army*.

[36] Chapman, *Cauldron of Resistance*; Miller, *Misalliance*; Philip Catton, *Diem's Final Failure: Prelude to America's War in Vietnam* (Lawrence: University Press of Kansas, 2003).

[37] Nu-Anh Tran, "Contested Nationalism: Ethnic Identity and State Power in the Republic of Vietnam, 1954–1963," ISSI Working Papers, Institute for the Study of Societal Issues, UC Berkeley, Jan. 3, 2012, www.escholarship.org/uc/item/1kb7z2vh.

[38] Robert J. Topmiller, *The Lotus Unleashed: The Buddhist Peace Movement in South Vietnam, 1964–1966* (Lexington: University Press of Kentucky, 2002), p. viii.

[39] Neil Jamieson, *Understanding Vietnam* (Berkeley: University of California Press, 1995).

through the making of the Paris Peace Accords.[40] The book also builds upon the work of scholars of Vietnamese history, including David Marr and Hue-Tam Ho Tai, who have examined Vietnamese political activism and nationalism in the early to mid-twentieth century.[41] The political diversity that defined urban RVN during the Vietnam War reflected a much older tradition of debate and activism over what an independent Vietnam should look like, more so than North Vietnam, where the government tightly controlled the media and other forms of speech.

Americans failed to recognize this political tradition. Instead of cultivating noncommunist activists and organizations, they focused on supporting the Saigon government even when government officials resorted to the suppression of dissent, including the imprisonment of political dissidents. Harsher state and police crackdowns on opposition groups in the late 1960s radicalized some Catholics and students, pushing them deeper into the camp that supported reconciliation and an end to war, even if it gave control of Vietnam to communists. Despite the results of fact-finding missions of American politicians, clergy, and NGO representatives that revealed evidence of arbitrary imprisonment and torture, US Embassy officials and some policymakers argued that such findings were overblown. For Saigon intellectuals, the choice appeared to be either an undemocratic government buttressed by US financial and military support, or a movement that positioned itself as purely Vietnamese and claimed widespread rural support, even if it was coerced support. The long-term consequences remain apparent in the twenty-first century, as bloggers and others willing to speak out against the Vietnamese government face surveillance, arrest, and imprisonment. Even some of those citizens who had opposed the Saigon government during the war and favored reconciliation eventually found themselves on the wrong side of the postwar regime.

Saigon at War also places South Vietnam and Saigon political activism in the context of the "global sixties." Scholars of the global

---

[40] Asselin, *Hanoi's Road to the Vietnam War, 1954–1965* and *A Bitter Peace: Washington, Hanoi, and the Making of the Paris Agreement* (Chapel Hill: University of North Carolina Press, 2002); Lien-Hang T. Nguyen, *Hanoi's War: An International History of the War for Peace in Vietnam* (Chapel Hill: University of North Carolina Press, 2012).

[41] David G. Marr, *Vietnam: State, War, and Revolution, 1945–1946* (Berkeley: University of California Press, 2013); *Vietnam 1945: The Quest for Power* (Berkeley: University of California Press, 1997); *Vietnamese Tradition on Trial, 1920–1945* (Berkeley: University of California Press, 1984). Hue Tam Ho Tai, *Radicalism and the Origins of the Vietnamese Revolution* (Cambridge, MA: Harvard University Press, 1992).

sixties have illustrated how the Vietnam War and images of National Liberation Front guerrillas inspired leftists throughout the world, including European youth, communist movements in Latin America, and the US antiwar movement. This book positions South Vietnam not just as a source of inspiration but as an actor: a nation and a people grappling with many of the same issues that motivated demonstrations and revolts elsewhere. Across borders during the global sixties, political activists tended to be middle class and fairly privileged by national standards and were focused on political freedom and independence. They were not typically the poor masses rising up to demand attention to their basic needs.[42] Activists were also "core political constituencies" – white-collar office workers, university students, housewives, religious leaders   not outright revolutionaries or "extreme figures." However, the actions of violent fringe groups such as the Weather Underground in the United States and the Red Army Faction in West Germany encouraged state officials to crack down on public protests across the board in harsh ways that were disproportionate to most activists' actual threats to domestic order.[43] "State authorities violently crushed a perceived threat from politically engaged citizens," historian Jeremi Suri argues.[44] All of these issues played out in South Vietnam even as the Vietnam War and romanticized ideas about Viet Cong fighters inspired political movements elsewhere.

---

[42] Jeremi Suri, "The Rise and Fall of an International Counterculture, 1960–1975," *American Historical Review*, Vol. 114, No. 1 (Feb. 2009) 47. Other studies of global protest movements in the 1960s and 1970s include Suri, *Power and Protest: Global Revolution and the Rise of Détente* (Cambridge, MA: Harvard University Press, 2005); Jeremy Varon, *Bringing the War Home: The Weather Underground, the Red Army Faction, and Revolutionary Violence in the Sixties and Seventies* (Berkeley: University of California Press, 2004); Michael Stewart Foley, *Confronting the War Machine: Draft Resistance during the Vietnam War* (Chapel Hill: University of North Carolina Press, 2003); Belinda Davis, "What's Left? Popular Political Participation in Postwar Europe," *American Historical Review*, Vol. 113, No. 2 (April 2008) 363–390; Jeffrey L. Gould, "Solidarity under Siege: The Latin American Left, 1968," *American Historical Review*, Vol. 114, No. 2 (April 2009) 348–375; Christopher Dunn, "Desbunde and Its Discontents: Counterculture and Authoritarian Modernization in Brazil, 1968–1974," *The Americas*, Vol. 70, No. 3 (Jan. 2014) 429–458; Valeria Manzano, "'Rock Nacional' and Revolutionary Politics: The Making of a Youth Culture of Contestation in Argentina, 1966–1976," *The Americas*, Vol. 70, No. 3 (Jan. 2014) 393–427; Vania Markarian, "To the Beat of 'the Walrus': Uruguayan Communists and Youth Culture in the Global Sixties," *The Americas*, Vol. 70, No. 3 (Jan. 2014) 363–392; Timothy Scott Brown, "The Sixties in the City: Avant-gardes and Urban Rebels in New York, London, and West Berlin," *Journal of Social History*, Vol. 46, No. 4 (Summer 2013) 817–842.
[43] Suri, *Power and Protest*, pp. 48–49.   [44] Ibid., pp. 61–62.

Much of the scholarship on the global sixties focuses on the New Left, and although there was not a definitive "New Left" in Saigon, we can apply some analytical frameworks from those studies to explorations of South Vietnam's political scene. Recent scholarship on the American New Left has sought to illustrate the movement's diversity beyond student activism, which had been central to the scholarship. Historian Van Gosse has called the New Left a "'movement of movements,' an overlapping set of individuals and institutions of varied origins."[45] The case of Saigon political activism illustrates the diversity of sixties and seventies political engagement, too. Catholic priests, Buddhists, and agitators in their thirties, forties, and fifties who had been involved in nationalist movements since the French era joined Saigon students in their protests against the Thieu government and the Vietnam War. That Vietnamese Catholics would join the anti-Thieu resistance and the peace movement in South Vietnam makes sense when placed in a global context that highlights a Catholic move to the left in the 1960s. In El Salvador, Catholic intellectuals helped to establish the Salvadoran New Left. Historian Joaquin M. Chavez argues that the transformations in the Catholic Church resulting from the Second Vatican Council, which began in 1962, and the Second Conference of Latin American Bishops (CELAM) in 1968 radicalized young Catholic intellectuals, causing them to break with conservative Catholicism. Transformations in the church brought together young Catholics and political revolutionaries because both sides wanted to reform the capitalist system. Catholic leaders critiqued liberal capitalism, the legacies of colonialism, and neocolonialism, and they invoked the "just war" theory to defend the use of revolutionary violence against oppression.[46] Latin American Catholicism, including liberation theology, shaped the thinking of some Vietnamese Catholics.

On January 27, 1965, the editors of the *Straits Times*, a Singaporean newspaper that closely monitored developments in Vietnam, published an opinion piece entitled "Saigon Struggle." In it, the writer mused about how history would treat the political situation in South Vietnam. "The historian of the future who tries to describe what has been happening in Saigon in recent months will be either foolish or uncommonly energetic,

[45] Daniel Geary, "'Becoming International Again': C. Wright Mills and the Emergence of a Global New Left, 1956–1962," *The Journal of American History*, Vol. 95, No. 3 (Dec. 2008) 711.

[46] Joaquin M. Chavez, "Catholic Action, the Second Vatican Council, and the Emergence of the New Left in El Salvador, 1950–1975," *The Americas*, Vol. 70, No. 3 (Jan. 2014) 459–487.

and certainly not likely to become a best-selling author," the journalist wrote. "In fact, all that will be interesting will be his conclusions about the effect of recent turmoil," the writer continued. "It will be fascinating to learn, for example, whether factional in-fighting led directly to a Communist take-over or whether South Vietnam found at the last moment sufficient unity to avoid this fate."[47] Ten years before the fall of Saigon, the *Straits Times* writer recognized both the chaos and the potential in South Vietnam's nation-building experiment. What the author did not predict was the war that would both buy time for Saigon to develop its political institutions and destroy popular will to resist a Hanoi-led reunification of Vietnam.

[47] "Saigon Struggle," *The Straits Times*, Jan. 27, 1965.

I

The Heart of South Vietnam

Saigon in the Sixties

During the rainy season in southern Vietnam, afternoon storms give way to breezy evenings that beckon people outdoors to enjoy a touch of cool in the thick tropical air. Friday, June 25, 1965, was one of those nights in Saigon. The riverfront across from Bach Dang Street and the Majestic Hotel, not far from the US Embassy, was alive with parents chasing children, young lovers strolling by the water, street merchants selling food and drink, and customers arriving for dinner at the My Canh riverboat restaurant. My Canh was packed that night, and Saigon businessmen dined on fresh seafood and drank French wine alongside American GIs and their Vietnamese girlfriends. Seated at a table with friends, trying to talk above the din of conversation, laughter, and silverware on dishes, a diner would not have noticed a bomb that was set to go off at 8:15pm. After it exploded, stunned patrons who were able to stumble down the gangway to get off the ship would not have noticed a second bomb attached to a bicycle that was leaning against a cigarette stand on the riverbank near the end of the gangway. It exploded shortly after the first bomb. Of the nearly fifty people killed by the two blasts, more than half were Vietnamese, mostly women and children. The bombing was not random; it was part of a broader National Liberation Front strategy to destabilize the political situation in Saigon. The city was a war zone, and the urban war was hot long before the Tet Offensive.

There were two currents of energy pulsating through Saigon when it was the capital of South Vietnam. One crackled and sparked from the friction between citizen political activism and the South Vietnamese government's measures to suppress dissent. The electricity generated a palpable buzz in a city that was one of the most dynamic in the world in

the 1960s and 1970s. The other was a high-voltage throb of danger that
reminded urbanites that Saigon was a city at war. The armies may have
been fighting in the villages, but in a guerrilla war, attacks on civilian
targets in cities left a psychological impact that could not be measured by
a body count. Throughout the war years, the two currents often were

FIGURE 1.1 Organized demonstration against the Viet Cong, Saigon, 1964.
Earl R. Rhine Collection, The Vietnam Center and Archive, Texas Tech University

inseparable. In some ways, South Vietnam was a nascent democracy where citizens grappled with multiple perspectives on Vietnam's postcolonial political identity as they attempted to establish a modern, republican political system. Yet government repression of known and suspected political opponents intersected with NLF determination to control, through violence if necessary, South Vietnam's capital city. The forces of political instability and NLF terrorism destabilized South Vietnam. Some days, Saigon residents went about their business spared of the brutality of rural combat. But then a bomb would go off in a movie theater, or a newspaper editor would fall victim to a drive-by assassination, and it would remind residents that their city was at war.

Through terrorism, the NLF aimed to instill fear in the citizenry and destabilize Saigon's political system, undermining efforts to establish a democratic society. The violence compounded the disorder in the capital city and other urban areas where students, intellectuals, and journalists protested the government's slow movement in enacting democratic political institutions and allowing citizens to elect a civilian government. Saigon officials responded to terrorist attacks by arresting and imprisoning political dissidents and assuming that anyone who spoke out against the government was a communist. The stifling of civil liberties in turn validated claims by the NLF and other anti-government groups that Saigon leadership was authoritarian – terrorism's mission accomplished.

SAIGON'S POLITICAL REVOLVING DOOR

The 1963 assassination of Ngo Dinh Diem left a political vacuum in Saigon that a coalition of generals worked to fill. After Diem's ouster, Duong Van Minh, a southern-born general, dissolved the National Assembly and formed the Military Revolutionary Council, a collection of military officers who sought to build up a base of political support that would give them an advantage in negotiations with the NLF.[1] At its inception, the new government enjoyed popular support from citizens happy to see the Diem regime come to an end. Public confidence in the government faltered, however, not long after Minh took power, as his lack of leadership skills became clear, and political infighting prevented the establishment of democratic institutions.[2] Meanwhile, at the Vietnam

[1] Mark Atwood Lawrence, *The Vietnam War: A Concise International History* (New York: Oxford University Press, 2008), p. 81.
[2] William J. Duiker, *Vietnam: Revolution in Transition* (Boulder, CO: Westview Press, 1995), p. 66.

Workers Party Ninth Plenum in Hanoi in December 1963, delegates had approved a resolution authorizing the use of military force as the main way to unify Vietnam, and the NLF sought to take advantage of the political instability in Saigon.[3] On January 29, 1964, General Nguyen Khanh overthrew Minh's government in a bloodless coup. At the end of 1964, People's Army Vietnam or North Vietnamese Army main force units began crossing the DMZ.[4]

Although Khanh had promised US advisors that he would wage a more effective war against the NLF, within just a few months of his taking power, Lyndon Johnson began to worry that the Khanh government was too weak to lead a stable state.[5] Emboldened citizens demanded a civilian government, protesters clogged the streets of Saigon and Hue, and ARVN desertions increased through to the end of 1964.[6] Late 1964 saw the move toward establishing a civilian government and a new constitution, but subsequent clashes between generals and civilian politicians led to several additional coups and urban unrest. US Ambassador to South Vietnam Maxwell Taylor pushed the various parties in Saigon to get their affairs in order or risk loss of US aid and easy defeat by the NLF. A year after the assassination of Diem, Saigon was "a mess," as an anti-Khanh pamphlet put it.[7]

Developments in South Vietnam were central on international radar screens, and in the early post-Diem years, conversations revolved around the issue of neutrality. In 1964, French President Charles De Gaulle proposed that Western nations work with China to establish a neutral political solution to the conflicts in Indochina as the only way to ensure peace. De Gaulle had broached the topic of a French-administered, neutral unification of the two Vietnams with John F. Kennedy in the summer of 1963, a few months before the assassination of Ngo Dinh Diem, but Kennedy rejected the idea as long as the NLF existed in South Vietnam. Lyndon Johnson's response was similar: He was willing to consider such

[3] Sophie Quinn-Judge, "The Search for a Third Force in Vietnam: From the Quiet American to the Paris Peace Agreement," *Vietnam and the West: New Approaches*, Wynn Wilcox, ed. (Ithaca, NY: Cornell University Press, 2010), 162–164. See also, Lawrence, *The Vietnam War*, p. 81; *South Vietnam, Volume 1: U.S.–Communist Confrontation in Southeast Asia, 1961–65*, p. 104.
[4] Duiker, *Vietnam*, pp. 66–69.   [5] Lawrence, *The Vietnam War*, pp. 84–85.
[6] Mark Philip Bradley, *Vietnam at War* (New York: Oxford University Press, 2009), p. 108.
[7] VNCH Phiếu Trình Thủ Tướng, v/v hoạt động chống chánh-phủ, 1–1965. Hồ sơ số 15406: về các hoạt động chống đối chính phủ VNCH, Việt Cộng tại Sài Gòn năm 1965. Phông Phủ Thủ Tướng Chính Phủ Việt Nam Cộng Hòa Từ năm 1954 đến năm 1975, Trung Tâm Lưu Trữ Quốc Gia II (National Archives II, hereafter TTLTQG II), Ho Chi Minh City, Vietnam.

a plan, but only if North Vietnam agreed to end the communist insurgency it directed in South Vietnam. Otherwise, any attempt at neutrality would facilitate a communist takeover of the country.[8] Duong Van Minh had desired neutrality for South Vietnam, and Nguyen Khanh justified his ouster in Saigon by arguing that deposing Minh was required as leader of South Vietnam to counter the forces of neutralism. US Senator Mike Mansfield had promoted the cause of neutralism to Congress, but Ambassador Henry Cabot Lodge, who replaced Taylor in 1965, asked De Gaulle to withdraw his proposal for the same reasons Kennedy and Johnson had dismissed it. "How can so-called 'neutralization' be attained if the aggressor is determined not to be neutralized, as is obviously the case as regards North Vietnam?" he wondered.[9]

Buddhist opposition remained a problem to the new Saigon government as it had been during the Diem era. In January 1964, politically active Buddhists formed the Unified Buddhist Church as a way to try and bring Buddhists together. Conflict among UBC members typically centered on the issue of neutralism. During the Cold War, some newly independent nations adopted a neutral stance on the United States–Soviet struggle to draw new allies into their respective orbits. The Non-Aligned Movement exemplified this position in its conference at Bandung in 1955 and in other efforts to assert independence from superpower meddling. As historian Fredrik Logevall has pointed out, in the South Vietnamese context, neutralism referred more to a general war weariness.[10] Peasants especially were interested in whatever approach would force both the Saigon government and the NLF to leave them alone. Britain's ambassador to South Vietnam wrote to London in 1963: "The peasants do not want Communism, but if the Government cannot protect them they will support the Communists. Urban populations felt the war exhaustion, too, as American and French officials suspected when they assessed the excitement over Diem's assassination. Some Vietnamese hoped that the collapse of his regime meant that the war would soon end.[11]

---

[8] *South Vietnam, Volume 1: U.S.–Communist Confrontation in Southeast Asia, 1961–65*, Lester A. Sobel, ed. (New York: Facts on File, Inc., 1973) 86, 97. See also, Lam Quang Thi, *The Twenty-Five Year Century: A South Vietnamese General Remembers the Indochina War to the Fall of Saigon* (Denton, TX: University of North Texas Press, 2001), p. 112.

[9] Quinn-Judge, *Vietnam and the West*, p. 162.

[10] On the nonaligned movement, see Robert B. Rakove, *Kennedy, Johnson, and the Non-Aligned World* (New York: Cambridge University Press, 2012).

[11] Fredrik Logevall, *Choosing War: The Lost Chance for Peace and the Escalation of the War in Vietnam* (Berkeley: University of California Press, 1999), p. 89.

Buddhist leaders were divided on the question of neutralism, but the concept gradually united Buddhists and student leaders who did not trust Nguyen Khanh. They worried that rumors of military officials plotting Khanh's overthrow would prove true, spinning the revolving door of the palace once again to seat another nonelected, noncivilian government. They supported a policy of neutralism that would force the United States to withdraw from South Vietnam and allow representatives of various political persuasions to negotiate an end to the war. Hanoi and NLF leaders also supported this approach, which made it all the more threatening to American advisers.[12] Thich Tam Chau, leader of moderate Buddhists, advocated a pro-government, anti-neutral stance. Thich Tri Quang, leader of Vien Hoa Dao, the Institute for the Propagation of the Faith, which was the political arm of the UBC, wanted the South Vietnamese government and the NLF to figure out a settlement to end the war. Increasing US involvement in Vietnam and violence throughout the country strengthened ties between the Buddhists and other activist groups, especially students.[13]

August 1964 was a particularly bloody month in Saigon. Protests against Nguyen Khanh's military government continued as part of a vicious cycle of citizen demonstrations, government crackdowns, rising citizen anger, and additional restrictions on democracy. Official proclamations authorizing police to move proactively against suspected security risks sometimes resulted in bloody attacks against groups that potentially were bases of support for the government. In late August 1964, officers shot and killed six Catholics who marched in front of the military's high command headquarters at Tan Son Nhut airport demanding representative government. Thousands of mourners turned out for the funeral procession several days later, and the government issued a statement acknowledging the "patriotism" of the slain demonstrators and admitting that the officers responsible had "lost their calm in crisis." Authorities offered 50,000 piasters to each family of the murdered protesters and promised to investigate the conduct of the officers involved in the incident.[14] At the same time, the Armed Forces High Command also issued a statement warning citizens that police would call in military reinforcements if crowds became unruly. Troops will have the authority to

---

[12] Logevall, *Choosing War*, p. 120–121.
[13] Robert Topmiller, *The Lotus Unleashed: The Buddhist Peace Movement in South Vietnam, 1964–1966* (Lexington: University Press of Kentucky, 2002), p. 7.
[14] "Services for Six Killed," *Saigon Daily News*, Monday, Aug. 31, 1964, p. 4.

blockade government buildings and other official installations, and if protesters attempt to cross the barricades, security forces would be "obligated to open fire to make the national authority respected."[15]

Authorities justified their harsh responses to citizen protests as necessary to bring order as government officials struggled to both establish new democratic political institutions and fight a war against the NLF. Yet state violence against civilians, even just in the form of threats, presented an image to Vietnamese citizens and the world of another example of authoritarianism taking root in the decolonizing world. South Vietnam's authoritarianism in the name of democracy enforced the notion that newly independent populations had only the choices between authoritarianism and communism for their political structures. Despite citizen protests and a vibrant press, South Vietnam looked reactionary. In the mid-sixties, leaders gave international observers little reason to believe that they were committed to building a democratic nation.

State suppression of civil liberties increased with US escalation in April 1964. The clash between US ships and North Vietnamese PT boats in the Gulf of Tonkin and subsequent US bombing of targets in North Vietnam resulted in Khanh's declaration of a state of emergency in South Vietnam.[16] Authorities imposed a curfew in Saigon and seized newspapers accused of printing anti-government articles. The Ministry of Interior issued a statement banning any object that could be construed as a weapon from public gatherings, and the ARVN High Command announced that troops would be deployed to aid police forces if police lose control of demonstrations. The stakes were high for civilians: Anyone caught with a weapon would be tried in a military court, and if troops were called in to assist police in riot control, they would be permitted to open fire on demonstrators "to make the national authority respected."[17] In the fall of 1964, the Khanh regime established a civilian High National Council, which appointed Tran Van Huong, former mayor of Saigon, premier of South Vietnam.[18]

[15] "High Command Issues Anti-Riot Warning," *Saigon Daily News*, Monday, Aug. 31, 1964, p. 2.

[16] *South Vietnam, Volume 1: U.S.–Communist Confrontation in Southeast Asia, 1961–65*, p. 101.

[17] "High Command Issues Anti-Riot Warning," "City Hall: Military Trial Awaits Armed Marchers," "Ministry Warns against Carrying Weapons," *Saigon Daily News*, Aug. 31, 1964, pp. 2–3.

[18] *South Vietnam, Volume 1: U.S.–Communist Confrontation in Southeast Asia, 1961–65*, Lester A. Sobel, ed. (New York: Facts on File, Inc., 1973) 106–107.

Though a civilian, Huong did not earn much support from politically active citizens, especially Vietnamese students. Huong increased draft calls, one of the main issues motivating student unrest, and demonstrations against the government continued, followed by arrests of protesters. Additional attempted coups removed Khanh from power for good in February 1965. That summer, a team of younger generals, led by Air Marshal Nguyen Cao Ky and Army General Nguyen Van Thieu, took control of the government and surprised Washington by bringing some stability to Saigon.[19] In February 1966, Thieu and Ky met with Johnson and other Americans in Honolulu to discuss strategies for building a base of popular support. Johnson promised to increase aid to help South Vietnam's economy and social issues, and Thieu and Ky agreed to make concrete efforts toward establishing a representative civilian government. Thieu and Ky promised that they would call for elections to a constituent assembly within the year. Voters elected a 117-member constituent assembly, which then drafted a new constitution – one of the demands citizen activists had wanted since Diem's assassination.[20] The government also established the processes for a nationwide presidential election. In September 1967, Thieu won the presidency with 35 percent of the vote, with Ky as his vice president. The second-place candidate, Truong Dinh Dzu, received 17 percent of the vote.[21]

LIFE FOR AMERICANS AND VIETNAMESE IN SAIGON

Saigon was a chameleon, able to be what observers and residents believed it to be, perhaps because it was so many things. Journalist Chin Koh Chong of the Pan-Asian Newspaper Alliance, saw a place that was oblivious to the war happening just beyond city limits. Its boulevards, shaded by tamarind trees, hosted busy outdoor cafes and shops that catered to local women of leisure, as well as foreigners, primarily American men, but in some cases their wives, too. Inside the crowded markets, shoppers bargaining for fruit, vegetables, and fish composed a noisy soundtrack that mixed with the near-constant rumbling of motorbikes and vehicles moving through the streets outside.[22] Political coups occurred without troops, tanks, or bloodshed. While Saigon residents went about their business one Saturday in February 1965, a group of

---

[19] Duiker, *Vietnam*, p. 68.   [20] Ibid.   [21] Bradley, *Vietnam at War*, p. 110.
[22] Chin Kah Chong, "A Coup D'Etat Is a 'Curious Custom' in South Vietnam," *Malayan Times*, April 17, 1965.

generals deposed Nguyen Khanh. They announced the regime change over the radio and promised that they intended to assemble a civilian government.[23] The illusion of being apart from the war made terrorist attacks even more jarring.

As Ann Laura Stoler has written, one way to trace power and power relations is to examine the "intimate" moments of daily life – instances when ordinary encounters among people define social hierarchies and categorize individuals for the sake of creating or maintaining power.[24] On the streets, in public places, and in private moments, Americans and Vietnamese, civilian and military personnel, women and men, mingled in trysts that were fraught with, to borrow Stoler's phrase, the "tensions of empire." Stoler identifies "the colonial" as the "settlement, exploration, and dominance of separate 'others' that transforms social organization, cultural convention, and private life."[25] In the neoimperial world of post-1945 US foreign relations, the American presence in Vietnam was not designed for territorial acquisition, but to protect and extend political and economic power. To do so meant that Americans would occupy Vietnam, and even though the occupation was always considered temporary, its impacts on Saigon were lasting.

For some Americans living in Saigon, the city was a place of comfort and leisure, which made terrorist attacks all the more jarring – and effective. Marion Williams, a journalist and nurse who went to Vietnam in 1967, wrote that there were two sides to the American war in Vietnam – the "non-combat luxury war" and the "field hardship war." "The bitching war is hell for the front line internment along the DMZ and the Mekong Delta," she wrote, "while in Saigon, Cam Ranh Bay, and many other places, the luxury men live high. They have nice living quarters, maid service, enlisted men's clubs, cold beer, T-bone steaks, J&B scotch, not to mention many other fine scotches and bourbons. Some even had automatic washers and dryers. Just like state-side living. If war could be like this for all men, it would become a pleasure to go to war."[26] Some American men found in Saigon a bachelor's life of good food, good

---

[23] Allington Kennard, "The City of Quiet Coups," *The Straits Times*, Feb. 28, 1965.

[24] Ann Laura Stoler, "Intimidations of Empire: Predicaments of the Tactile and Unseen," in *Haunted by Empire: Geographies of Intimacy in North American History*, ed. Stoler (Durham, NC: Duke University Press, 2006).

[25] Ibid., p. 32.

[26] Marion L. Williams, *My Tour in Vietnam: A Burlesque Shocker* (New York: Vantage Press, 1970), p. 36.

liquor, and a Vietnamese woman to keep their apartments tidy, and provide other services.

The black market for entertainment for foreigners in Saigon flourished thanks to men like William Crum. Crum was in the business of entertainment, running companies that distributed liquor, dry goods, and games such as slot machines. The son of an American Yangtze River pilot, Crum was born in Shanghai in 1915 and lived there until 1935, when his family moved to California. The military fascinated him, and he tried to enlist in the Navy when the United States entered World War II, but muscular dystrophy kept him out of the service. By the time of the Korean War, though, Crum had figured out a way to get close to the military and almost feel a part of it. He pitched his business to post exchanges, officers' clubs, and enlisted men's clubs in hopes of getting distribution contracts for military installations. When the United States escalated the war in 1965, Crum saw an opportunity to expand his business ventures.[27]

In bidding to win military contracts, Crum did more than submit proposals. He had skilled himself in the art of bribery. The practice almost caught up with him in Korea, where a sergeant in charge of the club system there was court-martialed for allegedly accepting bribes from Crum. Crum fled Korea in 1960 and made his way to Vietnam, where he found other military officers willing to accept his kickbacks. In late 1965, the Army and the Air Force ran the post exchange (PX) system in Vietnam, and five American men – one military officer and four civilians – oversaw the operations there. As a 1971 Senate inquiry into corruption in the club and PX systems stated, "when these men arrived in Vietnam, William Crum and his associates were ready to make their stay more comfortable."[28]

Upon arrival of Lieutenant Colonel John G. Goodlett Jr. and his civilian assistants Peter B. Mason, Richard Llewellyn, and Clarence Swafford in the fall of 1965, Crum provided them accommodations in a villa in Saigon. The two-story home featured five bedrooms, a living room, dining room, three bathrooms, two maids, and a cook. According to Senate investigations, it appeared that the men did not pay Crum for lodging. In a letter to Mel Peterson, vice president of Jim Beam, Crum wrote that he and the men were "getting along like peas in a pod" and

---

[27] "Fraud and Corruption in Management of Military Club Systems: Illegal Currency Manipulations Affecting South Vietnam." Report of the Committee on Government Operations, United States Senate, Permanent Subcommittee on Investigations (Washington, DC: U.S. Government Printing Office, 1971), pp. 9–11, 13, 93.
[28] Ibid., p. 97.

that he "showed them the brand new house I am decorating for them and they are absolutely delighted." The men lived together and partied together, with Crum sparing no expense to "cultivate the good will of PX personnel in Saigon." He entertained "lavishly" and always provided "good food, plenty of liquor, and female companionship."[29] Theirs was a bachelor pad for grown men living in a city known for its "outlaw spirit" and "all-or-nothing mentality."[30]

Based in Saigon, Denby Fawcett, twenty-four-year-old reporter for the *Honolulu Advertiser*, lived in a small apartment above a souvenir shop. In the bedroom, a ceiling fan hung above a king sized bed to stir a breeze in the thick Saigon heat. A balcony looked out over the busy bar and entertainment district on Tu Do Street, where Americans threw back whiskey and beer, ate continental cuisine prepared by Chinese chefs, and played in nightclubs that beckoned them with neon signs and, often, Vietnamese women. In English, "tu do" translates to "freedom." Fawcett hung out at the French café Brodard's, where she listened to "California Dreamin" and other American tunes on the jukebox. At night, she dined on pepper steak and fresh vegetables shipped in from the resort city of Da Lat and prepared by a French-trained cook at a restaurant called Aterbea. Sometimes she went to Caruso's, which featured candlelight dinners, French and Italian cuisine, and imported French wine. After a meal, she liked to join friends at Jo Marcel's, a nightclub where rich Vietnamese young women danced in miniskirts and drank Coca-Cola. When columnist Ann Landers came to Vietnam to visit wounded soldiers, she invited Fawcett to have dinner with her at the posh Caravelle Hotel's rooftop restaurant. They ate frogs' legs, rice, and chocolate éclairs, and they sipped espresso high above Saigon, far from the war waging in the distance.[31]

Americans in Vietnam enjoyed a variety of leisure activities. When a day's work was done, there was time for golf in Saigon, according to Ann Morrisy Merick, a white American journalist with ABC news stationed in Vietnam in 1967. The Golf Club of Saigon, near Tan Son Nhut Airport, offered eighteen holes on a relatively flat, easy course. The most challenging parts of the course weren't sand traps or lagoons, but rather the occasional outpost where ARVN soldiers stood on guard, watching for VC infiltrators. Barbed wire, land mines, and armed guards protected the

[29] Ibid., pp. 104, 98, 102.
[30] Tad Bartimus, *War Torn: Stories of War from the Women Reporters Who Covered Vietnam* (New York: Random House, 2002), pp. 253–254.
[31] Bartimus, *War Torn*, pp. 6, 22–24.

outposts, so landing a golf ball near one was akin to landing a ball in a pond. The caddies were "sturdy Vietnamese women not much bigger than the bags they carried," Merick observed.

For those who did not care to play golf, there was the Cercle Sportif, a sprawling athletic club in downtown Saigon left behind by the French. Restless diplomats and tired embassy employees could pick up a tennis match or relax by the pool with a gin and tonic. Adventuresome Americans and wealthy Vietnamese went waterskiing on the Saigon River, skimming past US Navy river boat patrols.[32] On weekends, some Americans hopped a plane or helicopter and retreated to Nha Trang, a coastal village turned resort town where lobster dinners, coconut trees, and glass-bottom boats awaited them.[33] Evenings meant cocktails and dinner parties. Merick noted that US Ambassador Ellsworth Bunker threw some of the best parties, featuring brandy, cigars, and imported Russian vodka. His soirees were for the "A-list" of Saigon, but for those without an invitation, there usually was a party going on somewhere, in the apartment of an American embassy worker or perhaps at the Rex Hotel. "It was a welcome break from being in the field, and we all got gussied up and partied," Merick said.[34]

Leisure activities, hotels, and imported goods were available for the foreigners occupying Saigon during the war. Vietnamese workers provided much of the labor that built the society in which Americans lived, worked, and played. Merick hired a French-trained Vietnamese cook and knew that "many correspondents had a houseboy or a woman who cooked for them. We all had seamstresses and tailors who could create a dressy outfit from the elegant silks and cottons that were available from our R&R shopping trips to Hong Kong and Bangkok."[35] A brochure for civilian employees of the US Air Force boasted that "one of the many pleasant aspects of duty in the Republic of Vietnam is the fact that one can afford servants." It listed the average costs per month in US dollars for hired help – cooks charged about $40–80, while maid service ran $35 to $60.[36] Vietnamese workers made clothes, kept house, and provided entertainment for Americans in Saigon.

[32] Ibid., pp. 118, 133.
[33] "Nha Trang," *Life in Vietnam*, No. 143, Dec. 16, 1967, 39, Glenn Helm Collection, Vietnam Archive, Texas Tech University, Lubbock, TX.
[34] Bartimus, *War Torn*, p. 117.   [35] Ibid.
[36] Pacific Air Forces Pamphlet, U.S. Air Force Civilian Employment, Republic of Vietnam, Area Information Pamphlet, Nov. 3, 1969, Sally Vineyard Collection, University of Denver Penrose Library, Special Collections, Denver, CO.

Ads in the English-language magazine *Life in Vietnam*, a publication distributed to US military installations in Vietnam and Vietnamese embassies throughout the world, showcased Saigon's amenities and painted a picture of what Saigon looked like during the US occupation of Vietnam. By the mid-1960s, the Saigon skyline was made of seven- and eight-story hotels that lifted guests high above the city and offered them panoramic views so that they could gaze down at the life below. The Mai Loan Hotel featured air-conditioned rooms with balconies, a snack bar with a panoramic view of Saigon, and a restaurant offering Chinese and American foods. While the Majestic Hotel also provided air-conditioned rooms and panoramic views, it also boasted "refined French cuisine" and the "attractive and talented Ngoc Nhi" performing every night in the bar on the fifth floor. Not to be outdone, the Manhattan Hotel and Restaurant stood in "the heart of Saigon's shopping area" and presented guests with a penthouse seventh floor restaurant and "delicious French and Chinese dishes by an excellent cook from Hong Kong." After settling into their accommodations, visitors might have strolled down one of the city's commercial boulevards to find a tailor and ensure they had proper party attire. The tailor shops Waloc and Ashoka both offered ready-to-wear and custom-made men's and women's clothing, and ads for the shops featured a drawing of a white man in a business suit. One stop at Beautex, and a visitor could walk out with the latest French hairdo courtesy of a Paris-certified stylist.[37]

Not all of Saigon's amenities developed as a result of the arrival of Americans. Some hotels, restaurants, and shops dated back to the days of French colonialism. But it is important to consider the colonial character of Saigon in the context of the American war in Vietnam because some US policymakers feared American involvement in Vietnam would appear colonial. In 1964, as the Johnson administration discussed sending more personnel to Vietnam, Ambassador Henry Cabot Lodge expressed concern that more Americans – particularly civilians – in Vietnam would give a "colonial coloration" to the US presence there.[38] Discussions about sending combat troops to Vietnam included fears that the conflict would look like "a white man's war against the brown."[39] And on the first day of

[37] *Life in Vietnam*, various issues, Glenn Helm Collection.
[38] Draft Memorandum by the Secretary of State's Special Assistant for Vietnam (Sullivan), Washington, June 13, 1964, *FRUS, 1964–1968*, 1:503.
[39] Telegram from the Embassy in Vietnam to the Department of State, Saigon, Jan. 6, 1965, *FRUS, 1964–1968*, 2:26.

1967, Maxwell Taylor wondered what the United States should do about the "growing 'colonialist' image of the white man."[40] Throughout the course of the relationship between the United States and Vietnam, some American government officials worried that the United States would appear to have imperial aspirations for Vietnam, but all the while, American women and men lived in a world in Saigon marked by a colonial character. Vietnamese workers labored in a service industry aimed at providing for the needs of Americans, many of whom were in Vietnam to aid the US effort to prevent communist rule from taking South Vietnam.

Viewed from the lives of its Vietnamese residents, Saigon revealed South Vietnam's class differences and some of the consequences of the war. Wealthy and middle-class Vietnamese lived, worked, and played alongside their American occupiers. Well-to-do families owned French-style villas with comforts such as electricity, running water, Western plumbing, and separate living quarters for domestic help.[41] They lived on tree-lined boulevards and spent hot, humid afternoons playing tennis or lounging by the pool at the Cercle Sportif country club. These were the generals and government employees and their families, and they moved in the same circles as US Embassy employees, independent contractors, and military personnel stationed in the city.[42] Journalists and newspaper editors tried to inform readers about their government's activities, even as authorities periodically shut down newspapers and arrested reporters who criticized the government. As of fall 1967, twenty-seven daily newspapers circulated throughout Saigon, each with a few thousand subscribers.[43]

Young Vietnamese frequented coffee shops on Tu Do Street, which ran from Notre Dame Cathedral near the Presidential Palace to the Saigon River. Young men brought their sweethearts, and groups of friends packed tables and drank coffee, smoked cigarettes, and listened to music. French artists remained popular into the American era, but Vietnamese musicians such as Trinh Cong Son became increasingly popular with the young coffeehouse set as the war dragged on. Son's songs and other popular

---

[40] Paper Prepared by the President's Special Consultant (Taylor), Washington, Jan. 1, 1967, *FRUS, 1964–1968*, 5:2.

[41] Duong Van Mai Elliott, *The Sacred Willow: Four Generations in the Life of a Vietnamese Family* (New York: Oxford University Press, 1999), p. 255.

[42] Bernard Weintraub, "Footnotes on the Vietnam Dispatches," *New York Times*, Oct. 20, 1968.

[43] Howard Moffett, "Reporting the Cool-Medium War," *Yale Alumni Magazine*, Oct. 1967, p. 29.

Vietnamese music of the day expressed a deep, if apolitical, longing for peace. Ballads told stories of young servicemen who missed their girl-friends and dreamed of being back in Saigon, at one of those cafes on Tu Do Street. Vietnamese employees of the US Embassy and American companies gathered at restaurants and bars and tried to make sense of America's intentions. Some gazed out over their coffee cups to the street outside, wondering what would happen to them if the Communists won. They worked for the enemy; would they be hung as traitors? The war had made life difficult, but the terms of peace that might come in the wake of an American departure terrified some Saigon residents. One American adviser remarked that a "peace scare" had begun to wash across the city as Americans made serious moves toward peace talks in 1968.[44]

For the poor – including the refugees the war drove from the country-side into the cities – Saigon was a constant reminder of their poverty and dislocation. By 1969, Saigon's population had increased from about 400,000 at the start of World War II to more than 2.5 million.[45] Before 1964, 80 percent of Vietnamese were rural farmers. By 1970, 40–50 percent of the population of South Vietnam lived in a city. Many were refugees, and they hoped to make some money off the wartime economy. The population surge took its toll on the city. Traffic jammed Saigon's streets, and sewage, garbage removal, telephone, and electrical systems struggled to keep up. While Saigon's wealthy families lived in "spacious villas solidly built of stone or brick and equipped with running water, electricity, and sanitary facilities," slums literally were built out of con-sumerism.[46] Sheets of rolled beer cans were reused as siding for homes. Aluminum shacks doubled as billboards for Miller High Life, Pabst Blue Ribbon, and Budweiser. Karen Offut, a stenographer in the Women's Army Corps who was stationed in Saigon for part of her tour of duty, noted that in Saigon, "there were just thousands and thousands of people and then there would be big mansions and right next to it would be these little three-sided houses or makeshift homes made out of flattened beer cans."[47] In 1970, about 158,000 Vietnamese worked for the US military

[44] Bernard Weintraub, "Saigon Mood Uneasy and Bitter in Face of Peace Moves by the U.S.," *New York Times*, April 6, 1968.
[45] *Army Civilian Employment: Living and Working in Vietnam* (Washington, DC: U.S. Government Printing Office, 1969), p. 6.
[46] *Area Handbook for South Vietnam*, 121–124.
[47] Ron Steinman, *Women in Vietnam: The Oral History* (New York: TV Books, 2000), p. 263; see also *Area Handbook for South Vietnam*, 136–137.

and civilian companies, while many others found income in war-related services from housekeeping to brothels.[48]

It was in this context that NLF terrorism played out in Saigon. While generals and politicians fought in the houses of government, and citizens demanded freedoms in the streets, foreigners living in the city provided targets and justifications for the NLF strategy of terror. Americans made use of the colonial economy their French predecessors had cultivated, presenting the appearance of yet another form of Western imperialism. The cafes and theaters they frequented offered convenient targets for bombings because they allowed the NLF to strike the city without necessarily targeting Vietnamese civilians. Vietnamese casualties always lay among the wreckage, and in cases like the My Canh restaurant bombing, sometimes were the majority of those killed, but the Western presence in Saigon bolstered the notion that the primary conflict in Vietnam was between Americans and the Vietnamese.

URBAN TERRORISM

Terrorism was a central component of NLF strategy. Douglas Pike made this argument in his studies of the National Liberation Front, which were grounded in more than a decade living in South Vietnam as an employee of the US Information Agency. Pike, a World War II veteran of the Pacific Theater, documented NLF uses of terrorism, including the massacre of several thousand civilians at Hue during the Tet Offensive. The seeming randomness of a car bomb here and an explosion in a market there belied the calculated, rational nature of the NLF's terrorism as a primary tactic in its war strategy.[49] In 1959, leaders in Hanoi decided that it was time to focus on "liberating the South ... to struggle heroically and perseveringly to smash the Southern regime."[50]

NLF sources justified the use of terrorism as being the only choice they had given the "warlike and terrorist policies of the enemy."[51] Ngo Dinh Diem, enabled by his American advisers, had unleashed a brutal secret police force on his citizens out of fear of popular political revolt against his regime, and NLF leadership, in its determination to bolster the

[48] "The Urban Trend," *Time*, Aug. 30, 1970, www.time.com/time/magazine/article/0,9171,876792,00.html.
[49] United States Mission in Vietnam, "Viet Cong Use of Terror: A Study," March 1967, p. 3.
[50] Ibid.	[51] Ibid., p. 5.

political struggle, argued that there was no other way to fight the enemy that stood in the way of Vietnam's destiny. Not all cadres agreed with the official policy; some believed that the political struggle alone could topple the Saigon government, and terrorism might actually have an opposite effect than what NLF authorities intended. An indoctrination pamphlet explained that violence was an essential ingredient in the recipe of revolution: "(T)he only correct way to organize revolutionary forces and make preparations in all areas to smash the enemy's machinery of violence is to use the appropriate form of armed struggle ... Emergence of this new struggle form not only meets an urgent demand, but is an inevitable result of the revolutionary movement. It does not contradict the political struggle, but supplements it and paves the way for the political struggle to develop."[52] Confidence in the preordained nature of Vietnam's communist revolution allowed the NLF to justify its commitment to violent struggle.

NLF leaders clearly believed their movement had the moral authority in Vietnam, as the statement that in order for the NLF's political struggle to take place, terrorism was necessary proved. The notion of having the right to Vietnam's future was a central part of the broader conflict that involved the governments in Saigon and Hanoi, the NLF, and Vietnamese and foreign citizens across the political spectrum. Historian Nu-Anh Tran has the concept of "contested nationalism," in which the DRV and the RVN offered competing expressions of Vietnamese nationalism as each side argued that it had authentic claim to Vietnamese heritage and nationhood.[53] Tran proposed the notion of contested nationalism in response to a pervasive bias in the historiography of Vietnamese nationalism and the Vietnam War that has cast the DRV as the rightful descendant of Vietnam's history. As Tran notes, scholars since the 1970s have assumed that "only one of the two Vietnams could be authentically nationalist and, by extension, politically legitimate."[54] What this approach is ultimately about, Tran argues, is not Vietnam, but US foreign policy. Historians' efforts to cast the DRV as the legitimate Vietnam have done so in order to critique US policies toward Vietnam and America's Cold War foreign

[52] "Viet Cong Use of Terror," p. 6.
[53] Nu-Anh Tran, "Contested Nationalism: Ethnic Identity and State Power in the Republic of Vietnam, 1954–1963," ISSI Fellows Working Papers, Institute for the Study of Societal Issues, UC Berkeley, Jan. 3, 2012, p. 9.
[54] Tran, *Contentested Nationalism*, p. 5.

policies more broadly.[55] The result is that writers have obscured the complexities of South Vietnam's political and social scenes.

Terrorism was central to the NLF's efforts to destabilize Saigon, and it compounded the chaos in the capital city and other urban areas where students, intellectuals, and journalists protested the government's slow movement in enacting democratic political institutions and allowing citizens to elect a civilian government. This was part of the reason why the NLF's urban terrorism strategy succeeded: Saigon already was chaotic, and the addition of terrorism influenced the government to crack down on free speech and assembly, two hallmarks of a democratic society. The stifling of civil liberties in turn validated claims by the NLF and other anti-government groups that Saigon leadership was authoritarian. On January 4 and 5, 1965, anywhere from three hundred to five hundred activists, including students, journalists, and Buddhists, marched in Saigon to protest the government, and authorities decided they must be proactive in preventing unrest. It would have to involve infiltration; the only way to stop conspiracies was to know who was leading them and what the plans were before they were put into action.[56]

NLF terrorists operating within three-person cells carried about assassinations, planted explosives, and launched grenades into crowded spaces. Skilled technicians from the provincial and zone headquarters built and detonated explosives and provided leadership to the cells.[57] The mythology surrounding the image of the NLF as an organic movement belied the planning, training, and expertise that shaped and executed the NLF's terror strategy. The NLF's policy of terrorism was intentional, and key evidence of that is that the NLF generally used terrorism "judiciously, selectively, and sparingly."[58] Cadres knew they walked a thin line between engendering fear in civilians and provoking hate. NLF leaders also worked to make it look as though terrorist activity was not connected to the NLF's political struggle. Authorities established "[c]landestine organizations for sabotage in urban areas" so that appear to have "no connection with political organizations."[59] NLF leaders knew their movement could lose credibility if its commitment to violent revolution became clear.

[55] Ibid.
[56] Viet Nam Cong Hoa, Thu Tuong Phu, Vo Phong Bien Ban Buoi, Hop Ngay 6/1/65. Ho so so 15333: Ve tinh hinh an ninh tai Sai Gon Gia Dinh nam 1965. TTLTQG II.
[57] "Viet Cong Use of Terror," p. 9.   [58] Ibid., p. 55.   [59] Ibid., p. 8.

The NLF aimed its terror strategy at achieving five goals, four of which were psychological. Successful terrorist attacks had the power to boost guerrilla morale and unit cohesion while at the same time destroying community structure and security. The latter made villagers feel that their government, from local chiefs to the Saigon regime, was unable to protect them. It also motivated the government to retaliate, another goal of the NLF's terror strategy. As a US study of NLF terrorism stated, "if the terrorist is effective and if the government sees itself in a crisis, it will almost inevitably use extra-ordinary repressive measures."[60] Terrorism also served as advertising and earned the NLF an international reputation. It was not always favorable publicity, though. In January 1966, Yugoslavia, the United Arab Emirates, and Algeria issued a joint statement urging the Hanoi government and the NLF to do away with their terror policy, as it harmed the reputation of the Vietnamese communist movement among their citizens. Finally, the NLF had a quantifiable goal, which was to "eliminate the entire leader class of Vietnamese villagers."[61] Assassinating village chiefs and rising leaders removed the greater threat to the NLF than high political authorities in Saigon because the countryside was where the NLF worked to establish control.

NLF terrorism targeted and disrupted rural and urban life. South Vietnamese and US government and military sources, news coverage, and International Control Commission reports documented the violence, although because the attacks tended to yield small numbers of casualties at a time, reports failed to garner much attention. This served the NLF well, as it ensured that the brutality of the organizations strategy was not central to the NLF's international image. The Front mainly targeted villages, especially hamlets it considered to be pro-Saigon, and the goal of an attack was typically to cause confusion and fear rather than to kill a large number of civilians. One of the methods for achieving this goal worked this way: Guerrillas approached a village and fired a few rifle shots. Self-defense forces and government security troops stationed there then had to decide whether it was an actual attack or simply harassment. If the commanding officer decided it was an attack that required a military response, troop attention would be diverted from another area, where the guerrillas would then stage an actual attack. If the commanding officer chose to not respond, believing the shots to be harassment, the lack of response would leave villagers worried that government troops were not

[60] Ibid., p. 52.   [61] Ibid.

committed to protecting them. It bred insecurity within the village, the ultimate goal of the small-scale terrorism, as bullets punctured daily life, if not human bodies.[62] When targeting individuals in rural areas, guerrillas focused on village and hamlet chiefs, government employees, teachers, and suspected "informants" and other "traitors," as well as foreigners including priests and other missionaries, humanitarian aid workers, and US government employees.[63]

Psychological destabilization was also the goal of terrorism in Saigon, and grenades and other explosives were the primary weapons. One report referred to a bicycle, its hollow frame packed with explosives, as an "instrument of death."[64] It was an apt description of the bicycle that caused the secondary explosion at the My Canh restaurant. Urban terrorism aimed to harm Americans and the Vietnamese who worked with them. On Christmas Eve 1964, NLF guerrillas drove a car loaded with explosives into a parking lot behind the Brinks Hotel Bachelor Officers Quarters in Saigon. When it detonated, the blast killed two US servicemen and wounded more than sixty American military personnel and Vietnamese civilians. Three months later, NLF terrorists again used an explosives-laden vehicle to bomb the US Embassy in Saigon, killing twenty and wounding more than one hundred eighty people.

The NLF bombing of the Kinh-Do Theater in February 1964 became a training case study for the Front and particularly rattled Americans living in Saigon. Located near the Presidential Palace in the busy center of the city, the Kinh-Do Theater served Americans, including dependents of US military and government personnel. The area surrounding the theater included a US dispensary, US Special Forces headquarters, and the homes of South Vietnamese civil servants and "the city bourgeois." A captured NLF document noted, in translation, that "attacking it will create a strong impression at home and abroad and will greatly affect the morale of Americans, both in Vietnam and in the United States."[65] A few minutes before the eight o'clock movie started on the evening of February 16, a team of three guerrillas arrived at the theater in a car. The first man to jump out was the leader: a sharpshooter and a judo expert who had combat experience. The other two guerrillas lacked the experience and skill of the leader, but they had proven their loyalty to the NLF cause. Once out of the car, the marksman pulled out a gun and shot a security guard while yelling to Vietnamese police officers near the theater, "We

[62] Ibid., p. 39.   [63] Ibid., pp. 16–38.   [64] Ibid., p. 40.   [65] Ibid., pp. 63–64.

attack the Americans. Run away brother policemen and agents."[66] Pan-icked moviegoers rushed from the lobby into the seating area as the other guerrillas lobbed grenades into the theater. Three American servicemen were killed and thirty-two patrons were injured in the blast, including three American women, two American children, and one British civilian.[67]

Urban terrorism, like its rural variety, also targeted Vietnamese who held esteemed positions in the community and were leaders or had leadership potential. The assassination of Tu Chung, editor of the news-paper *Chinh Luan (Political Discussion)*, on December 30, 1965, was an example of that goal. *Chinh Luan* leaned anti-communist, but it also criticized the Saigon government and US intervention. Chung and editor in chief Dang Van Sung received death threats at the newsroom, and when a letter arrived in mid-December announcing a "last warning," the editors published it, along with a reply stating that the paper was com-mitted to balanced news coverage and would critique groups, individuals, governments, and nations that deserved criticism. This stand cost Tu Chung his life. As he stepped out of his car in front of his home, NLF guerrillas shot him four times, killing him, before fleeing the scene on a motorbike.[68]

Although the image of the black pajama-clad guerrilla seems most well placed in a rural setting, the city by its nature was perhaps an easier target for NLF terrorism and infiltration. More than two million people lived in Saigon, and the population swelled as war refugees fled the fighting in the countryside. Even despite security checkpoints on the outskirts of the city, ID checks, and house-to-house inspections throughout town, Saigon offered anonymity to NLF guerrillas who organized terror cells, infil-trated political activist groups, and smuggled drugs and supplies out of the city. Prime Minister Nguyen Cao Ky emphasized development as the key to defeating the NLF, authorizing the building of a housing project for the urban poor. Youth volunteer groups ministered to Saigon's needy and worked in community organizing, but NLF worked through the well-connected elites as much as it did the disaffected poor.[69]

Attacks on Saigon had continued through 1964 as did discussions of what to do with American dependents. Due to NLF infiltration of political

[66] Ibid., p. 77.   [67] Ibid., p. 79.
[68] Ibid. pp. 47–49. For an in-depth analysis of *Chinh Luan*, see Nu-Anh Tran, "South Vietnamese Identity, American Intervention, and the Newspaper *Chinh Luan* [*Political Discussion*], 1965–1969," *Journal of Vietnamese Studies*, Vol. 1, No. 1–2 (Feb./Aug. 2006), 169–209.
[69] Robert Shaplen, "Letter from South Vietnam," *New Yorker*, March 1966, p. 58.

groups and protest movements, it was not always clear to the CIA or other outsiders who exactly was behind the unrest in Saigon. In August, CIA agents uncovered orders from the NLF's Saigon/Cholon/Gia Dinh special committee instructing cadres to foment unrest among Saigon's high school and university students. Cadres were to infiltrate student and Buddhist organizations and encourage opposition to the government.[70] Yet embassy and CIA reports also indicated agitation by politicians and others not affiliated with the NLF.

Late November saw a series of demonstrations in Saigon, some of which escalated to violence as citizens protested the government of Tran Van Huong. A march on November 22 grew particularly large, spiraled out of control, and resulted in violence. US Embassy officers observed demonstrators leaving the National Pagoda, and as they marched toward Gia Long Palace, a government residence, the crowd swelled to between 200 and 300 marchers. Security forces struggled to contain the protest. When city firefighters opened fire hoses on the crowd, demonstrators grabbed the hoses and turned them on the firemen. Anti-riot troops armed with nightsticks arrived, and the crowd dispersed, but later that afternoon, anti-government protesters returned to the streets with an even larger crowd. A US Embassy report estimated the number of protesters in the afternoon demonstration at 2,000, marching from the National Pagoda to Cong Ly Boulevard into the city center. Some of the protesters drove a truck with a loudspeaker in the march, calling for Huong's resignation. Security officers attempted to drown out the protesters with their own sound truck, but the vehicle stalled, and once they restarted it, it turned out that the speaker was no match for the protest's blaring loudspeaker. Violence erupted between civilians and police, grenades were thrown, and Huong eventually called in airborne troops, who arrived with tear gas and live ammunition. Nearly sixty civilians, police, and military personnel were injured, and one fifteen-year-old boy named Nguyen Van Khuong was reported dead. An embassy assessment of the demonstration suggested that opposition political figures and Buddhist leaders were involved in planning and instigating the event.[71]

---

[70] CIA Intelligence Information Cable, Viet Cong Plans to Further Anti-Government Demonstrations in the Saigon Area, Sept. 6, 1964, 2120319003, Douglas Pike Collection: Unit 01 – Assessment and Strategy, Folder 19, Box 03. The Vietnam Center and Archive, Texas Tech University.

[71] Telegram 19182 from AmEmbassy Saigon to SecState Washington, DC, Nov. 23, 1964. Lyndon B. Johnson National Security Files: Vietnam, 1963–1969, 998Micro00295, The Vietnam Center and Archive, Texas Tech University.

Students were especially angry because of Huong's orders increasing draft calls. On November 24, a group of several hundred Vietnamese students seized Le Quy Don School in Saigon and held an American woman teacher hostage in protest of the draft. It was a school that educated the children of Saigon's wealthy families. Huong retaliated by sending armed military police out into the city's streets to try and prevent subsequent demonstrations, but unrest continued. Students also occupied five other schools throughout the city, including one owned by the director of a Saigon radio station.[72] CIA agents searched for evidence of NLF involvement in the demonstrations, and although they reported nothing conclusive, embassy officers asserted that they must "assume VC hand" guided the unrest. Embassy officials asserted that the work of the "young punks" who participated in the school seizures and street protests did not represent the general will of Saigon residents.[73]

On February 7, 1965, President Lyndon B. Johnson announced that all American dependents of US personnel in Vietnam were to be evacuated immediately from the country. The directive came in the wake of growing anti-American sentiment, violence against Americans, and sneak attacks in Saigon. Most dependents were wives and children of American diplomats and advisors, and the vast majority lived in Saigon, the heart of US operations in the early 1960s. Members of the Johnson administration had been in talks about evacuating American dependents since January of 1964 "in light of recent terrorism against Americans in Saigon." By February 20, 1964, Americans had reported fifteen attacks, including the bombing of a softball game in which five Americans died and more than fifty, including dependents, were wounded, in addition to the incident at the Kinh-Do Theater.[74] But despite the attacks on Americans, some officials opposed the evacuation of dependents from Saigon because they feared it would cause panic among Vietnamese who might consider the evacuation a sign that the United States was preparing to abandon them.[75] Others, such as General William Westmoreland, worried that

[72] "Students Seize School in Saigon," *New York Times*, Nov. 24, 1964, p. 1.
[73] Telegram 021248 from AmEmbassy Saigon to SecState Washington, Nov. 25, 1964. Lyndon B. Johnson National Security Files: Vietnam, 1963–1969, 998Micro0295, The Vietnam Center and Archive, Texas Tech University.
[74] Message from the Ambassador in Vietnam (Lodge) to the President, Saigon, Feb. 20, 1964, *Foreign Relations of the United States, 1964–1968* (Washington, DC: U.S. Government Printing Office, 1992) 1:94–95. [Hereafter *FRUS*, followed by year and volume].
[75] Memorandum from the Secretary of Defense (McNamara) to the President, Washington, March 16, 1964, *FRUS, 1964–1968*, 1:153–167.

sending wives and children home would harm the recruiting efforts of some agencies and prevent personnel from staying in Vietnam beyond a one-year tour of duty.[76] From the perspectives of some of Johnson's advisors, evacuating dependents held serious consequences for the US mission in Vietnam.

In 1966, the NLF launched an urban strategy called the "1966 Revolution." It emphasized that the political struggle in the cities was of equal value to the armed struggle in the countryside. The strategy specifically targeted urban youth to enlist them as the foot soldiers in the urban confrontation between authorities and citizens.[77] NLF terrorism motivated the US government and military to relocate Americans away from Saigon. In August 1966, US President Lyndon Johnson ordered the military to reduce its presence in the city. The plan, known as "Operation MOOSE" for "Move Out of Saigon Expeditiously," relocated the majority of US Army personnel from Tan Son Nhut air base in Saigon to the base at Long Binh.[78] It also made Saigon off-limits to combat GIs on R&R and to all incoming troops. According to a *Time* magazine report, Operation MOOSE cut the number of American soldiers in Saigon from about 71,000 to about 36,000 by the end of 1967.[79] In March 1972, as US troops gradually left Vietnam due to President Richard Nixon's "Vietnamization" plan, the mayor of Saigon announced that all "hostess bars" catering to Americans must move out of downtown Saigon. The mayor ordered the clubs to the city's ninth precinct, across the Saigon River. The only way to get there was by boat.[80]

Writing for the *Yale Alumni Magazine* in October 1967, Howard Moffett offered an astute observation about Americans' understanding of the Vietnam War: "There has never been a more difficult war to cover, but it is nevertheless startling to realize that *Newsweek*'s most successful

---

[76] Summary Record of a Meeting, Honolulu, June 1, 1964, *FRUS, 1964–1968*, 1:422–433.

[77] Quinn-Judge, *Vietnam and the West*, pp. 165–166.

[78] Memo, Department of the Army, 28 Headquarters, USA Regional Communications Group Vietnam, "Report of MOOSE Action, FY69," Oct. 31, 1968, National Archives, Records of the United States Forces in Southeast Asia. Record Group 472, Box 116, Folder 1378 – "Project Moose Reports." See also, Memo, "United States Army, Vietnam MOOSE Plan, FY 70," April 1, 1969. National Archives, Records of the United States Forces in Southeast Asia. Record Group 472, Box 116, Folder 1378 – "Project Moose Reports."

[79] "Cleaning Up Saigon," *Time*, Dec. 1, 1967, www.time.com/time/magazine/article/0,9171, 712011,00.html.

[80] "Closing Time," *Time*, March 20, 1972, www.time.com/time/magazine/article/0,9171, 942505,00.html.

treatment of Vietnam came in this summer's special issue on 'The Vietnam War and American Life.' We have almost given up trying to understand what is happening over there and are now simply trying to explain what effects it has had here at home."[81] Moffett casts South Vietnam's problem as one similar to the tensions felt in Iran, Afghanistan, and other countries where an educated, worldly, urban elite clashed or was disconnected from the rural populace, which tended to be conservative in their politics and traditional in their culture. He called it "the conflict between traditionalism and modernism in a developing society." Colonialism had widened the gap by concentrating the best schools in the cities. Rural youth whose families could afford to send them to urban schools often never returned home, having fallen under the spell of the city's charm, and, on a practical level, found that the kinds of professional and civil service jobs their education prepared them for existed primarily in the cities. Educated young adults stayed in the cities rather than returning home and serving as a bridge between city and country across which they could share ideas and build a common worldview. The influx of rural refugees into cities because of the war remained isolated, and their circumstances were not conducive to establishing connections between country and city. It was unclear whether they were loyal to the government or the NLF.[82]

Americans involved with the US intervention in Vietnam ignored or dismissed the educated elites, conceiving of all Vietnamese as simple peasants. Americans' inability or unwillingness to acknowledge their Vietnamese friends' cultural refinement – indeed, that they were "civilized" – constituted one of the most significant missed opportunities of the Vietnam War. Educated Vietnamese resented that Americans did not treat them as equals, and this reduced the effectiveness of US intervention.[83] Complicating matters further were regional divisions and resentments among the Vietnamese. Born-and-raised Southerners, who comprised the majority of South Vietnam's population, took offense to what appeared to be minority northern control in Saigon. The one million refugees who fled the north in 1954 – including Nguyen Cao Ky – seemed to dominate. Activists in Hue longed to return it to the capital of Vietnam, demoting Saigon to a second-rate city.[84]

South Vietnam was also split into political factions, from religious groups such as Catholics, Buddhists, the Cao Dai, and the Hoa Hao;

---

[81] Howard Moffett, "Reporting the Cool-Medium War," *Yale Alumni Magazine*, Oct. 1967, p. 26.
[82] Ibid., pp. 26–27.   [83] Ibid., p. 27.   [84] Ibid., p. 28.

the Army; and old-line political parties such as the Dai Viets and the VNQDD. Some of these groups were even splintered within.[85] The media represented the political prism that was South Vietnam. In the fall of 1967, thirty newspapers were published in the country, twenty-seven of them in Saigon. Most represented a particular political point of view, and the circulation of multiple perspectives made it difficult for any one group to unify the population as the Hanoi government had united North Vietnam under one highly centralized ideology.[86]

Even as the American presence in Saigon dwindled, and even after the indecisive Tet Offensive of 1968, the NLF understood the importance of Saigon. In 1971, NLF cadres in the Saigon area began making plans to launch a mass uprising in the capital city, believing it was key, more so than the villages, to the ultimate success of the communist movement. Saigon was a powerful cultural, political, and military symbol of South Vietnam, and with more than three million people concentrated in a fairly small area compared to two to three million rural dwellers spread throughout the Mekong Delta region, the political impact of a Saigon uprising would be greater. NLF leaders also speculated that the political engagement of Saigon's middle class would be more significant given its location in the seat of the federal government, and so convincing this group to abandon their primarily neutral stance and join the communist front would constitute a major NLF victory.[87]

Though confident, the cadres in and around Saigon knew that gaining the support of the urban middle class was not a foregone conclusion. Pro-communist sympathies had never been the primary motivation of political unrest in the city. Opposition to the draft brought students into the streets, and austerity measures, including higher taxes, alienated small business owners and other members of the "petty bourgeoisie."[88] As frustration with President Nguyen Van Thieu spread to the political right, NLF leadership in the cities, especially Saigon, instructed cadres to try and capitalize on anti-Thieu sentiment in order to control rightist groups that would not otherwise feel any connection to the communist cause. In order to do so, the NLF would need to strengthen its leadership, build closer relationships with urban contacts, and convince the noncommunist anti-

[85] Ibid., p. 28.   [86] Ibid., p. 29.

[87] VC Plan for Taking Over Saigon through a Large-Scale Mass Uprising, May 18, 1971, Folder 03, Box 16, Douglas Pike Collection: Unit 02 – Military Operations, The Vietnam Center and Archive, Texas Tech University (hereafter Vietnam Archive).

[88] Ibid.

Thieu element to join the NLF in demanding complete US withdrawal, not just troop withdrawal, from Vietnam.[89] Capturing Saigon, NLF leaders concluded, would take a deeper political effort aimed at convincing their fellow countrymen that theirs was the right side.

There were some experienced nationalists in Saigon who would help. Educated elites like the lawyers Ngo Ba Thanh and Nguyen Long had participated in the peace movement that dated back to the Diem era. They opposed foreign support for the Saigon government and believed the NLF better represented the southern population than the US-backed Saigon government. Some joined the NLF and established anti-government organizations meant to appear independent of the Front even though their members worked secretly with the Communists. When questioned by police or Americans, the southern nationalists asserted that they were not members of Hanoi's Communist Party, called the Vietnam Workers Party or Lao Dong, which was true for many of them. For them, communism was not the point. Freedom to decide Vietnam's future was the point.

The name of the organization that Thanh and Long helped establish expressed their philosophy clearly. In 1964, they founded the Movement for the People's Self-Determination, announcing in a leaflet that the group supported "America for Americans. South Vietnam for South Vietnamese. We demand that the NLF and the government negotiate peace between the two brothers. South Vietnam must have the right to determine its own future."[90] Members believed that if they supported the NLF, they would accumulate political capital and favor with Hanoi, which they could use if the war ended in a northern victory. Neither house arrest nor prison nor exile sapped their commitment to self-determination. They asserted their claims to nonaligned nationalism from their prison cells, during their hunger strikes, and at their press conferences. Yet what Americans and Saigon authorities saw were dangerous activists whose vision of independence would undoubtedly unify Vietnam under a communist government.

[89] PRP C.C. Strategy for Political Struggle in Cities, Sept. 15, 1974, Folder 02, Box 34, Douglas Pike Collection: Unit 01 – Assessment and Strategy, Vietnam Archive.

[90] Truong Nhu Tang, *A Viet Cong Memoir: An Inside Account of the Vietnam War and Its Aftermath* (New York: Vintage Books, 1986), p. 93.

2

A Tradition of Activism

At a dinner party in early 1965, a group of Saigon elites decided to submit a cease-fire petition to the government of South Vietnam. The party was held in the Saigon suburb of Gia Định, at the villa of forty-two-year-old Trương Như Tăng, director of Hiệp Hòa sugar company. The attendees recognized their privilege, that, as "educated patriots and industrialists," they were at the top of Saigon society. They lived the good life but believed it should not be just for them. Twenty years of war had brought so much sorrow to the Vietnamese people that it was now time to figure out how to end the bloodshed and bring lasting stability to Vietnam. The group assembled at the dinner party included doctors, lawyers, engineers, professors, wealthy industrialists, and government officials. Nguyen Long, a lawyer who had been active in the peace movement of the 1950s and whose son had joined the National Liberation Front in 1962, led the discussion. In 1964, Long had founded the Movement for People's Self-Determination, and most of the people at the dinner party were members.[1] A Catholic in the group noted that Pope Paul VI had sent a message to bishops and priests throughout the world urging peace, an encouraging bit of news as they thought about how they might shape Vietnam's future.[2]

Long's self-determination movement was not grassroots. It was a legal organization, properly registered with the Saigon government, and

---

[1] Members of the Peace Movement, 1967, Folder 04, Box 12, Douglas Pike Collection: Unit 08 – Biography, The Vietnam Center and Archive, Texas Tech University.

[2] Ủy Ban Vận Động Hòa Bình, 15-2-1965. Ho so so: 30223, Về họat động của Ủy Ban Bảo vệ Hòa Bình và Phong trào Dân tộc Tự quyết năm 1965–1968. Tập 1: Điều tra, họat động. TTLTQG II.

secretly attached to the NLF. Tang and his associates saw an opportunity to exploit the political chaos in Saigon after the death of Diem, and especially during Nguyen Khanh's fragile reign in 1964. The Movement for Self-Determination aimed to mobilize disgruntled citizens frustrated by dysfunctional government and US intervention. By concealing the movement's connection to the NLF, leaders hoped to reach as many citizens as possible who hoped the Vietnamese would be left alone to determine their fate. Ideology was not important so long as all members and activists agreed with the demands for freedom and independence.[3]

Long, Tang, and most of the other partygoers were experienced rebels. Many had been active in the Viet Minh against France after World War II. Long and others had gotten into trouble during the Diem presidency because of their involvement with the Saigon peace movement, and Tang was one of the founders of the National Liberation Front.[4] Another member, Pham Van Huyen, had also been associated with the Viet Minh, but after the war, Michigan State's Wesley Fischel encouraged Ngo Dinh Diem to appoint him Commissioner General for Refugees, putting Huyen in charge of refugees who fled the north after the partition of Vietnam in 1954.[5] They considered themselves nationalists, and some were either openly or covertly associated with the NLF.

Elites such as those who attended Tang's party vindicated Americans' and the Saigon government's reluctance to trust Vietnamese political activists who were not explicitly pro-government. Both anticommunists and those affiliated with the NLF called themselves nationalists. Because the NLF portrayed itself as an organic southern movement, not one under Hanoi's direction, its members and affiliates could argue that they represented South Vietnamese citizens, not the will of Hanoi. Members of the self-determination movement had the resumes to suggest commitments to both nationalism and communism. Many had joined the Viet Minh against the French and then later got involved in movements against the presidency of Ngo Dinh Diem. During the Vietnam War, leaders of groups affiliated with the NLF, such as the Movement for People's

---

[3] Truong Nhu Tang, *A Viet Cong Memoir: An Inside Account of the Vietnam War and Its Aftermath* (New York: Vintage Books, 1986), p. 92.

[4] For an in-depth account of Tang's role in the NLF and self-determination movement, see Tang, *A Viet Cong Memoir*.

[5] Tu Pham Van Huyen, Da Nang 15-3-1965, Kinh goi: Thien Tuong Tu Lenh Quan Doan I, Kiem Tu Lenh Vung I Chien Thuat, Kiem Dai Bieu Chinh Phu Trung Nguyen Trung Phan Da Nang. Ho so so: 30226, Ve hoat dong cua Uy ban Bao ve Hoa Binh va Phong Trao Dan Toc Tu Quyet. TTLTQG II.

Self-Determination and the Alliance of National, Democratic, and Peace Forces asserted that they sought to provide a political home for non-Communist intellectuals and other middle-class South Vietnamese who opposed the Saigon government. What was unclear to American and international observers was whether those who did not officially belong to the Vietnam Workers Party, the official name of the Communist Party headquartered in Hanoi, were willing to adhere to Communist ideology if an end to war would lead to a Communist takeover of South Vietnam.

Contemporary journalists and observers, and scholars after the war, used the term "third force" in reference to political groups that appeared to be neither pro-Saigon government nor pro-Communist. Ngo Dinh Diem had used it to describe his vision of a South Vietnam that was neither Communist nor colonized. The idea that a third force could exist in South Vietnam would later be codified in the Paris Peace Agreement of 1973. The treaty stipulated that a coalition government be formed in Saigon including neutral third force members until a permanent administration could be implemented. Some organizations that were tied to the NLF used the third force nickname as a disguise and asserted their neutrality.

This is what made the situation tricky for Americans in Saigon and Washington, as well as for Saigon government officials. Key members of these groups were not members of a Communist political party such as the Vietnam Workers Party or Lao Dong, the Communist party that ruled Hanoi. They talked of democracy, self-determination, and freedom, the same ideals that Americans and the Saigon government claimed to espouse, so it was difficult for Americans to determine which individuals and groups they might cultivate. Even if US Embassy or USAID workers on the ground in Vietnam identified potential political leaders, Vietnamese in general did not want Americans meddling in their affairs. That included doing things that Americans considered helpful, like attempting to groom someone to become a politically connected US ally. Americans understood this, and they tried to work behind the scenes, although the strategy often failed as it did when Ted Britton attempted to develop a Vietnamese peace corps. It was easier to manage one leader, such as President Thieu, than to assess and respond to the multiple personalities that existed in any citizen group. Part of fostering South Vietnam's independence was letting the president deal with his country's internal affairs, and that meant it was up to him to deal with political dissent.

Truong Nhu Tang's dinner party of middle-aged Vietnamese nationalists illustrates a link between an earlier phase of anti-colonial activism against the French and the political struggles in South Vietnam during American intervention over what courses of action to take to ensure

Vietnamese independence. As historian Robert K. Brigham has shown in his seminal work on NLF diplomacy, North Vietnam's communist party, called the Vietnam Workers Party (VWP) or Lao Dong, guided the establishment of the NLF in order to unite Communists and noncommunists in opposition to foreign intervention, including foreign-backed leaders in Saigon. Party leaders identified existing political structures, such as the anti-Diem movements like the fifties peace movement, through which to build the NLF. Quoting historian Huynh Kim Khanh, Brigham has written that the NLF was meant to be the VWP's "architectural façade," which would "promote the Party's ideological values and policies as widely as possible" while hiding its direct connection to the VWP.[6] In order to conceal the VWP's role in anti-government activism in South Vietnam, the NLF used groups and activists who denied affiliation with or were not actually Communists or allies. Brigham's analysis of the NLF diplomatic corps has revealed that its members were middle- to upper-middle-class-educated Southerners, and they had the ability to travel around the world and interact with international audiences to gain international support.[7] They had what Pierre Bourdieu called social capital, an elite standing that came from education, economic well-being, and international connections, and they set out to establish civil society in South Vietnam, from which they would assert control over the political fate of Vietnam. These activists became important after the assassination of Diem, when the Saigon government was up for grabs.

In South Vietnam, there were political activists aligned with the NLF and Hanoi who called themselves nationalists and argued that their main desire was self-determination. Whether freedom from foreign influence would allow communism to take hold in Saigon and lead to the reunification of the North and the South under Hanoi's control was not a goal that they necessarily admitted to holding. Doing so could land them in in jail or force them into exile. So they used the rhetoric of self-determination and asserted their belief that Vietnamese people should be left to decide their own national fate, free of outside influence. American advisers and their associates in the Saigon government worried that all political activism was of this type. If they trusted a leader or a movement, there was no guarantee that the long-term outcome would be a free and democratic nation that would be friendly to the United States.

---

[6] Robert K. Brigham, *Guerrilla Diplomacy: The NLF's Foreign Relations and the Viet Nam War* (Ithaca, NY: Cornell University Press, 1999), p. 11.
[7] Ibid., p. 22.

Vietnamese of various political persuasions fought the battle over who was the rightful representative of the southern people with words. The ideas embedded in the rhetoric were the same across groups: freedom, democracy, independence, the right of the Vietnamese people to control their destiny. Self-determination activists pointed to their long history of involvement in nationalist movements as proof of their commitment to Vietnamese freedom, and their elite status gave them access to local and foreign media and international political networks. With global attention focused on Vietnam as an example of how Cold War geopolitics affected the formation of postcolonial nations, the international mood mattered. Americans, the South Vietnamese government, the NLF, and self-determination activists all sent delegates abroad to plead their cases to the world.

As South Vietnam attempted to build a new government regime after the murder of Diem in November 1963, the revolving door into and out of the presidential palace exacerbated the country's political chaos. The South Vietnamese government labeled all groups and their members Communists and set out to persecute them. CIA investigations were less conclusive, in some cases finding no evidence of Communist connections. This speaks to the success of the NLF in presenting the image of independent anti-government political action in South Vietnam. Americans' inability to pinpoint the political affiliations of elite Saigon activists led them to work on establishing a solid head of state first, en route to building a democratic government. US Embassy officers and other American advisers focused their efforts on cultivating individual leaders so as to avoid the risk involved in using a diverse civil society as the channel through which to establish democratic political institutions and processes. Southern elite activists could then use America's risk aversion to argue that the United States was simply interested in supporting an authoritarian regime in South Vietnam against the will of Vietnamese citizens.

American choices determined the course of the Vietnam War, but only to a point. International mood mattered, and members of the Movement for People's Self-Determination, also referred to as the Movement for Self-Determination, used rhetoric that spoke to a global public that was skeptical of, if not hostile to, US interventions in the affairs of other countries. Self-determination rhetoric was the weapon in the political struggle alongside the NLF violence and terrorism that constituted the urban struggle. Members of the self-determination movement spoke of freedom, peace, democracy, and the right of the Vietnamese to decide among themselves how to govern their nation. They criticized foreign influence, deliberately naming not just the United States, but also the Soviet Union, China, and France. Activists' emphasis on the themes of freedom and peace, buzzwords that had universal appeal across political lines, challenged American intervention in Vietnam by asserting that US involvement got in the way of achieving what Americans claimed to want for the Vietnamese, the ability to choose their future. The rhetoric resonated with activists throughout the global sixties. While Madame Ngo Ba Thanh, one of the leading members of the self-determination movement, was in prison for her political activities, she received a letter from Japan, signed by a supporter named Tsuyashi Sugihara, telling her that Thanh's statement, "tu do hay la chet" – "freedom or death" – inspired the Japanese people who want peace.[8] Freedom or death – live free or die – what could Americans say in response to words that were central to their national identity?

As Brigham and historian William Duiker have shown, the Movement for Self-Determination had its roots in the anti-French struggles of the late 1940s and the peace movement of the 1950s. Cultivating support among the southern urban middle class was always central to the mission of the Hanoi-based Vietnam Workers Party, formerly the Indochinese Communist Party. Le Duan often referenced the importance of the southern middle class, stating that in South Vietnam, "the school and university students, the writers, artists, the intellectuals and scientists all enjoy a social prestige vis-à-vis the people of other strata in the cities." Because of this, he argued, central to the southern mission must be figuring out a way to "best rally the bourgeoisie with the National Front for Liberation."[9] One strategy was to draw urban elites into non-Communist organizations that were open to collaborating with the VWP.

Many urban activists had been part of the Viet Minh in the war against the French. After the partition of Vietnam in 1954, a group of non-Party leftists and former Viet Minh operatives established the Movement for the Protection of Peace, also known as the Saigon-Cholon Peace Committee, in order to consolidate middle-class political activity in Saigon. Party operatives believed that a united front of Communist and non-Communist anti-government activists was the best tactic as part of a broader effort to destroy South Vietnam. Members of the peace

---

[8] Letter to Ngo Ba Thanh from Tsuyashi Sugihara, date unknown. Ho so so 18525: ve hoat dong chinh tri cua ba ngo ba thanh nhu danh tran thanh van chu tich "phong trao phu nu doi quyen song" nam 1967–1974. TTLTQG II.

[9] The Leadership of the PRG, the NFLSV and Their Affiliated Organizations, 1973, April 1973, p. 3. Folder 03, Box 10, Douglas Pike Collection: Unit 05 – National Liberation Front, The Vietnam Center and Archive, Texas Tech University.

movement went on to form the NLF in 1960.[10] One such peace activist turned NLF leader was Nguyen Huu Tho, who had been active against the French and had led an anti-American demonstration in 1950. Tho was born in Cholon in 1910 to a civil servant family. He studied law in France before returning to Saigon in 1934.

In 1950, Tho led a demonstration of intellectuals, students, and civil servants against French suppression of civil liberties. He claimed to be working for peace between the French and the Viet Minh, but colonial police arrested and imprisoned him and he was arrested and imprisoned in a northern jail for two years, during which time he went on a hunger strike, which gained international attention. In 1954, he was back in Saigon practicing law and organizing the Committee to Encourage Peace, which led to another arrest before he joined the NLF. Tho eventually was made president of the NLF, but his public persona was one of a non-Communist intellectual and lawyer.[11] He had contacts in the international peace movement, and supporters included Americans Norman Cousins and Jonathan Mirsky, Paul Barraud of the French peace movement, and Sumi Yukawa, wife of Nobel Prize–winning Japanese physicist and peace activist Hideki Yukawa.[12]

Ngo Ba Thanh, a Columbia University–educated lawyer, was one of the most high-profile advocates for self-determination. She was born Pham Thi Thanh Van in 1931 in Hanoi and moved to Paris with her father, Pham Van Huyen, a physician, in 1949. In 1950, she married the director of fisheries for the South Vietnamese government, and she went on to graduate from the University of Paris and receive a Ph.D. in comparative law from Columbia University.[13] Both she and her father had worked for the Diem government – Huyen as the commissioner of refugees, Thanh as chief

[10] William J. Duiker, *The Communist Road to Power in Vietnam* (Boulder, CO: Westview Press, 1996), pp. 183–184. See also, Brigham, *Guerrilla Diplomacy*, pp. 4–11.

[11] Viet-Nam Documents and Research Notes, Document No. 111 – The Leadership of the PRG, the NFLSV and Their Affiliated Organization, 1973, April 1973, Folder 31, Box 01, William Duiker Collection, The Vietnam Center and Archive, Texas Tech University.

[12] Viet Nam Cong Hoa Bo Ngoai Giao, Kinh gui: Ong Dong Ly Van Phong Phu Thu Tuong, Trich yeu: v/v hoat dong chinh tri cua Ong Nguyen Huu Tho, 13-2-68. Ho so so 30227: ve hoat dong cua ong Nguyen Huu chu tich Mat Tran Dan Toc Viet Nam Tranh Dau Cho Thong Nhat Doc Lap Trung Lap Trong Hoa Binh. TTLTQG II.

[13] Embassy Saigon to Department of State, Telegram 08980, May 23, 1973, Central Foreign Policy Files, 1973–1979/Electronic Telegrams, 1973, RG 59: General Records of the Department of State, National Archives (accessed June 10, 2016).

judicial adviser.[14] After the assassination of Diem, Huyen and Thanh got involved with the peace and self-determination movements in Saigon.

Fluent in English and French and a skilled communicator, Ngo Ba Thanh, president of the Comparative Law Institute of Saigon Law University, became one of the main public faces of the self-determination movement and traveled easily between Western and Vietnamese circles. She was regularly invited to diplomatic meetings, including one held at the British Embassy in late 1964 or early 1965, where the main topic of conversation was Operation Rolling Thunder, the US plan to bomb North Vietnam. Also in attendance were British Ambassador Gordon Etherington-Smith, counterinsurgency expert Robert Thompson, US Ambassador Henry Cabot Lodge, General William Westmoreland, and ambassadors and military attachés from the Australian and New Zealand embassies. Thanh was the only Vietnamese person and the only woman in the room, and the men wanted to know what she thought of bombing strategy. You're a very clever woman, they told her, and we understand your desire for peace and self-determination, but we're going to the root of the problem. She assured them that a military approach would push more people over to the Communists.[15]

She was arrested in 1965 for her participation in the peace movement, and then in June 1966, she was arrested during a protest at Saigon University. She served two years in prison, only to be arrested again in 1971.[16] The groups with which she associated – the Committee for Peace, the Movement for Self-Determination, the Women's Movement for the Right to Live, and the Committee for Prison Reform – all billed themselves as noncommunist movements that opposed foreign intervention and, as the war continued, were increasingly antiwar. In the late sixties and early seventies, she worked with the Saigon Student Union, a group which in the early to mid-sixties had taken a moderate, primarily anticommunist stance on the political situation in South Vietnam but had grown antiwar and pro-reconciliation under the leadership of Huyen Tan Mam. US Embassy officers understood Madame Thanh and others

[14] Tang, *A Viet Cong Memoir*, pp. 95–96.
[15] "Vietnam: A Television History; Interview with Mrs. Ngo Ba Thanh, 1981," March 15, 1981, WGBH Media Library & Archives, accessed June 11, 2016, http://openvault.wgbh .org/catalog/V_0C7B0EF2BA92408985FB01E19CD727DB.
[16] Embassy Saigon to Department of State, Telegram 08980, May 23, 1973, Central Foreign Policy Files, 1973–1979/Electronic Telegrams, 1973, RG 59: General Records of the Department of State, National Archives (accessed June 10, 2016).

in these groups to be "non communist Leftist Saigon intellectuals," and they seemed to believe her admission that she and her groups were more popular with the international intelligentsia than with the average Vietnamese citizen. Madame Thanh was a member of the Women's International League for Peace and Freedom, and she had cultivated a wide network of friends and supporters in the United States and Europe.[17]

Ngo Ba Thanh's connection with high-ranking American and Western operatives did not protect her from the South Vietnamese government's efforts to go after suspected communists and other potential insurgents. In the political chaos of Saigon in 1964 and 1965, members of the fifties-era peace movement regrouped to form the Movement for People's Self-Determination and the Committee to Encourage Peace. A CIA report on the "fluid and complex" situation in South Vietnam in September of 1964 indicated that there was still hope for clearing the chaos if the right leader could take and keep power as head of state.[18] Meanwhile, Buddhists, students, intellectuals, politicians, and military leaders were all asserting themselves into the volatile mix and trying to get their voices heard. While the disarray stemmed in part from the freedom to assemble publicly and protest, liberties unavailable to citizens of North Vietnam, the political instability was exhausting, and neutralism, with its seductive promise of peace, attracted many in the south. CIA agents also saw more expressions of anti-Americanism. The chaos offered opportunities for Communist "mischief making," the CIA observed, and made it easy for Communists to influence the political situation in South Vietnam.[19]

Some activists used the press to make their voices heard. Journalist and housewife Le Thi Ngoc Suong wrote in the newspaper *Self-Determination* (*Tu Quyet*) that the war in 1965 was becoming more serious and was pitting brother against brother, taking young people from their families. She wrote on behalf of all Vietnamese women who, though not on the battlefield, were experiencing the war up close because their sons, brothers, and husbands were fighting and dying. "'Where is my son?' 'Where is

---

[17] Embassy Saigon to Department of State, Telegram 08980, May 23, 1973, Central Foreign Policy Files, 1973–1979/Electronic Telegrams, 1973, RG 59: General Records of the Department of State, National Archives (accessed June 10, 2016).

[18] Central Intelligence Agency, Subject: SNIE-53-64. "Chances for a Stable Government in South Vietnam," Sep. 8, 1964, p. 4. Lyndon B. Johnson National Security Files Vietnam 1963–1965, Item 998Micro0294, DS557.4.L96, Vietnam Archive.

[19] Central Intelligence Agency, Subject: SNIE-53-64. "Chances for a Stable Government in South Vietnam," Sep. 8, 1964, pp. 10–11. Lyndon B. Johnson National Security Files Vietnam 1963–1965, Item 998Micro0294, DS557.4.L96, Vietnam Archive.

my husband?' These are our questions," she wrote in February 1965.[20] In another newspaper, *Truth (Chan Ly)*, a writer named Vu Quang Hung blamed the escalating war on foreign countries that had influenced the governments of North and South Vietnam. Hung argued that most rural Vietnamese follow neither the Saigon government nor the NLF. The conflict between the two sides was crushing them.[21] Even though neither writer overtly expressed support for Communists or the NLF, Saigon police asserted that the newspapers were NLF organs and ordered monitoring of the writers.

On February 25, 1965, members of the Committee to Encourage Peace and the Movement for Self-Determination held a press conference at Thanh The restaurant in Saigon to announce that they had been collecting signatures on a cease-fire petition.[22] Thanh served as translator for the international journalists invited to cover the event. Police raided the event and arrested Thanh, Huyen, founder Nguyen Long, and others. The Ministry of Domestic Affairs instructed the national police to deal harshly with members of these groups and to assume they were associated with the Communists.[23] Police also went after signers of the cease-fire petition who had not been at the press conference

By early March, authorities had arrested twenty-nine people, including members of government administration offices, a juror, military officers, engineers in the public works ministry, directors of companies, professors, teachers, journalists, artists, doctors, and housewives. Most of the accused were in their fifties and sixties, with a few students in their late teens and early twenties among them.[24] By mid-May, the arrest count was

---

[20] Le Thi Ngoc Suong, "Vai cam nghi cua nguoi phu nu trong mot mua xuan khoi lua," *Tu Quyet*, 2-2-1965. Ho so so: 30226, Ve hoat dong cua Uy ban Bao ve Hoa Binh va Phong Trao Dan Toc Tu Quyet. TTLTQG II.

[21] Vu Quang Hung, "Dan Toc Viet Nam co mong uoc chien tranh khong?" *Chan Ly*, undated. Ho so so: 30226, Ve hoat dong cua Uy ban Bao ve Hoa Binh va Phong Trao Dan Toc Tu Quyet. TTLTQG II.

[22] Danh sach nhung nguoi bi bat vi co Lien He Den Phong-Trao, Phong Trao Dan Toc Tu Quyet, 2 thang 3, nam 1965. Ho so so: 30226, Ve hoat dong cua Uy ban Bao ve Hoa Binh va Phong Trao Dan Toc Tu Quyet. TTLTQG II.

[23] Biên Bản Tóm Tắt Phiên Họp Hội Đồng Chánh Phủ, Đông Lý Văn Phòng Le Đức Hợi. 26-2-1965. Ủy Ban Vận Động Hòa Bình, 15-2-1965. Ho so so: 30223, Về hoạt động của Ủy Ban Bảo vệ Hòa Bình và Phong trào Dân tộc Tự quyết năm 1965–1968. Tập 1: Điều tra, hoạt động. TTLTQG II

[24] Danh sach nhung nguoi bi bat vi co Lien He Den Phong-Trao, Phong Trao Dan Toc Tu Quyet, 26-2-65 cua Bo Noi Vu. Ho so so 30224: ve hoat dong cua Uy Ban Van Dong Hoa Binh va Phong Trao Dan Toc Tu Quyet, nam 1965–1968. Tap 2: Danh Sach nhung nguoi bi bat, bi cau/luu. TTLTQG II.

up to sixty-nine, and sentences varied.[25] Nguyen Long received ten years hard labor followed by five years in exile. Le Thi Ngoc Suong got five years house arrest, and student Nguyen Van Ram got two years house arrest.[26] In addition to prison sentences, house arrest, and exile, some members and supporters of the self-determination and peace movements lost their jobs. A military court released Ngo Ba Thanh, but her imprisonment had gotten attention outside Vietnam, and two Spanish lawyers, Felipe de Sola Canizares and Francisco Vega, had sent telegrams to the South Vietnamese government asking that she be treated fairly.[27]

The CIA took a more measured approached to the activists. While a US government fact-finding mission in February 1965 concluded that urban political opposition to the government was driven by the NLF, a CIA report from March 3 stated that the degree to which Communists controlled Saigon political movements, if at all, was unclear. Americans knew that the South Vietnamese government had labeled the Movement for Self-Determination "Communist-inspired" and was particularly concerned about the cease-fire petition. A cease-fire would lead to an easy Communist takeover of the government, officials worried. The link between a cease-fire and a Communist takeover reinforced government suspicion that the self-determination movement was a Communist front.[28]

The national police decided to make an example of three members of the self-determination movement, including Thanh's father, Pham Van Huyen. A military court sentenced him, along with literature professor Ton That Duong Ky and journalist Cao Minh Chiem, to be expelled to North Vietnam for their involvement in the self-determination and peace movements. On the morning of March 14, Huyen, Ky, and Chiem, along with other self-determination activists, sat in a police interrogation room in Saigon. As officers gathered the three men to take them to the airport for a flight to Da Nang, and then, over the seventeenth parallel, Thanh,

[25] Viet Nam Cong Hoa Bo Noi Vu, Nha Tong Giam Doc Canh Sat Quoc Gia, 8 thang 6, nam 1965. Kinh goi: Ong Tong Truong Bo Noi Vu Sai Gon, trich yeu: v/v tong ket ho so ve Phong Trao Hoa Binh. Ho so so 30224. TTLTQG II.

[26] Danh sach nhung nguoi co Lien He Trong Phong Trao Dan Toc Tu Quyet Hien Con Giam Giu Hoac Truy To Truoc Toa-An Quan-Su Mat Tran va Tong Xuat Ra Bac. Ho so so 30224. TTLTQG II.

[27] Viet Nam Cong Hoa, Bo Noi Vu, Nha Tong Giam Doc Canh Sat Quoc Gia, June 2, 1966, so 017814. Ho so so 30235: ve hoat dong cua nhom tri thuc nam 1963–1968. TTLTQG II.

[28] CIA Weekly Report: The Situation in Vietnam, March 3, 1965, Folder 19, Box 04, Douglas Pike Collection: Unit 01 – Assessment and Strategy, The Vietnam Center and Archive, Texas Tech University. Item #2120419001.

Nguyen Long, and others began to scuffle with police, demanding first that the court should reconsider the men's sentence, and then that they should go to the North, too. To do so made sense to police officials; why not rid South Vietnam of all the members of these Communist-leaning groups? Nguyen Long and Ngo Ba Thanh were particular nuisances, but the Ministry of Domestic Affairs decided it would just be the three men who would be expelled, and they set the date for March 19.[29]

The original sentence had Huyen, Ky, and Chiem parachuting from 12,000 feet into North Vietnam, but the men and their families pleaded for a different mode of expulsion. The men were too old to act like paratroopers, they argued. They were just old men wearing glasses, Huyen wrote in his testimony to the national police. If we cannot see, how can we be expected to jump out of an airplane?[30] Chiem wrote that, as a journalist, his hands and feet were soft, not calloused like a soldier's who has parachuting experience.[31] The men convinced the court to modify their sentences so that they would walk across the Ben Hai River at the seventeenth parallel. Where they failed was in their attempts to convince the court that they were innocent. Huyen reminded authorities that he had worked with Michigan State's Wesley Fischel, a clear example of his anticommunist position. He and others had signed the cease-fire petition because they were tired of war and death. They wanted Vietnam to get back to business, to rebuild and enter the global community of nations. They were patriots, Huyen argued, and the government slandered them by calling them communists. Tossing them out of a plane into North Vietnam would be a wonderful gift for the real Communists, not only from a propaganda perspective, but also because they and other self-determination activists were South Vietnam's educated professionals. North Vietnam will put them to work in ways that will not benefit South Vietnam.[32]

Ky also maintained his innocence and argued that his desire for peace did not make him a communist sympathizer. He had opposed Ngo Dinh Diem, but it was because he believed that Diem had trampled on democracy rather than cultivating it. Because he had never been a communist, he

---

[29] Viet Nam Cong Hoa Bo Noi Vu, Nha Tong Giam Doc Canh Sat Quoc Gia so 09480, 20-3-65. Ho so so 30226.

[30] Handwritten testimony of Pham Van Huyen, 14-3-1965, Da Nang. Ho so so 30226. TTLTQG II.

[31] Handwritten testimony of Cao Minh Chiem, 14-3-1965, Da Nang. Ho so so 30226. TTLTQG II.

[32] Handwritten testimony of Pham Van Huyen, 14-3-1965, Da Nang. Ho so so 30226. TTLTQG II.

wondered how he would live among them in North Vietnam. If the police refused to allow him to stay in the South, he hoped he would at least be able to send farewell letters to his literature students and his eighty-seven-year-old mother. He also hoped he could see his wife one last time to make sure her affairs were in order for her and their children.[33] Ky's wife wrote to the Minister of Domestic Affairs, accusing the government of disrespecting human rights and acting undemocratically.[34] Cao Minh Chiem also insisted that he was a patriot, and that he and his family were committed to fighting against the communists.[35]

Prime Minister Phan Huy Quat allowed the men to see their wives on March 18, and I Corps military authorities confirmed plans to escort the men across the Ben Hai River the following day. At 10am on March 19, the Minister of Domestic Affairs, a representative from psychological warfare, military officers, journalists, family members of the accused, the Quang Tri province chief, and curious Quang Tri residents assembled near the Ben Hai Bridge. North Vietnamese guards waited for them on the other side. Members of the crowd on the south side of the bridge taunted the men as they crossed, calling them communists, shouting that they got what they deserved, denouncing the NLF and Ho Chi Minh. Police shoved the men forward as they walked.[36] A CIA agent observing the event noted that the NVA guards "warmly greeted" the men and mused that the three might "lend themselves to Hanoi's propaganda purposes." Public opinion in South Vietnam appeared to favor the deportation.[37]

South Vietnamese officials argued that the government had the right to expel citizens if they posed a threat to national security.[38] Because of evidence that some members of the self-determination and peace

[33] Handwritten testimony of Ton That Duong Ky, 14-3-1965, Da Nang. Ho so so 30226. TTLTQG II.
[34] Letter from Ba Tran Xuan Hue Phuong, wife of Ton That Duong Ky and on behalf of their nine children. 13-3-1965, Kinh goi: Quoc Truong Viet Nam Cong Hoa. Ho so so 30226. TTLTQG II.
[35] Handwritten testimony of Cao Minh Chiem, 14-3-1965, Da Nang. Ho so so 30226. TTLTQG II.
[36] Telegram 20-3-1965 from Trung Tam Truyen Tin #1696. Ho so so 30226. TTLTQG II.
[37] "The Situation in South Vietnam," March 24, 1965, Intelligence and Reporting Subcommittee of the Interagency Vietnam Coordinating Committee, p. 1. Folder 19, Box 02, Central Intelligence Agency Collection, The Vietnam Center and Archive, Texas Tech University.
[38] Mat Dien Den, 15/3/65. Ho so so 30226: ve hoat dong cua Uy ban bao ve Hoa Binh va Phong Trao Dan Toc Tu Quyet, nam 1965–1968. Tap 4: Tong xuat Ong Pham Van Huyen, Duong Ky, Cao Minh Chiem ra bac. TTLTQG II.

movements had ties to the NLF, self-preservation from a government standpoint meant cracking down on those groups. South Vietnamese intelligence had intercepted NLF documents directing propaganda agents to encourage educated and wealthy Saigonese to join the self-determination movement. All South Vietnamese wanted peace, and most wanted foreigners out, the directive argued, so a neutral peace stance could be attractive to a wide swath of the population, even those who had close ties to the Americans and the French and were anticommunist. Intelligence analysts realized the group was similar to the 1950s peace movement, and its founder, the Saigon lawyer Nguyen Long, had been involved in the earlier group. These connections justified surveillance and arrests, the police asserted.[39] This included censoring newspapers and spying on suspected members of the self-determination movement. Self-determination activists were well-connected elites who had prior experience in anti-imperial, anti–foreign intervention uprisings, some going back to the era of French occupation. Their past experiences likely put authorities on higher alert than students did, although students posed a threat, too, in part because self-determination activists courted young people to their side. The Ministry of Education was to encourage deans, professors, and teachers to explain to students the consequences of joining the movement, and government offices were to fire known or suspected members.[40]

World opinion was never far from the minds of Saigon officials, and activities of the self-determination and peace movements encouraged the Ministry of Psychological Warfare to consider ways of improving South Vietnam's reputation globally. One idea was to send delegations throughout the world, especially to countries in Africa and Europe, where South Vietnam lacked support. If delegates would try to convince world leaders that South Vietnam was the victim of a Communist invasion.[41] Using print media, a propaganda campaign would aim to convince citizens that the

[39] Viet Nam Cong Hoa Bo Noi Vu Nha Tong Giam Doc Canh Sat Quoc Gia hoi Canh Sat Dac Biet So Ke Hoach, 26-2-1965, Kinh Goi: Ong Tong Truong Bo Noi Vu Saigon, Trich yeu: v/v Viet-Cong thanh lap "Mat Tran Dan Toc Tu Quyet." Ho so so 30223: Ve hoat dong cua Uy Ban Bao Ve Hoa Binh va Phong Trao Dan Toc Tu Quyet, nam 1965–1968, tap 1: Dien tra, hoat dong. TTLTQG II.

[40] Bien Ban Tom Tat, Phien hop hoi dong chanh phu, 26-2-1965. Saigon 3-3-1965, Dong Ly van Phong Le Duc Hoi. Ho so so 30223. TTLTQG II.

[41] Bo Tam Ly Chien Viet Nam Cong Hoa, Kinh goi: Thu Tuong Chanh Phu, trich-yeu: v/v de nghi goi Phai-doan Quan Dan Chinh ra ngoai quoc 26-3-1965. Ho so so 29402: ve hoat dong cua Bo Thong Tim Tam Ly Chien nam 1965. TTLTQG II.

peace self-determination activists demanded was a "fake peace."[42] If the government sentenced more suspected Communists to exile in the North, South Vietnam officials believed peace would have a chance in Vietnam. Because it would have been impossible to round up every Communist and ally, the Psychological Warfare ministry suggested that the government include students, civilians, and military and paramilitary personnel, to cultivate international contacts and spread the word to other countries about all that was good about South Vietnam. It was important for South Vietnam to gain the support of US public opinion, Psychological Warfare asserted. Vietnamese were also responsible for boosting the morale of American troops and allied forces stationed in-country. South Vietnam also needed more young people to join the Army.[43]

According to a national police report, word on the street in Saigon was that the government was not dealing harshly enough with members of the Committee to Encourage Peace and the Movement for Self-Determination. More than 300 people had signed the cease-fire petition, but the government only exiled three to the North. People wondered if the government was really taking a firm stance against Communists and their allies. The police report indicated that average citizens wanted the government to be firm with those suspected of having Communist ties and expel them to North Vietnam.[44] The CIA report of the citizen reaction to the Ben Hai Bridge affair seemed to confirm this finding.

Hanoi did try to put the exiles to work. In June 1966, Japanese diplomat Masuyuki Yokoyama told Edwin Reischauer, US Ambassador to Japan, of a recent meeting with his old friend, Pham Van Huyen, in Phnom Penh. It was the height of American, Vietnamese, and international efforts to establish peace terms following a major expansion of US combat forces in Vietnam. Yokoyama had been surprised to see him in Cambodia, having heard about his exile to North Vietnam. As the CIA agent observing the expulsion had predicted, Hanoi had welcomed him and treated him as an "honored guest." A few months ago, a government official had approached Huyen and told him the government trusted him

[42] Bo Tam Ly Chien Viet Nam Cong Hoa, 7-4-1965, trich-yeu: v/v mo chien dich chong am muu van dong hoa binh o Viet Nam cua Cong San, thuc dan va cac phan tu co hoi khynh to o Phap. Ho so so 29402. TTLTQG II.
[43] Viet Nam Cong Hoa Bo Thong Tin Tam Ly Chien, 27-4-1965. Trich-yeu: v/v phuc tinh cong tac cua Uy Ban Hon Hop Tam Ly Chien. Ho so so 29402. TTLTQG II.
[44] Viet Nam Cong Hoa Bo Noi Vu, Nha Tong Giam Doc Canh Sat Quoc Gia, 22-3-1965, so 09523. Ho so so 30225: ve hoat dong cua Uy Ban bao ve hoa binh va Phong Trao Dan Toc Tu Quyet nam 1965–1968. Tap 3: Ngung chuc cong chuc co lien he. TTLTQG II.

and wanted to send him on a peace mission to the Americans.[45] That Huyen was now an agent of Hanoi must have confirmed some suspicions about the links between the self-determination and peace movements, the NLF, and North Vietnam.

Huyen knew that Yokoyama was also on a mission on behalf of Japanese Prime Minister Eisaku Sato to explore peace options for Vietnam, and he hoped that his trusted old friend might help him contact Americans secretly. Reischauer wrote to Assistant Secretary of State William Bundy telling him Yokoyama's story sounded legitimate and worth pursuing. Ho Chi Minh was in Beijing at the time discussing Chinese aid to North Vietnam and the course of the war, but Huyen said the Chinese knew nothing of his peace mission, so if Hanoi could enter into secret talks with Washington and come to an agreement, they could present Beijing with the done deal.[46] The Chinese government loudly criticized US peace overtures as fake efforts designed to hide America's real goal, the expansion of the war and permanent colonization of South Vietnam. North Vietnam's Foreign Ministry parroted China's accusations, so it was imperative that officials keep their attempts to talk with Americans secret from North Vietnam's major patron.

The Hanoi government also put Ton That Duong Ky to work on its behalf. A representative contacted him shortly after he crossed the seventeenth parallel in exile, and soon the government shipped him off to Paris. From there, he slipped back into Saigon and became secretary-general of the Alliance of National, Democratic, and Peace Forces when it was established in 1968. The purpose of the organization was to bring together the small political and paramilitary groups that had developed throughout South Vietnam and were affiliated in varying degrees with the NLF. Front leadership sought to portray the Alliance as a non-Communist, grassroots political movement that illustrated the will of the people against US intervention and the government of Nguyen Van Thieu, who was elected president in 1967. An Alliance spokesman explained to a Japanese reporter that the group's ultimate goal was to restore peace in Vietnam. Members were "non-Communist nationalists and patriots, who do not belong to the Liberation Front" but were cooperating with the NLF to achieve peace, he said. They were primarily

[45] Incoming telegram 06813, Department of State from U.S. Embassy Tokyo, June 7, 1966. NARA RG 59, Box 2923, Folder 2.
[46] Incoming telegram 06813, Department of State from U.S. Embassy Tokyo, June 7, 1966. NARA RG 59, Box 2923, Folder 2.

intellectuals, students, "the progressive bourgeoisie, and the progressive elements of various political parties and religious groups."[47] Later, during the Paris peace talks, the Alliance would put itself forth as a "third force" able to bridge the divide between the NLF and the Saigon government.

The expulsions of Huyen, Ky, and Chiem did not stop self-determination activists. US air strikes against North Vietnamese targets and the arrival of US combat forces in South Vietnam in March 1965 compounded the disorder. International efforts aimed at ending the conflict in Vietnam included plans by UN Secretary-General U Thant, the British government, a group of nonaligned nations, and a France–Russia partnership, as well as the United States, South Vietnam, North Vietnam, and the NLF, which was trying to assert itself as the true representative of the South Vietnamese people. Disagreements over peace terms stymied the efforts, and the political situation in Saigon remained in flux. As peace talks moved in fits and starts into 1966, members of the self-determination movement continued to cultivate local and international support. In May 1966, Ngo Ba Thanh wrote a declaration announcing the mobilization of South Vietnam's urban intelligentsia for the causes of "freedom, democracy, and sovereignty." The government oppressed non-Communist patriots and allowed foreigners to divide the Vietnamese people by meddling in their affairs.[48]

Thanh's manifesto demanded what the self-determination and peace movements had been calling for since the assassination of Diem, if not before: an election to seat a national assembly, an end to war, and an emphasis on a political solution that would lead to the reunification of Vietnam. The war amounted to genocide in defense of a dictator regime, Thanh argued.[49] The message presented the core ideals that the United States used to justify its foreign policies not just in Vietnam but in the broader Cold War world. Yet with the self-determination movement counting among its members and friends NLF leaders, neither the Saigon government nor the United States could reach out to the group without undermining the strategy of solidifying South Vietnam as a viable non-Communist state. In June 1966, Thanh was arrested during a protest at

---

[47] Douglas Pike, *War, Peace, and the Viet Cong* (Cambridge, MA: MIT Press, 1969), p. 21.
[48] "Dat To," 26-5-1966. Ho so so 30235: ve hoat dong cua nhom tri thuc nam 1963–1968. TTLTQG II.
[49] "Dat To," 26-5-1966. Ho so so 30235: ve hoat dong cua nhom tri thuc nam 1963–1968. TTLTQG II.

Saigon University, and she served two years in prison.[50] Tapping in to student activism was useful, though, because the Saigon Student Union was veering to the left politically under the leadership of a student named Huynh Tan Mam.

Nguyen Huu Tho used similar language in 1967 in the run-up to the presidential election as he sought to develop his international support base. He spoke of Vietnam being divided and thus families being divided. He blamed the governments in both Hanoi and Saigon for hurting the Vietnamese people by holding stubbornly to their respective ideologies. Foreign interventions on both sides of the seventeenth parallel only weakened Vietnamese sovereignty, Tho argued in a manifesto he issued in the summer of 1967. The NLF was the group that would end the war, unite the two Vietnams, and implement the type of government that the majority of citizens wanted. Speaking to a global audience, Tho said he wanted the world to hear the truth about Vietnam and its history from a patriot and a soldier in the fight for world peace. The fact that Vietnam was still divided and at war was not the fault of the Vietnamese, Tho argued, but of the United States, which sent its troops in when it realized the ARVN could not defeat the NLF. Tho claimed that the majority of Vietnamese citizens favor neutrality because they believed it would prevent foreign meddling and allow the Vietnamese to establish democracy themselves. Tho called on the UN, peace and humanitarian organizations throughout the world, and the powerful nations to support the NLF.[51]

In April of 1968, the NLF established the Alliance of National, Democratic, and Peace Forces, which specifically targeted urban intellectuals. The organization pledged to work for an end to the war, the establishment of an independent and neutral government in South Vietnam, and the eventual reunification of the two Vietnams.[52] Representatives of the Alliance of National, Democratic, and Peace Forces made statements and

[50] Embassy Saigon to Department of State, Telegram 08980, May 23, 1973, Central Foreign Policy Files, 1973–1979/Electronic Telegrams, 1973, RG 59: General Records of the Department of State, National Archives (accessed June 10, 2016).

[51] Tuyen ngon cua Mat Tran Dan-Toc Viet Nam Tranh Dau Cho Thong Nhat Doc Lap Trung Lap Trong Hoa Binh cho chien cuoc Viet Nam do Ong Nguyen Huu (no date). Ho so so 30227: ve hoat dong cua Ong Nguyen Huu – chu tich Mat Tran Dan-Toc Viet Nam Tranh Dau Cho Thong Nhat Doc Lap Trung Lap Trong Hoa Binh. TTLTQG II.

[52] "Viet-Nam Documents and Research Notes," U.S. Mission, Vietnam, Sep. 1968, Document No. 42, 2310814010, Douglas Pike Collection: Unit 05 – National Liberation Front, folder 14, box 08, The Vietnam Center and Archive, Texas Tech University.

issued proclamations asserting that when war ends, South Vietnam will be a "democratic, non-Communist, neutral country, independent of North Vietnam."[53] In a July 1968 interview, an Alliance spokesman promised that the organization "calls for democracy, neutrality, and noncommunism," and that "the political platform of the Liberation Front will not force communism on South Vietnam." He went on to defend the Alliance's affiliation with the NLF, stating that the Alliance was collaborating with the Front only because its actions and goals were "compatible with the desires of the South Vietnamese people."[54] Yet Alliance members were mainly members of the southern middle class and elites, not rural people, and Alliance statements showed little to no evidence of close connections with representatives of the majority of Vietnamese citizens.

Both sides used the rhetoric of freedom and democracy even as neither upheld the principles. In March 1967, the South Vietnamese Constituent Assembly approved a new constitution that called for the election of a civilian government. It was to be the first election since the national referendum that elected Ngo Dinh Diem president. The constitution authorized the election of a president, vice president, and bicameral assembly comprised of a Senate and a House of Representatives. It also provided guidelines for local village elections, which were to begin in April. National elections were to be held in September and October.[55]

From the start, accusations of corruption tarnished the campaign season. Civilian candidates accused the Army of trying to thwart a political rally in Quang Tri province by diverting a military plane carrying candidates to the town of Dong Ha rather than the city of Quang Tri, where more than 1,000 people had gathered to hear from the candidates. Rivals Nguyen Van Thieu and Nguyen Cao Ky agreed in June to join together on one ticket led by Thieu even though Ky had announced his candidacy for president a month earlier. Ky faced allegations that he had used his position as premier in the military government to advance his presidential campaign, including using friendly journalists to promote him in the media and attempting to censor Thieu's announcement of his candidacy. Once word of his fraudulent activity got out, Ky found that his best opportunity for high political office was to sign on as Thieu's second in command.[56] Hanging over all this was a provision in the constitution

[53] Pike, *War, Peace, and the Viet Cong*, p. 23.   [54] Ibid., p. 23.
[55] *South Vietnam: Volume 2, U.S.–Communist Confrontation in Southeast Asia, 1966–1967*, Lester A. Sobel, ed. (New York: Facts on File, 1973) pp. 455–456.
[56] Ibid.

that prohibited "persons who work directly for communism or neutralism" from running for office.[57]

Despite this limitation on democratic politics, Saigon authorities sought to portray an air of commitment to democracy in word and deed. The preamble to the 1967 constitution lauded the "patriotism, indomitable will, and unyielding traditions of the people," and called for "a republican form of government of the people, by the people and for the people." Nguyen Huu Tho, Ngo Ba Thanh, or anyone else from the self-determination movement or NLF could have written its words. They spoke of years of "foreign domination" and its division of Vietnam, and how it was time for the Vietnamese to take control of their country and "unite the nation, unite the territory and assure independence, freedom, and democracy."[58] The only difference between the two sides was the method.

Officials also reached out to the UN and requested election observers who could certify that the process passed muster according to the standards of democratic practice. In June 1966, Nguyen Duy Lien, South Vietnam's permanent observer to the UN, petitioned for UN election observers in an effort to confirm the government's good-faith effort to conduct fair, free elections. The UN rejected Lien's request for several reasons. The provisions of the Geneva Agreements had already designated the International Control Commission to oversee elections in Vietnam, but the South Vietnamese government had refused to hold elections in part because of Poland, with its Eastern Bloc ties, had delegates on the ICC. Among members of the General Assembly, the main sentiment was one of opposition to UN involvement in Vietnam. Members feared that UN intervention would only hinder the peace process because it would anger North Vietnam and China. Only adherence to the terms of the Geneva Agreement would bring peace.[59]

Furthermore, UN delegates questioned whether it was even possible for fair elections to take place in South Vietnam. By banning Communists and neutralists from running for office, South Vietnam violated the UN provision that elections not restrict candidates on political grounds. South

---

[57] USAID Public Administration Bulletin Vietnam, No. 37, May 1, 1967. Folder 11, Box 01, Glenn Helm Collection, The Vietnam Center and Archive, Texas Tech University.

[58] USAID Public Administration Bulletin Vietnam, No. 37.

[59] "Note on Observers for the Elections to the Constituent Assembly in Viet-Nam," June 14, 1966. Folder "Peacekeeping Operations Files of the Secretary-General: U Thant-Vietnam, Request by Government of South Vietnam for Observers during Elections," Series S-0871, Box 1, File 4, United Nations Archives, New York, NY.

Vietnam was in "open civil war with thousands of political prisoners, wide areas of the country in military rebellion, and the largest religious group in more or less open revolt. There is no need for United Nations observers to go to South Viet-Nam to discover that the situation is not conducive to a free political campaigning and voting." In addition to the political principles involved, UN delegates also worried about the safety of observers. The NLF had threatened to harm election observers, but even without that risk, sending observers into a war zone would require the UN to also send a security contingent, which could compromise the objectivity of the observation. Free elections would not be possible as long as Vietnam was at war, UN Secretary-General U Thant concluded.[60]

UN members had reason to worry about the safety of election observers in South Vietnam. The NLF used terrorism to disrupt the springtime village elections, dispatching agents to attack voters and kidnap and kill candidates. The violence continued throughout the presidential campaign season leading to the 1967 election. NLF operatives killed 200 civilians during the campaign and on election day. At Nguyen Van Thieu's inauguration party on October 31, three NLF mortar shells exploded on the grounds of Independence Palace in Saigon, injuring three people.[61] The attacks were in keeping with the NLF's strategy of inciting violence to destabilize South Vietnam's political situation.[62]

While NLF cadres on the ground intimidated villagers and urban dwellers and attempted to challenge the US presence by targeting places where Americans lived and worked, including the US Embassy, leadership worked with self-determination and peace activists to present an image of an organization committed to Vietnamese freedom. NLF representatives and associated self-determination activists argued that the NLF was the rightful representative of the South Vietnamese people. Yet just like the Saigon government, they were not elected, nor did NLF leadership consist primarily of average Vietnamese. The founders were the elites of South

---

[60] "Note on Observers for the Elections to the Constituent Assembly in Viet-Nam," June 14, 1966. Folder "Peacekeeping Operations Files of the Secretary-General: U Thant-Vietnam, Request by Government of South Vietnam for Observers during Elections," Series S-0871, Box 1, File 4, United Nations Archives, New York, NY.

[61] *South Vietnam: Volume 2, U.S.–Communist Confrontation in Southeast Asia, 1966–1967*, 456, 461, 465.

[62] Sep. 6, 1964, Central Intelligence Agency, Intelligence Information Cable, Subject: "Viet Cong Plans to Further Anti-Government Demonstrations in the Saigon Area," Folder 19, Box 03, Douglas Pike Collection: Unit 01 – Assessment and Strategy, the Vietnam Center and Archive.

Vietnamese society, like Truong Nhu Tang. He and others argued that because the NLF had established leaders at the province and district level in some places, it was the true representative of the people.[63] The line between nationalist and Communist was blurry, making it difficult for Americans and the South Vietnamese government to offer definitive proof of an individual or group's affiliation and respond accordingly.

The election of Thieu to the presidency in 1967 brought an end to the game of political musical chairs that had been going on in Saigon since the assassination of Ngo Dinh Diem. For the self-determination movement and the Alliance, the Thieu presidency provided a clear target at which it could take aim in front of an international audience that was growing more and more vocal in its opposition to the war in Vietnam. Ngo Ba Thanh and other activists focused on political repression, especially the political prisoners the Thieu regime locked up. She knew what it was like, having served multiple sentences in South Vietnamese jails, and her international reputation drew foreign correspondents to her story. Cosmopolitan, well-educated, and articulate, Madame Thanh embraced the media spotlight. Madame Thanh always maintained that she was not a communist. She was never a member of the Party in Vietnam, and in the years after the fall of Saigon, as the two Vietnams transitioned to reunification under Hanoi, Madame Thanh and other third force activists were required to take a course in Marxism-Leninism, a milder form of reeducation than that which military personnel and Saigon government associates endured in the camps.[64] Party operatives monitored her activities even though she was elected to the National Assembly after the war ended.[65] Some leftist and self-determination activists, including student leader Huyen Tan Mam and Catholic priest Chan Tin, also found themselves under Party surveillance years after the war ended because they demanded political freedoms. During the war, none had the benefit of hindsight to know what postwar Vietnam would be like, and at the time, what had seemed most important was the removal of foreign influence in Vietnamese affairs.

From the perspective of US Embassy officers and other Americans who had close contact with South Vietnamese political activists, the fluidity of

---

[63] Tang, *A Viet Cong Memoir*, p. 86.
[64] Patrice De Beer, "Vietnam Two Years Later," *Le Monde*, April 24, 1977, p. 3.
[65] Situation in South Vietnam According to Refugees: November 1975, Folder 11, Box 25, Douglas Pike Collection: Unit 06 – Democratic Republic of Vietnam, The Vietnam Center and Archive, Texas Tech University.

the third force political identity made it difficult for Americans to identify allies and potential leaders who could establish a stable, secure, noncommunist government in Saigon. By backing military governments and Nguyen Van Thieu's presidency, Americans limited their opportunities to establish trust with urban elites, especially during Thieu's presidency because of his imprisonment of political dissidents. The ability of third force leaders such as Ngo Ba Thanh to use international opinion to their advantage raised the third force profile, and third force connections to the antiwar movement in the United States and Europe increased American advisers' suspicions about third force motives.

As Ambassador Ellsworth Bunker observed, Thieu did not have the ability to act freely as the military dictators that preceded him did. With an elected National Assembly in place and "a public opinion that has a surprising latitude for expression," Thieu could not simply issue proclamations that became laws.[66] That openness and the checks on Thieu's behavior allowed for the flourishing of a political movement that opposed the Thieu presidency. Because US Embassy officers could not identify an overarching political ideology with which to define third force groups, and because some third force operatives had connections to communist networks, Americans cast the third force as a phenomenon to be viewed with suspicion rather than movement for political modernization. Instead, Americans continued supporting Thieu, while occasionally scolding him about political repression and corruption. From the perspective of the United States, if the goal of US intervention in South Vietnam was to establish a viable noncommunist state, then supporting self-determination activists would have been too great a risk, even if the alternative was to only lightly chide the Saigon government for its persecution of suspected political dissidents. As President Nixon said, Thieu could do whatever he wanted if it helped the war effort. The cultivation of civil society likely would have led to the same result, reunification under Hanoi. Antigovernment activists used US opposition to their advantage in international propaganda by positioning themselves as democratic peace groups to an audience that already was skeptical of or opposed US intervention in Vietnam.

Older elites had connections and political experience, but they alone would not bring down the Saigon government. Saigon students also expanded their international contacts, and the student antiwar movement

---

[66] Telegram from the Embassy in Vietnam to the Department of State, Saigon, Jan. 24, 1969, 0444Z, document 7. *FRUS, 1969–1976, Vol. VI*, 16.

in the United States, along with other American antiwar groups, began publicizing information about Thieu's political prisoners in order to show that the Saigon government was far from being a functional democracy. South Vietnamese students told of military courts sentencing student leaders to hard labor "for having weakened the country's anticommunist spirit." They protested the government's shuttering of *Sinh Vien* (*Student*), Saigon's main student newspaper, in the summer of 1968. They accused the government of murdering students, such as Tran Quoc Chuong, a medical student who fell from the third story of the Saigon medical school to his death in August 1968. The twenty-two-year-old Chuong was the son of Saigon judge Tran Thuc Linh, and he had participated in protests against the government's involvement in university affairs and in favor of the use of Vietnamese as the primary language of university instruction. Chuong was "studious and peaceful," the Alliance argued, but government henchmen cut him down because of his "nationalist ideals." Alliance students issued a statement holding the Thieu government responsible for Chuong's death, and accusing Americans of having his blood on their hands, too. The statement offered a grisly account of how the students believed he died. Government agents kidnapped him, bound his hands and feet, and dropped him from the third floor of the medical school. The fall crushed his skull and shattered his bones, but it did not kill him instantly, according to the students' testimony. He writhed in a pool of his blood for a few moments before he died.[67] The Alliance understood the potential impact vivid stories like this could have in driving international public opinion against the Thieu government. Chuong was one of many young people fighting for Vietnam's freedom and independence, the students argued. Police had gunned down others in the streets, "martyred" prisoners in jail, and exiled outspoken youth to nearby islands.[68]

Established members of the peace, neutrality, and self-determination groups reached out to the city's young people. The elder activists understood the impact of images of young people marching in the streets in protest of an oppressive, foreign-backed government. Student groups had been vital to the dismantling of the Diem regime, and they remained vocal and visible in the aftermath. Ngo Ba Thanh was arrested for the second

---

[67] "Student Members of Alliance Rap Youth's Death," Liberation Radio in Vietnamese to South Vietnam, Aug. 5, 1968. Folder 10, Box 10, Douglas Pike Collection: Unit 05 – National Liberation Front, The Vietnam Center and Archive, Texas Tech University.
[68] Ibid.

time when she was caught in a protest at Saigon University, where she met student leader Huynh Tan Mam. The Alliance established a student wing to protest the Thieu government on behalf of high school and university students. Student members called themselves nationalists and patriots, and they accused Thieu and his American allies of ruining young people's lives by forcing them into military service to further "the American scheme of killing the Vietnamese people."[69] Alliance students worked to bring stories of government oppression of students to the world, reaching out to the World Youth Union, the World Students' Association, and other international youth and student groups to publicize stories of abuse.

Among those students was Nguyen Huu Thai, an architecture and law student who was president of the Saigon Student Association from 1963 to 1964. Like his older counterparts, Thai opposed US intervention in Vietnam's affairs, and he organized student protests in Saigon against the government. There was little unity of vision among students in the years after the fall of Diem, although continued foreign influence frustrated even the anticommunist students. For the NLF, the fractures among student activists were openings for cadres to slip in and, eventually, take control. When Huynh Tan Mam, a medical student at the University of Saigon, took control of the Saigon Student Union in 1967, he was an undercover agent for the NLF. The political chaos in Saigon, the government's targeting of young activists for arrest and imprisonment, and unpopular increases in draft calls made it increasingly easy for the NLF to gain youth support.

[69] Ibid.

3

South Vietnam's Sixties Youth

One morning in early November 1965, student leader Nguyen Huu
Thai visited US Embassy officer Melvin Levine at his Saigon apartment.
Thai was the president of an architecture students' organization at
Saigon University and former Saigon Student Union president, and he
hoped to explain to Levine why there had been so much student unrest,
not just in Saigon, but in Hue and other cities as well. Thai had made a
trip to Hue to try and get a clearer sense of the student perspective
there, and what he found was that the war was more real to students in
Hue than it was to their peers in Saigon. Hue students were concerned
about and frustrated by the large American military presence in Da
Nang, and the fighting in the I Corps rural areas felt closer to them than
perhaps the fighting in the Mekong Delta felt to Saigon students, Thai
explained. Thai wanted to see the rural areas for himself, so he took a
car trip through Quang Ngai and Quang Nam, and he talked with
peasants who believed that the ongoing artillery fire and air strikes
were indiscriminate rather than targeted at known NLF areas. Peasants
also felt squeezed by the growing refugee population and accused
refugees of harvesting their crops; that American troops often took
their farming tools, suspecting that they were weapons, compounded
the peasants' frustrations.[1]

---

[1] Telegram from the U.S. Embassy Saigon to the Department of State, Subject: Attached
Memoranda of Conversation, Nov. 10, 1965, Confidential U.S. State Department Central
Files. Vietnam, February 1963–66. Part I: Political, Governmental and National Defense
Affairs, Feb. 1, 1963, Stacks DS 556.58 .U55 C66 2000, Vietnam Archive Collection, The
Vietnam Center and Archive, Texas Tech University.

FIGURE 3.1 University Student volunteers made the concrete blocks with which they are shown building a dormitory for war orphans at the Buddhist Institute of Social Affairs in Saigon, undated.
Douglas Pike Photograph Collection, The Vietnam Center and Archive, Texas Tech University

All of this contributed to Hue students' opinions that the Saigon government had lost control of the country to the Americans and that the only way to bring peace at this point was to negotiate with the communists. Students also continued to demand an elected government, something they had wanted since the overthrow of Diem. Levine replied that representative government did not just happen "by snapping one's fingers." South Vietnamese leaders were working on it, but political agitation and chaos in the streets got in the way. Citizens needed to be patient; rapid change would only lead to chaos, Levine told Thai. It was not as though Americans were happy about the situation in Vietnam. Americans were paying the price in blood and treasure, and that earned US officials the right to give advice and have that advice taken seriously. They all wanted peace, Levine said, but the communists were the ones who started the war, and if they do not agree to stop, the only way to end the war is to either surrender to communist rule or allow the United States to help South Vietnam gain both peace and freedom from communist oppression. Reflecting on the conversation later, Levine thought that Thai had seemed anxious to be friendly, but while he did not dispute Levine's points too strongly, Levine worried that Thai had become attracted to neutralism.[2] What Levine did not realize was that Thai was already working with the NLF.

South Vietnamese student attitudes in the sixties spanned the political spectrum from anticommunist to communist and included opposition to foreign intervention and US assistance. The myriad opinions were on display at a conference of South Vietnamese university students in February 1965 in Saigon, where heated debates erupted over how students should respond collectively to political unrest, foreign intervention, and war. During a discussion on these issues, one student argued that they had to act; to do nothing would be to dig their own graves. Another student asserted that after twenty years of war against the French, the Vietnamese people were too tired to keep fighting. It was time for peace. If they advocated peace, though, they had to make sure it truly was peace and not simply a Communist takeover, countered a participant. The biggest problem was foreign intervention, someone else declared. Vietnamese citizens should not allow the United States, the Soviet Union, Britain, France, or any other nation to determine Vietnam's future. Antiwar students accused the war makers of pitting brother against brother, widowing women, and orphaning children. They pointed out that international leaders such as Pope Paul VI, US Secretary-General U Thant, the prime ministers of India and Burma, and even some Americans, were calling for an end to the war.[3] Ultimately, the conference delegates decided to issue a statement asking the South Vietnamese government and the NLF to end the fighting and come to a political solution to what one student characterized as a war of ideologies.[4] The diversity of opinions among students made it easy for NLF associates like Nguyen Huu Thai to operate undetected and difficult for Saigon authorities and

[2] Ibid.

[3] 15-2-1965, Sài Gòn Uỷ Ban Vận Động Hòa Bình. Ho so so: 30223, Ve hoat dong cua Uy ban Bao ve Hoa Binh va Phong trao Dan toc Tu quyet nam 1965–1968. Tap 1: Dien tra, hoat dong. TTLTQG II.

[4] 27-2-1965, so: 709, Canh sat Quoc Gia Saigon Giam-Doc Nha Canh-Sat Quoc Gia Saigon, De-muc: v/v Buoi hoi thao cua Luc Luong Hoc sinh chong chien tranh Lien truong Gia Dinh-Tan Dinh, 26-2-65. Ho so so: 30223, Ve hoat dong cua Uy ban Bao ve Hoa Binh va Phong trao Dan toc Tu quyet nam 1965-1968. Tap 1: Dien tra, hoat dong. Trung Tam Luu Tru Quoc Gia II (Vietnam National Archives II), Ho Chi Minh City, Vietnam.

American advisers to determine which students they might be able to cultivate as a base of support for the government.

The range of student opinions reflected South Vietnam's political scene in the mid-sixties. From the assassination of Ngo Dinh Diem in November 1963 to the election of Nguyen Van Thieu in September 1967, Saigon was up for grabs as a succession coup d'etat rotated heads of state through the government. American escalation of the war during this period increased the frustration of students who believed that a stable, civilian government and freedom from foreign intervention were the two keys to Vietnam's independence. For some students, independence included freedom from Communist control. Some students, including those who had ancestral roots in the North but fled south with their families in the 1954 exodus, demanded all out war against North Vietnam.[5] Like young people throughout the world in the 1960s, students in South Vietnam embodied the spirit of the global sixties as a hopeful moment in which the possibility of freedom energized those demanding political change. South Vietnam's university students staged protests, wrote letters, and drew up plans of action that tried to unite the disparate political interests among the nation's young people as politicians and generals in Saigon attempted to establish a viable national government.

American advisers on the ground in South Vietnam paid close attention to students, but Americans' tendency to conflate anti-government activism with Communist insurgency, combined with students' sensitivity to anything that appeared to be foreign control, caused the United States to miss opportunities to cultivate a young, vibrant, educated political base in the cities to support a non-Communist government in Saigon. University student unions were the most visible youth associations in South Vietnam and existed at the public universities in Saigon, Hue, and Dalat. At the forefront of youth activism in the 1960s, like US organizations Students for a Democratic Society (SDS) and the Berkeley Free Speech Movement, was the Saigon University Students Union, or Saigon Student Union (SSU). It developed as a politically active organization in early 1963 alongside Buddhist opposition to the Diem regime. SSU members demanded that the government protect the right to free speech, including that which criticized Diem and his policies.[6] Government agents

[5] Howard Moffett, "Reporting the Cool-Medium War," *Yale Alumni Magazine*, Oct. 1967, p. 28.

[6] Van Nguyen-Marshall, "Student Activism in a Time of War: Youth in the Republic of Vietnam, 1960s–1970s," *Journal of Vietnamese Studies*, Vol. 10, No. 2 (Spring 2015) 51–53.

infiltrated the group, which resulted in a decline in membership and influence once the government involvement was discovered. After Diem's assassination in November 1963, student leaders revived the SSU and began publishing the weekly newsletter *Sinh Vien (Student)*, which American and Vietnamese officials read regularly to try and understand the student position on national issues.[7] SSU was a fairly moderate group prior to the Tet Offensive, but by the late 1960s, students affiliated with the NLF had begun infiltrating the union, and articles in *Sinh Vien* grew increasingly critical of US intervention.[8]

Student efforts at forcing political change in South Vietnam would only go so far, though, partly because there was no broad consensus among students regarding how they should mobilize and who should lead them. University students tended to advocate for a moderate course of action and to urge restraint in vocalizing their message, while high school students were prone to public demonstrations and rioting, and it was in the latter that the NLF saw potential recruits. That the students themselves were not united, and in some cases were each other's adversaries, complicated the situation, making it at once more difficult for Americans to identify potential allies and easier for the NLF to exploit divisions among students in order to bring converts over to its side. From 1964 until the 1967 election, student unrest was largely due to the desire for a democratically elected civilian government, including the reinstating of the National Assembly. Contributing to the instability was the fact that the students themselves were divided by religion and politics: Catholics and Buddhists, leftists and moderates, university and high school students. Regarding the latter division, university students, as well as US Embassy personnel and other Americans in Saigon, considered high school students to be less serious, less aware of South Vietnam's political realities, and more susceptible to NLF recruitment efforts.

The story of South Vietnamese student activism illustrates the double paradox at the heart of nation building in South Vietnam – Americans knew that local leadership, buy-in, and action were crucial if any US-backed nation-building effort were to succeed, but they could not bring themselves to relinquish more than a modicum of control to the

[7] "Studies of Entrepreneurship and National Integration in South Vietnam," Feb. 1968, pp. 44–50, Folder 25, Box 18, Douglas Pike Collection: Unit 06 – Democratic Republic of Vietnam, The Vietnam Center and Archive, Texas Tech University. Accessed Jan. 12, 2016. www.vietnam.ttu.edu/virtualarchive/items.php?item=2321825004.

[8] Nguyen-Marshall, 55.

Vietnamese. Saigon government officials understood the need for public
support to prove that they, not the NLF, represented the will of the
people, but the government's repeated stifling of student activism turned
some of the brightest future leaders against it. As government repression
increased following student protests against the 1967 election, and as
Nguyen Van Thieu increased draft calls and funneled more young people
into the civilian self-defense forces in the wake of the 1968 Tet Offensive,
some students began to think about peace at any price.

* * *

In the 1960s, university students were an elite minority within the broader
population of South Vietnam, but their outspokenness and use of the
media kept them on the minds of Vietnamese officials in Saigon and
American observers and advisors. Four public universities in Saigon,
Hue, Dalat, and Can Tho, and the private Buddhist Van Hanh University,
served students, but enrollment was small. During the 1965–1966 academic year, for example, only one quarter of 1 percent of South Vietnamese youth aged nineteen to twenty-five was enrolled at a university.[9]
Student populations consisted mainly of the children of middle- and
upper–middle class urban families because it was too expensive for most
rural families to send their children to the cities where the universities
were located. This changed slightly during the war thanks to the wartime
economy, which brought prosperity, if only temporarily, to some families
that would otherwise not have been able to afford university. Often those
families had been country people who migrated to the cities to escape the
war, putting them in close proximity to the universities and thus elimin-
ating travel expenses.[10]

The broader result was that more country youth entered college in the
1960s, a strange consequence of the war. For the wealthiest students,
wartime restrictions on exit visas meant that more of them attended
Vietnamese universities rather than studying overseas.[11] War also served

[9] "Studies of Entrepreneurship and National Integration in South Vietnam," Feb. 1968,
    pp. 6–7, Folder 25, Box 18, Douglas Pike Collection: Unit 06 – Democratic Republic of
    Vietnam, The Vietnam Center and Archive, Texas Tech University. Jan. 12, 2016, www
    .vietnam.ttu.edu/virtualarchive/items.php?item=2321825004.
[10] "Studies of Entrepreneurship and National Integration in South Vietnam," Feb. 1968,
    pp. 6–7, Folder 25, Box 18, Douglas Pike Collection: Unit 06 – Democratic Republic of
    Vietnam, The Vietnam Center and Archive, Texas Tech University. Jan. 12, 2016. www
    .vietnam.ttu.edu/virtualarchive/items.php?item=2321825004.
[11] "Studies of Entrepreneurship and National Integration in South Vietnam," 11–13.

to equalize the gender breakdown of university student bodies. Because young men were subject to the draft, universities began admitting more women. The tightening of draft regulations meant that even the wealthiest of families could not guarantee that they could keep their sons out of the military. Staying in college indefinitely also did not protect young men from the draft.[12] In 1964, the government increased military service requirements to three years for all men between the ages of twenty and twenty-five.[13] The war's effect of increasing South Vietnam's university population contributed to the growing importance of students as a political force.

Sixties-era students followed in the footsteps of their predecessors, furthering a long tradition of the educated elite as a traditional source of political activism and protest. Going back to the 1880s, the "scholar-gentry" had voiced concerns about the impact of French colonialism on Vietnamese society, although it was not until the 1920s that a sense of Vietnamese nationalism began to develop among young middle- and upper-class intellectuals.[14] Student strikes and protests took aim at broad political issues and more personal affronts such as the poor treatment of Vietnamese students by French teachers in colonial schools.[15] In the 1920s, students signed amnesty petitions in support of the imprisoned revolutionary nationalist Phan Boi Chau and organized mourning ceremonies when he died in 1926.[16] Students also protested the arrest and imprisonment of Vietnamese nationalists in the 1920s and 1930s.[17] Frustrated young people found themselves trapped in the tension between the burgeoning ideas about national independence and the traditional culture that demanded deference to one's parents and a commitment to the family as central to one's life. Parents often did not like hearing anti-colonial talk from their children, and Phan Boi Chau had encouraged young people to make their own living rather than relying on their parents or a spouse. For many young intellectuals, it felt as though they had to cut ties with either tradition or modernity to release the tension, when what they wanted

---

[12] Ibid., p. 14.   [13] Nguyen-Marshall, 48.

[14] David Marr, *Vietnamese Anticolonialism, 1885–1925* (Berkeley: University of California Press, 1971), pp. 4–6.

[15] Micheline Lessard, "More Than Half the Sky: Vietnamese Women and Anti-French Political Activism, 1858–1945," *Vietnam and the West: New Approaches*, Wynn Wilcox ed. (Ithaca, NY: Cornell University Press, 2010), p. 100.

[16] David G. Marr, *Vietnamese Tradition on Trial, 1920–1945* (Berkeley: University of California Press, 1981), pp. 19–21.

[17] Ibid., pp. 387–388.

most was to move into a new political era without completely losing their connection to their families and customs.[18] Sometimes the impulse to rebel was as much of a motivator as was true patriotism, and revolutionary organizations in the 1920s used this to their advantage, emphasizing their ability to release youth from the clutches of "parental tyranny" in order to recruit members.[19] This generational tension reflected a global trend that continued after World War II into the sixties and seventies, shaping politics and culture in the United States, Europe, Latin America, and the decolonizing world.

Since the creation of South Vietnam in 1954, the South Vietnamese government had realized that students were a potential source of national energy and support. Authorities had been trying to mobilize students, especially as a way to counter the NLF's youth mobilization efforts that began in the early 1960s, but intergenerational skirmishes repeatedly erupted between students and older government representatives. Students wanted a sense of autonomy, but the government agents did not want to relinquish control.[20] The rift between students and the government widened during the Diem era, and students were key activists in the anti-Diem movement in the early 1960s. They united with the Buddhist opposition, forming what Americans believed to be a major cause of Diem's downfall. Diem felt their threat, and he deployed his secret police to infiltrate student groups, creating a vicious cycle in which police surveillance bred student distrust that caused students to try and organize secretly, which fed Diem's suspicions about them. When his police arrested students, it motivated other youth to join anti-Diem groups, which led to more arrests. Students' experiences with Diem-era repression created a strong bond among them and a perception that they as students were an effective and strong political force.[21] That self-image inspired post-Diem activity and made some student activists believe that "if the students but spoke, it seemed, the world trembled."[22] They saw themselves as the vanguard of a new order, but the chaos that followed the assassination of Diem smothered opportunities for sweeping democratic changes in South Vietnam, leaving once optimistic students disillusioned.

---

[18] Ibid., pp. 333–334.
[19] Hue-Tam Ho Tai, *Radicalism and the Origins of the Vietnamese Revolution* (Cambridge, MA: Harvard University Press, 1992), pp. 158, 198.
[20] "Studies of Entrepreneurship and National Integration in South Vietnam," 74.
[21] Ibid., p. 16.   [22] Ibid., p. 17.

US Embassy officials and advisers in South Vietnam paid attention to students as they worked to identify noncommunist Vietnamese they could enlist in their nation building efforts. Saigon featured the largest student population in the country, and their location in the heart of South Vietnam's political action made them of particular interest to embassy officers. Sources of young Vietnamese leaders included the military, Buddhist clergy, student and youth groups, municipal government offices, labor organizations, and teachers. Hoang Van Chi, a Vietnamese anticommunist intellectual, told a US Embassy official that the student political activism of 1964 was a good thing. Americans should cultivate student, as well as Buddhist, political engagement while also distancing itself from corrupt generals and older government officials. Doing so would give the United States "the best hope of producing a viable independent state provided U.S. support does not waver after the presidential elections," Chi argued.[23]

A reporter covering a student meeting for the *Hong Kong Tiger Standard* wrote that, having seen political repression under Ngo Dinh Diem, "students have no desire to see a repressive Communist regime here."[24] Students expecting an elected government after the coup against Diem would have to wait through a series of government upheavals in 1964, 1965, and 1966. After removing Diem, the coup organizers, led by Major General Duong Van Minh, established a military junta and dissolved the National Assembly and constitution. A subsequent coup in January 1964 deposed Minh and replaced him with another general, Nguyen Khanh, who censored the press and imposed a nationwide curfew due to unrest and violence. The previous December, at the Vietnam Workers Party Ninth Plenum in Hanoi, delegates had approved a resolution authorizing the use of military force as the main way to unify Vietnam, and the NLF sought to take advantage of the political instability in Saigon.[25] Late 1964 saw the move toward establishing a civilian

[23] Telegram from American Embassy Paris to the Department of State, Sep. 24, 1964, Subject: Miscellaneous Vietnamese Topics, NARA RG 59, Box 2916, Folder 7, "Gen. Policy Background."
[24] Gavin Young, "Discontent of young Vietnam," *Hong Kong Tiger Standard*, Oct. 14, 1965.
[25] "The Search for a Third Force in Vietnam: From the Quiet American to the Paris Peace Agreement," *Vietnam and the West: New Approaches*, Wynn Wilcox, ed. (Ithaca, NY: Cornell University Press, 2010) 162–164. See also, *South Vietnam, Volume 1: U.S.–Communist Confrontation in Southeast Asia, 1961–65*, 104. See also, Sophie Quinn-Judge, *The Third Force in the Vietnam War: The Elusive Search for Peace, 1954–1975* (London: I. B. Taurus, 2017).

government and a new constitution, but subsequent clashes between
generals and civilian politicians led to several additional coups and urban
unrest, while US Ambassador to South Vietnam Maxwell Taylor pushed
the various parties in Saigon to get their affairs in order or risk loss of US
aid and easy defeat by the NLF. A year after the assassination of Diem,
Saigon was "a mess," as an anti-Khanh pamphlet put it.[26]

* * *

One of the issues that motivated student unrest in 1964 was French
president Charles De Gaulle's Indochina neutrality proposal. As far as
some Vietnamese students were concerned, the French threat was as bad
as any other that year. De Gaulle had proposed that Western nations
work with China to establish a neutral political solution to the conflicts in
Indochina as the only way to ensure peace. Angry students tore down a
French military statue in Saigon in response to De Gaulle's neutralism
proposal. De Gaulle had broached the topic of a French-administered,
neutral unification of the two Vietnams with John F. Kennedy in the
summer of 1963, a few months before the assassination of Ngo Dinh
Diem, but Kennedy rejected the idea as long as the NLF existed in
South Vietnam.

De Gaulle's neutrality proposal was on the agenda of the National
Students Committee conference in June 1964 in Dalat, where 160 university students from Saigon, Hue, and Dalat met to discuss various issues,
from their desire for freedom university autonomy to national politics.
They demanded freedom of speech and assembly, as well as freedom
from government, religious, and any other outside control. They also
encouraged all students as well as the government to stand up against
De Gaulle's call for neutrality. It was a "fake peace" campaign, like all
policies of neutrality, the students argued. To be sure, the students wanted
peace, and eventual reunification, but not by handing South Vietnam over
to the communists. The executive board of the Saigon Students Union was
especially vocal in its opposition to communism. The delegates also called
upon their fellow young people to serve the nation, through both military
service and support of the troops. Student-run charity groups that ministered to soldiers in the field would be good for the morale of those on the

---

[26] VNCH Phiếu Trình Thủ Tương, v/v hoạt động chống chánh-phủ, 1-1965. Ho so so
15406: về các hoạt động chống đối chính phủ VNCH, Việt Công tại Sài Gòn năm 1965.
TTLTQG II.

front lines, the students stated. If they were going to serve the country, though, they wanted representation in government.[27] Student representation in government would require the transition from what was essentially a military dictatorship to some form of republican democracy, and students had been demanding that since the toppling of the Diem regime. However, also in 1964, a Saigon University official told a US Embassy officer that a neutralist solution to the conflict was growing in popularity among students and urban intellectuals.[28] Such a wide range of opinions – and comments from those who believed they knew the various opinions – contributed to the mystery, and the chaos, that characterized Saigon's political scene.

Unrest in Saigon in the summer of 1964 led Buddhist and Catholic students to come together and urge student unity in the midst of unrest among high school students. In a joint statement, the student wings of the Saigon Archdiocese and the Institute for the Execution of the Dharma called upon Saigon students to avoid violence and rioting and obey city and national laws. Students also called for intergenerational cooperation, arguing that disagreements and infighting of any kind only help "communists and colonialists" and could eventually contribute to the destruction of South Vietnam.[29] Le Khac Quyen, a Hue University professor and Buddhist, took control of the Buddhist People's Council of National Salvation, a political party that opposed neutralism and communism, supported war against the NLF, and demanded a civilian government and constitution. That fall, the Khanh regime established a civilian High National Council, which appointed Tran Van Huong, former mayor of Saigon, premier of South Vietnam.[30]

Even though Huong was a civilian, which was one of the criteria antigovernment protestors had demanded for a new leader, citizens launched major protests against the Huong government. Buddhists, Catholics, students, journalists, and some members of the High National Council criticized Huong for assembling a Cabinet without consultation, resulting in a body that did not represent a diversity of political and regional

---

[27] "Phiếu trình, Thử-tướng, Bầu cử Ban Chấp hành tổng hội sinh viên niên-khoa, 1964-65." Hồ sơ số 29870: Về tổ chức và hoạt động của tổng hội sinh viên Sài Gòn năm 1964-1967. TTLTQG II.

[28] Central Intelligence Agency Weekly Report, Aug. 27, 1964. Central Intelligence Agency Collection, Box 2, Folder 13, The Vietnam Center and Archive, Texas Tech University.

[29] "Student Groups Appeal for Interfaith Unity," *Saigon Daily News*, Aug. 31, 1964, 2.

[30] *South Vietnam, Volume 1: U.S.–Communist Confrontation in Southeast Asia, 1961–65*, Lester A. Sobel, ed. (New York: Facts on File, Inc., 1973), pp. 106–107.

positions. Opponents of Huong also complained that it included too many members of the Diem regime and Diem's secret police. A military junta no longer controlled the government, but authorities had yet to establish a democratic political system that would allow citizens to elect government officials. Huong tried to calm the demonstrators, but on November 13, he used the police and military to quell a student protest, the first time the state had moved aggressively against protesters since the unrest that previous summer. The students dispersed peacefully, but they remained angry at Huong.[31] The Ministry of Defense issued a proclamation warning students that if they were caught protesting against the government or encouraging others to protest the government, they would be drafted into the military immediately. Huong justified the harsh punishment by maintaining that unrest only benefitted the communist insurgency.[32]

A November 1964 investigation into student demonstrations conducted by the US Military Assistance Advisory Group (MAAG) concluded that much of the unrest among young people was the result of manipulation by "various political and even religious groups." By political, American advisers meant opposition to the Saigon government and to US intervention. It didn't have to be Communist-led, inspired, or affiliated; US advisers disliked activism of any kind. Demonstrations and protests could and often did descend into chaos, and opposition to the sitting regime in Saigon threatened the political stability Americans hoped to bolster. Establishing and preserving stability required at least a temporary suspension of the kinds of civil liberties such as free speech and assembly that Americans expected within their own democracy.

MAAG personnel suspected Buddhists and the NLF were involved in inciting students, and the report particularly scrutinized mass protests and rioting in which high school–age students were the majority, noting that "impressionable youths are easy to manipulate." The report indicated that demonstrations were large – from hundreds to thousands of participants – and in some cases, marchers carried clubs, lead pipes, and machetes. The MAAG report indicated that some of the protesters in recent marches had been hired. Local and international publics did not

[31] Intelligence note, Department of State, To: the Secretary, From: INR – Thomas L. Hughes, Subject: Political Crisis in Saigon, Nov. 27, 1964, The Lyndon B. Johnson National Security Files, Vietnam, 1963–1965, Nov. 1, 1963, Stacks DS 557.4 .L96, Vietnam Archive Collection, The Vietnam Center and Archive, Texas Tech University.
[32] "Demonstrating Students to Be Called Up, Government Warns," *Saigon Daily News*, Nov. 16, 1964, 2.

see that because protest organizers had been careful to present an image of teenagers and school children participating in the democratic process and becoming victims of political repression and police brutality because of it. The challenge for the South Vietnamese government, MAAG advisors believed, was finding the right balance between toughness and tolerance, which neither Diem nor Khanh had found.[33]

Mass protests threatened national stability and distracted the goal of establishing a viable nation, and so it was in the government's interest to prevent student demonstrations from happening, the MAAG report recommended. One way to do that would be to make military service a penalty for organizing and participating in a public protest. The organizers had to be punished, too, MAAG advised, because they were the ones recruiting children as young as eight to march "in the streets protesting against 'military dictatorship,'" when marchers that young likely had no idea what that meant. Forcing agitators into military service would help make up for the shortfall that existed at that point when ARVN was getting only about twelve responses for every 100 draft calls. University students were exempt from the draft, so making protest punishable by conscription depending on the nature of the protest could curb student involvement in anti-government activism. Young women were active in the political protest movements, too, and since conscription did not apply to them, MAAG suggested creating a Civil Defense Corps and drafting young women into it. The report noted that South Vietnam needed to mobilize "womanpower to care for the sick and wounded and serve in many administrative functions in the defense against the Viet Cong insurgency," and this type of noncombat personnel was a key component of counterinsurgency. It was women's work – nursing, social welfare, clerical – and there was a shortage of personnel to do those jobs.[34]

The MAAG report revealed advisors' contempt for student protesters. It chided students for "turning away from their own civic task, that of study, which would develop them into a productive and respectable element of the nation." In discussing the mobilization of young women, the report stated that "for anyone familiar with the work of women auxiliaries in Western countries during wartime, it is difficult to view with

[33] Confidential MAAG report, "Student Demonstrations: An Appraisal," 1–2. 28-1-65, Bo Quan Luc, Dong Ly Van Phong, v/v cac bien-phap do MACV de nghi de doi pho voi cac cuoc bieu-tinh cua sinh vien hoc sinh. Ho so so 29547: ve ke hoach doi pho voi phong trao bieu-tinh cua hoc sinh sinh vien do MACV de nghi nam 1964-1965.TTLTQG II.
[34] Confidential MAAG report, "Student Demonstrations: An Appraisal," 5–6.

anything but disdain the hundreds or even thousands of Vietnamese girl students parading in anti-government demonstrations, while their country is fighting for survival." The report also blamed prosperity and its attendant leisure time for urban student protests. "There is obviously a large segment of the population consisting mainly of young men and women who are generally well fed, well dressed, and available to be marshaled for demonstrations, by the thousands, even while their country is at war. Prosperity, normally an asset, in this case has actually become a political liability." The report concluded by asserting that "youths, with time on their hands and influenced by the characteristic need of the adolescent for rallying to a cause, are easily aroused and manipulated. Unless the government finds a way to harness their excess energy and turn it toward national goals, dissident and seditious groups will continue to use them for their own purposes."[35]

The report's characterization of politically active youth mirrored the criticisms of American students. By the mid-sixties, Students for a Democratic Society, the Free Speech Movement at the University of California, Berkeley, and student involvement in the civil rights movement had become well-known fixtures on America's political landscape. In 1966, a speech Ronald Reagan gave during his California gubernatorial campaign illustrated the disdain older Americans had for those of the "baby boom" generation, especially the ones who used their college years to rebel against the political and cultural status quo. Reagan chastised Berkeley students for the apparent "morality gap" that encouraged sex, drugs, and demands for free speech on campus. The Berkeley Free Speech Movement, which had begun in 1964, demanded that the university's administration repeal its ban on political action on campus and support students' rights to free speech and academic freedom. Reagan and others accused the movement of being communist and of precipitating a "deluge of filth."[36] It was just one example of how the "establishment" disparaged American youth political activism.

MAAG advisors' attitudes regarding students limited United States and South Vietnamese government opportunities to mobilize a pro-government student movement. It considered students as a monolith, with only passing acknowledgment of the diversity of political attitudes and approaches that existed among South Vietnamese students. University

[35] Ibid., pp. 4, 6–8.
[36] Jon Savage, "1966: The Year Youth Culture Exploded," *The Guardian*, Nov. 15, 2015, www.theguardian.com/culture/2015/nov/15/1966-trip-good-vibrations-pop-revolution.

students, particularly in Saigon, led by SSU, had sought to limit the use of public protest as a political tool because they, like the government, worried about the potential of demonstrations to become riots and to be susceptible to NLF infiltration. The report also shows the generational divide that characterized so much sixties activism throughout the world. It amounted to an older generation scolding a younger generation for being the beneficiaries of national prosperity and access to global networks in a time when anti-colonial activism was a defining feature of the world at large. The attitudes outlined in the MAAG report hindered the cultivation of what could have been an important source of government support for the reasons the report detailed – education, prosperity, and leisure time – even though university students were a minority in South Vietnam's population. Developing relationships with key SSU members and representatives from student unions in Dalat and Hue could have pushed the NLF-supported groups to the fringes and made them easier to identify and suppress.

Along with MAAG, the US Embassy in Saigon also analyzed South Vietnamese youth behavior. As MAAG officers collected and examined data for their report, US Embassy press secretary Barry Zorthian reflected on what he had learned about Vietnamese students. Student activism was not new in Vietnam; students had been an important part of the fall of Ngo Dinh Diem, and they had been inspired by student protests against government corruption and for constitutional liberties in South Korea and Japan in 1960. Zorthian believed the SSU was nationalistic, strongly anticommunist, and in favor of "democratic" government. Members were also anti-French, anti-neutralist, and anti–foreign involvement, including US intervention. Their opposition to foreign influence was how university students expressed their anticommunism, Zorthian explained, and they were often uncompromising in their suspicion of outsiders. Zorthian believed students were genuine in that regard, not under the influence of "anti-American elements" in South Vietnam.

Students' suspicion stemmed in part from their confusion about what America's purpose in South Vietnam actually was. They said they wanted a military victory for the South Vietnamese government, and Zorthian believed them even though the students also wanted to avoid military service, expecting others to do the fighting.[37] "The importance

---

[37] Telegram from Barry Zorthian, Counselor of Embassy for Public Affairs, U.S. Embassy Saigon, to Department of State, Subject: Emphasis on Youth, Oct. 23, 1964, Confidential U.S. State Department Central Files. Vietnam, February 1963–66. Part I: Political,

of the leaders of student and youth organizations, both for the immediate present and the long-range future of Vietnam, cannot be over-
emphasized," Zorthian concluded in his report. "They must be
recognized as prime sources for future leaders." Teachers, especially
young teachers, were important because of their contact with Vietnamese youth, and so US advisors should include them in long-range plan
regarding Vietnamese youth. High school teachers were especially
important given that high school students were major targets of NLF
recruitment efforts.[38]

The arrests of twenty high school and university students in December 1964 for disorderly conduct and carrying anti-Huong pamphlets
inspired protests that ushered in 1965. Students staged a series of
demonstrations and strikes in early January to protest the continued
existence of an unelected government in Saigon, as well as Huong's
expansion of the draft in preparation to widen the war against the
NLF. One of their protest slogans was "Better to die for freedom and
democracy than live under fascism."[39] Students demanded an end to
police suppression of dissent, an end to military rule, and an end to
foreign intervention in Vietnam. The organizers planned the uprising
to coincide with the fifteenth anniversary of the murder of Tran Van
On, an eighteen-year-old student who had died protesting French
colonialism. Born to a family of poor farmers in 1931, On had grown
up in Ben Tre province in the Mekong Delta and was a student at
Petrus Ky High School in Saigon in the late 1940s when he joined the
student movement against French occupation. On January 9, 1950, he
joined about 6,000 students and teachers in a march to demand the
release of students who had been arrested and imprisoned for allegedly
speaking out against French colonialism. Police confronted the protesters, and in the chaos that ensued, an officer shot On in the stomach,
killing him. His funeral became a subsequent protest, and French
journalists wrote of thousands of mourners lining the streets to pay
their respects. The NLF youth league had made him a legend, telling
stories of how On and other older students took police baton blows

Governmental and National Defense Affairs, Feb. 1, 1963, Stacks DS 556.58 .U55 C66
2000, Vietnam Archive Collection, The Vietnam Center and Archive, Texas Tech
University.
[38] Ibid.
[39] 27-2-1965, so: 709, Canh sat Quoc Gia Saigon Giam-Doc Nha Canh-Sat Quoc Gia
Saigon, De-muc: v/v Buoi hoi thao cua Luc Luong Hoc sinh chong chien tranh Lien
truong Gia Dinh-Tan Dinh, 26-2-65. TTLTQG II.

and stoning in order to protect younger students before officers opened fire on the demonstrators.[40]

On January 6, 1965, Nguyen Cao Ky met with students at the office of the Saigon Student Union in his new capacity as chairman of the Armed Forces Council liaison.[41] He told the students they were a "most important and dynamic force" and assured them that his top priority was to find a solution to the political crisis in South Vietnam. Students pressed him on the status of those who had been arrested in the November protests, and he told them that he sympathized with those arrested and would work to secure an early release for them. Maxwell Taylor took this with a grain of salt, knowing that Ky was prone to "demagogic tendencies" and might be trying to cultivate favor for future political use.[42] Police released the twenty students on January 15, but authorities encouraged parents to monitor their children's behavior and keep them in line. Student unrest was not helping the anticommunist cause in South Vietnam.[43]

To keep students in line, the Saigon government curtailed civil liberties. Authorities issued an order stating that the government should monitor newspapers with an eye toward any articles or opinion columns that appeared to support the NLF. Any groups calling for self-determination, including student groups, should be considered communist-infiltrated, and the Ministry of Justice should deal with them harshly. The Domestic Affairs office took charge of spying on the SSU, and if need be, that would include spying on their parents. The Ministry of Education encouraged administrators, professors, and teachers to warn students of the penalties for associating with suspected communist groups. All government offices were ordered to immediately fire and turn over suspected NLF collaborators to authorities. Only by knowing

[40] Công Điện, Chuyển Tay, Sài Gòn, 1-1965. Ho so so 29541: Về Hoạt động chống Chính phủ của sinh viên, học sinh, tháng 1, 1965. TTLTQG II.

[41] Nha Canh-Sat Quoc-Gia Do-Thanh Saigon, ngay 7, thang 1, nam 1965, Giam-Doc Nha Canh-Sat Quoc-Gia Do-Thanh, Kinh goi: Thieu Tuong, Tong-Tran Saigon-Gia Dinh, Dong kinh goi: Ong Do-Truong Saigon, Ong Tong Giam-Doc Canh-Sat Quoc-Gia, De-muc: v/v cuoc tiep-xuc cua Thieu-Tuong Nguyen Cao Ky voi dai-dien sinh-vien cac Phan-Khoa Saigon tai so 4 Duy-Tan hoi 17 gio 50 ngay 6.1.1965. Ho so so 29541: Về Hoạt động chống Chính phủ của sinh viên, học sinh, tháng 1, 1965. TTLTQG II.

[42] Telegram from the U.S. Embassy Saigon to the Department of State, Jan. 7, 1965, Armed Forces Council creation of liaison subcommittee headed by Ky, The Lyndon B. Johnson National Security Files, Vietnam, 1963–1965, Nov. 1, 1963, Stacks DS 557.4 .L96, Vietnam Archive Collection, The Vietnam Center and Archive, Texas Tech University.

[43] "20 sinh vien hoc sinh duoc tra tu do," *Long Dan*, 15-1-1965. Ho so so 3209: Tap bao trong nuoc dua tin ve cac nguyen vong cua nguoi dan nam 1965. TTLTQG II.

about student protests beforehand will the government be able to prevent them.[44] Students caught striking were to be immediately drafted into military service at the infantry level regardless of how much education they had. Meanwhile, other government agencies, such as the Ministry of Culture, Youth, and Sports, must help instill nationalism into South Vietnam's young people.[45] Americans denied knowledge of such order given to police.[46]

Student-led protests against Tran Van Huong's government continued until he resigned at the end of January 1965. Anti-Americanism increasingly became a theme of the demonstrations as students and their Buddhist supporters demanded an end to US intervention in South Vietnam. In one of the more dramatic anti-Huong demonstrations, a crowd of 5,000 students and Buddhists in Hue marched on the US consulate, and about forty of the protestors broke into the building, smashing windows, breaking furniture, and setting fire to books in the library. Buddhists demanded the removal of US Ambassador Maxwell Taylor from his post and encouraged Hue restaurant and store owners to turn away American customers.[47] Government infighting, including clashes between civilian and military leaders, and Catholics and Buddhists, continued into the summer, and amidst the chaos, Nguyen Cao Ky and Nguyen Van Thieu began to emerge as leaders. In June, Thieu took control of the National Leadership Committee, the governing body that functioned as the legislature, and Ky assumed the premiership.[48] Students remained agitated as the game of revolving premiers and lawmakers continued to stray off the path toward elected government.

[44] Phieu Trinh Thu Tuong Trich-yeu: Buoi le mat Ban Chap Hanh Tong hoi Sinh Vien Saigon Nien-Khoa 1964-65. Ho so so: 29870, Ve to chuc va hoat dong cua Tong Hoi Sinh Vien Sai Gon nam 1964-1967. TTLTQG II.

[45] Bo Quan Luc, Dong Ly, Van Phong, v/v cac bien phap do MACV de nghi de doi pho voi cac cuoc bieu tinh cua sinh vien hoc sinh, 28-1-65. Ho so so 29547: Ve ke hoach doi pho voi phong tra bieu tinh cua hoc sinh, sinh vien do MACV de nghi nam 1964-1965. TTLTQG II.

[46] Telegram from the U.S. Embassy in Saigon to the Department of State, Subject: Struggle Movement Developments, Sep. 4, 1965, Confidential U.S. State Department Central Files. Vietnam, Feb. 1963–66. Part I: Political, Governmental and National Defense Affairs, Feb. 1, 1963, Stacks DS 556.58 .U55 C66 2000, Vietnam Archive Collection, The Vietnam Center and Archive, Texas Tech University.

[47] *South Vietnam, Volume 1: U.S.–Communist Confrontation in Southeast Asia, 1961–65*, Lester A. Sobel, ed. (New York: Facts on File, Inc., 1973), p. 197.

[48] Ibid., p. 202.

FIGURE 3.2 Students at Phan Rang High School, undated.
Jerry L. Harlowe Collection, The Vietnam Center and Archive, Texas Tech University

* * *

Student frustration with US intervention extended from politics to social organizations. Case in point was the Summer Youth Program (SYP), which Edward "Ted" Britton, a professor of education from Sacramento State College, helped to establish in 1965 as a consultant with the RAND Corporation studying youth in South Vietnam. Britton had prior experience working with Vietnamese youth. From 1959 to 1961, Britton had served as an education adviser to Diem and had helped Diem's government standardize South Vietnam's secondary education system. In 1964, when student anti-government activism was particularly aggressive, RAND hired Britton to figure out a way to channel youth energy toward national causes. Britton arrived in Saigon in mid-October 1964 with instructions to interview youth leaders, students, and government officials about the relationship between South Vietnamese young people and the state.[49]

[49] Duong Van Mai Elliott, *RAND in Southeast Asia: A History of the Vietnam War Era* (Santa Monica, CA: RAND Corporation, 2010), p. 121.

While conducting his fieldwork, Britton established SYP in 1965. Part New Deal Civilian Conservation Corps, part Peace Corps, SYP featured 200 work camps throughout South Vietnam staffed by 8,000 youth volunteers. SYP volunteers built roads, schools, bridges, orphanages, and homes for refugees. It was successful enough to catch the attention of McGeorge Bundy, Lyndon Johnson's national security advisor. Bundy had been concerned about youth unrest and its threat to South Vietnam's internal security, and he reported to Johnson that SYP was "well received by various political and religious groups" in South Vietnam.[50] Keeping students occupied with service to their fellow countrymen would not only minimize their involvement in political demonstrations but also perhaps instill in them a sense of national duty, Bundy and other US officials mused.

Britton, along with assistance from the US Embassy in Saigon, made it a point to include representatives from Vietnamese youth organizations from Hue, Dalat, and Saigon and to remain behind the scenes as much as possible so as to give students a sense of ownership and prevent accusations of US meddling. In Hue, SYP brought together Catholic and Buddhist adversaries and had the support of Vien Hoa Dao. Britton reported that the young people of South Vietnam were the best hope for the future and thus for USOM. Americans needed to see that students were "the only element in the society which could develop mutual understanding and leadership for the coming years."[51] USOM needed to convey the importance of nation-building activities to Vietnamese students and needed to show the American public what USOM programs were doing to help the Vietnamese people.[52]

Still, anti-American sentiment simmered just below the surface among some students. Even though the creators invited student leaders to be on the founding committee, students considered it an American rather than a homegrown initiative, and those who had not been asked to assist with the founding felt slighted. Articles in *Sinh Vien* alleged misuses of funds, corruption, and the exploitation of Vietnamese youth by Americans. Once again, the "Yankee dollar" triumphed over local efforts, disgruntled

[50] Ibid., p. 122.

[51] Memorandum of Conversation, Department of State, "Youth Programs in Vietnam," Jan. 28, 1966, Confidential U.S. State Department Central Files. Vietnam, February 1963–66. Part I: Political, Governmental and National Defense Affairs, Feb. 1, 1963, Stacks DS 556.58 .U55 C66 2000, Vietnam Archive Collection, The Vietnam Center and Archive, Texas Tech University.

[52] Ibid.

students contended. The NLF knew about the friction and worked to exploit it, both through propaganda campaigns quoting negative statements by students about SYP and by attempting to disrupt the travel of student volunteers throughout the twenty-six provinces the SYP served. Those Yankee dollars were powerful, though, and they supported an SYP so successful that it was expanded in 1966.[53]

One of the problems was that South Vietnam already had a youth volunteer program, the National Voluntary Service. Motivated by the floods that ravaged villages along Vietnam's central coast, some students pressed for an emphasis on social service work over political action and formed NVS. Saigon University students had been planning a demonstration against the Huong government in November 1964, but the flooding pulled them away from politics for a moment. There had always been tension between those students who believed they should focus on social services and those committed to political activism, and when a typhoon crashed down on the central coast, killing more than 6,000 people, Saigon students answered the calls for help. They took action in part out of humanitarian concern, but also because of the notion that the NLF could exploit any disaster or hardship in order to fuel pro-communist sentiment.[54]

Nguyen Hy Van, student leader of the group, had hoped to transform the NVS, which had managed agricultural, health, and other sorts of social service programs at the village level into a type of peace corps. However, the military had snatched up many NVS volunteers, leaving it with only about 100 when Britton was there observing it. As far as he could tell, the group was nonpolitical and independent of the South Vietnamese government. Britton thought the group would be ideal for working in refugee areas throughout the country. Britton stressed that anything the United States did in Vietnam should be behind the scenes and should appear to be the workings of the South Vietnamese government. When praising South Vietnam, the United States should be careful to praise the Vietnamese people generally, not Ky or his government. From the US Embassy's perspective, Britton needed to stress that his work was with Vietnamese students as a whole, not favoring one group over another.[55] The US Embassy's Zorthian believed that the NVS was

[53] "Studies of Entrepreneurship and National Integration in South Vietnam," 73.

[54] "Troops Brace for Saigon Demonstrations," *Saigon Daily News*, Nov. 16, 1964, 4.

[55] Memorandum of Conversation, Department of State, "Youth Programs in Vietnam," Jan. 28, 1966, Confidential U.S. State Department Central Files. Vietnam, February

one student group the United States could count on. Members were anticommunist, anti-neutralist, and pro-American, and they demonstrated strong potential to be future leaders of Vietnam, Zorthian maintained.[56]

For some of the student volunteers, service to rural peasants would provide an avenue through which they could connect with the "traditional wisdom and culture of their country."[57] The desire to feel close to a traditional Vietnamese past was especially acute at a time when some students worried about the encroachment of Western culture on Vietnamese society. Students' anti-Americanism reflected not just their resentment of foreign intervention in South Vietnam's affairs but also broader insecurities that were facts of life for residents of an unstable nation whose legitimacy and claim to a Vietnamese heritage were under attack at the same time that the country was at war. They associated Americans with materialism and immorality, blaming US advisors and military personnel for prostitution, traffic jams, the black market, and the mini-skirt, although some young Vietnamese would adopt Western style. By the mid-1960s, students had mostly stopped linking "American" with "modern," an association that had contradicted their desire to build a strong, independent nation. At times, they felt helpless, wanting to change South Vietnamese society for the better but not knowing exactly how to do it, and this frustration grew as they watched American social scientists, engineers, political advisers, and others come in and establish programs in areas students had hoped to work, like the rural social services initiatives. As a result, some students began to see themselves as victims of a power struggle between the US-led "free world" and the communist world backed by the Soviet Union and China. That male students were subject to the draft only increased their anxieties.[58]

* * *

1963–66. Part I: Political, Governmental and National Defense Affairs, Feb. 1, 1963, Stacks DS 556.58 .U55 C66 2000, Vietnam Archive Collection, The Vietnam Center and Archive, Texas Tech University.

[56] Telegram from Barry Zorthian, Counselor of Embassy for Public Affairs, U.S. Embassy Saigon, to Department of State, Subject: Emphasis on Youth, Oct. 23, 1964, Confidential U.S. State Department Central Files. Vietnam, February 1963–66. Part I: Political, Governmental and National Defense Affairs, Feb. 1, 1963, Stacks DS 556.58 .U55 C66 2000, Vietnam Archive Collection, The Vietnam Center and Archive, Texas Tech University.

[57] "Studies of Entrepreneurship and National Integration in South Vietnam," 19.

[58] Ibid., pp. 91–93.

Despite frustrations with United States involvement in South Vietnam's affairs, some students hoped that American allies could help them and wanted to demonstrate to Americans that student groups, including peace groups, were not communist. Ted Britton and Barry Zorthian had stressed the importance of cultivating student support for the Saigon government, and some US officials agreed. In October and November 1965, the US Embassy in Saigon and the US Youth Council, an organization the CIA secretly funded, sponsored a delegation of five Vietnamese university students who traveled throughout the United States to try and show American students what was really happening in South Vietnam. Local and national media outlets covered the delegation's visit. The students spoke English but the language barrier still existed and likely prevented more national media coverage of their speeches. Antiwar groups refused to participate in activities with the Vietnamese students, so audiences tended to be like-minded rather than skeptics or opponents whose minds needed changing.

The students had not been adequately prepared to answer questions about why some Vietnamese thought it was necessary to fight communism. Some US antiwar students accused the delegates of being "stooges" of the South Vietnamese government, and the delegation did not demonstrate the diversity of South Vietnam's political milieu. African-American audiences reacted negatively to one of the students who seemed to be reactionary.[59] A US State Department evaluation of the Vietnamese student delegation tour concluded that students were more effective in conveying the political situation in South Vietnam to American students than South Vietnamese or US government officials, but their US audiences tended to be made of up people who already supported South Vietnam. Antiwar US student groups refused to meet with the Vietnamese delegation. However, they received more requests for speaking engagements than the delegation could fill, so there clearly was interest among Americans to hear from Vietnamese students. In a meeting with University of California, Berkeley students, the Vietnamese students tried to explain that it was difficult for those who did not live in Saigon to understand the situation there.[60]

[59] Telegram from the Department of State to the U.S. Embassy Saigon, Nov. 26, 1965, Confidential U.S. State Department Central Files. Vietnam, February 1963–66. Part I: Political, Governmental and National Defense Affairs, Feb. 1, 1963, Stacks DS 556.58 . U55 C66 2000, Vietnam Archive Collection, The Vietnam Center and Archive, Texas Tech University.

[60] Ibid.

While the Vietnamese student delegates traveled to the United States trying to convince American college students that South Vietnam was legitimate and worth defending, SSU members back in Saigon launched other campaigns to make the anticommunist perspective heard. SSU wanted to send a South Vietnamese delegation to the Afro-Asian Conference in Algiers in 1965 so they could explain their staunch anticommunist position. They asserted that they would be able to present the facts of the conflict in Vietnam to other students, although the issue ended up being moot because the conference was never held.[61] In October of 1965, the members of SSU wrote an open letter to American students explaining their perspective on the situation in Vietnam. The letter was aimed at students who were concerned about the escalating US military commitment to Vietnam, and SSU wanted Americans to understand that North Vietnam and the NLF were a threat to South Vietnam's existence. The way they saw it, Ho Chi Minh and others were exploiting Vietnam's victory over France in 1954, arguing that nationalists had opposed France but were not necessarily communists. Calling North Vietnam the Democratic Republic of Vietnam was misleading, the SSU students argued, because democracy cannot exist without freedom of speech, multiple political parties, and other civil liberties, none of which the DRV allowed. They pointed to the differences in quality of life in East and West Germany for evidence of the oppressive nature of communist governments. The United States and its allies have already turned their backs on Hungary and Tibet in a war between the communist bloc and the free world, the letter accused. Regardless of what NLF propaganda or North Vietnamese representatives might say, most Vietnamese are not communists, the letter contended. The NLF is simply taking advantage of rural war-weariness and fear. Anyway, if communism is such a good thing, why does the NLF not call itself communist?[62]

American advisers understood the value of cultivating the anticommunist wing of student activists in the cities, but they struggled to make sense of the neutralist students and student peace movements. It was unclear to

---

[61] Telegram from the U.S. Embassy Saigon to the Department of State, June 2, 1965, Saigon Student Union invitation to attend World Youth Festival in Algiers, The Lyndon B. Johnson National Security Files, Vietnam, 1963–1965, Nov.1, 1963, Stacks DS 557.4 .L96, Vietnam Archive Collection, The Vietnam Center and Archive, Texas Tech University.

[62] Tu Tong Hoi Sinh Vien Sai Gon, 28-10-65. Ho so so: 3207, Tap ban tin VTX, bao cat cua bao Hong Konh ve hoat dong cua Tong hoi sinh vien Saigon, Hue, nam 1965. TTLTQG II.

Americans whether neutralism meant the desire for self-determination without foreign influence, or whether those who called themselves neutralists and wanted Americans out of Vietnam were just communists in disguise. In October 1965, Hue students proposed establishing an anticommunist peace force as a way to prove to the Untied States that not all peace movements were communist. Vinh Kha, head of the Hue Buddhist Student Association and a past president of the Hue Student Union led the movement. American officials in Hue knew that Kha was one of the most popular student leaders in the area, and thus he had the ability to gain widespread support for his ideas.[63] Student leaders, including avowed and suspected neutralists, met with US Embassy officials to try and convince the Americans that they were not communists.

The day after Thai had called on US Embassy officer Melvin Levine, Le Doan Kim, a friend of Thai's and a neutralist activist, appeared at Levine's door. Kim began by contending that the Vietnamese people wanted peace, and so the United States should assist the South Vietnamese government in starting peace talks. Lyndon Johnson wanted peace, too, Kim argued, so Kim's position reflected not only that of the majority of Vietnamese people, but also of the US president. Levine reminded him that the Vietnamese people were also fighting for their freedom against communist oppression, and it was the communists who launched the war. An olive branch was essentially a white flag in this case. Just as he had told Thai, Levine asserted to Kin that everyone involved wanted peace, but all sides would have to agree to end aggression in order to have true peace. From the US perspective, the communists were not going to agree to that unless they were given full control of South Vietnam. Yes, Johnson called for peace, but only with the condition that South Vietnam's sovereignty be respected – by communist Vietnamese as well as by the United States.[64]

---

[63] Telegram from the U.S. Consulate in Hue to the Department of State, Subject: Hue University Student Leader's Ideas for Formation of "Peace Force," Oct. 8, 1965, Confidential U.S. State Department Central Files. Vietnam, February 1963–66. Part I: Political, Governmental and National Defense Affairs, Feb. 1, 1963, Stacks DS 556.58 .U55 C66 2000, Vietnam Archive Collection, The Vietnam Center and Archive, Texas Tech University.

[64] Telegram from the U.S. Embassy Saigon to the Department of State, Subject: Attached Memoranda of Conversation, Nov. 10, 1965, Confidential U.S. State Department Central Files. Vietnam, February 1963–66. Part I: Political, Governmental and National Defense Affairs, Feb. 1, 1963, Stacks DS 556.58 .U55 C66 2000, Vietnam Archive Collection, The Vietnam Center and Archive, Texas Tech University.

As the conversation continued, Kim asserted that his whole reason for calling for immediate negotiations between North and South Vietnam was to place the blame for the war on the NLF, to shine a light on NLF aggression. Levine told Kim that reaching out to the DRV and NLF was self-defeating. The communists were doing the attacking; the South Vietnamese government, with US assistance, was acting defensively, which was understandable, they argued. It was perfectly acceptable for the South Vietnamese government and military, along with their allies, to fight back in self-defense when attacked by communist forces. Aware that Americans saw neutralism and communism as interchangeable, Kim tried to convince Levine that not only was he not a communist, but that communists did not like him. Communist delegations at the Indochinese People's Conference annual meeting in Phnom Penh had called for his expulsion from the group because he published a neutral, noncommunist newspaper called *Strict Neutrality*, in which he suggested that communist calls for neutrality were not actually neutral. Kim also emphasized that he had the support of Father Hoang Quynh, an anticommunist Catholic activist, and Thich Tam Chau, a moderate Buddhist leader. As the men said their goodbyes, Levine stressed to Kim that he should not construe any aspect of their conversation to suggest that the US Embassy supported Kim's position.[65]

* * *

Unrest in Saigon, Hue, and Dalat, led by students, Buddhists, and Catholics, escalated along with the US military presence in South Vietnam in 1966. Another military junta, this one with Nguyen Cao Ky at the head, was in power in Saigon, and the country still lacked a constitution despite promises by Ky, echoing his predecessors, that a constitution and an election were forthcoming. In the spring of 1966, Buddhist-led demonstrations in Saigon and Hue drew crowds of 10,000 protesters. At the same time, more than 1,500 students clashed with police in Saigon, burned US jeeps, and stoned a building where US military personnel lived. In Dalat, 3,000 students occupied a government radio station and burned the building before moving on to seize a police station. The students demanded Ky's ouster, and they wanted US troops to stop using Dalat as an R-&-R spot. Catholics who worried that a national election would bring communists to power staged a protest in Bien Hoa, a town just

[65] Ibid.

north of Saigon, demanding that the government put down the Buddhist and student riots. As protests continued into May, as many as ten Buddhists self-immolated, including a seventeen-year-old girl named Nguyen Thi Van in Hue.[66] With the cities in chaos, it was difficult to determine the politics of any of the angry individuals or groups. The loudest demands were for elected government, and as the US military presence in South Vietnam increased, demonstrations increasingly took on an anti-American tone.

US Embassy officials scrambled to make sense of it all and to understand the student perspectives. The US Embassy's Youth Committee closely monitored student activities and tried to convince members of SSU to continue on a moderate course despite agitation by "hard core" Buddhist student and youth leaders' efforts to draw students into their camp. The Buddhists wanted the current government out and were willing to use violence if necessary to be heard. From an embassy perspective, the students were becoming more and more polarized, and the anti-government Buddhists were to blame.[67] US Embassy telegrams reported to the State Department that the angry student movement was in Hue. The students demanded the removal of Ky and Thieu. Secretary of State Dean Rusk directed embassy personnel to remain in close contact with SSU and monitor Buddhist efforts to steer students off a moderate path. Rusk wondered if sending Ted Britton back to South Vietnam to work with students would be helpful.[68]

Judging student attitudes was difficult in part because students' statements about their political perspectives were often vague. Richard Critchfield, a reporter for the *Washington Star*, got in with some Buddhist students who had rioted in Hue. Critchfield met the students where they were staying, a large hall with mattresses lining the floor. The students were intense, and their minds were on revolution, but Critchfield was not

[66] *South Vietnam, Volume 1: U.S.–Communist Confrontation in Southeast Asia, 1961–65,* Lester A. Sobel, ed. (New York: Facts on File, Inc., 1973), pp. 210–230.

[67] Telegram from the U.S. Embassy in Saigon to the Department of State, May 25, 1966. Confidential U.S. State Department Central Files. Vietnam, February 1963–66. Part I: Political, Governmental and National Defense Affairs, Feb. 1, 1963, Stacks DS 556.58 . U55 C66 2000, Vietnam Archive Collection, The Vietnam Center and Archive, Texas Tech University.

[68] Telegram from the Department of State to the U.S. Embassy Saigon, May 24, 1966, Confidential U.S. State Department Central Files. Vietnam, February 1963–66. Part I: Political, Governmental and National Defense Affairs, Feb. 1, 1963, Stacks DS 556.58 . U55 C66 2000, Vietnam Archive Collection, The Vietnam Center and Archive, Texas Tech University.

entirely sure what they meant when they said they were ready to go at any time. When he asked them if they took orders from leftist Buddhist Thich Thien Minh, they glared at him and denied it. Yet they also asserted that they did not trust Ky and did not believe that he would reinstate the National Assembly. Their attitudes reflected the dominant mindset since the overthrow of Diem, but Critchfield could not tell what the students' specific political goals were and to what degree, if at all, communists had influenced them.

Back in Saigon, SSU leaders had been urging restraint regarding the use of public demonstrations to protest the South Vietnamese government. Massive marches could too easily devolve into chaos, they argued, and that would only play into the hands of the NLF. SSU and the Vietnamese Student Solidarity Forces, a Catholic group associated with Father Hoang Quynh, met in April and issued a proclamation calling for solidarity between the military and civilians and a solution to the strife between the government and anti-government forces. Conflict only helped the communist cause, they argued. In exchange for ending the demonstrations, the government must respect freedom of the press, the United States must honor Vietnamese independence, and students must appreciate the work of allied troops in the struggle against communist forces, the proclamation asserted. While university students could show restraint, SSU representatives and other university student leaders worried that high school students were easily incited and could be easily swayed by NLF operatives.[69]

NLF youth set out to infiltrate and disrupt the activities of student organizations that were not intractably anti-government. At the April 5, 1966, general meeting of representatives from various Saigon student groups, several unfamiliar faces in the audience began pushing hard for a resolution authorizing anti-government street protests. SSU members managed to keep control of the meeting but left shaken by the aggressive nature of the new delegates; they did not seem to be university students. Two days later, a telegram from the Dalat Student Union confirmed their suspicion that nonstudent elements were working to undermine student leadership. On April 6, a group of unidentified youths had kidnapped and

[69] Telegram from the U.S. Embassy Saigon to the Department of State, April 15, 1966, "Saigon Student Political Activities," Confidential U.S. State Department Central Files. Vietnam, February 1963–66. Part I: Political, Governmental and National Defense Affairs, Feb. 1, 1963, Stacks DS 556.58 .U55 C66 2000, Vietnam Archive Collection, The Vietnam Center and Archive, Texas Tech University.

beaten two Dalat University students and threatened others. Earlier, the DSU had issued a statement in support of SSU's position on mass protests, and leaders of both groups speculated that the muggers in Dalat and the strangers at the Saigon student meeting were part of a broad effort to thwart student activism. Since the assassination of Ngo Dinh Diem in 1963, a broad coalition of South Vietnamese students had been demanding the establishment of a democratically elected, noncommunist national government in Saigon. Student leaders worried about the impact rioting would have on stability before such a government took hold, so they sought to limit the use of street protests. The events in Saigon and Dalat suggested to them that national instability was exactly what the unknown operatives wanted. This, combined with nearly three years of waiting out a revolving door of appointed governments that kept promising elections and a constitution without delivering in any meaningful way, was making it harder and harder for some students to stay the moderate course they had been advocating.[70]

US Embassy officials working with the Saigon mayor's office had noticed an increase in young street urchins and high school–age delinquents from slum neighborhoods near the Saigon River marching in the streets and trying to convince other youth to join them. The vice president of the Saigon City Council told an Embassy contact that he saw a group of about 100 such youth marching with a banner calling others to join a march with Buddhist Institute members.[71] Divisions between the moderate SSU and anti-government Buddhists came to a head in April 1966 when Thich Thien Minh accused the SSU of receiving a bribe of five million piasters from the South Vietnamese government. SSU chairman Lai Chanh launched a hunger strike to protest Minh's accusation, and the move won sympathy of other students, who began fasting in twenty-four-hour shifts. Dalat students issued a statement in solidarity with SSU, demanding that Minh and the Hue Buddhists stay out of Dalat and Saigon students' affairs. As a result of the hunger strike, Lai Chanh slipped into a coma and was rushed to a hospital on April 18, while other students kept up the fast on his behalf. Although Minh eventually apologized for his accusation, he later maintained that "reactionary and

[70] Telegram from the U.S. Embassy Saigon to the Department of State, "Student and Youth Political Activities," April 9, 1966, Confidential U.S. State Department Central Files. Vietnam, February 1963–66. Part I: Political, Governmental and National Defense Affairs, 01 February 1963, Stacks DS 556.58 .U55 C66 2000, Vietnam Archive Collection, The Vietnam Center and Archive, Texas Tech University.
[71] Ibid.

counter-revolutionary elements" were exploiting Saigon students. US Embassy officials believed the hunger strike had brought enough negative publicity on Minh to strengthen SSU's moderate position.[72]

In an effort to calm the student rivalry, SSU representatives met with Minh and Ky on April 13, 1966, to try and show that it was neither pro-government nor associated with anti-government Buddhists. Minh tried to convince the students that the Buddhist fight was over the issue of elections and demand for a civilian government, something that SSU also wanted. For his part, Ky said the government was working toward its promise of transferring power from the military to a civilian assembly within six months. Meanwhile, some nonaligned students began leaning toward the Buddhist position, although Catholic students still remained connected primarily to SSU. When the government announced on April 15 that elections and a constitutional convention would be held, students were excited and felt as though they had accomplished something. But euphoria would be short lived if the government did not make good on its promises. Buddhist student leaders did not believe the government proclamation and said they would only accept Thieu and Ky's resignations and exclusion from the government.[73]

September 1966 brought a political breakthrough as voters cast their ballots for a Constituent Assembly. The implementation of a form of political democracy seemed to inspire student groups to work for peaceful coexistence. When the new officers of the Buddhist Students Association were inaugurated at a ceremony on November 20, 1966, the newly elected president, Pham Phi Long, a medical student, encouraged students regardless of religion or position regarding the government to join with Buddhist students and focus on social service work. The inauguration took place at the Buddhist Youth Center, and the presidents of the Saigon Student Union, the Vietnam Youth Council, National Voluntary Service, and the Voluntary Youth Association attended. One wall of the main

[72] Telegram from the U.S. Embassy Saigon to the Department of State, April 22, 1966, "Saigon Students vs. Thich Thien Minh," Confidential U.S. State Department Central Files. Vietnam, February 1963–66. Part I: Political, Governmental and National Defense Affairs, Feb. 1, 1963, Stacks DS 556.58 .U55 C66 2000, Vietnam Archive Collection, The Vietnam Center and Archive, Texas Tech University.

[73] Telegram from the U.S. Embassy Saigon to the Department of State, April 15, 1966, "Saigon Student Political Activities," Confidential U.S. State Department Central Files. Vietnam, February 1963–66. Part I: Political, Governmental and National Defense Affairs, Feb. 1, 1963, Stacks DS 556.58 .U55 C66 2000, Vietnam Archive Collection, The Vietnam Center and Archive, Texas Tech University.

room in the Buddhist Youth Center was covered with paintings by Chinese Buddhists living in Cholon. On another wall hung photographs from various charity programs the Buddhist students participated in, as well as photographs from student gatherings. After the inauguration ceremony, students and their guests enjoyed light refreshments and a live band performing rock and roll music. The JUSPAO Youth Officer from the US Embassy was a sport when some students called him on stage twice to sing Vietnamese songs. Students cheered him on both times, and the party atmosphere would not be ruined by politics that night. It was as though the Buddhist students went out of their way to show that they were more interested in providing social services than the protests that had rocked Saigon earlier that spring and summer.[74] It seemed to be a glimpse at the potential of unity across political differences for the good of the nation. If South Vietnam could accomplish that writ large, perhaps it could show the world that it could be a legitimate representative democracy.

***

Seeking to find out as much as they could about South Vietnamese student attitudes, Pentagon officials commissioned a study. D. Jane Pratt, a doctoral student in political science and development at the Massachusetts Institute of Technology and a Defense Department consultant, spent several months in 1967 conducting research on South Vietnamese students in order to report back to the Pentagon about the attitudes of university students since the end of the Diem regime. Pratt had been a student at the University of Saigon during the turbulent final months of Diem's presidency, and that experience solidified an interest in Vietnam, inspiring her to return to the university for the 1965–1966 academic year. She traveled throughout South Vietnam, became friends with Vietnamese students, and interviewed government officials about their perceptions of South Vietnam's youth and hopes for how they might support the nation. Conversation after conversation with her Vietnamese friends revealed the same attitude: The government could not be trusted because it refused to

---

[74] Telegram from the U.S. Embassy in Saigon to the Department of State, Subject: Inauguration Ceremony for New Buddhist Student Association Officers, Dec. 22, 1966. Confidential U.S. State Department Central Files. Vietnam, February 1963–66. Part I: Political, Governmental and National Defense Affairs, Feb. 1, 1963, Stacks DS 556.58 .U55 C66 2000, Vietnam Archive Collection, The Vietnam Center and Archive, Texas Tech University.

give students the freedom to organize on their own. This overall suspicion discouraged students who supported the government to openly collaborate with it for fear of losing the respect of their peers. Those who did work through state channels were sometimes accused of selling out and accepting government payments to work against student interests.

In conversation, Pratt's Vietnamese associates were often vague. She reported that her friends and other interviewees spoke in general sound bites and idealistic terms without necessarily seeming to have an understanding of the complex realities the government faced. By 1967, when she was finishing her report, Pratt found that students had become more realistic but still clung to the notion that "if only good and virtuous leaders could be found to run the government, the solutions for all of their country's problems would follow almost magically as a matter of course."[75] Yet it seemed as though no one in the South Vietnamese government could win with students. Their ongoing criticism fluctuated between casting the government as undemocratic, harsh, and repressive or soft, weak, impotent, and corrupt.[76]

As for the relationship between South Vietnamese students and the US government, Pratt concluded that it was one of mutual suspicion. US advisers tried to hide their efforts to observe students because if the students caught them, they would have accused Americans of spying. So Americans tried to fake disinterest, and they asserted that the United States would stay out of student affairs. Pratt believed that approach was a mistake. It prevented Americans from engaging with students in ways that could have benefited nation-building efforts. Pratt also suggested that if Americans seemed disengaged or risk averse, Vietnamese students could read that as weakness or lack of courage. Some of the students Pratt knew felt to a certain degree that Americans in Vietnam truly did want to help and work with Vietnamese students.[77] By 1967, when Pratt completed her fieldwork, her overall assessment of the student mood in South Vietnam was gloomy, an unfortunate devolution from the sense of hopefulness that marked the period after the fall of Diem. That generation of students had known war their whole lives, and with no end to war in sight, it was hard to believe politics could change. Overall, Pratt concluded that the failure of the Untied States and the South Vietnamese government to mobilize students in nation-building efforts was a "tragic waste."[78] There had been windows of opportunity, and US Embassy

---

[75] "Studies of Entrepreneurship and National Integration in South Vietnam," 77–80.
[76] Ibid., p. 80.   [77] Ibid., pp. 103–104.   [78] Ibid., p. 96.

officials and other Americans on the ground in Vietnam had recognized the anticommunist leadership potential among young, educated Vietnamese, but suspicion and risk aversion had prevented Americans from cultivating would-be leaders.

In the years of political upheaval that followed the assassination of Diem, Nguyen Cao Ky and Nguyen Van Thieu emerged as the next best hope for American advisers attempting to keep South Vietnam on a democratic path. Both men were military officers, and students loved neither. Hoping to come to a deeper understanding of the university student mindset toward Ky and Thieu, Deputy Ambassador U. Alexis Johnson and embassy officer Melvin Levine met with Bui Tuong Huan, the rector of Hue University and former Minister of Education. Huan told the Americans that students disliked Thieu because they believed he would establish a "fascist" government, although it was unclear how the students were conceptualizing fascism. To the students, Thieu seemed aloof and impenetrable, and he kept showing up every time there was a governmental transition in Saigon, so they suspected him of being part of some sort of conspiracy. Nguyen Cao Ky, on the other hand, struck students as young and open, and so they trusted him more.[79] After the presidential election of 1967, disillusionment with South Vietnam's political system and the ongoing war would push some student leaders further to the left and open the door to both open and secret partnerships with the NLF.

As it was for so many aspects of the Vietnam War, the Tet Offensive was the death knell for the relationship between South Vietnamese students and their government. Some student leaders were killed, other were kidnapped by NLF agents, and some defected to the NLF, including, most notably, the president of the Saigon Student Union, Huynh Tan Mam. For some educated young people, the Tet Offensive made them decide that reconciliation was the only way to end the war, even if it ultimately meant reunification under a Communist government. Activists of this mindset joined the Alliance of National, Democratic, and Peace Forces, a pro-NLF group that emerged in the wake of Tet and recruited

[79] Memorandum of Conversation, Participants: Deputy Ambassador U. Alexis Johnson, Mr. Bui Tuong Huan, Rector of Hue University and former Minister of Education, Melvin H. Levine, Embassy officer, Aug. 26, 1965, Ambassador Johnson's office, Confidential U.S. State Department Central Files. Vietnam, February 1963–66. Part I: Political, Governmental and National Defense Affairs, Feb. 1, 1963, Stacks DS 556.58 .U55 C66 2000, Vietnam Archive Collection, The Vietnam Center and Archive, Texas Tech University.

intellectuals, students, artists, journalists, and other urban elites.[80] Other South Vietnamese students connected with American and international antiwar movements. All of this led the government to ramp up surveillance, going so far as to send the National Police to raid campus offices and headquarters and disable telephone lines.[81] Defection to the NLF did not necessarily indicate support for the Front's objectives. As reports spread throughout South Vietnam of NLF kidnappings and executions of student activists and young teachers in Hue during Tet who allegedly refused to join the Front, we can deduce that at least some of the defectors turned to the NLF as a matter of personal survival, not ideological commitment.[82] This was exactly the result the NLF's strategy of urban terrorism was supposed to yield.

Could things have happened differently in 1967 to rally student energy, idealism, and nationalism to South Vietnam's cause? Rather than dealing in counterfactuals, we can take away a couple lessons from this story. One is that for all the military might the United States imposed upon Vietnam, its dealings with young activists reveal America's insecurity in its Vietnam policy. Had Americans been confident in their Vietnam strategy and in their choice of ally, perhaps they would have trusted young Vietnamese leaders. Second, the Saigon government squandered a potential base of support in its hard-line approach to student activism, it drove young citizens into the arms of its adversary, and it lost an opportunity to win the support of the rural poor through youth voluntary programs. This is a crucial missed opportunity given that both ARVN troops and the NLF harassed and abused the peasantry. This quote from John Donnell, the former US Information Service public affairs officer who conducted a study of South Vietnamese students in 1967, sums up the central problem in the government-student relationship, and in South Vietnam's brief history more broadly: "It does appear ironic that just about the time the GVN perceived the necessity to prepare for political competition ... with the NLF, that it should squeeze the voluntary youth organizations out of the picture, with their demonstrated potential for engaging the social and political commitment of considerable numbers of young people."[83]

The Saigon government and the US Embassy did try to use students as representatives of South Vietnam before international audiences.

---

[80] John Donnell, "Vietnam's Youth Associations–Social Commitment and Political Promise," p. 63. Vietnam Center and Archive. 0721005002 1969 Box 10, Folder5. John Donnell Collection. The Vietnam Center and Archive, Texas Tech University.
[81] Ibid., p. 80.   [82] Ibid., p. 64.   [83] Ibid., p. 81.

Audacious youth activism was a hallmark of the sixties, and not just because of left-wing movements. American students from the conservative Young Americans for Freedom traveled to South Vietnam and throughout Southeast Asia to meet with anticommunist youth. In 1965, the US State Department sponsored a group of South Vietnamese students who toured Europe and the United States in support of the Saigon government. World University Service sent pro-government South Vietnamese students to India, Pakistan, Israel, Switzerland, France, West Germany, Denmark, Norway, and Sweden, where they networked with Vietnamese students living abroad and met with non-Vietnamese students to discuss the political situation in South Vietnam and rally support.[84] When several young men defected from North Vietnam and sought help from the US Embassy, State Department officers wondered if they would make good advocates for South Vietnam. Authorities in Saigon, as well as American advisers, knew South Vietnam needed international support to survive.

[84] Memorandum of Conversation, Participants: Do Pham Hanh – Secretary-General, Saigon University Student Union, Ralph R. Moore, Embassy Economic Officer, Subject: Student Activities, Sep. 14, 1964, Confidential U.S. State Department Central Files. Vietnam, February 1963–66. Part I: Political, Governmental and National Defense Affairs, Feb. 1, 1963, Stacks DS 556.58 .U55 C66 2000, Vietnam Archive Collection, The Vietnam Center and Archive, Texas Tech University.

4

South Vietnam and the World

A crowd of several hundred students and other protesters in Radhus Square in Copenhagen on an October afternoon in 1965 quieted as a North Vietnamese student stepped to the podium. His comments were expected to validate the demonstrators' opposition to US involvement in Vietnam, and that seemed to be the case as he declared in German that the United States must get out of South Vietnam. When he followed that statement with "after, of course, the Communists get out of South Vietnam, for it is they who started the terror and the war there," confused chatter from the audience rose to a din as protest organizers scrambled to make sense of what was going on. The Vietnamese student made several more pro-South Vietnam, pro-American statements before organizers pulled him from the podium. US Embassy Copenhagen officer Cord Hansen-Sturm was parking his car at the square and saw it happening. He had arrived to meet a Vietnamese student who had called the embassy seeking a German-Danish translator because the student wanted "to talk to the demonstrators and enlighten them to what was really going on in Vietnam." The turnaround was too quick for the embassy to deliver a translator who could not be traced back to the Americans, but Hansen-Sturm and other embassy officers thought the student might be a good contact to have. As Hansen-Sturm watched the protest organizers drag him off the podium, he knew their meeting would have to wait.[1]

[1] Department of State Airgram, No. A-290, Oct. 17, 1965, from AmEmbassy Copenhagen, Subject: Presence of Vietnamese Anti-Viet Cong Students in Copenhagen. Foreign Service Officer Cord Hansen-Sturm. Memorandum of conversation, subject: Vietnam and Denmark, place: Copenhagen, date: Oct. 2, 4, 5, 1965, participants: Phan Phuc Vinh, North

The student was Phan Phuc Vinh, a North Vietnamese defector who, along with three other defectors, had been living and going to school in West Germany. They came from Hanoi, but their bloodlines were southern. They were from southern families who had supported the Viet Minh against the French and had traveled north to support the resistance. The Hanoi government had sent all four of the young men to attend universities in Eastern Europe in the early 1960s, and it was from there that they defected from East Germany to West Germany in 1964. They had become disillusioned by what they saw as communist totalitarianism, and the government's seizure of their families' wealth frightened them. They did not want the United States in South Vietnam forever, but they believed that a noncommunist government would best represent Vietnamese nationalism and facilitate the country's growth as an independent nation.[2]

South Vietnamese and American officials hoped figures such as the student defectors would successfully plead South Vietnam's case to the world. The global stage was the third battlefield, along with the internal political war and the military war in Vietnam, on which South Vietnam fought to justify its existence. In the February 21, 1965, edition of the *Malayan Times*, a reporter wrote of South Vietnam: "The Americans have more than a tiger by the tail. This tiger has two tails: the war against Communist Viet Cong and the unending political war inside South Vietnam itself." The metaphorical tiger actually had a third tail: international public opinion. Liberals and conservatives throughout the world closely monitored developments in South Vietnam, and Vietnamese political activists, writers, and students worked international connections and foreign media in a global war of ideas over which side rightfully represented the future of South Vietnam. In an era of decolonization, the ability of a group to convince the world of its moral authority was as powerful as military hardware.

The North Vietnamese and the National Liberation Front were already working the international scene in the mid-sixties. As Robert K. Brigham has shown, the nonaligned movement and neutralist sentiment in Western Europe and the Third World inspired the NLF to begin presenting a

---

Vietnamese student, Hung Nguyen Thanh, North Vietnamese student, Cord D. Hansen-Sturm, third secretary of Embassy. NARA RG 59 – Central Foreign Policy Files, 1964–1966, Political and Defense, Pol 7-29, folder "Pol 12 – Political Parties," Box 2923.

[2] "North Viet Defectors Will Speak on Red China's Influence Tonight," *The Stanford Daily*, Feb. 28, 1966, Vol. 49, No. 20, p. 1. Bill Rorabaugh, "North Vietnamese Students Censure Hanoi," *The Stanford Daily*, March 1, 1966, Vol. 149, No. 21, 1.

neutralism platform to other countries in 1962. This "third way" appealed to many noncommunists in South Vietnam, too, because they saw it as an alternative choice to communism or the Saigon government.[3] Groups such as the Movement for Self-Determination claimed to be part of the third force so as to conceal their connections to the NLF.[4] UN Secretary-General U Thant expressed the notion that the adversaries in Vietnam might use diplomacy rather than war to decide the country's postcolonial fate, but Lyndon Johnson resisted, saying a meeting at the bargaining table would simply "ratify terror."[5] Yet America's ally in Saigon, Nguyen Khanh, secretly reached out to the NLF in December 1964 with the hope of negotiating a political settlement and ending the fighting. Khanh eventually fled to France in exile, and American advisers began searching for a more loyal head of state. NLF leaders pointed out that their neutralist platform had caused the collapse of Saigon governments.[6]

It shaped European and Southeast Asian attitudes, too. Americans had expected broad international support and were surprised by the popularity of neutralism as a solution to the Vietnam question. NLF representatives addressed groups and rallies in Europe and argued that the introduction of US ground troops to South Vietnam meant that they had to abandon neutralism and focus on battlefield victory.[7] NLF leaders traveled to Finland, Czechoslovakia, Syria, and Japan on public relations tours to gain support, and Western journalists covered their trips. In response, Johnson sent representatives to thirty countries to speak with representatives of more than 100 nations.[8] Given Khanh's willingness to hold secret talks with the NLF, Americans turned to nonstate actors to explain that the free Vietnam they wanted was a noncommunist one.

Hanoi also sought to sway international opinion while attempting to resist Soviet and Chinese influence. Pierre Asselin argues that both superpowers viewed their relationship with North Vietnam in light of US actions in the region. In 1964, France and China normalized relations with each other, which angered the United States. The same year, PAVN units crossed into South Vietnam to aid PLAF and topple the Saigon government.[9] Through Resolution 9, which placed the "liberation" of the South on the same level as industrial transformation in the North,

[3] Robert K. Brigham, *Guerrilla Diplomacy: The NLF's Foreign Relations and the Viet Nam War* (Ithaca, NY: Cornell University Press, 1999), pp. 19–20.
[4] Ibid., p. 35.   [5] Ibid., p. 35.   [6] Ibid., pp. 35–37.   [7] Ibid., pp. 39–41.
[8] Ibid., pp. 52, 55.
[9] Pierre Asselin, *Hanoi's Road to the Vietnam War, 1954–1965* (Berkeley: University of California Press, 2013), pp. 228–229.

Hanoi asserted itself to wage "offensive military struggle waged by main-line forces."[10] Asselin has called Resolution 9 Hanoi's equivalent of Washington's Gulf of Tonkin Resolution.[11]

When Le Duan, Le Duc Tho, and others went to Moscow to discuss Resolution 9, Khrushchev, hoping to avoid a confrontation with the United States said that the Soviet Union did not approve and would not provide military equipment. Soviet leaders did not want the conflict to become a confrontation with the United States. Mao, on the other hand, supported Resolution 9, viewing it as an example of North Vietnam siding with China in the Sino-Soviet split. China authorized military and economic assistance to North Vietnam.[12] This left North Vietnam in a bind as leaders sought to maintain relationships with both superpowers. Closeness with the Soviet Union was crucial because of North Vietnam's reliance on trade from Eastern Europe.[13]

Managing international opinion was part of the process. China warned Hanoi that negotiation with the United States, especially after escalation, would appear to be "weakness in the face of American imperialism" because the Johnson administration's call for peace talks was just a ruse to "deceive public opinion."[14] The Soviet Union and Eastern European countries pushed for negotiations, even after US escalation.[15] Hanoi leaders understood that international, including American, public opinion was crucial, and North Vietnam had to make sure it convinced the world of its moral authority in order to maintain international support. North Vietnam had to present itself to the world as a nation that sought peace but would not turn from its revolutionary objectives in the face of American aggression.[16] Recognizing North Vietnam's need for support from both superpowers, Hanoi leaders did not publicly disparage either China or the Soviet Union.

As Lien-Hang T. Nguyen has argued, North Vietnamese leaders brought and kept superpowers in the mix, but the Sino-Soviet split had a major impact on North Vietnam's socialist transformation. Hanoi proved the power of "small power" global politics by frustrating and undermining US diplomatic efforts.[17] Meanwhile, according to Robert K. Brigham, southern communists worried that "northern doves" would sacrifice the South in a political settlement with the United States intended

---

[10] Ibid., p. 229.   [11] Ibid., p. 230.   [12] Ibid., pp. 235–236.   [13] Ibid., p. 237.
[14] Ibid., p. 266.   [15] Ibid., p. 267.   [16] Ibid., p. 266.
[17] Lien-Hang T. Nguyen, *Hanoi's War: An International History of the War for Peace in Vietnam* (Chapel Hill: University of North Carolina Press, 2015), p. 4.

to avoid a war. Some northerners worried that US bombing would harm northern industrial development, and some leaders wondered if the southern insurgency was worth it, so in 1965, the party approved secret talks with the United States despite divisions among hawks and doves. It all illustrated the complicated and indirect nature of diplomacy, which worked in fits and starts as representatives refused to meet with certain diplomats, letters sat unopened, and talks took place in secret.[18]

American, North Vietnamese, South Vietnamese, and NLF leaders all recognized the importance of winning international support for their political causes. South Vietnamese and American officials hoped to foster global public sympathy for a non-Communist government in South Vietnam. They needed spokespersons who could explain, even to skeptical crowds, why southern non-Communists opposed the NLF and northern influence and why they needed temporary American assistance. They had to attest to the legitimacy of the Saigon government and of South Vietnam as representing the will of Vietnamese people. Diplomatic teams visited Asian, African, and European countries hoping to convince especially the newly independent world that they could be allies. In turn, some countries reached out to South Vietnam, offering words of support and more. US allies such as South Korea, the Philippines, Australia, and New Zealand supported the military war, but South Vietnam also sought validation in the international court of public opinion. Diplomats and young people were key to demonstrating that South Vietnam was more than a collection of generals in Saigon who had the support of American policymakers. In an era of popular uprisings and movements against the status quo, nongovernmental actors were critical. In the sixties, youth mattered, especially to audiences in the United States and Europe. Youth was also important given the roles of young people and the social activism of the time, even if it was more image than reality.

The defectors, Pham Phu Oanh, Phan Phuc Vinh, Nguyen Thanh Hung, and Nguyen Khe, might have appeared to live the charmed lives of favored sons in Hanoi, but they had become disillusioned by North Vietnam's close association with China, and they felt trapped by the government's stifling control of every aspect of people's lives. They also worried about the devastating consequences of the government's land reform program and other economic initiatives. So when they slipped into West Germany in 1964, they joined the Association of Vietnamese

---

[18] Brigham, *Guerrilla Diplomacy*, pp. 41–45.

Students there. Members soon elected Phan Phuc Vinh president.[19] They sought refuge in South Vietnam's embassy in Bonn, and they worked as waiters, clothes washers, and poster artists in the city to earn money.[20] Vinh's call to the US Embassy in Copenhagen on that October afternoon in 1965 put the students on the State Department's radar screen.[21]

Vinh had been sitting at a cafe on Radhus Square, angrily awaiting the four o'clock start time of the anti-American protest he had planned to crash. He wanted to communicate with the demonstrators about what it was really like in Vietnam, "the more communism, the worse the life."[22] He and Nguyen Thanh Hung had traveled from Bonn to Copenhagen hoping to disrupt a conference hosted by the Studentersamfundet, at which two NLF representatives had been set to be the keynote speakers. Vinh and Hung, armed with leaflets and three films defending US involvement in Vietnam, visited Inge Nielsen, international secretary of the Studentersamfundet, in hopes of getting on the program. She told them that the conference, originally scheduled for October 2, had been postponed to November 15 because the NLF delegates were delayed on a visa technicality. They would veto Vinh and Hung's participation anyway, she continued, so the students should not expect an opportunity to speak at the conference. Perhaps not, but the defectors decided their voices would be heard, and they made plans for Vinh to address the protest scheduled for that afternoon.[23]

On October 11, Phan and Hung held a press conference sponsored by the Democratic Alliance, an anticommunist youth group in Copenhagen. Vinh and Hung told reporters that the communist movement in Vietnam was not a popular uprising but a movement orchestrated by infiltrators from China and the Soviet Union. South Vietnamese students and rural

[19] "North Viet Defectors Will Speak on Red China's Influence Tonight," *The Stanford Daily*, Feb. 28, 1966, Vol. 49, No. 20, p. 1. Bill Rorabaugh, "North Vietnamese Students Censure Hanoi," *The Stanford Daily*, March 1, 1966, Vol. 149, No. 21, 1.

[20] Incoming telegram, Department of State, 006033, Jan. 9, 1966, from AmEmbassy Saigon to Washington. RG 59 – Central Foreign Policy Files, 1964–1966, Political and Defense, Pol 7–29, folder "Pol 12 – Political Parties," Box 2923.

[21] "North Viet Defectors Will Speak on Red China's Influence Tonight," "North Vietnamese Students Censure Hanoi."

[22] Ibid.

[23] Memorandum of conversation, subject: Vietnam and Denmark, place: Copenhagen, date: Oct. 2, 4, 5, 1965, participants: Phan Phuc Vinh, North Vietnamese student, Hung Nguyen Thanh, North Vietnamese student, Cord D. Hansen-Sturm, third secretary of Embassy. RG 59 – Central Foreign Policy Files, 1964–1966, Political and Defense, Pol 7-29, folder "Pol 12 – Political Parties," Box 2923.

people only joined the NLF out of fear, the young men asserted.[24] Yet they were unable to answer questions about allegations of torture by South Vietnam's national police against suspected NLF operatives. Press reaction was much less favorable than embassy officials had hoped. Even the conservative *Berlingske Tidende* thought the students were too emotional and not effective in their presentation. The US Embassy in Copenhagen was keeping its distance from the students so as not to dilute their effectiveness if anyone thinks they are mouthpieces of the US Embassy. It might be a good idea for the US Embassy or the Vietnamese Embassy in Bonn to speak with the students about the value of the "soft sell" in Denmark once they return to West Germany.[25]

US Ambassador Henry Cabot Lodge saw spokesman potential in the defectors and encouraged Secretary of State Dean Rusk to put them to work for US and South Vietnamese interests. Rusk hesitated initially, worried that observers would question the men's authority on anything related to North or South Vietnam because they had all been out of the country for so long. Lodge countered that their experiences in the other communist countries such as China and East Germany along with their time spent in Western Europe gave them a unique perspective to be able to compare life on both sides of the iron curtain. The men's marriages showed their worldliness: Vinh's wife was Japanese, Hung's was Italian, and Oanh had married a Hungarian woman.[26] As defectors, the young men had made the personal choice to flee the communist sphere, and they showed conviction in "invading communist speakers' platform in Copenhagen," Lodge argued. West German authorities had agreed to contribute to financing a speaking tour for the defectors. Rusk eventually agreed, and US Embassy officers began planning a tour with stops in South Vietnam, Taiwan, Japan, the Philippines, and the United States[27]

In early January 1966, the trio began its speaking tour in South Vietnam, where the men met with members of the Ministry of Psychological Warfare, ARVN personnel, local journalists, and JUSPAO officials, who

[24] "The Vietnamese People Do Not Stand Behind the Front of Liberation," translated from *Berlingske Aftenavis*, Oct. 11, 1965.
[25] Department of State Airgram, No. A-290, Oct. 17, 1965, from AmEmbassy Copenhagen, Subject: Presence of Vietnamese Anti-Viet Cong Students in Copenhagen. Foreign Service Officer Cord Hansen-Sturm.
[26] Incoming telegram, Department of State, 006033, Jan. 9, 1966, from AmEmbassy Saigon to Washington.
[27] Incoming telegram, Department of State, 21471, Dec. 29, 1965, from AmEmbassy Saigon to Washington. Joint JUSPAO/Embassy message.

called them "personable, intelligent, articulate, superior to any other Vietnamese team we have assisted."[28] They also traveled to Da Lat and Hue to meet with student groups. The JUSPAO officer escorting them reported that they were "extremely effective" in describing conditions in North Vietnam and other communist countries to show why they defected.[29] An audience of two hundred students in Da Lat was receptive, while Hue students were skeptical, some wondering how the young men could know what things were like in North Vietnam when they had not lived there in years, others questioning the purpose of the trip and its funding sources. The Voice of America planned to air their interviews in Mandarin, Vietnamese, German, and Hungarian. While in Saigon, the students attended briefings at the embassies of Taiwan, the Philippines, Japan, and the United States before leaving South Vietnam for the rest of their tour.[30]

In the United States, the defectors visited Washington, DC, New York City, and California, where they gave a talk and held a press conference at Stanford University in February 1966. They told their audiences that although their families had fought in the anti-French Viet Minh resistance, they defected because the NLF and North Vietnam were fighting for communism, not nationalism, and were under China's influence.[31] Oanh said he wanted to "live a normal life as a free student with initiative," communism was "unnatural" to him, and he opposed the brutality of the North Vietnamese government's land reform program. Hung argued that North Vietnam was being set up as a bastion of communism not for the Vietnamese people but to spread communism throughout Southeast Asia.[32]

The defectors said they wanted to return to South Vietnam after they complete their studies and participate in the "social revolution" that they saw happening when they were in Saigon for their briefing. They all said they are staunchly anticommunist, but they also said they were not interested in American "ideology or political ideals." South Vietnam

[28] Incoming telegram, Department of State, 006033, Jan. 9, 1966, from AmEmbassy Saigon to Washington.
[29] Incoming telegram, Department of State, 014187, Jan. 18, 1966, from AmEmbassy Saigon to Washington.
[30] Ibid.
[31] "North Viet Defectors Will Speak on Red China's Influence Tonight," *The Stanford Daily*, Feb. 28, 1966, Vol. 49, No. 20, 1.
[32] Bill Rorabaugh, "North Vietnamese Students Censure Hanoi," *The Stanford Daily*, March 1, 1966, Vol. 149, No. 21, 1.

needed US military and medical aid, but that was it. If the United States tried to remain in South Vietnam after defeating the NLF, the South Vietnamese people would fight the Americans.[33] A journalist present pointed to 96,000 desertions a year from the South Vietnamese military as proof that the people support the NLF, but Vinh said they were deserting because they were needed in their villages and on their farms, not because they were for the NLF.[34]

In the meeting with the Stanford Committee for Peace in Vietnam (SCPV), Hung emphasized North Vietnam's role in guiding the NLF. He argued that the NLF was composed of North Vietnamese infiltrators. An SCPV member argued that the communists would win the war, identifying the NLF with the people. SCVP delegates and the defectors argued over the extent to which Hanoi controlled the NLF. Vinh said he was not enthusiastic about the Ky government in Saigon but preferred it to the Hanoi leadership. Under Ky, there was "at least a chance to criticize or praise, while Hanoi is totalitarian." Comparing Vietnam to Cuba, Hung said the Cuban revolution was an internal one, and therefore the United States had no right to intervene, but North Vietnam had invaded South Vietnam, and so South Vietnam had requested American help. "South Vietnamese students feel American student demonstrators who cry for peace are crying out of fear," Vinh said.[35]

The story of the deserters illustrates the ineffectiveness of anticommunist Vietnamese voices in a time when there was a broad global consensus, including in the United States, on the moral authority of the NLF. The government in South Vietnam did not have a well-organized propaganda machine that could spin a winning message, and it was short on dynamic representatives who could persuade international audiences to listen. US Embassy officers seemed ready to pounce on anyone, especially young people, willing to stand before the court of international public opinion on behalf of South Vietnam, but this further suggests a lack of such representatives. Vinh, Hung, and Oanh did not seem to convince many skeptics that South Vietnam was a legitimate creation of the Vietnamese people. Mass anti-government demonstrations in Saigon and other South Vietnamese cities made the defectors seem so in the minority that it was no wonder some audiences accused them of being mouthpieces of the government. Reports of the imprisonment and torture of political dissidents had gotten out to the world, which only made it more difficult for

[33] Ibid.   [34] Ibid.   [35] Ibid.

pro-South Vietnam voices to convey their message. By contrast, reports of NLF violence against civilians were muffled by the rising tide of antiwar, anti-US involvement in Vietnam, voices who believed the NLF was the true representative of the South Vietnamese people, not a puppet of Hanoi.

South Vietnamese officials, with US assistance, sought to tell their side of the story to audiences in Africa and Latin America. The results were predictable; as was the case regionally, right-wing governments were open, but left-leaning regimes were skeptical if not resistant. Part of the problem for South Vietnam was that the northern, and especially the NLF, story was more compelling in the context of decolonization. US intervention in South Vietnam was obvious and provided validation of the critique that the RVN was simply an American invention. Like the defectors, South Vietnam's other representatives often seemed defensive, and their message lacked the focused polish and progressive spirit that appealed in an era marked by challenges to the colonial status quo.

A comparison of visits to Hokkaido, Japan in June 1965 by delegations from both North and South Vietnam illustrates the differences. John Sylvester, American Consul in Hokkaido, wrote a report about the two visits in an effort to understand why South Vietnam struggled on the international stage whereas DRV and NLF representatives seemed to be better received. The Japanese were polarized in their views of North and South Vietnam, Sylvester wrote, and the DRV delegation along with its Japanese sponsor had much stronger public relations than the RVN and Japanese conservatives. South Vietnam's delegation consisted of a government official, an army officer, a student leader, and an army nurse, and although the representatives interacted well with small audiences, their sponsor, the conservative Jiji Press, was unwilling to allow them to meet with students, professors, or others who might espouse leftist ideas. By contrast, North Vietnam sent a "cultural delegation" of three professors, and they were received by a large and enthusiastic mass meeting at a local university gymnasium, arranged by Japanese socialists and communists.[36]

To Sylvester, it seemed that Japanese conservatives and business leaders had given up foreign relations to the left. They generally believed that that students, professors, and the media were "leftist beyond redemption," and so any effort to build support for non-communist governments in Vietnam

---

[36] Department of State Airgram, No. A-37, June 24, 1965, from American Consulate (Amconsul) Sapporo to Department of State, Subject: Visit of Delegations from the two Viet Nams. Joint State/USIS message.

or elsewhere should focus on the business community. Yet conservatives and those in business did not show interest in rallying to make the RVN delegation's visit a successful one. Jiji Press representatives who sponsored the delegation wanted to avoid arguments or scuffles with leftists, and even just the threat of leftist agitation was enough to move them to cancel a meeting. This prevented the South Vietnamese delegation from meeting with supportive students at a local university because the Jiji Press sponsors worried that leftists might plant agitators in the audience.[37]

By contrast, Consul Sylvester observed that Japanese sponsors of the DRV delegation had a "conspicuous ability" to organize effective mass meetings. DRV events were well run, well staged, and well attended, and the students and labor unionists who attended responded enthusiastically to slogans denouncing US imperialism. The polish of the DRV tour made South Vietnam's visit seem "pitifully inadequate." From the standpoint of the American Consulate, the main lesson was that USIS should quietly assist local sponsors on future visits to ensure the constant presence of good interpreters and the arranging of more polished presentations.[38] American diplomats understood the importance of South Vietnam appearing independent in all things, including its appeals to the world for recognition, but they also worried about the public relations skills of the groups willing to sponsor a South Vietnamese delegation. It was difficult to match the left's compelling message of anti-imperialism and self-determination when the image of South Vietnam in the global mind's eye was that of an American client.

Sanshichi Hanyu, a Japanese politician and member of the Japan Socialist Party, explained to Far Eastern Affairs Secretary William Bundy that many Europeans, at least those he met in France, Romania, and Yugoslavia, believed that peace was up to the United States. They believed that the United States jumped to bombing without attempting other responses to Hanoi, and that made it appear that the United States was not necessarily committed to peace. Yet Hanoi was the aggressor, Bundy retorted. Hanoi authorities were sending 5,000 troops per month to South Vietnam, and the number was not larger only because of US bombing. Americans were always willing to stop, Bundy asserted, if only North Vietnam would, too. Hanoi had erected the roadblocks to peace – refusing to remove its troops and operatives from South Vietnam and demanding that the United States recognize the NLF as the sole legitimate

[37] Ibid.   [38] Ibid.

government of South Vietnam. Perhaps some conversation through a mediator, such as a neutral French official, Hanyu offered, would help the sides agree to a peace settlement. Britain was too obviously a US ally, and Hanoi leaders assumed that most of Southeast Asia was pro-United States, Hanyu added. France's neutralism was exactly part of the problem, Bundy countered, and in any case, the United States already had direct contact with North Vietnam. If Hanoi, the Communist sphere, Europe, or elsewhere worried that the United States intended to establish a permanent military presence in South Vietnam, they need look only to Japan as an example of America's willingness to withdraw when the time was right, Bundy argued. Just negotiate; why was a country as powerful as the United States worried about losing face, Hanyu wondered. Losing face was the least of America's worries, Bundy assured him.[39]

Japanese authorities suggested that they might assist in some infrastructure projects in the Mekong Delta and elsewhere in South Vietnam. Japanese Embassy counselor Takeo Arita spoke with John T. Bennett, first secretary of the US Embassy in Saigon, about how Japan might assist on a hydroelectric project in the Central Highlands city of Ban Me Thuot, the port of Da Nang, and the construction of the My Thuan bridge in the delta. Arita worried that the bridge would be a wasted investment because it would be an easy bombing target, and Bennett conceded that it would need a defense plan as it would be the main route into the delta. Japanese technicians were already slated to travel to Saigon to work on salvage operations to recover Japanese ships sunk during World War II. The equipment had already arrived in South Vietnam, and the project would employ about fifty Japanese and several hundred Vietnamese workers in Saigon, My Tho, and Da Nang. The Japanese government promised to turn over any recovered precious metals to the South Vietnamese government, while Japan would sell scrap iron domestically or in Hong Kong.[40]

In the spring and summer of 1965, South Vietnam sponsored goodwill missions to African nations in hopes of cultivating sympathy, if not alliances, to counter North Vietnamese and NLF efforts to court Africans during the same time period. The delegation was scheduled for

[39] Department of State, Memorandum of Conversation, Sep. 21, 1966, AmEmbassy Tokyo, Subject: U.S. Policy on Viet-Nam: William Bundy, Assistant Secretary for Far Eastern Affairs, NARA RG 59, Box 2923, Folder 1.
[40] Memorandum of Conversation, Subject: Japanese Aid, Dec. 17, 1964. NARA RG 59, Box 2923, Folder 1.

stops in Cairo, Madagascar, Nigeria, Kenya, and Tunisia.[41] Saigon
officials hoped that sending delegates to Africa, where people were more
skeptical than supportive, would make the skeptics see South Vietnam
as a victim of a communist invasion.[42] RVN charge d'affaires Buu Kinh
traveled to Madagascar to meet with President Philibert Tsiranana, a
member of the Joint African and Malagasy Organization (OCAM –
Organisation Commune Africaine et Malgache), an organization of
former French colonies in Africa that the US Embassy in Morocco
considered a moderate group.[43] The organization emphasized regional
cooperation and solidarity, political, economic, social, and technical
development of members, respect for national sovereignty, and an
opposition to Chinese intervention in Africa. Yet some members also
worried that if the group took too hard-line a political stance it would
harm individual member nations' relationships with Communist countries.[44] So much of the decolonizing world played the balancing act of
maintaining sovereignty while ensuring the aid and alliances that would
most help them develop as independent states.

Allegations of wrongful imprisonment, torture, and other abuses by the
RVN government against citizens tempered African leaders' sympathy for
South Vietnam. Tunisian diplomat Ahmed Mestiri told a US Embassy in
Tunis official that Tunisian President Habib Bourguiba understood what
the United States hoped to accomplish in Vietnam and that "South Vietnam's problems with communists today could become Africa's tomorrow."[45] Mestiri also said he hoped that the Johnson administration
would move forward in its efforts to negotiate an end to the fighting in
Vietnam. To that end, the US Embassy official hoped that Tunisia could
act as an intermediary and convince China and North Vietnam to respond
to Johnson's overtures. The problem for Tunisia were the rumors of
poison gas use by the RVN government and the talks of escalation.
Tunisia had maintained a moderate tone regarding Vietnam, but its

[41] Incoming Telegram, Department of State, 00464, May 1, 1965, From AmEmbassy Rabat to Washington. NARA RG 59, Box 2923, Folder 1.
[42] Bo Tam Ly Chien Viet Nam Cong Hoa, kinh goi: Thu Tuong Chanh Phu, trich yeu: v/v de nghi goi Phai doan quan dan chinh ra ngoai quoc, 26-3-1965. Ho so so 29402: ve hoat dong cua Bo Thong tin Tam Ly Chien nam 1965. TTLTQG II.
[43] Incoming telegram, Department of State, 004157 June 4, 1965, From AmEmbassy Rabat to Washington, DC. NARA RG 59, Box 2923, Folder 1.
[44] "Joint African and Malagasy Organization," *International Organization*, Vol. 20, No. 4 (Autumn 1966) 857–859.
[45] Incoming telegram, Department of State, 12322, April 14, 1965, From AmEmbassy Tunis to Washington. NARA RG 59, Box 2923, Folder 1.

neighbors wondered how it could continue to do so when such stories were in circulation, Mestiri chided. He reminded his American counterpart that Ho Chi Minh had once been a hero in Tunisia when both Tunisia and Vietnam fought for independence from France. That Vietnam had become a "testing ground for communist aggression" saddened Mestiri, Bourguiba, and other Tunisians, Mestiri said. A DRV delegation was set to visit Tunisia soon as part of a tour of African nations, but Mestiri promised that Bourguiba did not intend to recognize North Vietnam or change its relationship with South Vietnam, which already had an embassy in Tunis. He had told as much to the Hanoi government.[46]

NLF representatives were also on a tour of Africa, hoping to convince countries to recognize the NLF as the legitimate government of South Vietnam. US Embassy officials in Cairo had word that Nguyen Van Hieu was in Cairo on his way to Algiers and was working to prove that the Front was not a Communist organization, but rather one that represented multiple political viewpoints. It was different from China, Hieu argued, because it aimed to establish "a neutral and democratic national state, postponing discussion of socialism until after liberation." The most important aim was the establishment of independence, democracy, and an independent national economy. Hieu also demanded that the NLF be allowed to attend Bandung II as the representative of South Vietnam, not as an observer. He argued that the Saigon government "changes every week" and only controlled one-fifth of the country, and only represented the United States, not the people of South Vietnam.[47] Hieu also criticized the Commonwealth peace initiative, arguing that it would only serve the American cause because Australia, New Zealand, and Britain supported the United States morally and with troops in Vietnam.[48]

Also while in Cairo, Van Hieu asked that "friendly countries" recognize it as the provisional government of South Vietnam. China, Indonesia, the Soviet Union, Czechoslovakia, East Germany, Cuba, and Algeria already had. The Arab Socialist Union had sponsored the NLF delegation's visit to Cairo, but the US Embassy in Cairo received a French tip that the Hanoi government had arranged the NLF tour. Khalid Muhyi al-Din, head of the ASU press syndicate, said the Egyptian government sympathized with

[46] Incoming telegram, Department of State, 12322, April 14, 1965, From AmEmbassy Tunis to Washington. NARA RG 59, Box 2923, Folder 1.
[47] Department of State Incoming Telegram, 23120, June 25, 1965, from AmEmbassy Cairo to Washington. NARA RG 59, Box 2923, Folder 1.
[48] Incoming Telegram, Department of State, June 24, 1965, Cairo. NARA RG 59, Box 2923, Folder 1.

African and Asian nations working to throw off imperialism and supported the NLF's efforts to establish independence and remove foreign
military occupation.[49] This had been Egypt's position since Nasser rose to
power in 1952, and although Egyptian leadership had assumed an official
policy of nonalignment, the country developed close ties with China. Zhou
En Lai visited Cairo in March 1963. Lutfi al-Khuli, a journalist and one of
the leaders of the ASU, argued that the organization should come up with
a solution to the conflict in Vietnam "for the sake of the unity of the
revolutionary peoples in Asia and Africa."[50]

DRV delegations traveled throughout Eastern Europe and signed
trade, arms, and other agreements with Czechoslovakia, Hungary,
Poland, and East Germany.[51] Meanwhile, a four-man DRV delegation
to Africa hoped to establish diplomatic relations with Egypt, Ghana,
Mauritania, Tanzania, Mali, Congo, and Central African Republic. The
mission, headed by Phan Ngoc Thuan, chairman of the Foreign Relations
Council of North Vietnam, spent ten days in February and March
1965 traveling through East and Central Africa to build economic and
trade relations between the DRV and those countries. Some African
countries, including Morocco and Congo, refused to receive the DRV
delegation. According to Reuters and local news reports, the CAR
government was downplaying the visit even though the Pham Ngoc
Thuan talked about the similarities between North Vietnamese and
CAR problems in postcolonialism and the Vietnamese effort against US
aggression in South Vietnam. An Agence France-Presse reporter covering
the delegation described Thuan as "sharp, clever, charming, persuasive,
well-educated."[52] The nonaligned conference in Bandung in 1955 may
have presented an image of Third World unity, but Afro-Asian engagement with the three Vietnamese sides to the Indochina conflict illustrated
that there was no Third World monolith. From the Joint African and
Malagasy Organization to the Arab Socialist Union, Africans, like their
Southeast Asian counterparts, had varying approaches to postcolonial
politics and international relations.

---

[49] Incoming Telegram, Department of State, 16654, June 18, 1965, from AmEmbassy Cairo
to Washington. Incoming Telegram Department of State, 14382, June 16, 1965, from
Cairo. NARA RG 59, Box 2923, Folder 1.

[50] Rami Ginat, *Egypt's Incomplete Revolution: Lutfi al-Khuli and Nasser's Socialism in the
1960s* (London: Frank Cass & Co. Ltd., 1997), pp. 90–91.

[51] Nguyen, *Hanoi's War*, pp. 186, 199.

[52] Department of State Airgram, from AmEmbassy Cairo to Department of State, March 6,
1965. NARA RG 59, Box 2923, Folder 1.

From time to time, a memo landed on a State Department desk from a US Embassy with information that illustrated how deeply the Vietnam conflict was embedded in the day-to-day activities of another country. In late September 1965, an officer from the US Embassy in Dakar, Senegal, reported that a Vietnamese man named Tran Van Ngo was deported from the country because of his alleged connections to an international Communist syndicate. He was an established resident of Senegal. He had lived in the country since 1943, was married to a Senegalese woman, had converted to Islam, and owned a Vietnamese restaurant called "Hanoi." Behind the scenes of this ordinary immigrant story in which a subject of French Indochina crossed continents and settled in French West Africa was a tale of Cold War intrigue. Tran Van Ngo's restaurant was a meeting place for reporters from the New China News Agency and African Independence Party (PAI) operatives. PAI was a Communist organization that American observers believed to have ties to China, and the New China News Agency was affiliated with the Chinese government. According to US Embassy officers, reporters for NCNA engaged in diplomacy on behalf of Beijing. Tran's expulsion was meant to serve as a warning to NCNA correspondents, who would be next if they continued their actions, warned Senegal's President Leopold Senghor. US Embassy observers had noticed a steady buzz of activity in Hanoi restaurant, with Tran as a prime contact between NCNA and the PAI.[53]

President Senghor would not have wanted Chinese influence in Senegal. Educated in France, he was a moderate who strove for retaining close ties with the West, especially Senegal's former colonial authority, France. Though he espoused what he called a distinctly "African socialism," Senghor opposed alliances with the Soviet Union or China and denounced the idea of the "dictatorship of the proletariat."[54] His presidency was an example of the political diversity of the newly independent world of the Cold War era. It was a world in which South Vietnam and the United States hoped to find enough widespread, vocal support for the RVN.

Much of what was at stake in the spring of 1965 revolved around an invitation to "Bandung II," the proposed follow-up conference to the Afro-Asian meeting held in Bandung, Indonesia, in 1955. Representatives

---

[53] Department of State Airgram from AmEmbassy Dakar, Sep. 25, 1965, Subject: Senegal Expels Manager of "Hanoi" Restaurant. NARA RG 59, Box 2923, Folder 1.

[54] Albin Krebs, "Leopold Senghor Dies at 95; Senegal's Poet of Negritude," *New York Times*, Dec. 21, 2001, www.nytimes.com/2001/12/21/world/leopold-senghor-dies-at-95-senegal-s-poet-of-negritude.html.

of countries that had participated in the first conference had begun meeting in 1964 to discuss plans for a second event to be held in Algiers in 1965, a decade after Bandung I. Attempts to organize the conference took place against a backdrop of large state competition for African nations' attention, with China, the United States, and the Soviet Union all working to guide developments in the Third World toward their respective interests. In 1964, Chinese Premier Zhou Enlai spent about two months in Africa, traveling to ten countries, a tour US Secretary of State Dean Rusk called "the most ambitious and extensive Chicom diplomatic offensive yet undertaken in (the) Free World."[55] In addition to vying with the United States and the Soviet Union for African allies, Zhou's efforts were part of a larger mission of resisting the UN, which recognized Taiwan as the legitimate China and thus had seated the ROC instead of the PRC. Due to the Sino-Soviet split, some nonaligned nations, notably India, favored the Soviet Union in discussions about which nations to invite to Bandung II. From the perspective of Americans in the State Department, the goal was to ensure that a second Afro-Asian conference did not become an anti-US, anti-Western meeting in which the central purpose was to denounce American "imperialism." State Department officials hoped delegates to Bandung II would focus instead on economic and political development.[56]

In addition to American concerns about the broad message of Bandung II, State Department officials also worried about whether the government of South Vietnam or the NLF would receive an invitation. Both the DRV and the RVN had been invited to Bandung I, but early planning meetings for Bandung II included discussions of welcoming "Nationalist Movements seeking independence," which made possible an invitation to the NLF as the representative of South Vietnam.[57] While in Madagascar, Buu Kinh asked President Tsiranana to make a pitch at the upcoming OCAM summit that moderate nations be invited to a possible Bandung II. Tsiranana dismissed any Bandung meeting as being run by Communists. South Vietnamese officials also broached the subject of Bandung II with representatives from Algeria, Morocco, and India to see if they might receive an invitation to the meeting.[58] It soon was a moot point, though,

[55] Eric Gettig, "'Trouble Ahead in Afro-Asia': The United States, the Second Bandung Conference, and the Struggle for the Third World, 1964–1965," *Diplomatic History*, Vol. 39, No. 1 (Jan. 2015) 129.
[56] Ibid., pp. 129–135.   [57] Ibid., p. 132.
[58] Incoming telegram, Department of State, 12322, April 14, 1965, From AmEmbassy Tunis to Washington. NARA RG 59, Box 2923, Folder 1.

because Bandung II never happened. At a planning meeting in late October 1965, arguments over whether to invite the Soviet Union, China, or neither country stalled planning, and Indonesia, a key ally of China, used the impasse to successfully lobby for postponing the conference.[59] The failure of Afro-Asian nations to organize a second Bandung conference illustrates the diversity of political attitudes and goals that existed throughout the decolonizing world. South Vietnam's diplomatic missions to Africa engaged in that diversity and hoped to gain allies from it.

In Latin America, Argentine anticommunist groups supported South Vietnam and US involvement in its affairs. Luis Cesar Parazzo, a politician in his late thirties who aspired to be in the National Assembly, held a meeting of his Frente Latino-Americano Anti-Comunista (FLA) in May 1966 to express support for US policy in Vietnam. FLA touted student membership, and US Embassy officials believed it was more selective in its membership than some of the other anticommunist organizations in Argentina, which were suspected of having large numbers of "exiled East European monarchists" and "former Nazis" among their members. About eighty-five people attended the meeting, held at a small Italian club in Buenos Aires because most of the universities Parazzo had approached for meeting space denied his request. Most of the attendees were in their thirties and forties, although about a quarter of them were in their twenties. Official types included an aide to Argentina's Secretary of the Navy and a representative of the Taiwan Embassy. At the start of the meeting, Parazzo recognized some "ex-combatants of the White Russian anti-communist army" in the room.[60]

The meeting featured three short speeches, including one by Cesar Alberto Cogorno of the Centro de Estudios e Investigaciones Sociales Juan XXIII. US troops in Vietnam were fighting for Argentina, too, he stated, and he chastised Communist infiltrators for drumming up anti-US sentiment in Buenos Aires and elsewhere in the country. Raul Zelo Zapata, representative of Amigos de Mayo, an offshoot of "32 Bloc" of democratic labor unions, decried the "campaign against liberty and democracy which is deforming the minds of (Argentine) youth." He spent most of his speech castigating the General Confederation of Labor, for its nondemocratic orientations, including its associations with Peronism, and

[59] Gettig, p. 150.
[60] Department of State Airgram, to Department of State, May 14, 1966, from AmEmbassy Buenos Aires, Subject: Anti-Communist Organizations Back U.S. Vietnam Policy. NARA RG 59, Box 2923, Folder 1.

for its failure to denounce Soviet "aggression" against Argentina while being very willing to denounce US intervention in Vietnam. In April, Argentine Navy ships pushed out Soviet whalers in Argentine territorial waters off Tierra del Fuego and Patagonia.[61]

Ellwood Rabenold, US Embassy counselor for political affairs, reported on the event, noting the Embassy and USIS paid attention to the FLA even though it was small because it was one of the few "strident-but-reasonable anti-Communist voices" in Buenos Aires. It also struck Rabenold that, despite much advance publicity, agitators, Communist or otherwise, did not disrupt the meeting. After the meeting, the student-age attendees stood on a street corner and quietly discussed the meeting and related items. The police had assigned four uniformed patrolmen to the event, and one worked the door while three others sat in a police car across the street from the venue and watched for signs of trouble. That they were a small security presence, and that riot police were not on standby, suggested to Rabenold that police had not expected trouble. It was a stark contrast to the anti-US, pro-NLF student demonstration at the opening of the University of Buenos Aires' new Ciudad Universitaria a couple weeks earlier. Several chiefs of diplomatic missions were among the honored guests at that ceremony, which perhaps gave an air of significance to the event that the FLA's meeting did not have. Rabenold also suggested that it could have implied that Communist efforts had limited reach and success in Buenos Aires, including among students.[62]

Perazzo had been working to unite a variety of anticommunist and Christian democratic groups under the FLA, including Organizacion Amigos de Maya, Centro de Estudios e Investigaciones Sociales Juan XXIII, Accion Liberal Argentina, Confederacion Universitaria Argentina Liberal, Instituto Coordinadora de Accion Social Christiana, and Union de Entidades Liberales Argentinas. In 1963 and 1965, Perazzo had run on the anti-Peronist UDELPA ticket for national deputy. Perazzo had been involved with more right-wing anticommunist groups but left them because he believed they were too McCarthyist, reactionary, and not discerning enough in their admission of members. He considered himself a liberal in the Argentine, nineteenth-century meaning of the word, and he had taken a strong stand against anti-Semitism. If there was a moderate anticommunist thread in Latin America, Perazzo seemed to seek it. He had connections with the Paraguayan Partido Liberal, which opposed

---

[61] Ibid.   [62] Ibid.

Paraguay's right-wing dictator but tried to "avoid falling under communist influence," according to US Embassy authorities in Buenos Aires. FLA and some of the other Argentine groups openly supported US intervention in the Dominican Republic and in Vietnam, and they spoke out against leftist Argentine groups that have protested US involvement in Vietnam.[63] Like in Africa, the diversity of political movements in South America provided opportunities for representatives of South Vietnam to seek support for the country.

REGIONAL RESPONSES

As the war between communist and noncommunist forces became a central fact of life in Vietnam, South Vietnam's neighbors and regional allies monitored the situation, seeing it as a Southeast Asian issue, not just a Vietnam issue. After the assassination of Ngo Dinh Diem at the end of 1963, the Asian People's Anti-Communist League, which was founded by the governments of Taiwan and South Korea in 1954 to resist what members considered to be communist insurgencies, turned its attention to the political situation in South Vietnam.[64] Beginning in 1964, the central subject of the organization's annual meetings was South Vietnam and how members of the APACL could assist the Army of the Republic of Vietnam. At the 1964 meeting in Taipei, conference goers decided to open a special APACL office in Saigon to demonstrate support for the Saigon government. Newspapers in Bangkok, Kuala Lumpur, and Manila published editorials supporting South Vietnam. An APACL youth conference featured delegates from the United States, including Tom Charles Huston and David Keene representing Young Americans for Freedom.[65]

---

[63] Ibid.

[64] Il Hyun Cho and Seo-Hyun Park, "Anti-Chinese and Anti-Japanese Sentiments in East Asia: The Politics of Opinion, Distrust, and Prejudice," *The Chinese Journal of International Politics*, Vol. 4 (2011) 284. See also, Peter Dale Scott, "Contragate: Reagan, Foreign Money, and the Contra Deal," *Crime and Social Justice*, No. 28/29 (1987) 110–148. For details on Malaysia's interest in the Vietnam conflict, see Pamela Sodhy, "Malaysian-American Relations during Indonesia's Confrontation against Malaysia, 1963–66," *Journal of Southeast Asian Studies*, Vol. 19, No. 1 (March 1988) 111–136; Sodhy, "The Malaysian Connection in the Vietnam War," *Contemporary Southeast Asia*, Vol. 9, No. 1 (June 1987) 38–53; Marvin Ott, "Malaysia: The Search for Solidarity and Security," *Asian Survey*, Vol. 8, No. 2 (Feb. 1968) 127–132.

[65] Tu Hoang Nam Hung, Hoi Khong Hoc Viet Nam, Kinh goi: Thu Tuong Chanh-Phu Viet Nam Cong Hoa, 7-12-1964; Hoi-Nghi Lien Minh A – Chau Chong Cong; Hoat-Dong Thanh-Nien. Ho so so: 29878, Cac ky hoi nghi cua Lien Minh A Chau chong cong tai Dai Bac, Dai Han, Philippin nam 1964–67. TTLTQG II.

Saigon officials took advantage of the friendly audience to portray a citizenry under attack by brutal Viet Cong. In preparation for the Manila conference in 1965, the Department of Psychological Warfare gathered photographs meant to depict the war's impact on South Vietnam. Pictures featured a one-year-old baby sitting near its mother's dead body, a monk in Binh Dinh who immolated himself in protest against the VC, and foreign troops building schools and bridges throughout South Vietnam. South Vietnamese delegates to the conference also brought a documentary called "Toi-ac Viet Cong" – "Crime of the Viet Cong" – to drive home the point that South Vietnamese citizens were suffering at the hands of the VC. The plan worked. Delegates in Manila issued a slogan, "Tat ca cho Viet Nam" – "All is for Vietnam" – and emphasized that candidates in upcoming Philippine elections must make South Vietnam a foreign policy priority.[66]

APACL's focus on South Vietnam illustrates the regional nature of the Vietnam War and situates South Vietnam in a broader context of political activism against communism in Southeast Asia. The region was a key example of postcolonial political movements to establish the identities of newly independent nations where communist and noncommunist movements clashed. Leaders and observers throughout Southeast Asia monitored the situation in South Vietnam as an example of how such conflicts might play out. Throughout 1965, the *Straits Times* of Singapore ran editorials about Saigon politics and relations between the government, the VC, and the United States The biggest problem for South Vietnam, the editorials lamented, was the government itself. Repeated coups, the imprisonment of students and rebel politicians, and infighting among government officials over how to deal with the VC would ensure that South Vietnam would enjoy no clear victory.[67]

In October 1966, South Vietnam's Ambassador to Malaysia Tran Kim Phuong told Malaysia's Deputy Prime Minister Abdul Razak that his country welcomed any deployment of Malaysian troops to fight the communist insurgency there. If South Vietnam defeated communism, all of Southeast Asia would win, Phuong declared. The Malaysian government offered verbal support to South Vietnam, but it was dealing with its own insurgency in Sarawak and Brunei, where 30,000 Malaysian troops

[66] 9-10-1965, Tong Thu Ky Chi Hoi Viet-Nam, Lien Minh A Chau Chong Cong, Kinh gui: Thieu Tuong Chu Tich Uy Ban Hanh Phap Trung-Uong. Ho so so: 29878. TTLTQG II.
[67] "Decisive Year," *The Straits Times*, Jan. 1, 1965; "Saigon Waits," *The Straits Times*, Jan. 12, 1965.

were fighting Indonesians. With the British withdrawing their forces, Malaysia did not have enough troops to send abroad. Malaysian officials also worried that, given the country's delicate racial balance, with ethnic Chinese Malaysians making up nearly 50 percent of the population, sending troops to South Vietnam would cause unrest in the Chinese Malaysian communities. Where Malaysia could help was in training, and the government offered to help train South Vietnamese police and military personnel in the methods of guerrilla warfare.[68]

Lyndon Johnson saw the value for the United States in promoting the idea that the Vietnam War was an international conflict. Although unsuccessful in his attempts to convince NATO allies, especially Great Britain given its counterinsurgency efforts during the Malayan Emergency, to commit troops to Vietnam, he enlisted the support of South Korea, the Philippines, Thailand, Taiwan, Australia, and New Zealand under his "more flags" program.[69] Some Johnson administration officials had hoped that the British might be willing to support US intervention in Vietnam in exchange for American assistance in dealing with the brewing crisis between Malaysia and Indonesia, but others worried that a US agreement to commit troops to Malaysia would amount to overreach that would outweigh the value of British military support in Vietnam.[70] When the Malaysian "confrontation" ended in 1966 after a coup overthrew Sukarno in Indonesia and replaced him with Suharto, who signed a peace treaty with Malaysia, Johnson thought that perhaps the British government would divert its forces in Malaysia to Vietnam, but economic and political constraints on British defense efforts ultimately prevented the formation of an Anglo-American military alliance in Vietnam.[71] The lesson learned was that South Vietnam was part of a larger Southeast Asian anxiety over the spread of communism. The political instability in Saigon from the murder of Ngo Dinh Diem in November 1963 to the election of Nguyen Van

---

[68] 5-10-1966, Viet Nam Cong Hoa Bo Ngoai Giao Trich Yeu: Yeu cau chanh phu Phu Ma Lai A gui quan sang Viet Nam; 12-10-1966 Viet Nam Cong Hoa Bo Ngoai Giao Trich Yeu: v/v chanh phu Ma Lai A cai chinh tin se gui quan sang Viet Nam. Ho so so 15899: Cac Quoc Gia gia Anh, Malaxia, Nicaragua, Tay Ban Nha, Thoi Nhi Ku du dinh va gui quan sang giup Viet Nam Cong Hoa nam 1966–67. TTLTQG II.

[69] Sylvia Ellis, *Britain, America, and the Vietnam War* (Westport, CT: Praeger, 2004), pp. 2–5. See also, Robert M. Blackburn, *Mercenaries and Lyndon Johnson's "More Flags": The Hiring of Korean, Filipino, and Thai Soldiers in the Vietnam War* (Jefferson, NC: McFarland, 1994).

[70] Ibid., pp. 12, 32–33.   [71] Ibid., pp. 155–156.

Thieu in September 1967 led regional observers to worry about similar conflicts between citizens and government, communists and noncommunists, in their own nations.

The political chaos that marked Saigon after the assassination of Ngo Dinh Diem caught the attention of the APACL and motivated members to make South Vietnam central to the group's agenda. At the Taipei conference in November 1964, delegates from other countries offered words of encouragement to the six South Vietnamese representatives to embolden them in the fight against Communism. Hoang Nam Hung, one of the six, had spoken with the APACL president and learned that the organization had decided to open a special office in Saigon given the situation there and what they considered a Communist invasion of South Vietnam.[72] Chairman Ku Cheng-kang of the China Council of the APACL issued a statement on May 9, 1964, stating that nations in eastern Asia should support South Vietnam's anticommunist government. He was echoing General Nguyen Khanh appeal for help defeating the Viet Cong. Support did not require troop commitments, Ku Cheng-kang wrote. The nations under siege could provide the manpower; they needed "logistical and material supplies." Ku affirmed Khanh's assertion that South Vietnam would not win if it only fought a defensive war. South Vietnam and its allies needed to move the war into North Vietnam. Although the conflict was an Asian one in 1964, Ku called on anticommunist nations throughout the world to support South Vietnam because South Vietnam was fighting for the "freedom of the world free world."[73]

The APACL was founded in 1954 by Syngman Rhee and Chiang Kai-Shek, two leaders who had been at the forefront of the early postwar struggle against Communism in Asia. Rhee's South Korea was still reeling from the war against North Korea, and Taiwan and China had been clashing over islands in the Taiwan Strait since the early 1950s. Leaders of South Korea, Taiwan, and the Philippines had been discussing the idea of establishing a regional defense pact similar to NATO to defend against Communist Chinese encroachment and other communist threats in the region since 1949. When Americans learned of this, they went in hoping to preserve their dominance in the region with bilateral

---

[72] Hoang Nam Hung of the Hoi Khong Hoc Viet Nam, 7-12-1964, Kinh goi: Thu Tuong Chanh Phu Viet Nam Cong Hoa. Ho so so 29878 – Cac ky hoi nghi cua Lien Minh A Chau chong cong tai Dai Bac, Dai Han, Philippin nam 1964–67. TTLTQG II.

[73] "APACL Leader Backing Up Vietnam's Appeal for Help," *Taiwan Today*, May 17, 1964, http://taiwantoday.tw/fp.asp?xItem=170113&CtNode=122.

agreements and their own plan to establish a defense pact.[74] The United States, along with France, Britain, New Zealand, Australia, the Philippines, Thailand, and Pakistan, founded the Southeast Asian Treaty Organization (SEATO) in 1954 in an effort to staunch the spread of communism in eastern Asia. Yet because most of the members were countries that had interests in the region but were outsiders, Rhee and Chiang called for an organization made up of members that directly faced the possibility of communist expansion in Asia. South Korea, Taiwan, the Philippines, Thailand, South Vietnam, Hong Kong, Macao, and the Ryukyu Islands were among the first members. Presidents held one-year terms, and the president's nation hosted the annual conference. Reflecting the Chinese diaspora that had followed the end of the Chinese Civil War and the victory of Mao's forces, many of the delegates were overseas Chinese. Fear of a perceived threat of China's imperialist goals motivated most of the APACL member nations.[75]

In 1955, the Bandung conference and the founding of the Afro-Asian nonaligned movement created another persuasion for the APACL to counter. Members envisioned the APACL as an alternative to the nonaligned movement, and the organization emphasized an "Asia first" strategy. The ideology manifested itself in opposition to foreign interference and was explicitly anti-American and anti-European at times.[76] That did not stop the APACL from accepting financing from private individuals and organizations, businesses, the governments of member nations, other anticommunist groups throughout the world, and the CIA and other foreign intelligence organizations funded the APACL.[77] The APACL's charter called for a struggle against communist imperialism and aggression and an end to communist expansion, cooperation between free Asian nations and the rest of the free world, destruction of the "Iron Curtain in Asia at an early date," national reunification of divided countries "so as to restore freedom to the enslaved peoples," and "to build a new Asia, where freedom, democracy, peace, and prosperity will prevail in cooperation with the rest of the free world."[78]

The APACL annual meetings were sometimes extravagant affairs. A European observer at the 1962 conference in Seoul reported:

---

[74] Torben Gulstorff, "Warming Up a Cooling War: An Introductory Guide on the CIAS and Other Globally Operating Anti-Communist Networks at the Beginning of the Cold War Decade of Détente," Cold War International History Project, Woodrow Wilson International Center for Scholars, Working Paper #75, Feb. 2015, p. 25.
[75] Ibid., pp. 24–26. [76] Ibid., p. 31. [77] Ibid., p. 34. [78] Ibid., p. 31.

The style of the conference was to an almost unjustified degree "enormous." The participants were accommodated in some of the few best hotels, constantly under supervision by clerks of the CIA ([South Korean] State Security Ministry) and accompanying interpreters (schoolgirls out of the best families of Seoul). The population was ordered to the roadsides several times, 200,000 people participated at a declaration at the stadium. Near the border with North Korea, a heavy infantry attack with live ammunition was presented to the delegates, the visit in Panmunjon was well prepared by the US-Army; transportation was conducted by helicopter. A parade took place in the military academy, to celebrate the visit. At the receptions—especially the ones at the president's house—the vanguards of military and civil administration as well as the diplomatic corps were present.[79]

At the 1964 APACL conference, the tenth anniversary of its establishment, delegates again discussed the idea of establishing an Asian defense pact, particularly in support of South Vietnam against Communist aggression. South Korea, Taiwan, Thailand, the Philippines, and South Vietnam agreed to be part of this. The members pledged to send a total of 400,000 troops to South Vietnam to fight the communist insurgency, indicating a sense that the United States was not able to win the war alone according to its current strategy.[80] At the twelfth conference in 1966 in South Korea, delegates began talking about expanding the organization to other continents and joining an international anticommunist network. They had also begun planning to open a West German office of APACL.[81] Also in 1966, the APACL participated with European and Latin American anticommunist groups in the founding of the World Anti-Communist League (WACL). Its goals were to support anticommunist leaders and groups with political and psychological warfare methods to "overcome the Communist menace."[82]

South Vietnamese officials understood the value of the APACL meetings as opportunities to provide their perspectives on the conflict and chaos in their country. In doing so, they hoped to gain sympathy from their neighbors in East Asia.[83] For the 1965 conference in Manila, authorities in the Ministry of Psychological Warfare compiled collections of photographs, films, and maps depicting Communist infiltration of South Vietnam, work and actions of ARVN troops, and foreign militaries building schools, bridges, and other infrastructure throughout

[79] Ibid., pp. 13–14.   [80] Ibid., p. 33.   [81] Ibid., p. 70.   [82] Ibid., p. 71.
[83] Letter from Trung Tuong (Lt. Gen.) Pham Xuan Chieu, Van Phong Uy Ban Lanh Dao Quoc Gia, Saigon 22-7-1965, Kinh goi: Thieu Tuong Chu Tich Uy Ban Hanh Phap Truong Uong. Ho so so 29878 – Cac ky hoi nghi cua Lien Minh A Chau chong cong tai Dai Bac, Dai Han, Philippin nam 1964-67. TTLTQG II.

the country. They selected graphic photos that illustrated NLF brutality against civilians. One picture captured a baby, about a year old, sitting next to the dead body of its mother, a victim of NLF. Another image showed a monk in a village in Binh Dinh province who immolated himself to protest NLF violence. Along with the photos, they planned to show a 1964 documentary called "Crime of the Viet Cong"/"Toi ac Viet Cong." If they could demonstrate the impact of NLF violence on civilians and civilians fighting Communists, then they could garner international sympathy.[84]

The efforts worked, and delegates to the Manila conference declared a new APACL slogan: "All is for Vietnam" – "Tat ca cho Viet Nam." The work of APACL must focus on supporting the government of South Vietnam. South Vietnamese representatives asked their counterparts to send specialists in agricultural development, as well as health, education, and other forms of social work to assist those Vietnamese civilians who fled the NLF. As far as the representatives of the meeting's host country, the Philippines, were concerned, South Vietnam was the main topic that candidates in its upcoming election must understand and address. Delegates also issued a statement of support in favor of US assistance to the South Vietnamese government and military. They hoped that US resolve in South Vietnam would encourage anticommunist movements elsewhere in the region.[85]

It was also at the 1965 Manila conference that delegates discussed prospects for forming a regional military cooperative for mutual defense. Its goal was to rid the region of communism and replace it with democracy. Such a collaboration could also foster closer political, economic, and cultural cooperation, like the Afro-Asian nonaligned movement tried to do among its members. APACL members believed their military alliance would be more effective than SEATO, which included only two Southeast Asian nations. Members hoped the United States would support the formation of an APACL military cooperative, but not to the degree that Americans would have license to direct it.[86]

---

[84] Statement from Bo Tam Ly Chien re: Manila Conference, 7-12-Sept-1965. Ho so so 29878. TTLTQG II.
[85] APACL Vietnam Chapter, 9-10-1965, Tong Thu Ky Chi Hoi Viet Nam Lien Minh A Chau Chong Cong, Kinh gui: Thieu Tuong Chu Tich Uy Ban Hanh Phap Trung Uong from Bac Si Pham Huu Chuong (APACL VN) Ho so so 29878. TTLTQG II.
[86] Letter written by APACL secretary-general Jose Hernandez to prime minister of South Vietnam, 15-12-1965. Ho so so 15721: Ton Thanh Khuyen nghi cua to chuc APACL ve thanh lap "Lien Minh cac Quoc Gia A Chau chong cong" nam 1965–66. TTLTQG II.

While taking care to keep the United States at arms length in terms of APACL decision-making, members understood the value of connecting with like-minded Americans. The group invited Tom Charles Huston, national chairman of the conservative student group Young Americans for Freedom, as well as YAF members Maureen Butler and Sylvia Griffith Sanders, to the Manila conference. The American Afro-Asian Educational Exchange sponsored their travels to both Manila and a pre-conference meeting in Seoul. Yale University professor David Rowe accompanied the students.[87] Huston, an Indiana University law student in his early twenties, attended as one of his first orders of business as YAF's newly elected national chairman. He was particularly interested in Southeast Asia and the situation in Vietnam. His uncle, a missionary, had been killed in China by Communist forces before World War II, and that remained on his mind as he assessed Communist movements in Asia. At the end of 1965, the APACL invited Huston back to Southeast Asia, and he met with US troops serving in Vietnam.[88] He also met with government and anticommunist youth group representatives in South Korea, the Philippines, and Taiwan, offering reassuring messages about the American commitment to South Vietnam and the fight against communism more broadly. Among other topics, Huston explained to his counterparts about YAF initiatives including a blood drive for Vietnam and the group's collaboration with the US Marines in Operation Hand Clasp to collect and distribute clothing, food, and other necessities to refugees throughout South Vietnam. Huston and his YAF colleagues hoped that they would boost the morale of young anticommunists throughout Asia if they convinced them that not all young Americans opposed US intervention in Vietnam or the broader global fight against communism.[89]

As part of the mission of opposing communist expansion throughout the world, the YAF had focused on Vietnam since the early 1960s. Board member Robert Harley had traveled throughout Southeast Asia in the summer of 1961 and while in to South Vietnam, he met Tran Tam, the Vietnamese representative of the APACL. Tam gave Harley a tour of Cholon, Saigon's Chinatown district, and Harley came to believe that the city's Chinese population was a major line of defense against communism.

---

[87] *The New Guard*, Nov. 1965, p. 20.

[88] Gregory L. Schneider, *Cadres for Conservatism: Young Americans for Freedom and the Rise of the Contemporary Right* (New York: New York University Press, 1999), p. 98.

[89] Irene Corbally Kuhn, "YAF Spearheads Rallies for Freedom in Viet Nam," *Human Events*, Jan. 22, 1966, p. 12.

Harley came away from his trip to South Vietnam convinced that supporting it was key to defending Southeast Asia. YAF members, like mainstream
politicians on both the left and the right, believed in the domino theory.[90]
After the assassination of Ngo Dinh Diem, YAF members wrote in the
group's official newspaper, *New Guard*, that the United States "must
first commit itself to total victory in South Vietnam."[91] YAF members
viewed the conflict in Vietnam as a struggle between communist aggression and an independent and free South Vietnam. YAF chapters put this
commitment into action, holding food and clothing drives for war
refugees in South Vietnam and book drives for soldiers. In early January
1966, thousands of people attended YAF rallies throughout the country
in support of US policies in Vietnam. YAF members also looked abroad
and reached out to international anticommunist groups.[92] Youth in
India, Taiwan, Japan, Hong Kong, South Korea, Australia, Thailand,
Vietnam, Denmark, Sweden, Norway, Honduras, Indonesia, France,
Italy, Spain, the Philippines, New Zealand, Burma, and Somalia held
anticommunist rallies to mark the YAF-sponsored "International Youth
Crusade for Freedom in Vietnam."[93]

With the assistance of Marvin Liebman, a conservative fundraiser and
major player in the China Lobby, Huston's work with the APACL
resulted in the founding of the international World Youth Crusade for
Freedom (WYCF). It was "a group committed to the defeat of Communism," founders declared at its initial meeting in Hong Kong on May 8,
1966. The WYCF established a Freedom Corps, similar to the Peace
Corps, in which American students would spend summers in Asian countries learning about the situations there and working with local youth. In
the first month, volunteers met and talked with political leaders and
activists to get a feel for the overall state of their host nation's affairs.
The American students spent the second month working in the villages in
various ways including teaching, working with local youth organizations,
and building infrastructure. Discussions at the Hong Kong conference
offer a fascinating glimpse at the delegates' different national attitudes
toward gender. The Indian and Taiwanese representatives asked for male
and female volunteers, respectively, to be placed in their respective countries. The delegate from the Philippines argued that women are better in
person-to-person diplomacy than men, and thus hoped for a woman
volunteer to be assigned to the country. The Japanese and Australian

[90] Schneider, *Cadres for Conservatism*, p. 95.   [91] Ibid., p. 96.   [92] Ibid.
[93] *The New Guard*, Dec. 1965, p. 22.

delegates requested men only; the Vietnamese representative did so, too, but because of the dangers of operating in a country at war.[94]

Students selected for the program would be among the college-educated elite – high grade point averages, award winning, multilingual. The inaugural group included delegates who were fluent in French and Chinese; Huston himself was Phi Beta Kappa at IU. They saw themselves as ambassadors, and they presented an image of American youth as worldly, intellectually curious, idealistic, and respectful.[95] Yet that image was not meant to suggest that Freedom Corps members would only operate in elite circles in their host countries. On the contrary, the volunteers would roll up their sleeves and get down to business in the villages, "ugly American" style as Burdick and Lederer conceived of that deeply misunderstood moniker. David Keene, at that time a first-year law student at the University of Wisconsin, was among the inaugural nine in the program, which sent him, along with fellow Wisconsin student, Richard Wright, to South Vietnam. Others went to Japan, Australia, the Philippines, India, Taiwan, Indonesia, Singapore, and Hong Kong.[96]

As the volunteers in South Vietnam got to know students in Saigon and other cities, they concluded that urban students were "not much different than young people anywhere else. Many use every means possible to stay out of the armed services of their country; others carp about government bureaucracy and corruption; still others have been indoctrinated by the communists."[97] It was in the countryside where they found people who had "seen the real face of Communism. They fear it and are prepared to fight to the death against it." Keene and Wright worked in villages throughout South Vietnam, and they reported encountering people in every part of the country who were willing to fight Communism so that they could live in peace. When Keene returned to the United States, he founded the Student Committee for a Free China and argued that China was the biggest threat in Asia. "If you believed that Communism was

[94] World Youth Crusade for Freedom, memorandum to: Senior American Advisory Council and Contributors, from: Tom Charles Huston, May 27, 1966, p. 8. Personal collection of Tom Charles Huston.

[95] Robert L. Riggs, "Old China Hands and Young Conservatives Team Up to Carry Anti-Red Gospel to Asia," *Louisville Courier-Journal*, June 5, 1966, p. D-3.

[96] World Youth Crusade for Freedom, memorandum to: Senior American Advisory Council, Supporters, and All Others Concerned, from: Tom Charles Huston, Nov. 18, 1966, p. 3. Personal collection of Tom Charles Huston.

[97] Schneider, *Cadres for Conservatism*, p. 99.

really a threat, then the national security state ... and our commitment to Vietnam were justified," Keene asserted.[98]

As part of their efforts to immerse themselves in local culture and develop their knowledge of the people with whom they worked in Vietnam, the young men both participated in a traditional tribal ceremony while working with Montagnards in the Central Highlands.[99] Yet it was not just a getting-to-know-you goodwill gesture. Keene and Wright were following the Edward Lansdale method of engagement and diplomacy that had worked so well in the Philippines yet was subject to a less patient timeline in Vietnam. As Huston wrote, the point was to train a local counterinsurgency force that was well-versed in political organization and economic theory, committed to the ideals of representative democracy, and trusting of Americans who arrived to help. Freedom Corps' endgame was the establishment of revolutionary local militias that had as much a right to determine Vietnam's future as the communists.[100] Writing for the conservative student journal *Insight and Outlook*, published at the University of Wisconsin–Madison, William A. Rusher compared the WYCF to the Young Communist International, founded in Berlin in 1919 to draw young people into service to the global communist movement. In Europe's colonial empires, young communists would heed Lenin's call to take up arms in indigenous rebellions against imperialism as part of the predetermined course of history Marx had envisioned. WYCF members disagreed with the notion that communist movements had the moral authority to establish the world's future, and they saw the Freedom Corps as the other side of the fight, having just as much right to guiding the Third World as the communists. Freedom Corps' central values included representative government, personal freedom, and economic development.[101]

In an effort to build on the momentum of the founding of the WYCF in May 1966, the APACL organized a youth conference held in conjunction with the 1966 annual meeting in Seoul. Young delegates from member countries attended, and representatives from India, Australia, Ukraine, and Congo, as well as Americans Keene and Huston, participated as

---

[98] Ibid., p. 92.

[99] *WYCF Report*, Vol. 1, No. 2, Nov. 1966, p. 1. Personal collection of Tom Charles Huston.

[100] Tom Charles Huston, "The Third Dimension of International Conflict," *WYCF Report*, Vol. 1, No. 2, Nov. 1966, p. 3. Personal collection of Tom Charles Huston.

[101] William A. Rusher, "Enter the World Youth Crusade," *Insight and Outlook*, Vol. IX, No. 2 (Dec.–Jan. 1966–1967) 4. Personal Collection of Tom Charles Huston.

observers. Attendees discussed the international youth attitudes toward the Vietnam War, and they were especially interested in the Vietnamese delegates' perspectives on anti-Americanism in Vietnam and what Vietnamese youth thought of the presence of free world forces in their country. Delegates invited Keene to speak about anticommunist youth in the United States. South Vietnam's youth delegation presented to South Korean veterans of the war a South Vietnamese flag with the signatures of hundreds of mothers. While in South Korea, Keene and Huston visited Yonsei University and Ewa Women's University and met with Korean students, and they traveled to Japan and met with students at Tokyo University.[102]

VU VAN THAI

Career diplomat Vu Van Thai, who became South Vietnam's ambassador to the United States in 1965, believed international recognition and regional cooperation were vital – required, even – for South Vietnam's survival. Thai was cosmopolitan, a world citizen. He was born in Hanoi in 1919 and went to university in Paris. He was a member of the Resistance, and in the 1940s and early 1950s, he was a left-wing noncommunist nationalist who joined the Viet Minh. He advised Ho Chi Minh at the Fountainebleau negotiations with France in 1945 but broke with Ho when he realized that behind his claims of nationalism was a commitment to communism. In 1947, Thai's father, Vu Van An, was a nationalist in North Vietnam and fled to the countryside with the Viet Minh in 1947, but he, along with other non-Communist leaders, was executed as the Communists successfully took over the Viet Minh.[103]

He left the Viet Minh when its communist character became clear and it became apparent that no noncommunist could influence the course of events. Thai narrowly escaped his father's fate. "He escaped capture and death by the skin of his teeth."[104] During the Diem era, Thai served beginning in 1954 as head of South Vietnam's Bureau of the Budget and Directorate General of Foreign Aid. He revolutionized South Vietnam's fiscal bureaucracy by implementing IBM equipment and processes aimed at improving efficiency and budget accuracy. His principled approach to

---

[102] Hoat Dong Thanh Nien APACL, no date. Ho so so 29878. Vietnam National Archives II.

[103] "Welcoming a Vietnamese Friend," *Vietnam Perspectives*, Vol. 1, No. 2 (Nov. 1965) 1–3.

[104] Jan. 28, 1966, Briefing Note for the President, Subject: Vietnamese Ambassador Vu Van Thai (pronounced "TIE"), Chester Cooper and McGeorge Bundy.

being a civil servant got him in trouble in the world of Diem and the Nhus. In 1960, Thai angered Ngo Dinh Nhu for not approving government expenditures for Nhu and his wife, which topped a list of grievances Nhu had against Thai for his willingness to criticize openly the government's corruption, inefficiency, and moves toward authoritarianism in the face of NLF attacks. Thai resigned from his post in September 1960, but government officers placed him under house arrest for nine months afterward, a sentence that culminated with Nhu ordering Thai's execution. Diem saved his life, authorizing an exit visa for Thai behind Nhu's back. Thai managed to slip out of the country and enter the United States as an exile. Impressed by the efficiency reforms Thai implemented while heading Saigon's budget office, the UN sent him to head its Technical Assistance Board in Togo.[105] He was married to a French woman. He was a high modernist who had deep faith in the power of science, technology, and economic development to transform societies for the better.

Thai's "chameleon-like ability to shift positions and survive" earned him the reputation of being somewhat of a Tallyrand, wrote Geoffrey L. Thomas in *The Harvard Crimson*. After all, Talleyrand spent the "Reign of Terror" following the French Revolution safe in the United States, and Thai spent the post-Diem coups and other political upheavals in Saigon as a UN staff member in Togo. Thai had once been an adviser to Ho Chi Minh, but now he was on the side fighting the Communists. He had worked in the Diem government, but now he worked for the regime that included people who had overthrown him. He talked out of both sides of his mouth, but as a diplomat, that was his job. In an interview with Thomas, Thai accused Americans who supported negotiations with the NLF of "causing a lot of headaches" because they had "no direct living experience with Communism." "When you bring Communists in, you have one party using coercion as a means of influencing the people, and the other party has to resort to the same," Thai said in the interview.[106] During his visit to Harvard, Thai told a member of the campus SDS chapter that if the communists in the north proved that they were independent from China, then southerners might be willing to consider reunification.[107]

[105] "Welcoming a Vietnamese Friend," *Vietnam Perspectives*, Vol. 1, No. 2 (Nov. 1965) 1–3.
[106] Geoffrey L. Thomas, "Vu Van Thai: Silhouette," *The Harvard Crimson*, Mar. 24, 1966, www.thecrimson.com/article/1966/3/24/vu-van-thai-pthe-french-are.
[107] "Vu Van Thai Hails Saigon Democracy," *The Harvard Crimson*, March 18, 1966, www.thecrimson.com/article/1966/3/18/vu-van-thai-hails-saigon-democracy.

As South Vietnam's ambassador to the United States, he enjoyed entertaining guests in his Washington, DC, apartment. At lunch one day with Edward Lansdale, he talked about having brought a year's supply of 4,000 cha gio – fried spring rolls – to Washington but having gone through it "in three months of entertaining hungry guests." He would not disappoint future visitors, though – with an entrepreneurial spirit, he now made cha gio at home using a paint roller to moisten the wrappers for rolling.[108] Thai's vision for South Vietnam was in line with that of his American counterparts. He had proposed creating a Specialist Corps in ARVN for engineers, chemists, and other highly educated technicians, who would be assigned to duties developing South Vietnam's economy. Thai believed urban light industries were the key to South Vietnam's economic future, and he pointed to the country's spinning mills, paper factories, and chemical and cement plants. He envisioned "the Hong Kong type of activities" based upon the export of products of light industries. That would benefit the cities at the expense of the countryside, but Thai hoped South Vietnam would reduce its economic dependence on agriculture, which would reduce its dependence on areas under NLF control.[109] Americans noted that Thai believed strongly in preserving South Vietnam's image as an independent nation. Therefore, he believed that the United States should keep South Vietnamese officials informed of US political and diplomatic intensions and moves and push the GVN to take the lead when possible.[110]

While ambassador to the United States, Thai emphasized that the political activists who worked to overthrow Diem, as well as subsequent protest movements, were examples of democracy and social justice in action. Some in the anti-Diem movement were involved with the NLF, but many of the activists worked through the existing channels of dissent that had a much longer tradition in Vietnamese political life than the communist movement, Thai argued. A common goal had united Catholics, Buddhists, students, and military personnel, especially under the leadership of moderate Buddhist Thich Tam Chau and Catholic

---

[108] Memorandum to Ambassador Lodge from Ed Lansdale, Subject: Talk with Thai, Aug. 5, 1966.

[109] Geoffrey L. Thomas, "Vu Van Thai: Silhouette," *The Harvard Crimson*, Mar. 24, 1966, www.thecrimson.com/article/1966/3/24/vu-van-thai-pthe-french-are.

[110] Jan. 28, 1966, Briefing Note for the President, Subject: Vietnamese Ambassador Vu Van Thai. Chester Cooper and McGeorge Bundy. Larry Berman Collection (Presidential Archives Research), Box 03, Folder 22, The Vietnam Center and Archive, Texas Tech University.

moderates Archbishop Nguyen Van Binh and Father Ho Van Vui. Students have moved from simplistic demands to giving serious thought about the most pressing issues South Vietnam faced, national survival and development. Military leaders hoped to position themselves as "prime movers of social and political reform." Thai asserted that students and the military "comprise the overwhelming majority of the young generation who must build the Vietnam of tomorrow."[111] Observers need look no further than the recent election of a constituent assembly of 117 representatives as evidence that South Vietnam was building the democratic institutions of a modern nation. Thai believed that the country's representative government and the commitment to social justice by clergy and lay social activists could be a model of an alternative to communism for emerging nations.[112]

Thai met with UN Secretary-General U Thant several times in the fall of 1966. He asserted that there was a genuine noncommunist element in South Vietnam, and that even though it was divided, the international community needed to hear it out, otherwise it would do everything it could to prevent the United States from leaving Vietnam. The ideal situation, Thai explained, would be elections under "international protection" after all foreign troops left, although U Thant reminded him that the South Vietnamese government had up to that point rejected the idea of elections under international protection as called for in Geneva.[113] The men met again in November, and they discussed what impact China's cultural revolution might have on Vietnam. Thai speculated that if Hanoi made concrete efforts to distance itself from China then perhaps Saigon would agree to concessions and negotiations, leading to a coexisting North and South Vietnam. U Thant wondered if North Vietnam would ask for foreign volunteers to fight the war, and Thai replied that while it was possible, it would signal Hanoi's desire to speed the move to the bargaining table. As for other Asian attitudes, Thai worried that Thailand's Thanat Khoman and the South Koreans would put dangerous pressure on Johnson to continue escalation. Overall, the next six months

[111] Vu Van Thai, "Vietnam: Nationalism under Challenge," *Vietnam Perspectives*, Vol. 2, No. 2 (Nov. 1966) 12. Published by the American Friends of Vietnam. 999Serial49392, Vietnam Center Collection, The Vietnam Center and Archive, Texas Tech University.
[112] Ibid.
[113] Sep. 23, 1966, "Conversation with Vu Van Thai (South Viet-Nam Ambassador to Washington)." Memos of the Special Assistant for National Security Affairs, McGeorge Bundy to President Johnson, 1963–1966. 998Micro0337, Sam Johnson Vietnam Archive Collection, The Vietnam Center and Archive, Texas Tech University.

could be a "crucial turning point" that could perhaps offer possibilities for peace.[114] Yet the war would drag on for much longer.

Thai's outspokenness and willingness to critique state behavior had gotten him in trouble during the Diem era, and it put him on the wrong side of the Thieu/Ky regime. Perhaps it was his speculation on the chance for North-South reconciliation, or perhaps it was his emphasis on social justice and peace, but Thai did not keep his ambassador position for long. Ky removed him in December 1966. Ky offered him a Cabinet position as Minister of Economics, but Thai went back to the UN instead to work on a development project in Senegal. He also signed on as a consultant to the RAND Corporation in 1967. In that capacity, he wrote several articles and papers between 1967 and 1969 about the situation in Vietnam. In all of them, his central argument was the same: Only a political solution would end the war in Vietnam. That meant South Vietnam and the United States must adopt the NLF's strategy of "fighting while negotiating."

In conversation with U Thant after his removal from his ambassadorship, Thai asserted that the Saigon government had replaced him with Bui Diem because it realized Thai wanted to play a personal role in diplomacy and negotiations for Vietnam's future. The Saigon government offered him various other posts, including economic minister, but he turned them all down so he could keep his autonomy. The Brookings Institute had offered him a position, but he turned it down, too. Thai noted that Saigon political life was revived by the upcoming presidential election, and that there were concerns among civilian politicians and some Army officers that Thieu was going to try and give constitutional legality to a "prolonged military dictatorship." Thai also speculated that the outcome of the election would affect peace negotiations, as a civilian government might be likely to negotiate with their fellow Vietnamese to the north, but a military government might be more likely to want to prolong the war. Regarding North Vietnam, Thai noted that China's cultural revolution would have unknown economic impacts that could shape its relationship with North Vietnam in that North Vietnam would realize China could not give it as much. The Soviet Union would not be able to match China's support, so Thai speculated that hopefully this might push North Vietnam to agree to coexist with a noncommunist

---

[114] Nov. 9, 1966, "Conversation with Vu Van Thai." Memos of the Special Assistant for National Security Affairs, McGeorge Bundy to President Johnson, 1963–1966.

South Vietnam and begin building economic relationships with it and other countries.[115]

Thai also told U Thant that he was disappointed by US escalation, and in his role as ambassador, he had encouraged Americans not to do anything that would prevent Hanoi from reaching out to negotiate. He considered Johnson a practical politician who was concerned more with the present moment than with long-term planning. Thai believed that crucial to a lasting peace was a dialogue between Vietnamese from various political perspectives. Only a political solution would allow the United States to leave. He believed that it was possible that a civilian government in Saigon would have enough support to enter into talks with North Vietnam and the NLF, but a military government would always need US support because there would always be citizen opposition to a military government.[116]

While the United States remained involved in Vietnam, it should focus significant efforts on strengthening Saigon's political institutions, alongside its military war. Unless the United States planned to keep a large troop presence in Vietnam forever, Thai argued, Americans should focus more attention on a settlement in which communists and non-communists could coexist peacefully. Nonaligned people were key in Thai's mind, particularly those who opposed communist aggression and Chinese expansion. Among the communists, negotiating could enhance the divisions – Russian and Chinese interests might diverge even more, and "a cooling off of relationships" between China and North Vietnam could happen. Thai even saw negotiations potentially causing a strain between Hanoi and the NLF. Although NLF loyalty to Hanoi was clear, the NLF might be willing to accept a settlement that gave it more autonomy, Thai argued.[117]

He also emphasized the importance of regional concerns. If stability could come to Vietnam, then perhaps leaders could transcend political differences and form a Southeast Asian cooperative organization like the European Economic Community in which members would pledge to support economic development throughout the region. Endorsements and support from the United States and the UN would be crucial, Thai

---

[115] UN archives folder "Vietnam (South) – Vu Van Thai 1966–1968," Series 0279, Box 24, File 3. Feb. 27, 1967, "Conversation with Vu Van Thai (former Ambassador of the Republic of Vietnam to the United States)," Feb. 27, 1967.

[116] Ibid.

[117] Vu Van Thai, *Fighting and Negotiating in Vietnam: A Strategy* (Santa Monica, CA: RAND, 1969).

stressed;[118] a regional alliance including communist and noncommunist Southeast Asian nations supported by the United States and the UN, which had remained on the sidelines for much of the Vietnam conflict up to that point. Thai's writing was prophetic. The United States and the Soviet Union were more than a year away from signing the Strategic Arms Limitation Treaty (SALT) and ushering in a period of détente. Nixon's historic visit to China was still four years away. It was as though Thai anticipated a Cold War thaw. The Vietnam War dragged on for nearly seven years despite Thai's clairvoyant diplomacy.

Although Ky removed Thai from his diplomatic post, Thai continued to put his ideas about Vietnam's future out into circulation by publishing works in RAND anthologies and foreign relations journals. In 1969, RAND published a collection of Thai's papers entitled *Fighting and Negotiating in Vietnam: A Strategy*. Throughout his writings, Thai argued that the United States could strengthen noncommunist political movements in South Vietnam by exploiting differences among communists and working toward a goal of peaceful coexistence between communists and noncommunists. Thai acknowledged the risk embedded in this strategy: Communists might eventually take over a unified Vietnam, via elections or via force. But it was a risk inherent in any foreigner's policy toward Vietnam, he argued. The communists had given no indication that they would abandon their mission of establishing a government over Vietnam, and no foreign involvement up to that point had shown any real potential for destroying the movement.[119]

Any viable solution had to include politicians focused on social justice and peace, which reflect more closely the desires of the majority of Vietnamese rather than a specific political ideology. Political leaders would have to prove to the public that they were not corrupt and that they cared first and foremost about national survival, not selfish power plays. Perhaps US withdrawal would enforce this upon would-be leaders, Thai mused.[120] It was crucial for Americans to remember that average Vietnamese associated anticommunism with a desire to conserve the privileges associated with having had access to the French system in the colonial days. If the current Saigon government wanted to ensure the survival of a noncommunist South Vietnam, it should embrace moderate politicians who advocate the types of social reforms that would appeal to the broader population.

[118] Vu Van Thai, "A Regional Solution for Viet Nam," *Foreign Affairs*, Vol. 46, No. 2 (Jan. 1968).
[119] Thai, *Fighting and Negotiating in Vietnam*, p. v.   [120] Ibid., p. vi.

Furthermore, if Saigon and Hanoi entered into negotiations independent of their respective foreign allies, Saigon representatives might exploit differences between Hanoi and the NLF. The latter group might be willing to accept a settlement that gave it more autonomy and guaranteed some of its survival.[121] Essential to any effort at political stability in South Vietnam was a show of unity of opinion among Americans, care for the morale of ARVN troops, and noncommunist South Vietnamese rallying to a moderate government.[122]

Thai saw the Vietnam question as a broader issue related to Southeast Asia's future. If the United States withdrew unconditionally from South Vietnam, they would either alienate themselves from Southeast Asia or have to work hard to reestablish the confidence of Thailand and other Southeast Asian allies that might decide to make their own deals with local communist movements.[123] China cast its shadow over regional relations and posed a more serious threat to regional security than Russia did. If a break in negotiations occurred and the war escalated, North Vietnam would have to move closer to China because it would need Chinese support to battle an American increased war effort. A softening of the US position and an offer of cooperation might send North Vietnam to the Soviet side, which is better than the China alliance.[124] Writing in *Foreign Affairs*, Thai argued that if South Vietnam fell, there would be significant ramifications throughout the region. Likewise, changing political conditions in Southeast Asia would affect the situation in Viet Nam. All the nations of Southeast Asia at that time were plagued with tensions and were battlegrounds for the world powers.[125]

The broader context of regional history and culture was crucial, Thai explained. In many Southeast Asian countries, Thai argued, deep-seated nationalism in these ancient cultures clashed with disillusionment with the postcolonial experience of the struggles against colonial invaders. People were expecting social and economic betterment after the overthrow of colonialism, but political independence had left social and political expectations unfulfilled. There were enough cadres to start revolts but not enough technocrats to build modern nations and speed economic growth. Various social groups – the old governing elite, the new technocrats, the military, the students, the religious groups – clashed, and marginalized ethnic minorities did not trust any regime in power.

[121] Ibid., pp. viii–ix.   [122] Ibid., p. xii.   [123] Ibid, p. 66.   [124] Ibid., p. 52.
[125] Vu Van Thai, "A Regional Solution for Viet Nam," *Foreign Affairs*, Vol. 46, No. 2 (Jan. 1968) 347.

Southeast Asia's strategic location made it susceptible to "triangular confrontations" of communism versus capitalism versus Sino-Soviet tensions. Thus, any settlement in Vietnam will shape and be shaped by regional issues.[126]

US troop withdrawal alone would not lead to peace in Vietnam or in Southeast Asia, Thai warned. Thai believed that the best hope for the region was diversification of external influences in Southeast Asia and regional cooperation of Southeast Asian countries aimed at collective security and peaceful coexistence.[127] Simply ending the war in Vietnam would end a "hot confrontation" but would not eliminate the source of tension throughout the region. China would remain a potential threat because it would work to "to spread revolution and trouble," and also because it possessed nuclear weapons that it could use against Southeast Asian adversaries.[128] US troop withdrawals from Vietnam and Southeast Asia would be a delicate and difficult process that would have serious ramifications. If US military forces withdrew from the whole of Southeast Asia, the resulting vacuum could prolong turmoil, endanger the implementation of a Vietnamese agreement, and possibly lead to an international crisis. Not even an international peacekeeping force could prevent that, Thai warned.[129]

Thai was not naive. He understood the obstacles in the way of achieving regional cooperation. Long histories of antagonisms existed between some of the countries. Their economies competed to export many of the same products, and the region was home to many different cultures, languages, and religions. He also knew that Southeast Asian leaders had attempted collaboration and drove into dead ends. In the late 1940s and early 1950s, Thailand's leaders had tried to arrange a conference to discuss a Southeast Asian union. Malaya's Tunku Abdul Rahman and Cambodia's Prince Sihanouk had both talked about a common Southeast Asian market. Leaders of Malaya, Indonesia, and the Philippines had discussed the possibility of forming a "Maphilindo" union. In 1961, Malaysia, the Philippines, and Thailand established the Association of Southeast Asia, a precursor to ASEAN, for mutual economic, cultural, educational, and other nonmilitary purposes. Since 1957, South Vietnam, Thailand, Laos, and Cambodia had worked together on a Mekong River project. An example of success was the Mekong River project between South Vietnam, Thailand, Laos, and Cambodia since 1957.[130] For any

[126] Ibid., pp. 348–351.   [127] Ibid, p. 355.   [128] Ibid., p. 357.   [129] Ibid.
[130] Ibid., pp. 359–360.

large-scale regional cooperative to work, Thai declared, an established international organization such as the UN would have to be involved, and the United States would have to support it.[131]

For Vu Van Thai, peace would only come to Vietnam through domestic and international political cooperation. The character of leaders mattered; he had served under corrupt regimes and made their hit lists. In his vision of a future Vietnam, leaders who emphasized social justice and the needs of the people were central. He believed foreign support was necessary, but only to the degree that it amplified the desires and decision-making of Southeast Asians. It was self-determination with the blessing of stronger nations. Thai was asking Americans and Vietnamese to take a risk on trust. Americans would have to trust the Vietnamese; South and North Vietnamese would have to trust each other. They all would have to trust that China would back down. Thai had journals willing to publish his ideas, but without an official diplomatic post, he had no guarantee that anyone in power would pay attention.

For ordinary South Vietnamese citizens, ideas about government were less important than what the government actually did. For them, especially in wartime, military families turned to the government to request benefits, to seek the relocation or release of loved ones who were needed back home, and to file complaints about perceived injustices done to them. Authorities sought to build stronger connections between villagers and Saigon by trying to codify a South Vietnamese identity and cultural heritage. In urban magazines and newspapers, calls to political action included encouraging readers to remember the plight of their rural sisters and brothers. Although conditions, attitudes, and action differed between Saigon and the provinces, both leaders and citizens knew the importance of trying to find common ground between city and country.

[131] Ibid., p. 361.

5

Building Connections between the People and the Government

It had been more than a week in May 1965 since Dang Nguyet Anh had learned that the Viet Cong had launched an attack in Phuoc Long province, where her husband, Second Lieutenant Nguyen Thanh Trac, was stationed at a military training center. In the time that passed, she did not hear from him, and the waiting soon became more than she should bear. So she took a local bus to the town of Dong Xoai in Phuoc Long province, and from there, she got a lift on an army vehicle heading to the training center where she believed her husband to be. On the way, VC troops attacked the vehicle, and Mrs. Anh was shot in both arms and suffered a broken foot. From her hospital bed in Saigon, she wrote a letter to South Vietnam's Ministry of National Defense, asking that her husband be transferred to the city so that he could help take care of their six children, the oldest of whom was eight. Mrs. Anh was still nursing the youngest two, and she had no relatives to help her with child care. While recovering from her war wounds, she needed help more than ever.[1]

Dang Nguyet Anh's letter was just one of many that South Vietnam's Ministry of National Defense received from wives, parents, and siblings of soldiers in the South's armed forces asking for their men to be reassigned to units closer to home, moved from combat positions in the field to desk jobs in Saigon, or released from service. The government also received letters from civilians asking for compensation and reporting corruption related to the militarization of South Vietnam. These letters

[1] Letter in Ho so so 4852: Tập lưu đơn thư của các quân nhân và gia đình xin cứu xét liên quan đến công tác nhân sự năm 1965 Tập 1, Trung tâm lưu trữ Quốc Gia II, Ho Chi Minh City, Vietnam.

and reports reveal several important characteristics about the impact of the Vietnam War on South Vietnamese civilians and the relationship between civilians and the government. The blurred lines between the home front and the battle front in South Vietnam allowed for an army wife to take a bus to find her soldier husband and get wounded in an enemy offensive in the process. The proximity of home to war made it conceivable that the Ministry of Defense might reassign a soldier closer to home so he could help with the planting and harvesting or care for an aging parent. Although a family member might request leave for a soldier stationed overseas or in a neighboring country, when the civilian world is adjacent to the military world, they bleed into one another and affect each other in immediate ways.

The blending of the home and battle fronts also shaped the relationship between South Vietnamese citizens and their government in Saigon. In South Vietnam, civilians viewed the national government as the institution responsible for various forms of social welfare needs related to the war and the resulting militarization of noncombatants' lives. Citizens sought compensation from the national government for injuries done to them, their loved ones, and their property by South Vietnam's military, the US military, and the NLF. They also reported corrupt local leaders embezzling funds, supporting brothels, and operating casinos to the national government. When they wanted a war-related problem solved, citizens turned to government ministries. Letters from citizens to the government seeking various types of wartime assistance illustrate that regardless of what they may have thought about the government, they turned to it for social welfare and expected it to respond to the needs of its constituents.

Examining South Vietnam's political institutions and civil society, historians Nu-Anh Tran and Van Nguyen-Marshall have argued that South Vietnamese citizens had expressed a distinct nationalism through civil society and political activism during South Vietnam's brief life. The actions of government officials, journalists, military officers, professors, religious figures, and average citizens together constituted aspects of a nation, even if not everyone was thinking that they were part of building a national culture. Tran offers the concept of "contested nationalism." The conventional wisdom says that noncommunist nationalism in South Vietnam was inauthentic or weak, whereas North Vietnam and the NLF represented true Vietnamese identity. Yet Tran argues that pro-government South Vietnamese combined anticommunism with Vietnamese cultural identity to craft a national character. By claiming to be the rightful descendant of Vietnam's cultural traditions, South Vietnam challenged the DRV's legitimacy, Tran contends. Theories of nationalism typically have linked common ethnicity with state power, but a partitioned state like Vietnam challenges that definition because there was a common Viet ethnicity on both sides. Tran's contested nationalism applies to the competition between North and South Vietnamese over which side had authentic claim to Vietnamese nationhood.[2] The citizens who wrote to the Saigon government ministries seeking wartime assistance demonstrated a sense that they had served the national war effort and now sought something from their government in return. The notion of a give-and-take relationship between South Vietnam's government and its citizens illustrates a sense of national identity and how the war facilitated the development of that national connection. The relationship between women and the state is particularly illustrative. As South Vietnam attemtped to prove to the world that it had earned its place at the table of modern nations, state media highlighted the women's support for the war effort that demonstrated political modernity without challenging traditional gender roles.

WOMEN, THE GOVERNMENT, AND SOUTH VIETNAM'S FUTURE

In a modern South Vietnam, there was a "new woman" who reflected the transformations happening in Vietnamese society as a result of the war. While not rejecting all the traditional women's duties such as marriage and motherhood, the new Vietnamese woman should be politically aware and active and should assist the war effort in any way that they could. This was the central message of the magazine *Phu Nu Moi* – "New Woman" – which was published weekly in Saigon from 1966 to 1975. Aimed at middle-class women, the magazine mainly published serial

[2] Nu-Anh Tran, "Contested Nationalism: Ethnic Identity and State Power in the Republic of Vietnam, 1954–1963," ISSI Fellows Working Papers, Institute for the Study of Societal Issues, UC Berkeley, Jan. 3, 2012; "South Vietnamese Identity, American Intervention and the Newspaper *Chính Luận* [Political Discussion], 1965–1969," *Journal of Vietnamese Studies*, Vol. 1, No. 1–2 (Feb./Aug. 2006) 169–209; "Contested Identities: Nationalism in the Republic of Vietnam, 1954–1963," Ph.D. diss., University of California, Berkeley; Van Nguyen-Marshall, "Student Activism in Time of War Youth in the Republic of Vietnam, 1960s–1970s," *Journal of Vietnamese Studies*, Vol. 10, No. 2 (Spring 2015) 43–81; *The Reinvention of Distinction: Modernity and the Middle Class in Urban Vietnam*, Van Nguyen-Marshall, Lisa B. Welch Drummond, and Danièle Bélanger, eds. (Singapore: Springer, 2012), "Tools of Empire? Vietnamese Catholics in South Vietnam," *The Journal of the Canadian Historical Association*, Vol. 20, No. 2 (2009) 138–159.

novels, advice columns, and fashion, beauty, and celebrity news, but each issue opened with an editorial that dealt with current political issues, the military, and how women could support the war effort and the government of South Vietnam. Editorials showcased women in the military, encouraged women to donate needed items to troops, and, after the Tet Offensive, participate in local People's Self-Defense Forces.[3] They also stressed the importance of women's political action, especially in the lead-up to the 1967 election that would place Nguyen Van Thieu in the presidency. An editorial in a July 1967 issue asserted that women were equally important to men in ensuring that democracy would thrive in South Vietnam. A September edition went further in emphasizing the importance of women to the democratic process. Women's political activism would highlight the progress and maturity of South Vietnam and would advance the cause of gender equality in the nation.[4]

Media outlets also worked to cultivate loyalty to the nation and a sense of citizenship, especially by connecting civilians to the war effort. One way was by emphasizing women's opportunities to participate in the political process and support South Vietnam's troops. The South Vietnamese government, like the communists, tried to argue that under its new way, women's lives would become modernized and changed from the old patriarchal ways. Modernizing women's lives and gender roles would help speed the nation's political maturation. In a modern South Vietnam, there was a "new woman" who reflected the transformations happening in Vietnamese society as a result of the war.

While not rejecting all the traditional women's duties such as marriage and motherhood, the new Vietnamese woman should be politically aware and active and should assist the war effort in any way that they could. Wives of government officials linked domesticity and patriotism and served as examples of a "modern Vietnamese version of republican motherhood."[5] It was a tradition Madame Ngo Dinh Nhu, sister-in-law of President Ngo Dinh Diem, began in the 1950s during Diem's presidency. Later, Nguyen Cao Ky's wife spoke about it in the mid-1960s and said women's support of their servicemen would help the war effort.[6]

[3] Various issues of *Phu Nu Moi*, 1966–1968. General Sciences Library, Ho Chi Minh City, Vietnam.
[4] "Khong nen dat la phieu vao may rui," *Phu Nu Moi*, July 21, 1967; "Vinh du cua phu nu trong thoi chien," *Phu Nu Moi*, Sep. 15, 1967, General Sciences Library.
[5] Robert K. Brigham, *ARVN: Life and Death in the South Vietnamese Army* (Lawrence: University Press of Kansas, 2006), pp. 115–116.
[6] Ibid., p. 116.

In reality, most women followed their ARVN husbands not out of patriotic duty but because either they wanted to take care of their men, or their villages were no longer safe due to the war.

The new woman sketched out in *Phu Nu Moi* editorials embodied the liberal modernity that would have complemented the modernization theory that influenced US nation building. She was to be politically engaged, aware of the plights of the less fortunate, and willing to offer assistance via fundraising or other types of advocacy. The consequences of the war on rural women should not be far from her mind, and it was up to middle-class urban women to demand that the government create programs to help rural women and their families, especially in the areas of health, education, and job training. Bettering rural women's lives would help counter another social issue new women should be concerned about – the rise of prostitution due to the presence of foreign troops in South Vietnam.[7] Earlier, in 1966, the magazine had responded to US Senator J. William Fulbright's statement that American troops had turned Saigon into a "brothel." His statement angered magazine staff members, and they countered by arguing that it was an irresponsible statement that would only help the enemy and hurt the relationship between the United Staetes and South Vietnam. Writers recognized the problem of prostitution in Saigon but maintained it was better to regulate it than to criticize it openly. The NLF would only latch on to such criticism and use it in its propaganda against South Vietnam.[8]

South Vietnam's Ministry of Defense took the idea of women's service to the nation and used it to respond to the needs of ARVN families in creating the Women's Armed Forces Corps (WAFC). Established in 1955 as the national army of the Republic of Vietnam, the ARVN originally focused on fighting the guerrillas of the National Liberation Front, which was founded in December 1960. As the US military took an increasingly central role in American intervention in Vietnam, the United States armed, funded, and trained ARVN soldiers and officers. At its height of personnel strength, ARVN servicemen numbered approximately one million, including draftees and volunteers. After the 1968 Tet Offensive, South Vietnam's National Assembly approved President Nguyen Van Thieu's proposal to change the draft minimum age from

---

[7] "Nen thanh lap that nhieu trung tam huan nghiep phu nu?" *Phu Nu Moi*, Dec. 7, 1967, General Sciences Library.

[8] "Nhan mot loi phe binh nong can cua mot nguoi My," *Phu Nu Moi*, June 14, 1966, General Sciences Library.

twenty to eighteen and the maximum age from twenty-five to thirty-eight in order to pull more men into the service. More than 200,000 ARVN soldiers died fighting in the war.[9]

As is the case in any military, ARVN soldiers' motivations and attitudes toward the conflict varied widely. Historian Robert Brigham speculates that of those troops who died fighting, some must have been committed to the fight, while others were committed to an alternative to communism even if they did not support the Saigon government. He argues that most ARVN soldiers were ambivalent about their service even if they opposed communism "because of lack of proper ideological training and the recognition that the RVN was not a legitimate political entity with a cultural or historical precedent in Vietnam, two requirements for a viable future."[10] ARVN enlisted men who thought the officers and Saigon government were corrupt and oblivious to the needs of the troops and their families. Coups and allegations of rigged elections further alienated ARVN soldiers.[11] Most ARVN troops wanted an independent South Vietnam and considered themselves southern patriots, but they lost confidence in the government and therefore could not believe that South Vietnam could become a stable, lasting nation.[12]

In his study of ARVN, Brigham offers a glimpse of the social world of South Vietnamese army families. For many ARVN soldiers, the war eventually became not about South Vietnam winning but about securing stability for their families, Brigham found.[13] Family camps at the battle-front, moving as troops moved, became more common as US forces began leaving South Vietnam in 1969 under Vietnamization. Wives set up "shantytowns" that stood in for soldiers' home villages and became the center of soldiers' social and cultural lives. Like the "camp followers" of the American Revolution Mayer studies, women did domestic work such as cooking and laundering uniforms for ARVN troops, and they also served as "the living inspiration for the war."[14] Historian Andrew Wiest has also found that family life remained central in the minds of ARVN soldiers, and that the "emasculating inability to care for one's family" because of low wages and lengthy separations contributed to high desertion rates. Wiest also found that while camp-following families may have

---

[9] Brigham, *ARVN*, p. xi; Gordon L. Rottman, *Army of the Republic of Vietnam, 1955–1975* (Oxford: Osprey Publishing, 2010), p. 40; "The ARVN," *Viet-Nam Bulletin* (U.S. Embassy in South Vietnam), Dec. 1969.
[10] Ibid., p. xi.   [11] Ibid., p. 109.   [12] Ibid., p. 120.   [13] Ibid., p. 109.
[14] Ibid., pp. 113–114.

provided some sense of comfort and inspiration to the troops, their presence near the battlefields caused soldiers to worry about their families' safety, lack of housing, lack of schools, and poor sanitation.[15] We may never know whether they agreed with their ARVN loved ones on the stability or legitimacy of the Saigon government, but their letters to the Ministry of National Defense make it clear that they viewed the national government as an institution from which they expected support in exchange for their family sacrifices.

When the Ministry of Defense established the Women's Armed Forces Corps on January 1, 1965, it included welfare services for military families as an MOS. The opportunities available to women through WAFC reflected the patriarchal gender structure that ordered Vietnamese families and society. It authorized women to serve in administrative, intelligence, medical, and social work positions to free men for combat and to provide support for troops' dependents. Officers served four-year tours; enlisted personnel committed to three years in. To enter the officers' corps, women had to be college graduates, while enlisted women needed a high school diploma. Recruits had to be unmarried and remain unmarried for their first two years of service. After that, they had to get permission from the RVNAF high command to get married. A lack of available records makes it difficult to know how many women served in WAFC, but according to US reports from the late 1960s, WAFC's strength was approximately 3,000 women at that time.[16] The WAFC had earlier counterparts in the Women's Auxiliary Corps and a women's paramilitary group organized by President Ngo Dinh Diem's outspoken and controversial sister-in-law, Madame Ngo Dinh Nhu, but WAFC was modeled after the US Women's Army Corps, another example of deepening US military intervention. Some of the first American WACs deployed to Vietnam went to help establish the WAFC and train recruits in Saigon for deployment to the provinces where military families had encamped with ARVN units.

For as much as we know about the Vietnam War and its consequences, we still know very little about the war's impact on Vietnamese women, especially those who supported South Vietnam. The southern women who have made it into the story are legends such as Madame Nhu, NLF

---

[15] Andrew Wiest, *Vietnam's Forgotten Army: Heroism and Betrayal in the ARVN* (New York: New York University Press, 2008), pp. 12, 40.

[16] Phung Thi Hanh, "South Vietnam's Women in Uniform," Saigon: The Vietnam Council on Foreign Relations, 1970.

leader Nguyen Thi Dinh, and Le Thi Hong Gam, the teenaged NLF sharpshooter from the Mekong Delta city of My Tho, who allegedly downed a US helicopter, as well as numerous troops, before being killed in a rice field in 1971 when she was not yet twenty. But the war touched the lives of millions of other southern women whose stories have not become part of the war's mythology. They include ARVN wives like Dang Nguyet Anh and the WAFC personnel who ministered to them. As war often does, the Vietnam War shaped southern women's lives where the home front and battlefront blurred and in the ways in which gender influenced women's military service.

WAFC's social welfare division ministered to ARVN families by placing servicewomen near family camps to provide childcare, basic health care, pharmaceutical services, and other social services support to troops' dependents.[17] That they were in the army but doing "women's work" illustrates one of the ways in which the Vietnam War expanded gender roles without completely transforming them. A war-era booklet published by the Vietnam Council on Foreign Relations entitled *South Vietnam's Women in Uniform* explained that wartime opportunities for women in WAFC and other defense services indicated a transformation occurring in South Vietnamese society. "Traditionally, the role of the Asian woman is a passive one," wrote Mrs. Phuong Thi Hanh, the author. "Kept in the background, girls are raised to be feminine and dependent, to stay at home caring for husband and family. Twenty years ago, the idea of a female soldier was even more far-fetched than that of a woman doctor or lawyer. But years of war have brought women into a man's world, partly by necessity, partly by choice."[18]

After the 1968 Tet Offensive, legislators introduced a bill in the National Assembly to draft all women aged eighteen to twenty-five, but members of the Assembly who felt that women should not be in the military other than in women's auxiliaries vetoed the bill. Women who wanted to take up arms could volunteer with their local People's Self-Defense Force unit and receive training in weapons and military tactics. Hanh estimated that by 1970, one million women served in PSDF units, more than 100,000 of them in combat roles. Although women could serve in PSDF combat positions, the gender hierarchy persisted. Mrs. Nguyen Hong Nguyet, commissioner of a Saigon PSDF unit, told Hanh that women are best suited for support roles.

[17] Hanh, p. 5.   [18] Hanh, p. 3.

Any broadening of women's options outside the traditional family structure that military service provided were limited. WAFC existed to provide support, not front line fighting. Even undertaking advanced training did not make a servicewoman eligible for a combat position. In 1970, a group of WAFCs completed the difficult ARVN Airborne School program, parachuting out of airplanes wearing fatigues as their male counterparts did. But as Hanh described them in her WAFC booklet, the "daredevil girls" would not have careers "dropping into combat zones." Major Ho Thi Ve, commander of the WAFC Training School, said the servicewomen took the Airborne course for fitness and fun.

Southern women enlisted in WAFC for all the same reasons as men joined the Army. Of the women Hanh interviewed, some wanted to help the war effort, while others saw the military as a viable career path. The lure of adventure also drew women to WAFC. When Lieutenant Ha Thi Tuoi graduated from high school, she decided to do her part to help the war effort. She enjoyed working with children, too, so she enlisted in WAFC and chose social work as her MOS. She was assigned to an ARVN dependents camp at Tan Son Nhut Air Base, which allowed her to continue living with her parents in Saigon. She ministered to ARVN families who lived in a shantytown near the base. Lieutenant Tuoi enjoyed her work, but she saw it as a temporary diversion along the road to a more traditional woman's life. She was engaged to an architecture student, and she planned to leave the military once she had a child. It was what her fiancé wanted.

The South Vietnamese government, like the communists, tried to argue that under its new way, women's lives would become modernized and changed from the old patriarchal ways. Modernizing women's lives and gender roles would help speed the nation's political maturation. In a modern South Vietnam, there was a "new woman" who reflected the transformations happening in Vietnamese society as a result of the war. While not rejecting all the traditional women's duties such as marriage and motherhood, the new Vietnamese woman should be politically aware and active and should assist the war effort in any way that they could. Wives of Saigon government officials linked domesticity and patriotism and served as examples of a "modern Vietnamese version of republican motherhood."[19] A tradition begun during the Ngo Dinh Diem presidency through Madame Ngo Dinh Nhu, Diem's sister-in-law, Nguyen Cao Ky's

---

[19] Brigham, *ARVN*, pp. 115–116.

wife spoke about it in the mid-1960s and said women's support of their ARVN men would help the war effort.[20] In reality, most women followed their ARVN husbands not out of patriotic duty but because either they wanted to take care of their men, or their villages were no longer safe due to the war. As they moved with their husbands' units, they remained connected to the Saigon government through letters requesting assistance for their families' needs.

LETTERS TO NATIONAL GOVERNMENT AGENCIES

Throughout the war, the Ministry of National Defense and the Ministry of the Armed Service received letters from ARVN families with various requests regarding their loved ones in the service. Families inquired about their ARVN loved ones' whereabouts after not hearing from them for a long time. Mothers of servicemen asked for their sons to be reassigned to posts closer to home. Widows sought compensation for the loss of their husbands. Wives requested additional welfare payments for their children while their soldier-husbands were away. Families asserted that they had done their patriotic duty and made the ultimate sacrifice to the nation by giving up their sons to the war effort, only to have them killed by the Viet Cong. The letters all indicate an assumption that the government was obligated to take care of citizens who were affected by the conflict and who were doing their part to support South Vietnam. Questions of political "legitimacy" did not appear to be on the minds of the letter writers. Everyday realities shaped their attitudes toward their government.

A common type of letter the ministries received during the war was one from parents asking for their sons to be reassigned closer to home, be taken out of the field and moved into a desk job, be given a promotion, or be dismissed. Mrs. Nham Thi My wrote a letter to the Ministry of the Armed Services inquiring about her son's demotion in the army. Her son, To Van Kiem, had been promoted to major but then demoted back to captain. Her letter does not detail the reasons for her son's demotion, noting only that her son had been told that a new law had gone into effect that increased the requirements for promotion and rendered some promotions provisional. Mrs. My noted that her son was a thirty-six-year-old married father of five who had attended the prestigious Dalat Military

---

[20] Ibid., p. 116.

Academy. He had served in the military for fourteen years, received a silver star and a bronze star, and had an unblemished record.[21]

Aged parents wrote to the Ministry of National Defense and Ministry of the Armed Services asking for their sons to be moved closer to home in order to help them and the household. Mr. Le Phuoc Dat, sixty, asked for his son, Le Phuoc Ngoc, to be reassigned from Hue to Gia Dinh, a suburb of Saigon, because he needed his son's help in his old age. He noted that his son-in-law was a pilot and was killed in action on December 10, 1964.[22] References to other children having served and died fighting show up in other letters as well. In 1965, sixty-four-year-old Nguyen Van Tich wrote to the Ministry of National Defense asking that his son, Nguyen Van Bien, be reassigned from Binh Tuy to Binh Dinh in Qui Nhon province where his family is. Mr. Tich's older son died fighting as a soldier in 1952, he explained in his letter, and therefore the family had already made its patriotic sacrifice for the nation.[23] Sometimes, a sibling wrote explaining the condition of aging parents and asking for a brother to be discharged or assigned closer to home to help care for their parents, especially if the brother was the family's only son. Nguyen Thi Kieu Hoa, a social worker in Dak Lak (Dar Lac), wrote asking for her brother to be moved near his home village to care for their parents because she had a job that the family relied upon for income.[24] On September 6, 1965, Nguyen Thi Hao, mother of Nguyen Trong Khiem, wrote and asked for her son to be discharged and given a less dangerous position in the Saigon police. She wrote again on September 27; her son was now wounded and in a hospital, and she asked the Army to post him to Saigon when he was released.[25] Vu Thi Chinh, an eighty-year-old mother from the Saigon suburb of Gia Dinh, lost four of her six sons in the war. She wrote to the army asking that one of her two remaining sons, Duong Van Tong, be sent home to help take care of her.[26]

Like Dang Nguyet Anh, who wrote to the defense ministry from a hospital bed in Saigon, ARVN wives wrote to the government seeking assistance for themselves and their families. Ngo Thi Tam lived in Hue, and her husband, Sergeant Nguyen Dac Xin had been serving in the army, mostly away from home, for ten years by 1965. She wrote to the

[21] One of numerous letters contained in Ho so so 4852: Tập lưu đơn thư của các quân nhân và gia đình xin cứu xét liên quan đến công tác nhân sự năm 1965 Tập 1, Trung tâm lưu trữ Quốc Gia II (Vietnam National Archives II), Ho Chi Minh City, Vietnam.
[22] Letters contained in Ho so so 4852.   [23] Ibid.   [24] Ibid.   [25] Ibid.
[26] Letter from Ho so so 4857: Tập lưu đơn thư của các quân nhân và gia đình xin giải ngũ năm 1965, TTLTQG II.

armed forces ministry from a hospital where she was recovering from injuries due to a VC attack near her home. Ngo Thi Tam hoped that her husband could be reassigned to an office job in Hue. In Tuy Hoa, Tran Thi Hao had been the lone caregiver for her five children and elderly mother for the eleven years her husband, Sergeant Nguyen Ngoc Anh, had been out in the field. She wrote to the armed forces ministry requesting that her husband be reassigned to the Tuy Hoa city center, closer to the family.[27] From the wives' perspectives, their families had clearly given to the war effort, and now the wives sought assistance from their government in return.

In some cases, requests from ARVN families on behalf of their loved ones involved other government ministries besides the defense and armed forces offices. On July 30, 1964, a journalist named Nguyen Thoi Nac wrote to the Ministry of National Education asking that his son, Nguyen Thoi Van, be allowed to keep his teaching position in Kien Giang and not be recalled to military service. Van had already served, and Nguyen Thoi Nac's two other sons, Nguyen Thoi Ban and Nguyen Thoi Duong were in the service. Ban was stationed at Tan Son Nhut air base, and Dưởng was a student at the military school in Thu Duc, just north of Saigon. Nguyen Thoi Nac received a reply stating that because Van taught part-time rather than full-time and had less than five years' teaching experience, he would be called up again. However, ARVN officials would consider placing him in Saigon rather than in the field.[28]

Soldiers also wrote letters on their own behalf asking for extra leave time and reassignments. In July 1965, Sergeant Mai Nhut, who had been sergeant for nine years, asked to be moved to an ARVN battalion near his family because the VC had killed his father and brother.[29] That same month, a group of soldiers who had been serving in the field in III and IV Corps wrote to the Republic of Vietnam's Central Executive Committee requesting that they be reassigned to desk jobs in Saigon. Describing the impact of the rain, heat, and diseases of the field on soldiers mentally and physically, the men argued that they had put in their time for the cause, some having served for two years already. It was only fair, they contended, that men in office jobs get to experience what it is like to be an

[27] Multiple letters in Ho so so 4853: Tập đờn thư của các quân nhân và gia đình xin cứu xét liên quan đến công, Tập 2,TTLTQG II.
[28] Letter in Ho so so 4853: Tập đờn thư của các quân nhân và gia đình xin cứu xét liên quan đến công, Tập 2,TTLTQG II.
[29] Letter in Ho so so 4857: Tập lùu đờn thư của các quân nhân và gia đình xin giải ngũ năm 1965,TTLTQG II.

infantryman. They speculated that those in office positions had paid for
them, and they suggested that rotating men out of the field while moving
support troops into combat positions would bring an end to corruption
and boost troop morale, which would inspire soldiers to fight more
fiercely.[30] By writing to the Central Executive Committee, the troops
went directly to the top, perhaps seeing that high office as having the
power to make real change.

Some servicemen who had deserted or been discharged and their
families wrote to the ministries asking to be reinstated. Some deserters
needed the military salary, while others feared punishments, such as being
placed in land force combat units if found. Among the letters, the typical
deserter was a soldier who had gone home to take care of an ailing family
member or who had been late returning from leave.[31] In some cases, a
serviceman fled his position during battle and later sought reinstatement.
Bach Van Chau was in Quang Tri when his area was bombarded, and he
left his position. The armed forces office denied his request, stating that by
deserting, he caused his comrades to lose their fighting spirit, which was
too great an offense to be readmitted.[32]

Letters came from servicemen asking to reenlist out of a need for extra
income, even if they were well beyond the draft age. The wife of a retired
fifty-five-year-old ARVN veteran from Nha Trang wrote to the armed
forces ministry asking if her husband could be readmitted to the service so
that the family could collect the associated income. They were struggling
to take care of their five children, and her husband had served the army
well as a mechanic, the wife wrote. The armed forces ministry denied her
request, saying that only men working in the most necessary specialties
could stay in after the age of fifty-five.[33] The ministries received various
types of letters related to salary issues, some coming from soldiers requesting more money for their families, others coming from wives explaining

---

[30] 21-7-65 – Kính Gởi: Thiến Tướng Chủ Tịch Uỷ Ban Hành-Pháp Trung Ương, Từ: Một số
quân nhân thuộc vùng ê và vùng ô chiến thuật. Ho so so 4852: Tập lủu đòn thư của các
quân nhân và gia đình xin cưu xét liên quan đến công tác nhân sự năm 1965 Tập 1.
TTLTQG II.

[31] Various letters in Ho so so 4853: Tập đòn thư của các quân nhân và gia đình xìn cưu xét
liên quan đến công, Tập 2, TTLTQG II.

[32] 6-10-64, Võ Phòng Phủ Thủ Tướng Phiến Trình Thủ Tướng Trung Ủy Địa Phương Quân,
Ho so so 4855: Tập lủu đòn thư của quân nhân và gia đình xin tái ngũ năm 1965,
TTLTQG II.

[33] Việt Nam Cộng Hòa Bộ Quân-Lực, Bộ Tổng Tư-Lệnh Quân-Lực VNCH, Phòng Tổng
Quản-Trị Kính Gởi: Bà Lê Thị Tân, Nha Trang, 27-4-65, Ho so so 4855: Tập lủu đòn thư
của quân nhân và gia đình xin tái ngũ năm 1965, TTLTQG II.

the conditions at home and family needs while their husbands were deployed. One group of army wives suggested that a soldier's pay should be divided, with one-third given to the soldier and two-thirds sent directly to the soldier's wife.[34] The letters highlight the impact of the war on ARVN families and demonstrate that wives, as well as some servicemen, believed the government of South Vietnam was obligated to assist them. Whether international observers considered the government legitimate was irrelevant to their everyday needs.

The South Vietnamese government recognized that attempting to meet some of the needs of ARVN families could prevent desertion, and in a 1964 cooperation plan, MACV advisers encouraged RVN officials to deal with these issues. General Maxwell Taylor, then US ambassador to South Vietnam, asserted that Vietnamese troops had to be on board with the war effort if South Vietnam were to have a chance at winning. Airplanes and weapons will not make the difference, Taylor argued, unless ARVN soldiers were committed to the fight. Vietnamese manpower, not American technological power, had to be central to the war effort. In order to increase ARVN personnel and decrease desertion, the South Vietnamese government agreed to increase the salaries and living standard of soldiers. It also would establish a housing program for soldiers' families and increase funding for WAFC social work initiatives for military families.

Stricter laws criminalizing desertion, as well as the public shaming of the families of deserters, would accompany the welfare programs.[35]

A 1971 Rand Corporation study of ARVN analyzed the issue of desertion and concluded that the desire to be with family, not an interest in defecting to the enemy, was the main motivator for potential deserters. "They object more to fighting *away from home* than fighting itself, for they often join local militia units to remain at home, defend their own families, and not be drafted again. The desertion rate of the Regional Forces, whose soldiers serve in their own provinces, is considerably lower than that of the regular army, and the desertion rate of the Popular Forces, whose soldiers serve in their own villages, is lower yet," the report explained. What could push ARVN veterans into the arms of the enemy,

[34] Various letters in Ho so so 4859: Tập lûu đờn thư của các quân nhân và gia đình xin của xét về lương bổng năm 1965, TTLTQG II.

[35] Quyết-định của hội-đồng Việt-Mỹ trong phiên họp ngày 16-10-1964, Tại ỦyBan Bình Định Trung-Ương (Bộ Tổng Tư-Lệnh), Ho so so 328: Tài liệu về các phiên họp Hội đồng cao cấp Việt-Mỹ năm 1964-1966, TTLTQG II.

the report speculated, was a lack of economic opportunities back in the civilian world.

Many of South Vietnam's soldiers have been in the army so long that they have no other profession, and they would not be absorbed easily into the civilian economy. Those that did not return to the family farm but drifted to the cities might simply add to the urban unemployment problem produced by the withdrawal of American forces. Groups of unemployed veterans could combine with the mobs of disabled veterans who are already demonstrating against the government. They might resort to banditry. There are increasing reports that idle soldiers are turning to looting and highway robbery, and able-bodied soldiers as well as disabled veterans openly engage in racketeering among businesses in Saigon. Rapid demobilization (without subsequent absorption of those released into the active labor force), or even a steep decline in the number of men inducted into the government forces, would furnish the Viet Cong a manpower pool. Persuaded that they had been exploited and then abandoned by the government, veterans today could become Viet Cong tomorrow.[36]

The report's findings suggest a need for national government initiatives to integrate veterans into society and continue providing for them and their families after they had completed their service.

One area in which the government established a concrete welfare program was children of ARVN soldiers killed in action. The Ministry of Defense, in partnership with the Ministry of Education, created a program to house and educate children up to the age of eighteen. The ministries furnished the children with books, clothes, and medicine, and boys and girls lived in single-sex dorms in Saigon and other cities throughout South Vietnam. One of the goals of the program was to instill in the children a sense of civic duty and love for South Vietnam, to mold the next generation of citizens. The defense ministry received letters from ARVN veterans asking to be relocated to Saigon so they could work with the children in this program.[37]

Concerns about ARVN salaries and military families' living expenses worried the RVN government until Saigon fell. US diplomats also noted the issue in its observations of the military situation in South Vietnam after America's military withdrawal. In May 1970, Thieu implored US President Richard Nixon to help South Vietnam's government increase

---

[36] Brian M. Jenkins, "A People's Army for South Vietnam: A Vietnamese Solution," Advanced Research Projects Agency, Rand Corporation, Nov. 1971, pp. 6–7. Folder 05, Box 04, Douglas Pike Collection: Unit 11 – Monographs, Vietnam Archive.

[37] Quốc gia nghĩa tử cuộc, Ho so so 3218: Tạp bản tin, VTX, báo cắt các báo trong nước về hoạt động Văn hóa, giáo dục, xã hội năm 1964-1965, TTLTQG II.

the salaries of ARVN troops. The existing salary rates were too low to ensure "them and their families a bare minimum for adequate living," Thieu wrote. He had wanted to increase ARVN salaries for a while, but doing so would only compound South Vietnam's budgetary woes, Thieu declared. The soldiers and their families needed American help, both in improving military housing and in providing financial aid earmarked for ARVN salaries. The United Staetes already supplied a protein food supplement for all members of South Vietnam's armed forces; Thieu's request was for more support. Thieu hoped that additional US assistance would come through and ameliorate living conditions for soldiers and their families in less than four years.[38] Nixon's reply to Thieu, as well as State Department cables, expressed sympathy with Thieu's position and acknowledged the morale boosting potential of helping ARVN troops provide better lives for their families.[39]

Despite the awareness by both US and South Vietnamese authorities of ARVN's paltry salaries, the inefficient back-and-forth of bureaucratic operations, as well as the overall cuts to American aid to South Vietnam, meant that ARVN troops were still struggling to support their families as late as November 1974. US Ambassador Graham Martin noted that "the average Vietnamese soldier" simply was not able to take care of his family on enlisted man pay. Cuts in US funding, along with the impact of worldwide inflation on South Vietnam's economy, made the low pay seem even worse. It was difficult to overcome a 63 percent inflation rate in 1973, even though it was down to 26 percent in 1974. Not even a 25 percent wage increase for military personnel and civil servants, enacted in June 1974, improved the standard of living for ARVN families, Martin acknowledged. He understood why some troops turned to the black market and other corrupt practices to supplement their incomes.[40]

The needs of service members and their families continued after military tours of duty ended, and veterans and war widows exercised their citizenship rights by demanding benefits and jobs from the government. Throughout the early 1970s, disabled veterans' organizations marched

---

[38] Letter from President Nguyen Van Thieu to President Richard Nixon, May 4, 1970, NARA RG59, Box 1873-DEF 1-1-70, Folder 2.

[39] Letter from Nixon to Thieu, May 20, 1970, RG59-snf-Box 1873-DEF 1-1-70, Folder 2. Confidential cable 11587 from U.S. Embassy Saigon to Secretary of State Washington, June 27, 1973, RG59, Box 1873-DEF 1-1-70, Folder 2.

[40] Cable 14644, from American Embassy Saigon to Secretary of State Washington DC, Nov. 23, 1974, NARA RG 59 – Central Foreign Policy Files, National Archives Access to Archival Databases, Electronic Telegrams, 1974.

and petitioned the government for benefits commensurate with the cost of living in South Vietnam. The General Association of Disabled Veterans, the largest veterans' organization in South Vietnam, claiming some 200,000 members, had held a series of demonstrations in Saigon in 1970 demanding increased veterans' benefits, and their activism had resulted in the passage of Law 08/70, which provided more government assistance to veterans. The government had not fully implemented the law as of late 1974, and GADV members, including amputees in wheelchairs and other visibly wounded veterans, got back out to protest in front of the National Assembly building, demanding that the government put the four-year-old bill into effect. In a separate demonstration, about 700 war widows staged a two-day demonstration in Qui Nhon in October 1974 demanding more government benefits for military families.[41]

Jobs were also high on veterans' groups' priority lists. In early October 1974, Da Nang veteran and city councilman Nguyen Dinh Hue led a march of about 100 veterans seeking jobs from the Association for the Development of the Da Nang Area. Members of Hue's group, the Da Nang chapter of the Vietnamese Veterans Association, submitted a list of names of veterans in need of jobs to representatives of ADDA, a US-funded initiative. A few weeks later, a representative of the Saigon chapter of the VVA presented a petition for jobs to the administrator of the Association for the Development of the Saigon Area. The Saigon petition requested 250 jobs for veterans.[42] Like their active duty counterparts and military families, veterans looked to the government to provide for them after they had completed the requirements of male citizenship.

Some servicemen chose to go on record and voice their opposition to Thieu's presidency. In October 1974, First Sergeant Dao Vu Dat told reporters that he no longer had confidence in Thieu's leadership. Dat later issued a statement saying he regretted the comment because it was detrimental to the Army, although he did not recant his declaration. A week later, Airman Third Class Ho Vuong Tuan spoke before the Lower House of the National Assembly, calling on Thieu to resign. Tuan had brought with him two open letters, which he read aloud in the Lower House chamber. The first declared his vote of no confidence for Thieu, and the

[41] Cable 13544, From American Embassy Saigon to Secretary of State Washington DC, Oct. 23, 1974, NARA RG 59 – Central Foreign Policy Files, National Archives Access to Archival Databases, Electronic Telegrams, 1974.
[42] Cable 13544, From American Embassy Saigon to Secretary of State Washington, DC, Oct. 23, 1974, NARA RG 59 – Central Foreign Policy Files, National Archives Access to Archival Databases, Electronic Telegrams, 1974.

second encouraged the youth of South Vietnam to avoid military service and return home. When Tuan finished reading his letters, opposition deputies escorted him out of the chamber and to air force headquarters at Tan Son Nhut. The assemblymen asked that Tuan have special protection, as he was simply exercising a right that Thieu promised when he gave a speech asking South Vietnamese citizens to let him know how he was doing as president.[43]

The government also received letters from civilians seeking compensation or help dealing with consequences of the war. As the US military presence in South Vietnam increased, civilian letters focused on needs resulting from American actions, especially the seizing and clearing of land to build US military bases. Hùynh văn Thương, a resident of the Mekong Delta city of Mỹ Tho, asked to be reimbursed for expenses incurred when he had to move to accommodate the building of a base in 1968. In Biên Hóa, also in 1968, Nguyễn Thị Hảo asked for compensation because members of the US ninth infantry division destroyed her rubber trees. She received a reply from a government office stating that it had no record of her case and therefore could not do anything for her. Farmers sought financial compensation for lost or destroyed land, including land destroyed as a result of chemical warfare, and other civilians asked for goods such as rice rather than money. Other citizens sought reimbursement for livestock killed by bombs. In the worst case scenarios, civilians wrote requesting compensation for the loss of family members killed by US or ARVN troops. Letters describe citizens run over by army vehicles, victims of "friendly fire," and other noncombat deaths. In the weeks and months after the 1968 Tet Offensive, citizens' letters focused on the loss of life and property as a result of that assault.[44]

Civilians also reported abuse by ARVN troops, especially during and after the withdrawal of US forces. In March 1974, the Ministry of Justice received letters from residents of Chau Doc and Buon Ma Thuot asking that members of the ARVN nineth division land force be prosecuted because they were extorting money and rice from civilians. The justice ministry also received reports of rapes by ARVN soldiers, arbitrary

[43] Telegram 13544 from AmEmbassy Saigon to Secretary of State, Oct. 23, 1974, Embassy Saigon Mission's Weekly. NARA RG 59 Central Foreign Policy Files, National Archives Access to Archival Databases, Electronic Telegrams, 1974.

[44] Various letters in Ho so so 294: Phiếu gửi đơn thư khiếu nại tố cáo hành vi tham nhũng hối lộ lạm dụng phương tiện, tẹợ cắp trộn thuế ỷ quyền hà hiếp bôi and Ho so so 239: Tập Công văn, phiếu gửi đơn thư khiếu nại tố cáo hành vi tham nhũng, mại dâm, xin hoãn dịch, xuất ngũ, xuất ngoại, trở cấp, bồi thường thiệt hại năm 1969–1971, TTLTQG II.

arrests and torture by police, and ARVN soldiers collaborating with or hiding VC. Other reports accused neighbors of hiding deserters and draft dodgers, named the location of brothels, and described a gangster-controlled drug and sex trade at casinos and brothels in Saigon.[45] Prostitution was a common theme in justice ministry reports. A complaint filed in March 1971 accused Nguyen Thi Long, wife of police officer Trương Van The, of operating a brothel in Saigon. In October 1973, a civilian named Tran Van Tho filed a police report accusing President Nguyen Van Thieu's secretary of running a Saigon brothel which lured female students and girls in to be prostitutes.[46]

The story of Mrs. Nguyen Thi Tung and the Hollywood Bar illustrates the complex ways in which war has gendered local economies. Mrs. Tung, owner of the Hollywood Bar in downtown Saigon in the 1960s, submitted to monthly police inspections as standard operating procedure in a city with a growing population of US servicemen. The troublesome inspections resulted from accusations by the occasional angry relative of a young hostess. In August of 1965, Saigon police investigated the bar after receiving an anonymous letter accusing Mrs. Tung of pimping hostesses to American men and bribing police to stay in business. She denied the accusation, stating that she never saw American customers take women to the rooms for rent upstairs, never forced a hostess to sleep with an American, and never paid a bribe.[47]

Mrs. Tung suspected that the letter was from the aunt of Pham Thi Tuong Phung, a former employee. Miss Phuong had left her rural hometown because the war had made it dangerous, and she had gone to live with her aunt, Tran Thi Tu, in Saigon. Mrs. Tu had brought Miss Phung to the Hollywood Bar to get a job, but when she heard that Miss Phung's father did not want his daughter to work there, she tried to convince her niece to quit. According to a police report, Mrs. Tu tried to have Miss Phung arrested after she refused to abandon her job. Saigon police officers concluded that there was not enough evidence to charge Mrs.

---

[45] Various reports in Ho so so 257: Chuyển đơn thư khiếu nại tối cáo về tham nhũng, bất chính, bắt bớ, hãm hiếp, xin bồi thương, tài sản, nhận mạng năm 1968-75, TTLTQG II.

[46] 25-10-73: Ông Tư-Lệnh Phó Cảnh Sát Quốc-Gia, Ho so so 257: Chuyển đơn thư khiếu nại tối cáo về tham nhũng, bất chính, bắt bớ, hãm hiếp, xin bồi thương, tài sản, nhận mạng năm 1968-75, TTLTQG II.

[47] Viet Nam Cong Hoa Bo Noi Vu, Nha Tong Giam Doc Canh Sat Quoc Gia, Khoi Canh Sat, 26-8-1965, Sai Gon, so 28896. Ho so so 15333: ve tinh hinh an ninh tai Sai Gon Gia Dinh nam 1965. Phong Phu Thu Tuong Chinh Phu Viet Nam Cong Hoa Tu nam 1954 den nam 1975.TTLTQG II.

Tung with any crime, so they went on their way.[48] With the influx of American male troops into Vietnam and the fighting on the countryside, a supply of young women and a demand for bars, restaurants, and heterosexual male pleasure altered the economies of Saigon and other cities in South Vietnam. As mentioned, in 1966, US Senator J. William Fulbright famously called Saigon itself a brothel.[49] Mrs. Tung was not the only Vietnamese woman who profited from the gendered economy. In 1971, Mrs. Tran Thi Phuong became the subject of a US Senate investigation into fraud and corruption in the US military club system for her efforts to operate a massage parlor that many believed was a front for a brothel.[50]

Complaints of corruption also made their way onto the desks of defense and armed forces ministry officials. Citizens reported abuse by local leaders and police, including instances of police brutality against unarmed civilians. A resident of the delta town of An Giang asserted in 1967 that the leader of his hamlet had embezzled federal government money that had been earmarked for bridge construction. Parents complained that local police were arresting and prosecuting their children as Viet Cong when the youths were not associated with the VC. Others reported neighbors allegedly helping youth to go abroad to avoid military service, and one anonymous letter asserted that draft resisters and deserters were hiding out in the Cho Lon district of Saigon. In response to these and similar reports, the South Vietnamese government established an anti-corruption committee in the late 1960s and encouraged village leaders to create local corruption prevention committees.[51]

In 1968, Thieu attempted to build a pro-government political coalition called the National Social Democratic Front/Lien Minh to counteract the NLF, and the United States covertly funded it, but members struggled to

---

[48] Viet Nam Cong Hoa Bo Noi Vu, Nha Tong Giam Doc Canh Sat Quoc Gia, Khoi Canh Sat, 26-8-1965, Sai Gon, so 28896. Ho so so 15333: ve tinh hinh an ninh tai Sai Gon Gia Dinh nam 1965. Phong Phu Thu Tuong Chinh Phu Viet Nam Cong Hoa Tu nam 1954 den nam 1975. TTLTQG II.

[49] Heather Marie Stur, *Beyond Combat: Women and Gender in the Vietnam War Era* (New York: Cambridge University Press, 2011), pp. 142–183.

[50] Ibid., p. 175.

[51] Various letters in Ho so so 294: Phiếu gửi đơn thư khiếu nại tố cáo hành vi tham nhũng hối lộ lạm dụng phương tiện, tẹ cắp trộn thuế ý quyền hà hiếp bôi and Ho so so 239: Tập Công văn, phiếu gửi đơn thư khiếu nại tố cáo hành vi tham nhũng, mại dâm, xin hoãn dịch, xuất ngũ, xuất ngoại, trợ cấp, bồi thường thiệt hại năm 1969–1971, TTLTQG II.

establish a meaningful following.[52] Arguing that South Vietnamese political leaders had "lost the respect of the people," Thieu envisioned Lien
Minh as a group that would emphasize social welfare projects as a means
of cultivating national unity in the face of NLF action. Yet infighting
among Lien Minh members prevented the group from building a political
following, and seven months after Lien Minh was founded, it remained
mostly unknown to the public.

Lien Minh was the type of program that exemplified what Partha
Chatterjee has called "political society," a social order in which the state
establishes programs and policies aimed at meeting the needs of the broad
population. Individual rights and other democratic principles are not
central to this structure as they are to civil society according to Chatterjee.[53] Chatterjee conceptualized political society as a way to more accur
ately describe the postcolonial condition for most people because he saw
civil society as the realm of a small elite. In South Vietnam, the mechan-
isms of civil and political society were often at odds because of US support
for the Saigon government. Regarding Lien Minh, the 303 Committee,
the American group responsible for overseeing covert funding, wanted to
ensure that US support remained hidden so as to not undermine the
program's efforts.[54] Even when the degree of US involvement was deep,
Americans understood the political liability of the US presence.

US Ambassador Ellsworth Bunker questioned Thieu's commitment to
the organization, wondering if the president actually believed Lien Minh
could neutralize the NLF, or if he offered verbal support simply because
he thought that was what Americans wanted to hear.[55] Part of the
problem, Bunker noted, was Thieu's personality – he was so risk averse
that he was unwilling or unable to support something unless he was
certain it would succeed. Thieu's ability to judge risk was questionable,
though. His decision to go after Tran Ngoc Chau, a legislator in South
Vietnam's National Assembly, because his brother was associated with

[52] Memorandum for the 40 Committee, Washington, Feb. 12, 1970, document 182. *Foreign Relations of the United States, 1969–1976, Vol. VI: Vietnam, January 1969–July
1970* (Washington, DC: U.S. Government Printing Office, 2006) 569.

[53] Partha Chatterjee, "Beyond the Nation? Or Within?" *Social Text*, No. 56 (Autumn
1998) 62.

[54] Memorandum from the President's Assistant for National Security Affairs (Kissinger) to
President Nixon, Washington, March 27, 1969, document 47. *FRUS, 1969–1976, Vol.
VI*, 61

[55] Backchannel Message from the Ambassador to Vietnam (Bunker) to the Under Secretary
of State for Political Affairs (Johnson), Saigon, Feb. 7, 1969, document 19. *FRUS, 1969–
1976, Vol. VI*, 61–64.

the Hanoi government, garnered negative publicity and cast Thieu as authoritarian rather than democratic. In order to demonstrate his opposition to any sort of coalition with communists, Thieu risked losing the support of those who believed in South Vietnam's democratic potential, including Americans, Bunker warned him.[56]

ARVN families and others looked to the Saigon government for support and to air grievances about their lives at war. After the Tet Offensive shocked Saigon, Americans, and South Vietnam's government, Thieu authorized his national police to crack down more forcefully on suspected enemies of the state. Meanwhile, the NLF set in motion its plans for taking Saigon by waging a political war in which its agents would establish organizations that appeared independent. NLF cadres also infiltrated existing groups. Anti-government activists worked to attract international attention to the plight of political prisoners in South Vietnam to prove the oppressive nature of the Saigon government. The chances that a democratic movement would develop in support of the sitting government seemed less and less likely as the dominant political activists in Saigon, as well as the international public, began demanding peace over all else. Increasing government repression eroded the trust citizens had in the Thieu regime, and media images of and stories about modern women and nascent democratic political institutions began to ring hollow and desperate as more activists demanded peace at any price, rather than continued war.

[56] Memorandum of Conversation, Washington, Mar. 8, 1970, document 198. *FRUS, 1969–1976, Vol. VI*, 654.

6

Saigon after Tet

On January 31, 1968, the night the Tet Offensive began, Sally Vinyard thought the noise she heard outside her villa in Saigon came from fire-crackers. She had been in Saigon as a civilian employee of the US Navy for a year and had experienced Tet 1967. So she ignored the booms and went to sleep. The next morning, Vinyard and her husband, John, who worked in Army intelligence, heard an announcement on the radio that Saigon was under attack. At first, they treated it like a lark, thinking they were getting a free day off for no good reason. The radio report advised listeners to stay indoors, but it was not until three or four days later that Vinyard knew what was happening. Her husband went to work the next day, and she did not hear from him for several days after that. Many of the city's phone lines had gone out, and so she had no idea if he had even made it to his office. Meanwhile, he was trying to call Sally's office but could not get through. A few days into the offensive, a bullet struck the wooden shutters on the outside of the Vinyards' villa while Sally was out in the courtyard. They had lost electricity, and inside the villa it was stagnant and stale without the fans going, so she had stepped out to get some fresh air.

On the third day of the Tet Offensive, a reporter from the weekly magazine *Phu Nu Moi – New Woman –* ventured out with a few ARVN soldiers to see what the attack had done. The magazine's staff had felt the effects of the fighting. A bomb destroyed an assistant director's house, and some reporters had been displaced because their homes were des-troyed. As the reporter and the servicemen crept through Saigon's streets, they encountered a pale and thin woman who bore a tattoo on her shoulder that read: "Sinh bac tu nam" – "born in the North, die in the

South." It was how they knew she was a communist.[1] In the days and weeks after the offensive, Saigon residents and workers tried to make sense of the attack that brought the war to the city even more forcefully than guerrilla terrorism had.

The Tet Offensive was a surprise assault by NLF forces on cities, South Vietnamese government offices, and US and ARVN military installations throughout South Vietnam. The attack got its name because it coincided with the Vietnamese New Year holiday, called Tet. In the United States, it turned American public opinion against the war and pushed President Lyndon Johnson to limit US troop escalation and bombing of North Vietnam. In the wake of Tet, Johnson conceded that he was open to direct negotiations with Hanoi, and he announced that he would not run for a second term as president. Johnson's decision opened the door to a Nixon victory in the 1968 election, and Nixon's policy of Vietnamization sought to turn the war over to ARVN while Americans negotiated a peace agreement with North Vietnamese diplomats.

For Saigon, the Tet Offensive was the culmination of urban unrest and violence that had defined the city's character for most of the sixties. As the fighting of Tet subsided and Americans committed themselves to peace talks, Saigon's mood grew tense, and then gloomy. Some city dwellers wondered what would happen to them if the Americans went home and the communists took over. Perhaps a new government would assume they had supported the American-backed Saigon government and persecute them. Saigon residents who worked for Americans were the most concerned, for there was evidence of their connection to the enemy. Students clashed more often with the government and police. Members of the self-determination and peace movements affiliated with NLF saw increasing opportunities to chip away at the tenuous hold Saigon authorities had on South Vietnam. NLF troops may have lost the Tet Offensive from a military standpoint, but the political tide had turned in its favor. As the grisly evidence of the NLF's massacre of thousands of civilians in Hue during the Tet Offensive were revealed in the spring of 1968, some American and Vietnamese observers began to worry that a US withdrawal from Vietnam would precipitate a bloodbath in the cities. Others maintained that the Communists would be too exhausted from the long fight to commit a Hue-style massacre in cities throughout South Vietnam.

---

[1] 29-2 to 6-3-68, so 88, "Loi uat nghen trong khoi lua mau than," *Phu Nu Moi*. General Sciences Library, Ho Chi Minh City, Vietnam.

In early May of 1968 and continuing through June, the Communists launched another attack on Saigon, and their military presence in III Corps signaled the city's importance in their overall strategy. US intelligence estimated that some 15,000 NLF and North Vietnamese Army troops were in the vicinity of Saigon, out of a total of about 37,000 Communist combat troops in III Corps. In addition, the CIA estimated anywhere from 30,000 to 40,000 enemy support troops were stationed in III Corps. In response, the United States moved 150,000 troops into III Corps and began directing bombing campaigns toward the city. The impact on Saigon life was clear. The city suffered more than 5,000 casualties by mid-June 1968, saw nearly 20,000 residences destroyed, and took in 180,000 refugees. Military mobilization had led to a labor shortage, so business and production in city industries had slowed. Saigon residents had seemed to take the attacks in stride, going about their daily business and life as they had in the midst of war for years, but CIA agents observing city life worried that subsequent attacks would break the morale of even the most stoic of Saigonese.[2]

The attacks were aimed at weakening the Saigon government. A government on the verge of collapse might push the United States to the bargaining table, where North Vietnam would sit with the upper hand. Saigon was key to this strategy. It was a symbol of the southern government, and it was the site of large-scale citizen protest since the coup against Diem. NLF operatives aimed to channel the political energy of the city toward their mission and capitalize on anti-government sentiment to make a case for themselves as the true representative of the southern people. To get in on the political action, the NLF created groups such as the Alliance of National, Democratic, and Peace Forces, which claimed to be nonaligned, anti-government, and antiwar. The NLF knew that attacks on Saigon would provoke US retaliation, which undoubtedly would result in collateral damage given the city's population density. Where a bomb dropped on a rural village might inadvertently take out a family, one aimed at enemy sites within a city likely result in more noncombatant injuries and deaths. It would not take many of these attacks for Saigon residents to lose trust in their government's ability to protect them. The last thing the government needed was more lost faith.[3]

---

[2] Intelligence Memorandum: The Impact of Communist Military Pressure on Saigon, Central Intelligence Agency, Directorate of Intelligence, July 5, 1968. F029200060431, Sam Johnson Vietnam Archive Collection, The Vietnam Center and Archive, Texas Tech University.
[3] Ibid.

NLF leaders knew that the power of their attacks on Saigon lay at least partly in the realm of the psychological. While destruction of the country-side caused rural South Vietnamese to question their government's commitment to protecting them, bombarding Saigon had the symbolic value of striking power where it lived. Then, as the government struggled to pick up the pieces of the ruined parts of the city, NLF cadres could tap into citizen discontent and facilitate a mass uprising against Thieu's government. All the chaos and fighting in the capital city would force the US and South Vietnamese armies to shift their attention away from the provinces, NLF leaders figured. If Saigon capitulated, the war would be over, a victory for Hanoi, so the Americans and South Vietnam would have to protect the city. Meanwhile, NLF troops would have easier access to the countryside.[4] During the May offensive, battalion-size NLF units attacked Saigon police stations and public facilities. Other heavy fighting involving NLF regiments occurred at the Saigon Golf Course, near bridges connecting the city to surrounding areas, and near Tan Son Nhut air base. Meanwhile, NLF and North Vietnamese main force units encir-cled the city.[5] Although life in Saigon had an idyllic quality when viewed from the swimming pool at the Cercle Sportif or a party at the villa of an American diplomat, the city was always at war, and always an integral part of NLF and American strategy.

In the weeks after the Tet Offensive, various municipal and national offices collaborated to help the victims of the attack and restore security in Saigon. City authorities enlisted young people to help get Saigon back on track. They suspended sports activities and put young athletes to work cleaning up trash and debris throughout the city, taking inventory of burned-out houses and other buildings, and distributing food at a recep-tion center for residents in need.[6] The government attempted to address the housing issue for Tet refugees as well as those misplaced by the May offensive. With the help of US AID funding, ARVN engineers, the Minis-try of Public Works, and US military personnel worked through the summer of 1968 to build more than 12,000 housing units in housing projects and apartment buildings. After the fighting in May and June subsided, American and South Vietnamese officials formed a joint recov-ery committee to assist refugees whose homes had been destroyed during the offensive. Both Tet and May offensive refugees received ten bags of

[4] Ibid.   [5] Ibid.
[6] O-Trinh Nguyet-De "B," Thang 02, nam 1968, Tinh-Hinh, Hanh-Chanh, Kinh-Te va Xa-Hoi, VNCH Do-Thanh Sai Gon So Ke-Hoach, Pttg 486 TTLTQG II.

cement, ten roofing sheets, and 10,000 piasters per family to rebuild their homes. Despite the government's efforts, 10,000 Tet refugees remained in camps in mid-June. Thieu opponents in the National Assembly criticized the government's inability to prevent attacks on Saigon and the additional destruction that US and ARVN retaliation caused. Others called for a tougher stance against Hanoi.[7]

The population of Saigon had swollen to two million by 1966 due to refugees streaming in to escape the war-torn countryside. NLF cadres targeted refugees as potential news recruits. The national police set up checkpoints throughout the city to stop and search pedestrians, vehicles, and motorbikes, but as was the case with anti-government political activists, it was difficult for the police to prove a suspect's direct connection to the Communists. The difficulty in regulating the movement and activities of the city's population meant that the NLF could traffic not only associates but also goods from Saigon to the provinces. Medicines were key commodities that cadres got in the city and took out to the rural areas. A cadre could go from pharmacy to pharmacy in Saigon and obtain penicillin because a centralized process for regulating pharmaceuticals did not exist until the government instituted the use of ration cards. The NLF had gained control of roads and waterways surrounding Saigon, too, and could control the flow of goods into and out of the city just as people moved between city and countryside armed with propaganda and terror tactics.

The urban cadres were bold, too. They not only attended civic meetings, they stood up and spoke at them. They planted bombs in police stations and threw grenades at officers out on patrol. Prime Minister Nguyen Cao Ky hoped that a new low-cost housing development would bring some order to one of the wards where the NLF was most active, and the government put youth voluntary organizations to work with refugees and others living in the slums. Neither effort prevented NLF agents from blending into the urban population and working in plain sight without authorities knowing. Before 1968, taking Saigon from within is what American observers assumed the NLF would do. The Communists would not risk the retribution they would face if they launched an all-out attack on the city, an American told journalist Robert Shaplen. Random acts of terrorism here and there would chip away at the government's hold on the

[7] Intelligence Memorandum: The Impact of Communist Military Pressure on Saigon, Central Intelligence Agency, Directorate of Intelligence, July 5, 1968. F029200060431, Sam Johnson Vietnam Archive Collection, The Vietnam Center and Archive, Texas Tech University.

city until it collapsed.[8] Those observers were not entirely wrong. The Tet Offensive was a surprise, but it did not destroy Saigon or the Thieu government immediately. Saigon was a sprawled out city with a population that was heavily refugee. A 1946 French census counted about 400,000 Saigon residents, and by 1972, the population had grown to more than three million – four million when including the adjacent suburb of Gia Dinh. The refugees had come in waves, beginning in 1954 with those who fled from above the seventeenth parallel when the Geneva Accords divided Vietnam in half. As the war in the South escalated, so too did the flow of refugees from the provinces into the cities. Saigon took them in, and they shaped the city in a variety of ways.

Refugee communities in Saigon provided some of the most fertile urban territory for NLF infiltration. One cadre told the story of meeting a refugee husband and wife in Gia Dinh, a suburb adjacent to Saigon. During the May 1968 offensive, the cadre got to know the husband, a farmer turned factory worker, who confided in him about the difficulties of a technical job he was still learning. He paid little attention to politics. His wife, however, had supported the Viet Minh against the French, and so the cadre saw in her a potential recruit. Winning her over would bring her husband along.[9]

Although Saigon did not have an organized working class with an articulated class consciousness, so many of the workers and "petty bourgeois" citizens relied heavily on the presence of Americans in South Vietnam. Americans ate their meals, lingered over their morning coffee, and imbibed in nightly cocktails at cafes, restaurants, and bars where Vietnamese waiters and waitresses served them. Pedicab drivers carted Americans from their villas to the Rex Hotel, the US Embassy, and other establishments. Housekeepers made Americans' beds, washed their dishes, dusted their shelves, and swept their floors. Owners of little shops whose goods spilled out onto Tu Do Street when the doors were open sold trinkets to Americans, like the man who bought for his wife back home a romantic picture of a Vietnamese girl in an *ao dai* who, the wife would never know, reminded him of a maid who knew very closely the rumpled and tangled sheets on his Saigon bed. Vietnamese workers took home meager salaries and tips, and occasionally an American lover, but with

[8] Robert Shaplen, "Letter from South Vietnam," *New Yorker*, March 12, 1966.
[9] "VC Plan for Taking Over Saigon through a Large-Scale Mass Uprising," Captured Enemy Document, Aug. 16, 1971. Box 21, Folder 05, Douglas Pike Collection: Unit 01 – Assessment and Strategy, The Vietnam Center and Archive, Texas Tech University.

Americans gone so would be their wages, no matter how paltry. Without any statement from Thieu or his officials about how the government would fill the financial vacuum, service workers were another potential source of urban support for the NLF.

Just the Tet Offensive was not the first violent attack on Saigon, it also was not the end of violence in the city. A little over a year after the offensive an NLF rocket attack on Grall Hospital on Nguyen Hue Street left dead and wounded casualties. Police noted that cadres on motorbikes threw grenades into city buildings and public spaces, and in response, city officials hired more security officers and put some of them on motorbikes, too. Police also responded violently to the violence. In March 1969, officers shot two women who tried to flee after police caught them throwing an NLF flag into a pagoda. That same month, officers had died when a bomb exploded on Nguyen Hue next to an NLF flag. Meanwhile, NLF supporters dropped leaflets and hung NLF flags in school buildings and on college campuses. Saigon was a city on edge, and innocuous items such as flags were emotionally charged and fear inducing. City officials reported that citizens were angry with the NLF, and some hated the organization and demanded that the government fight harder against it.[10]

In April 1969, 9,000 troops from Saigon's civil defense forces conducted sweeps around the southern border of Saigon in order to prevent VC from infiltrating the city. The offensive included a leaflet drop to explain to urban residents what the army was doing to protect them in the midst of constant danger. City officials had raised a civil defense army of about 250,000 citizens out of an urban population of three million to counter NLF advances around the edges of Saigon.[11] Following the skirmishes that marked spring 1969 in Saigon, June saw enough of a lull in the violence that city employees completed some public works projects and street improvements. People's Self-Defense Forces (NDTV) were largely responsible for a decline in crime and gang activity, a municipal report noted.[12] It would prove to be a short-lived peace, for violent activity in July disrupted public works projects and public safety, and in

[10] Ho So So 594: To trinh Nguyet de thang 01-12 1969 cua Do Thanh Sai Gon. Nguyet De A: Tinh hinh chinh-tri va an ninh trong thang 3 nam 1969. TTLTQG II.
[11] "9000 Soldiers Guard Routes to Saigon," Associated Press, April 7, 1969. Douglas Pike Collection: Unit 02 – Military Operations, Folder 01, Box 14. The Vietnam Center and Archive, Texas Tech University.
[12] Ho So So 594: To trinh Nguyet de thang 01-12 1969 cua Do Thanh Sai Gon. Nguyet De A: Tinh hinh chinh-tri va an ninh trong thang 7 nam 1969. TTLTQG II.

response, government officials enacted stricter regulations for movement in and out of the city.[13] Yet after a height of violence for the year in July, a calm began to settle on Saigon in September. Street vendors returned with their booths and carts as more pedestrians ventured out on foot. City officials anticipated that four new apartment buildings under construction would open in 1970, and plans for urban beautification projects were in the works.[14]

Saigon's population was about three million in 1972. Authorities had imposed a one o'clock in the morning curfew. The sound of ambulance and police sirens were part of the city's soundtrack, and their jarring song announced not just another bombing. They signaled protest marches that swelled to numbers that made police officers nervous. That was how the fighting went in Saigon after the Tet Offensive.[15]

The political war in Saigon remained a two-pronged conflict. Thieu and his government fought with citizens on matters of free speech, and NLF leaders began emphasizing the political war as the way to win the city. Thieu hated that rumors about the fate of the Saigon government in the wake of the Paris peace talks and American departure spread in whispers and shouts. Free speech was a culprit, and police punished journalists who published what they had heard about the government's intentions and actions. In March, police seized at gunpoint copies of the newspaper *Doc Lap* (*Independence*) from newsstands because it had published a report alleging that the Saigon government was considering a peace proposal that involved coexisting with the NLF. The controversial article quoted Senator Hoang Xuan Tuu, a well-known anticommunist politician, saying that Americans were planning to move quickly with their withdrawal, and in turn, North Vietnam would stop its military actions in the South. Any discussion or speculation about the war's end and Vietnam's future was taboo if it did not come in the form of official government statements. More than 10,000 angry students staged a three-day boycott of classes to protest the jailing of Huynh Tan Mam because he was an undercover agent for the NLF.[16]

[13] Ibid.
[14] Ho So So 594: To trinh Nguyet de thang 01-12 1969 cua Do Thanh Sai Gon. Nguyet De A: Tinh hinh chinh-tri va an ninh trong thang 9 nam 1969. TTLTQG II.
[15] Robert Shaplen, "We Have Always Survived," *New Yorker*, April 15, 1972. Douglas Pike Collection: Unit 06 – Democratic Republic of Vietnam, Box 17, Folder 25. The Vietnam Center and Archive, Texas Tech University.
[16] "Peace Plan Considered, Saigon Paper Claims," *Washington Post*, March 26, 1970, p. A26.

The outspoken opposition to Thieu's government, the willingness of Assembly members to think out loud about potential negotiations with North Vietnam, student protests, and newspaper coverage of it all were the components of a nascent democracy, messy as it was. Americans in Saigon reported back to Washington with this type of evidence. In late 1973, 58 of the 158 members of the lower house of the Assembly were openly opposed to the Thieu government. In the upper house, 29 of 70 lawmakers were oppositionist. As a group, they had blocked or forced the amendment of some bills even though pro-government representatives outnumbered them. Although Thieu had banned the Communist Party from operating in South Vietnam, American observers noted that several political parties existed, including leftist and anti-government parties. Leaders of those groups could often be found at marches and quoted in newspaper articles, further proving that the government was trying to allow democratic action, Americans asserted. Ngo Ba Thanh could be counted on to appear with a microphone at a protest, while Father Chan Tin, a Catholic priest, sent letters to US lawmakers and antiwar groups decrying the imprisonment of political dissidents in South Vietnam. As of late 1973, Americans counted fifteen daily newspapers in Saigon, three of which were specifically oppositionist. Others routinely criticized the government and published articles about various political activities despite regular censorship, which the US report acknowledged.[17]

There was a contradiction embedded in Saigon's political life. The government made democracy available to its citizens. Citizens protested government policies, oppositionists ran for public office and won elections, newspapers published articles about political developments and ran editorials expressing a variety of opinions about the government and Vietnam's future. The government had abided by the 1967 constitution calling for elections to be held at regular intervals from the national to the village level. Outside observers have deemed the elections as being generally fair. Pro-government candidates had won more seats than oppositionists, but the report attributed that to the fragmented nature of the opposition, not to government meddling. Most convincing of all, the report argued, was the 500,000-strong armed People's Self-Defense Force. If the government feared for its own existence, it would not have handed out weapons to half a million citizens. "No widely unpopular

---

[17] "Evidence of Political Freedom in South Viet-Nam," undated report, Douglas Pike Collection: Unit 02 – Military Operations, Folder 11, Box 23. The Vietnam Center and Archive, Texas Tech University.

regime, facing a strong military and political threat within its own borders, would dare to pass out so many guns which might readily be turned against it."[18] LBJ said that even though the 1967 election might not be "without blemish," the United States could not "impose impossible standards for a young nation at war."[19]

Yet all of these actions could and did land citizens in prison, where they might languish without a trial date or be tortured by prison police. It was difficult to convince Vietnamese citizens and global observers, including US lawmakers who had the power to grant or withhold funds from South Vietnam, that the Saigon government was making a good-faith effort to implement democracy. National leaders had relied so heavily on American support that when the Paris peace talks began and it looked as though Americans were open to settling with North Vietnam and withdrawing from South Vietnam, the self-preservation instinct overtook any commitment to fostering democracy. Fear that communists were behind student protests motivated the government to crack down. Anti-Thieu activists like Huynh Tan Mam and Ngo Ban Thanh insisted that they were not communists, and even those known to be official members of the NLF argued that they were not communists. What they meant was that they were not official members of the Hanoi party, called the Vietnam Workers Party or Lao Dong. Thieu and his American advisers knew that Hanoi leaders directed the NLF, but there was no real way to prove that Mam, Thanh, and others were communists, even if enough evidence linked them to the NLF. So the government and the US Embassy decided that anti-Thieu meant pro-communism. South Vietnam's was an insecure young government, and it feared democratic expression more than it fostered it.

The contradiction in South Vietnam's attempt at allowing freedom of the press dated back at least to the Nguyen Khanh era. Upon taking control of the government in Saigon at the end of January 1964, Khanh introduced Decree 2/64 to regulate the press. While the first article of the law called freedom of the press "a basic right in the Republic of Vietnam," article 5 stipulated the punishments for any journalistic expression that government officials deemed a threat to national security or offensive to "good mores." Khanh's government allowed political parties that were registered with the Ministry of the Interior to publish newspapers, seeing the move as a way to demonstrate Saigon's openness to multiple political

---

[18] Ibid. [19] "The Organization Man," *Time*, Aug. 25, 1967, p. 22.

parties. Yet the government had no standards determining what constituted a political party and what type of expression Khanh would allow. Later that spring, Khanh established a press council comprised of five publishers and four reporters to advise the government on issues of press freedom. He also provided rules for obtaining a permit to publish a newspaper, but the criteria were so narrow and difficult to measure that it would be nearly impossible for any prospective publisher to meet them all.

Repression bred resentment, which played into the hands of the NLF in the years after the Tet Offensive. NLF leaders learned from offensive that taking Saigon would require a political movement of several hundred thousand to a million people to do what a military attack could not. Rather than recruiting new personnel from the provinces, NLF leaders decided to use Saigon's political chaos to their advantage. Agents had already infiltrated activist groups in the city and established ostensibly independent organizations, but now the NLF would coordinate those efforts more closely. The NLF's goal was to win over the members of the middle class who had been disengaged from politics. In August 1971, NLF leaders announced that the future goal of the Sub-Region 6 Party Committee, which included Saigon, was to create a popular political movement that would lead to a mass uprising.[20]

Because Saigon was the capital of South Vietnam and its cultural, political, and military center, NLF leaders believed they must capture it in order for their revolution to succeed. It symbolized South Vietnam, and even if the revolution succeeded in other cities and in the rural areas, without Saigon, it would not be a success. Political action in Saigon would affect the central government more deeply than it would elsewhere because the government was there, and disrupting the central government was the revolution's most important task. There was a ripple effect that occurred in Saigon because news of disturbances traveled fast. If a group of thirty university students marched in front of the National Assembly, reports of the demonstration would likely reach high school students and inspire them to their own forms of unrest. The NLF had long targeted high school students, with their teenaged passion and impulses toward dramatic expression, as ripe for recruitment to the Communist cause.[21]

---

[20] "VC Plan for Taking Over Saigon through a Large-Scale Mass Uprising," Captured Enemy Document, Aug. 16, 1971. Box 21, Folder 05, Douglas Pike Collection: Unit 01 – Assessment and Strategy, The Vietnam Center and Archive, Texas Tech University.
[21] Ibid.

Because Saigon was the seat of government, any uprising, be it students, workers, or the population in general, would gain more attention than in any other city. In Saigon, three and a half million people concentrated into the boundaries of the city could make a dramatic statement about citizen dissatisfaction with the Thieu government. It would surely be louder than any political noise twenty million villagers scattered across the countryside could make. Saigon did not have a mobilized working class, the NLF speaker acknowledged, but workers were not the NLF's prime target. Middle-class residents, with their precarious hold on a standard of living that depended almost entirely on American spending, offered perhaps even a stronger source of support. Not that the urban poor did not have a place in the NLF's plan for taking the capital city. The slums on the outskirts of town bled into rural areas, and the porous borders allowed for rural cadres to connect with impoverished city folk.[22]

Saigon was also important to NLF strategy because it was South Vietnam's center of diplomacy. Ambassadors and embassy officers from around the world met, talked, ate, and drank together in the city, and those international communications and interactions could build support for the Thieu government, or some sort of noncommunist regime in South Vietnam. Mass demonstrations, especially those that threaten to explode into full-on riots, could stymie international relations, NLF leaders believed. Blocking access to an embassy, surrounding the vehicle of a visiting head of state, shouting at diplomats as they attempt to walk outside all could not only thwart tangible diplomatic engagements but also present to the world an image of an angry populace driven to chaos by an unpopular government.[23]

Two years after the Tet Offensive, the NLF, with guidance from Hanoi, began to put into action a plan for a mass political uprising in Saigon to overthrow the Thieu government. Once a cease-fire was enacted, agents would move to oust Thieu and establish a pro-Communist provisional government that would not include Thieu, Vice President Nguyen Cao Ky, or any of their close associates. As mass demonstrations unleashed chaos on the streets of Saigon, the NLF would launch a widespread series of attacks in the provinces. High-ranking NLF operatives and their advisers in Hanoi were confident that the United States would eventually agree to a cease-fire because the Americans only ever wanted to ensure peaceful coexistence between North and South

[22] Ibid.   [23] Ibid.

Vietnam. With a cease-fire in place, the NLF could concentrate on its political war while the NVA advanced south to Saigon.[24]

NLF authorities knew they could not assume loyalty from any group in Saigon, even those that had organized demonstrations and spoke out against the government. Students, some of the most boisterous, were not necessarily pro-Communist, the NLF recognized, and in the earlier sixties, many student leaders were decidedly anticommunist. It took government retaliation, in the form of arrests and imprisonment of student activists, to turn them against the state. Thieu's paranoia about maintaining his power would push him to work for the NLF without realizing it.[25] It was almost as though it was too easy for the NLF to win over Saigon's citizens without firing a shot. The Tet Offensive had not inspired a mass anti-government uprising in the city, but Thieu could bring his regime tumbling down by stifling the kind of expression that defined a democratic society.

Even as the student anti-Thieu movement rose to a dominant voice in the Saigon political scene, NLF operatives were aware of pro-government students who worked to sabotage the agenda of students who supported the NLF. NLF authorities named Doan Kinh and Pham Hoa Quang as leaders of the pro-government student wing. They were popular among their peers, and the NLF accused them of collaborating with the CIA after the defeat of Huynh Tan Mam in the Saigon Student Union elections. Mam was a student leader who had secretly joined the NLF and who had served several prison terms as a political dissident. An NLF leader accused Kinh and Quang of election fraud that led to Mam's defeat.[26]

NLF leaders also knew that they could not employ in Saigon and other cities the tactics they used to force rural people to their side. Agents of the national government could not keep watch over every village in every province, so NLF cadres could wield violence on those who did not participate in revolutionary meetings or other activities, collected taxes on agricultural yields, and perform labor for the Communists. Those who refused were at the mercy of the NLF. Cadres sentenced some disobedient peasants to indoctrination meetings. They murdered others. In Saigon, where the municipal and national police monitored citizens' activities throughout the city, it would be much more difficult for NLF cadres to threaten and kill uncooperative citizens without attracting attention.[27] Absent the anonymity of the countryside, the NLF had to rely on riling up

[24] Ibid.   [25] Ibid.   [26] Ibid.   [27] Ibid.

citizens behind the scenes and by infiltrating political movements to call attention to the population's disillusionment with the Thieu government and the war. As citizens expressed their dissatisfaction, and the government responded by silencing and arresting protesters, NLF front organizations like the Alliance for National, Democratic, and Peace Forces could assert themselves as having the best interests of the people in mind as they demanded an end to the conflict.[28]

The Tet Offensive influenced the NLF's approach to students and youth mobilization in Saigon. Just as NLF operatives established the Alliance for National, Democratic, and Peace Forces after Tet to consolidate groups friendly to the communists, cadres established student front organizations to try and reach the city's young people. Tet had hurt the NLF's Saigon youth movement as it had its military forces. Before the offensive, the City Youth Group boasted some 500 members, but by 1972, there were only about fifty members. Many of the members of the City Youth Group had been killed in the Tet Offensive, and the NLF failed to replenish its strength in numbers. The loud and chaotic anti-government struggle that the NLF had waged quieted. In 1971, NLF officials established several front organizations that earned legal approval from the government. Huynh Tan Mam headed the Saigon Association of Secondary School Students, and other groups included the Vietnam University Students Association, the South Vietnam Students Press Association, and the Committee for the Protection of Democratic School Activities.[29]

City Youth Group activities in 1971 had succeeded in frightening city residents with terrorist acts, but the government retaliated by arresting and imprisoning key operatives in the various front organizations. Street demonstrations that included the burning of American vehicles reminded residents of terrorism's ability to generate fear and showed the NLF's strength among students. Yet mass arrests of activists, including Huynh Tan Mam, prevented further significant unrest. Only about fifty City Youth Group agents remained in Saigon in 1972. Beginning in that year, Communist activism went underground and worked its way back into Saigon society through the front organizations. Meanwhile, student agents who realized that the government suspected them, and who found themselves under police surveillance, fled to the nearby provinces of Chau

[28] Ibid.
[29] "PRP Political Work among Saigon Youth, 1968–1973." Box 11, Folder 07, Douglas Pike Collection: Unit 05 – National Liberation Front, The Vietnam Center and Archive, Texas Tech University.

Doc and Hau Nghia to escape the attention and avoid arrest. NLF authorities sent thirty of the Saigon crew to Can Tho to continue their training for urban recruitment efforts among urban youths. Other young agents traveled to the Cambodian border for training on engagement with third force personalities such as Duong Van Minh. After training, their supervisors sent them, along with the Can Tho contingent, back to Saigon to work. The student agents arrived back in the city with a new emphasis on young soldiers. Members of the Troop Proselytizing Element tried to convince young men to dodge the draft or to desert. Some agents infiltrated the Army itself.[30]

In the heat of it all, a scandalous love affair developed between two of the primary Youth Proselytizing Section cadres. Nam Trang was in her late twenties when Ba Van, secretary of the City Youth Group in Saigon, recruited her. She was a true believer in Communism, and she took the risks she believed necessary to fight for the cause. National police officers had arrested her, but she escaped prison. She was married when she met Ba Van, but they fell in love, and they both left their spouses to be with each other. He was two years her junior, and they operated under aliases. In 1969, Trang became the deputy secretary of the City Youth Group, but in 1972, she was transferred to workers' and women's proselytizing sections. Van had a prison record, too, having been arrested and escaped twice, once in 1969 and again in 1971. He brought scandal on the City Youth Group with his affair with Trang, and the Current Affairs Committee accused him of giving her a high position in the CYG simply because he was in love with her. In 1973, he was demoted to the position of research cadre for his region, and left cynical and disillusioned.[31]

Some Vietnamese worried about reprisals at the hands of the North Vietnamese military, while others opposed President Richard Nixon's policy of Vietnamization and US withdrawal because it would place the military burden on Vietnamese young men. The departure of US troops did not mean the war was ending, they soon realized. Thieu was going to continue to fight, and as American ground forces left Vietnam, Vietnamese soldiers would have to take their place. That meant increasing draft calls, which many young men, especially university students, were quick to oppose. While attending Harvard University, a Vietnamese student named Ngo Vinh Long wrote articles for an English-speaking audience about Vietnamese student protests and the government's oppressive

30 Ibid.   31 Ibid.

responses. Long and other Vietnamese students at Harvard had founded a
magazine and connected with the Indochina Resource Center, a watchdog
organization that reported on conditions in Vietnam. Long offered the
perspective of Vietnamese who believed that the real goal of Vietnamization was not to bring peace to Vietnam but to save American lives and
money. The funds saved by removing US troops could be diverted to the
development and deployment of war technology such as bombing and
defoliants, keeping the United States involved and prolonging the war.[32]

Students understood this and began speaking out as soon as Nixon and
his associates announced the start of Vietnamization in 1969. As Long
had heard, opposition to Vietnamization began in the cities. War had
ravaged the countryside, so rural war-weariness was to be expected. In
Saigon, though – from an outside perspective, it might appear that Saigonese were in a bubble of safety, only hearing the war in the distance.
Intense fighting in Hue during the Tet Offensive had brought that city
directly into the war much more so than the attacks on Saigon had. Urban
terrorism in Saigon was unsettling, but life went on as usual. Yet some
urban residents had much to lose in Vietnamization. Leading the protests
were students because they opposed the government's plan to increase
conscription in order to fill the void left by departing American troops.
Police responded to student protests by arresting demonstrators, and that
angered students even more. They continued to march, now demanding
both an end to war and the release of imprisoned students whose crime
was having exercised freedom of speech.[33]

Repression and torture had become so troublesome that even anticommunist Catholics began speaking out against the government's
approach to student protesters. In April 1970, Father Nguyen Quang
Lam published an article in the conservative Catholic newspaper, *Xay
Dung*, describing imprisoned students' testimonies of torture. That same
month, the Catholic daily *Tin Sang* (*Morning News*) began a two-month
series publishing diaries of incarcerated students. The more outcry in the
papers and in the streets, the more the government and police cracked
down on protests. State-sanctioned violence was a form of terrorism,
Long asserted. Just like in the provinces, where villagers faced harassment
by ARVN troops by day and NLF cadres by night, Saigon residents

[32] Ngo Vinh Long, "The Urban Opposition," *American Report*, Feb. 18, 1972, Douglas
Pike Collection: Unit 03 – Antiwar Activities, Folder 08, Box 09. The Vietnam Center and
Archive, Texas Tech University.
[33] Ibid.

endured both state and NLF terrorism. Besieged by violence from all sides, some Saigon residents hoped that if the war ended, they at least could stop worrying about their personal safety.[34]

The mess of the situation in Saigon was clear in June 1970, when a dockworkers' strike, student unrest, and violent retaliation against the young demonstrators by American MPs and Saigon police all came to a head at the same time. On June 9, striking dockworkers shut down the port of Saigon, and a week later, 60,000 workers from Saigon and the nearby suburb of Gia Dinh went on a twenty-four-hour general strike. During the same timeframe, students threw Molotov cocktails at armed US MPs and burned two US military vehicles. Representatives of the Saigon Student Union held a press conference on June 16, in which they chastised the American MPs and demanded the release of all students jailed as political dissidents. The students built upon the momentum of their press conference by organizing a national student congress later in the month. Delegates issued a statement calling for an immediate end to the war and "a total revolution in every aspect of national life." They also demanded an end to all military training programs. The congress elected Mam as its leader, and he led a group of representatives to meet with some of the organizers of the workers' strike. The students pledged their support for the strikers, and both groups called for immediate peace. Thieu responded with an angry statement denouncing the calls for peace, but he did not prevent new opposition groups from forming. In July of 1970, Ngo Ba Thanh established the Women's Movement for the People's Right to Live. Thanh's founding statement called for the withdrawal of all Americans from South Vietnam and the establishment of a coalition government in Saigon.[35] Coordinated protests against Thieu and his American supporters continued almost daily throughout 1970 and 1971. Long argued in his article that the urban opposition was even more radical than the NLF, whose representatives still claimed to be open to a negotiated settlement with the Saigon government. Launching a unified urban struggle was a primary tactic in the NLF's political war, and Thieu's heavy-handed response to protests, as well as Americans' inability to cultivate a viable anticommunist political base to counter the NLF, played into the NLF's overall plan.

The story that Ngo Vinh Long told of Saigon after Tet and as Vietnamization began was one of uncertainty and danger. Throughout 1971,

[34] Ibid.   [35] Ibid.

protesters in Saigon set American vehicles on fire, sometimes daily. Over the course of October 19 and 20, a group of women students set ten US vehicles on fire in Saigon. According to a report in *Tin Sang*, Saigon residents warned their Americans colleagues and friends that the only way to stay safe was to wear a symbol showing a broken M-16. It signified peace, and it would deter would-be attackers from targeting wearers. Long explained that the purpose of the chaos in Saigon was to convince Americans that not only do South Vietnamese citizens want them out of Vietnam, they also want peace, not continued war through Vietnamization. As long as Americans remained in the country to implement Nixon's policy, there would be no peace. It was important for city people to show their opposition to the war so that Americans and the Thieu government would know that it was not just rural Vietnamese who wanted the fighting to end because they bore the brunt of it. Urban residents hated the chaos that the war brought to Saigon, Long argued.[36]

As American personnel left South Vietnam, the withdrawal of US financial support hit Saigon hard. South Vietnam suffered a 65 percent inflation rate in 1973, and it continued to rise into 1974. The disintegrating economy left some Saigonese desperate. At the end of April 1974, Vo Van Nam set himself on fire in a park across from Notre Dame Cathedral in one of the busiest sections of Saigon. Nam, a father of five and an army veteran, did it during the evening rush hour to ensure the optimal number of passersby would witness his desperate act. He and his wife had been struggling to provide for their family. She sold lottery tickets, and he had driven a pedicab since getting out of the army a few years earlier. When he did not have enough customers to make ends meet, he sold his blood at a local hospital. One day while Nam was selling his blood, a thief stole his pedicab. When Nam walked outside and discovered it missing, he broke down. A few days later, he pawned his watch, used the money to take his children see a movie, and then set himself ablaze.[37] The story of Nam illustrates the consequences of both US intervention and withdrawal. The war rocked Saigon before, during, and after the major US military presence in South Vietnam. It was not just bombs and artillery fire that destroyed Vietnamese lives. The economic impact of US intervention and withdrawal hurt Saigon, South Vietnam's commercial center, especially severely. Many of the city's residents had

[36] Ibid.
[37] David K. Shipler, "Saigon Father of 5, Unable to Feed Family, Seeks Death by Fire," *New York Times*, May 1, 1974.

made a living in industries aimed at foreigners living there. When they and their country's money disappeared, so did jobs.

By mid-1974, 20 percent of South Vietnam's workforce was unemployed. Inflation had risen another 25 percent on top of the more than 60 percent inflation rate of 1973. In Saigon's slums, poor people tore bark off of trees to build fires for cooking because kerosene was too expensive. American agricultural advisers had introduced a high-yield type of rice several years earlier, but after US withdrawal, Vietnamese farmers could no longer access fertilizer, pesticides, and equipment they needed to plant, grow, and harvest the rice. The country's army of more than one million men comprised one-fifth of South Vietnam's workforce. By the mid-1970s, South Vietnam produced very little for export, and its exports were just one-tenth of its imports. The fuel crisis of the 1970s affected South Vietnam, too. Citizens had remained fairly quiet about the decline in their quality of life, but President Thieu authorized his security forces to crack down on political activities at their discretion. Politicians and officials in the Thieu administration feared that it was just a matter of time before hungry citizens began to rise up. Saigon's mayor, Brigadier General Do Kien Nhieu, implemented broader police surveillance of citizens to bolster security.

Café Givral, located at the corner of Tu Do and Le Loi streets in the heart of Saigon, was one of the casualties of the city's economic downturn. The café was known as the city's rumor mill because of the gossip journalists and politicians traded at its tables over coffee every day. Vietnamese and foreign reporters traded secrets that they then published in their newspapers, angering the politicians who were the subjects of their articles. Assemblymen, undercover police, and Thieu associates also planted themselves at Givral's tables, hoping to catch their names, or those of their rivals, in snippets of chatter between journalists. By 1974, the cacophony of competing conversations had quieted a bit, some believed because of Thieu's limiting of press freedom. Others attributed the rumor mill's slowed production to the departure of foreign journalists who left as US troops did. The most scandalous rumor of 1974 was that Givral's would close. The café was a metaphor for Saigon. The noise, the politics, the spying, and the rumors together constituted a microcosm of Saigon's political energy.[38]

Meanwhile, members of the Joint Military Commission, a group comprised of delegates from the NLF and Saigon government and tasked with

---

[38] James H. Markham, "Rumor Has It Saigon Rumor Mill Is Closing," *New York Times*, May 13, 1974.

implementing the cease-fire of the Paris peace agreement, struggled to find common ground on which to meet. Saigon government officials accused the NLF of violating the Paris agreement, continuing the war, and spreading anti-government propaganda. In retaliation, authorities canceled the NLF representatives' weekly press conferences, cut their telephone lines, and banned flights from Saigon to the NLF headquarters in Loc Ninh. Saigon's isolation of the PRG was also a violation of the peace agreement. The JMC was meeting at Tan Son Nhut air base in Saigon. Talks resumed in June after Thieu lifted the ban on press access to the NLF, and negotiations continued in fits and starts.[39]

A year after the signing of the cease-fire negotiated in Paris, neither the Saigon nor the Hanoi government was satisfied with the outcome. North Vietnamese troops continued to move into the South, seeming to close in on Saigon. US ground forces had departed, and in return, received some prisoners of war from Hanoi. Some South Vietnamese looked cynically on their ally, wondering if the release of American POWs was its only goal all along. Those South Vietnamese citizens speculated that Americans' priority was assuaging domestic public opinion and saving their political careers, not the fate of South Vietnam. The fatalism was unsurprising in those who went about their days in Saigon wondering how much closer northern troops had encroached the night before. Perhaps the new US Ambassador, Graham Martin, was a true friend. He focused on catching Communist violations of the treaty rather than calling out South Vietnam for its own disobedience. Thieu opposed the formation of a National Council of National Reconciliation and Concord, which was meant to oversee the implementation of the treaty's terms, including elections that potentially could unite Vietnam. It was all a ruse to weaken South Vietnam, Thieu asserted. The third force that the peace agreement called for had not materialized, although now that Ngo Ba Thanh was out of prison, she was out on the public stage trying to organize a third force that Thieu would be willing to accept.[40]

Madame Ngo Ba Thanh seemed to enjoy a freedom in 1974 that had been out of her reach for nearly a decade. She had been imprisoned in 1965 for six months, and then she served a two-year term beginning in 1967, and another beginning in 1971. Her crime was always the same – speaking out against the sitting government in Saigon and demanding

---

[39] "Vietcong Walks Out on Talks," *Philadelphia Inquirer*, May 11, 1974.
[40] Henry S. Bradsher, "Year Shows Holes in Viet Pact," *Washington Star-News*, Jan. 14, 1974, A12.

that a third force be taken seriously as a negotiating party in the talks for Vietnam's future. Interestingly, her two two-year sentences coincided with the two presidential elections that Thieu won. A reporter for the *Christian Science Monitor* wondered if there was a connection. After spending so much time locked up, Thanh in 1974 was one of the most visible spokespersons for the third force that she and her associates argued they had a rightful place at the political table according to the Paris peace agreement. Cynical, or perhaps realistic, observers believed that Thieu left Thanh alone as evidence of political freedom in South Vietnam without opening the door to substantive political action by opposition parties.

Thanh's ease in the spotlight had made her a symbol of the political opposition that had been making noise in Saigon since the early 1960s. Now as the founder of the Vietnamese Women's Movement for the Right to Live and co-president of the People's Front Struggling for Peace, some in the national government and the US Embassy wonder what exactly her goals were for Vietnam. Again, Thanh was consistent. She argued that the fight between Communists and anticommunists was a creation of "foreign powers," and only a neutral third way would bring peace to Vietnam by mediating a compromise that would end the destruction of the country. But US and South Vietnamese leaders worried that neutrality was just a step on the road to communism. As Catholics, once stalwart anticommunists, began reaching out to leftists, peace activists, and communists in the late 1960s and early 1970s, it seemed that not even supporters could be trusted.[41] Catholics like Father Chan Tin were connected with Ngo Ba Thanh and other members of the self-determination movement, and they worked their international connections to draw attention to the plight of political prisoners and other examples of political oppression. Fr. Tin published dramatic testimonies of former political prisoners in a monthly journal, and he met with American politicians and religious leaders who traveled to South Vietnam in the 1970s to learn more about political prisoners. John Conyers, Leo Ryan, and others took fact-finding trips South Vietnam, and Fr. Tin found time to sit down with them all.

---

[41] Takashi Oka, "The Woman Who Opposes President Thieu," *Christian Science Monitor*, May 6, 1974.

7

The Catholic Opposition and Political Repression

Fr. Chan Tin, a Catholic Redemptorist priest in his fifties, had played the role of confessor often; it was part of his vocation. So he sat and listened as a young woman described how the guards at Thu Duc prison tortured her. They began by blindfolding her and asking her if she worked for the communists. They beat her with a night stick as she tried to respond, and the beating only increased when she said no, that she did not work for the communists. Unsatisfied with her responses, the guards then applied electric shock treatments to her armpits, breasts, and vagina. They were especially brutal on the days when she was menstruating. The woman believed the torture she endured in prison had caused her infertility.[1]

This was not the usual confession, in which Fr. Tin would determine a penance, grant absolution, and send the sinner on her way. The woman had confessed not her sins, but the sins of the Thu Duc prison guards, and, by extension, the sins of Nguyen Van Thieu, whose government and security officers arrested and imprisoned political dissidents without trial or sentencing. It was not the first time Fr. Tin had heard about torture in Thu Duc, Con Dao, and other South Vietnamese prisons. There would be no absolution; instead, Fr. Tin wrote about the woman's experience and other testimonies of torture and published them in the monthly magazine, *Doi Dien (Face to Face)*. Fr. Tin also formed the Committee to Reform the Prison System in order to draw international attention to political repression and torture in South Vietnam.

---

[1] *Doi Dien*, August 1970, Thu Vien Khoa Hoc Tong Hop (General Sciences Library), Ho Chi Minh City, Vietnam.

Even before the human rights turn of the 1970s, Chan Tin spoke and wrote about political prisoners to draw international attention to human rights violations in South Vietnam. American politicians, US Embassy officers, and CIA agents took note of Chan Tin's activism and sought to counter his estimates of political prisoners with their own. His emphasis on political prisoners linked Chan Tin with members of the "third force," including Ngo Ba Thanh, Nguyen Long, and Huynh Tan Mam, all of whom had served time in the system. Tin wrote a number of letters to South Vietnam's Minister of the Interior demanding the release of political prisoners. In early 1974, he advocated on behalf of student leader Huynh Tan Mam, who was in solitary confinement at Chi Hoa prison. In Paris, a group of Vietnamese expats led by Fr. Nguyen Dinh Chi, worked to call international attention to political oppression in South Vietnam.

According to the conventional wisdom, Catholics in South Vietnam were staunchly anticommunist and blindly pro-government. Historians have acknowledged Catholics and Catholicism in studies of Ngo Dinh Diem's family and presidency, John F. Kennedy's Vietnam policy, and US Catholic supporters of Vietnam War, notably Cardinal Francis Spellman. But a closer look at Vietnamese attitudes and activity on the ground in South Vietnam reveals a more complex reality.[2] Like so much of the action in the Vietnam War, two factors mattered – time period and international opinion. Where strict adherence to anticommunism might have been a characteristic of some Vietnamese Catholics in the 1950s and early 1960s, by the late sixties, a combination of war weariness and liberation theology nudged some Catholics toward reconciliation and even into the NLF camp. Fr. Chan Tin was one of the leading Catholic opponents of Nguyen Van Thieu's government, and he served as a link between liberal Vietnamese Catholics and members of the Movement for Self-Determination. Antiwar Americans and Vietnamese expats seized upon Chan Tin's reports of political prisoners and torture as evidence supporting their opposition to continued US support of South Vietnam's government. Among Vietnamese Catholic laity, Assemblyman Ngo Cong Duc was one of the most vocal critics of the Thieu government, and his outspokenness cost him his political career.

---

[2] Important studies of Vietnamese Catholics include Peter Hansen, "Bac Di Cu: Catholic Refugees from the North of Vietnam, and Their Role in the Southern Republic, 1954–1959," *Journal of Vietnamese Studies*, Vol. 4, No. 3 (Fall 2009) 173–211; Van Nguyen-Marshall, "Tools of Empire? Vietnamese Catholics in South Vietnam," *The Journal of the Canadian Historical Association*, Vol. 20, No. 2 (2009) 138–159.

On October 15, 1969, a group of ninety-three Vietnamese Catholics living in Europe issued a statement in which they declared that the US military presence in and bombing of Vietnam violated Vietnamese human rights and was the primary reason for the problems and violence in Vietnam. About one-tenth of the Vietnamese population was Catholic. During the French colonial period, the French fostered the development of a French-oriented Catholic professional, military, and bureaucratic elite. By the late 1960s, there were two main Catholic peace organizations in South Vietnam: Catholics for Peace, made up primarily of middle-class professionals, and Young Catholic Workers/Catholic Labor Youth, which consisted of working-class youth and Catholic soldiers. The Catholic youth wanted self-determination, and they said that even older refugee Catholics from the North were beginning to turn against the war. They had sent their sons to fight what they believed to be a war against the communists, but as the war dragged on without any end in sight, they began to question American policies, motives, and plans. While many bishops, older priests, and older laity continued to support the war, younger Catholics and priests had begun to join the opposition. Archbishop Nguyen Van Binh's Christmas 1970 message was a call for peace: "One speaks of peace with victory, of peace with honor. I don't understand what those are. We want simply peace, a peace accepted by both sides. It isn't just Catholics, but all the people who desire peace, for there has been too much killing, in the North as in the South."[3]

SOUTH VIETNAM'S CATHOLICS

Politics and religion were deeply intertwined throughout the course of South Vietnam's history. As Jessica Chapman illustrates in her work on South Vietnam's political scene during the Diem era, "politico-religious" groups including the Cao Dai, Hoa Hao, and Buddhists challenged the rule of the Catholic Diem. Diem found a convenient excuse for authoritarian repression in the tension and violence that this volatile mix produced, and he explained that security forces had to act harshly to bring order to South Vietnam. It also allowed Diem to link communist insurgency to the religious struggles and thus casting Catholicism as clearly

[3] George Wald, "The South Vietnamese Catholics," *New York Times*, Jan. 11, 1972, http://jfk.hood.edu/Collection/White%20Materials/Indochina/Indochina%200353.pdf.

anticommunist. That Catholicism shared a basic moral foundation with Western values made Diem more familiar to Americans.[4]

However, as Chapman points out, Catholic attitudes had a history of being more complex than Diem, foreigners, and historians have portrayed them. In the 1940s, Catholics joined with other politico-religious groups, as well as secular nationalists and Trotskyites, to form the United National Front, an independence movement.[5] Tensions between nationalist Catholics, other noncommunist nationalist groups, and the Viet Minh continued through the war with France. When Diem took power in 1954, he installed family members, who happened to be Catholic and often lacked experience, in government positions, creating the image of religious favoritism and a religious minority controlling South Vietnam.[6] Opposition groups accused Diem of trying to "Catholicize" Vietnam, emphasizing that not only the American government, but US Catholic organizations, funded Diem's efforts to consolidate his power.[7] It is no surprise that by the time of Diem's assassination, Vietnamese Catholics had an image of a monolithic, pro-government segment of South Vietnam's population.

Also contributing to the image of Catholics as a favored, pro-government group was the issue of northern refugees. In 1954, nearly one million Vietnamese Catholics fled south from the Democratic Republic of Vietnam across the seventeenth parallel into South Vietnam. As they arrived in South Vietnam, the Catholic refugees established communities that created de facto segregation from their southern peers. Some of the northern Catholic refugees became ARVN officers and civil servants, while others appeared to dominate academia and other professions.[8] Because of the involvement of Edward Lansdale and the CIA in the migration, it appeared that the exodus was an American ploy and the northern Catholics, dupes.

Yet as Peter Hansen's research has concluded, closer examination reveals that the migrants were more complex than the conventional

---

[4] Jessica Chapman, *Cauldron of Resistance: Ngo Dinh Diem, the United States, and 1950s Southern Vietnam* (Ithaca, NY: Cornell University Press, 2013), p. 7. See also, Seth Jacobs, *America's Miracle Man in Vietnam: Ngo Dinh Diem, Religion, Race, and U.S. Intervention in Southeast Asia, 1950–1957* (Durham, NC: Duke University Press, 2005); Van Nguyen-Marshall, "Tools of Empire? Vietnamese Catholics in South Vietnam," *Journal of the Canadian Historical Association*, Vol. 20, No. 2 (2009) 138–159; Peter Hansen, "Bac Di Cu: Catholic Refugees from the North of Vietnam, and Their Role in the Southern Republic, 1954–1959," *Journal of Vietnamese Studies*, Vol. 4, No. 3 (Fall 2009) 173–211.
[5] Chapman, *Cauldron of Resistance*, p. 28.   [6] Ibid., pp. 75–76.   [7] Ibid., p. 170.
[8] Hansen, p. 175.

wisdom had portrayed them. They made their own decisions regarding the move south, where they would live, and who they would support politically.[9] As Hansen points out, northern Catholics moved south at various moments in the first half of the twentieth century for multiple reasons, including the desire to establish farms on uncultivated land, the need to escape famine, and fear of the Viet Minh. So while religious freedom and fear of communism might have motivated some Catholics to leave the North in 1954, they were not the only reasons, and the 1954 migration was not unprecedented. Food shortages and concerns about employment opportunities motivated some migrants, for both urban professionals and the rural poor, in the mid-fifties. Saigon and South Vietnam looked to be more promising.[10]

This context is important because it illustrates a history of the diversity of Vietnamese Catholic attitudes toward politics, society, and their place in South Vietnam. With this in mind, it is less surprising that a group that had seemed staunchly pro-government during the Diem era would have members move to the left by the late 1960s and join the movements for peace and reunification. The other context that matters is international. That some Vietnamese Catholics would join the anti-Thieu resistance and the peace movement in South Vietnam makes sense when placed in a global context that highlights a Catholic move to the left in the 1960s. In El Salvador, Catholic intellectuals helped to establish the Salvadoran New Left. Historian Joaquin M. Chavez argues that the transformations in the Catholic Church resulting from the Second Vatican Council, which began in 1962, and the Second Conference of Latin American Bishops (CELAM) in 1968 radicalized young Catholic intellectuals, causing them to break with conservative Catholicism. Transformations in the church brought together young Catholics and political revolutionaries because both sides wanted to reform the capitalist system. Catholic leaders critiqued liberal capitalism, the legacies of colonialism, and neocolonialism, and they invoked the "just war" theory to defend the use of revolutionary violence against oppression.[11] Latin American Catholicism, including liberation theology, shaped the thinking of some Vietnamese Catholics.

Catholic clergy in Latin America officially articulated the concepts of liberation theology at the Latin American Episcopal Conference

---

[9] Hansen, p. 182.   [10] Hansen, pp. 186–187.
[11] Joaquin M. Chavez, "Catholic Action, the Second Vatican Council, and the Emergence of the New Left in El Salvador, 1950–1975," *The Americas*, Vol. 70, No. 3 (Jan. 2014) 459–487.

(CELAM) in Medellin, Colombia, in 1968. The central tenet of liberation theology was the Catholic Church's "preferential option for the poor" and its commitment to radical social change. It was the culmination of many prior years of collaboration between clergy and laity in rural areas and barrios throughout Latin America.[12] Such networks and other Catholic activist organizations helped facilitate the emergence of the liberation theology movement in Latin America. The CELAM conference, at which clergy discussed how to apply the outcomes of the Second Vatican Council to Latin America, inspired the formation of new Catholic groups such as Argentina's Movement of Priests for the Third World.[13]

In the case of South Vietnam, the existing activist networks that provided Chan Tin and others with a framework for Catholic opposition to the government were secular political organizations such as the Movement for Self-Determination and the peace and reconciliation movements. As Philip Roberts argues in his work on Catholic political activism in Brazil, "the unrest of the subaltern classes in Brazil, as social inequality and political violence worsened after 1968" inspired Brazilian Catholic clergy to mobilize against state oppression. Men of the cloth such as Helder Camara, Bishop of Recife, became a crucial voice in Brazilian politics and society as well as religion.[14] They saw themselves as "the voice of the voiceless," especially as Brazil's authoritarian government increased its persecution of subversives.[15] Chan Tin and other Catholic activists assumed the role of voice of the voiceless in their activism on behalf of political prisoners. Camara influenced Tin's thinking, and Tin reprinted articles by Camara in his magazine, *Doi Dien*. Tin's efforts to discuss political prisoners in terms of human rights reflected liberation theology's emphasis on human rights.[16]

---

[12] Jeffrey L. Gould, "Solidarity under Siege: The Latin American Left, 1968," *American Historical Review*, Vol. 114, No. 2 (Apr. 2009) 372–373.

[13] Robert Sean Mackin, "Liberation Theology: The Radicalization of Social Catholic Movements," *Politics, Religion & Ideology*, Vol. 13, No. 3 (Sep. 2012) 33.

[14] Philip Roberts, "Passive Revolution in Brazil: Struggles over Hegemony, Religion, and Development, 1964–2007," *Third World Quarterly*, 2015, Vol. 36, No. 9 (2015) 1663–1668.

[15] Jan Hoffman French, "A Tale of Two Priests and Two Struggles: Liberation Theology from Dictatorship to Democracy in the Brazilian Northeast," *The Americas*, Vol. 63, No. 3 (Jan. 2007) 410.

[16] Leila Celis, "The Legacy of Liberation Theology in Colombia: The Defense of Life and Territory," *Latin American Perspectives*, Issue 208, Vol. 43, No. 3 (May 2016) 69.

CHAN TIN, *ĐỐI DIỆN*, AND POLITICAL PRISONERS

In the fall of 1969, a reporter for the Saigon-based magazine *Đối Diện*, a monthly Catholic publication edited by Fr. Chan Tin, interviewed Fr. Nguyễn Ngọc Lan about his position on the Vietnam War and prospects for peace. Fr. Lan was a known peace advocate, which had led some to label him communist-leaning. When the reporter asked him about the accuracy of the label, he replied that if desiring peace and caring for the poor made him a communist, so be it. The way Fr. Lan saw it, if a peace settlement led the warring halves of Vietnam to be united under a communist government, that would be better than to remain at war while a corrupt noncommunist government continued to hold power in Saigon. What should we choose, the priest asked, if given the choice between war and peace? Lan could not imagine how peace of any kind could damage Vietnam any more than the war had. The reporter asked Lan if he ever thought he should trade his clerical garb for a soldier's uniform. No, Lan said. He believed he could not do more for his country in any other position than in his role as a priest.[17]

Not all Vietnamese Catholics believed the issue was that simple. While the theme running through most issues of *Đối Diện* was the desire for peace and an end to foreign intervention in Vietnam, some writers – priests and laity – worried that peace under communism would strip Vietnamese Catholics of the freedom to practice their religion. The March 1970 issue of the magazine featured an article about a letter Archbishops Nguyen Van Binh from Saigon and Pham Ngoc Chi from Danang sent to Paris, where American and Vietnamese delegates were struggling to agree on terms that would end the war. The archbishops wrote that while Vietnamese Catholics wanted peace, they also wanted to ensure that religious freedom would remain even if a communist government took control of Vietnam as a whole. Peace without freedom is a "fake peace," the archbishops argued.[18]

The articles in *Đối Diện* offer a fascinating look at how traditional Catholicism, liberation theology, communism, and the postcolonial struggle to establish independence and identity converged and existed in tension in Vietnam in the late 1960s and early 1970s. Although a

---

[17] "Phan chien? Nguy Hoa? Lam chinh tri? Thien Cong?" *Doi Dien*, Oct. 1969. Thu Vien Khoa Hoc Tong Hop (General Sciences Library), Ho Chi Minh City, Vietnam.
[18] "Buc thu ngo goi phai doan hoa dam Ba Le," *Doi Dien*, March 1970. Thu Vien Khoa Hoc Tong Hop (General Sciences Library), Ho Chi Minh City, Vietnam.

minority group, Vietnamese Catholic intellectuals wrote widely about
politics for publications such as *Đối Diện* and others, and Catholicism
in Vietnam had gained international attention due to the exodus of
Catholics from northern Vietnam in 1954 and during the presidency of
Ngô Đình Diệm, a Catholic. In the case of Vietnam, Catholicism in the
1950s and early 1960s tended to be associated with anticommunism, but
by the late 1960s, liberation theology had made its way from Latin
America to Southeast Asia, and it gave some Vietnamese Catholics a
way to reconcile their faith with their support for peace even if it brought
communist control of Vietnam. *Đối Diện* published interviews with Brazilian bishops Helder Camara and Dom Fragoso, both of whom adhered
to the tenets of liberation theology and emphasized that Catholicism and
communism or socialism are not inherently adversaries. When Fr. Lan
spoke with the *Đối Diện* reporter, he mentioned Bishop Camara as
someone whose beliefs were similar to his, although Fr. Lan noted that
while some called Bishop Camara a "red bishop," Fr. Lan himself was
only "đỏ đỏ" – "reddish," "a little bit red."[19]

In a country that had been at war in some form or another for decades,
and where foreign interventions continued to wreak havoc on the landscape and the economy, there was an audience open to the teachings of
liberation theology. There was no consensus among South Vietnam's
Catholics about what their relationship to the peace movements and
communism could or should be, but that is just one example of the
diversity of opinions within South Vietnam about Vietnam's postcolonial
future. He would not have been speaking for all Vietnamese Catholics,
but to the question "can a Vietnamese Catholic be a communist?" Fr. Lan
likely would have said yes, if it meant peace. For others, the fear of
religious persecution made it difficult to support a peace agreement that
paved the way for a communist takeover of Vietnam in its entirety.

In the late 1960s and early 1970s, Chan Tin published in *Doi Dien*
interviews he conducted with former inmates of South Vietnam's prisons.
The conversations revealed details of the torture they experienced at the
hands of prison guards during their sentences. Tin warned that the news
of police torture of imprisoned students had reached the public, and local
and global audiences were paying attention. Students recounted to Tin
their experiences being tortured to unconsciousness, and having water
poured into their nose, mouth, and ears. Interrogators drove nails under

their fingernails and beat them on their kneecaps and ankles. Some inmates were electrocuted and burned with chemicals. Some of the prisoners were taken to a hospital by ambulance after being tortured. A lack of food at the prisons only made the situation worse for inmates. The state news service, VTX, accused the student inmates of pretending to be injured, arguing that they were healthy enough to show up in court to plead their cases, but Chan Tin instructed readers to go to the hospital and see the evidence of torture.[20]

Tin acknowledged that some of the prisoners were associated with communist organizations. In March 1970, officers arrested Huynh Tan Mam, president of the Saigon Student Union and a member of Thanh Doan Thanh Nien Sinh Vien va Hoc Sinh Giai Phong, a communist youth group.[21] Mam's arrest was part of a police raid on the organization's headquarters, in which officers discovered explosives and documents detailing plans to bomb the US Embassy, Saigon police departments, and a military command post in the city. Members also infiltrated student organizations to build support for the NLF and the overthrow of the Saigon government. Authorities accused members of planting bombs in hotels, restaurants, and schools throughout Saigon, and officers arrested nearly forty students in addition to Mam. Not to be deterred by the very authorities they sought to topple, students sent a cable to American antiwar students asking for their support, and they issued a statement in Saigon declaring that if police failed to release Mam and the other students, Thieu's regime would face the same fate as Diem's government had.[22] Emboldened by the peace conferences in Paris and the support from older activists such as Fr. Tin, Mam and other students stood firm in the face of political repression by their government and drew global attention to the authoritarian practices of leaders who sought to set South Vietnam apart from the totalitarian North.

One of the questions Chan Tin and other Vietnamese Catholics debated in *Doi Dien* and other venues was how to reconcile Catholicism with political leftism that bled into communism. Tin turned to the Brazilian Bishop Helder Camara and published his thoughts in the magazine.

[20] *Doi Dien*, May 1970, Thu Vien Khoa Hoc Tong Hop (General Sciences Library), Ho Chi Minh City, Vietnam.
[21] Van Nguyen Marshall, "South Vietnam Had an Antiwar Movement, Too," *New York Times*, Sep. 15, 2017, www.nytimes.com/2017/09/15/opinion/south-vietnam-had-an-antiwar-movement-too.html.
[22] *Doi Dien*, April 1970. Thu Vien Khoa Hoc Tong Hop (General Sciences Library), Ho Chi Minh City, Vietnam.

Camara argued that the idea that socialism is anti-Catholic and capitalism is linked with Catholicism was a false dichotomy. He asserted that the Latin American Catholic leaders who met at Medellin in 1968 agreed that justice was a condition for peace. There was no justice for the majority of people under capitalism, a system where corporations such as General Motors and Standard Oil made profits greater than some countries' budgets, Camara argued.[23]

Tin also reprinted an article that a Chilean magazine, *Pastoral Popular*, had run about the increase in political activism of Latin American Catholic priests. The article discussed Camara, Colombian priest and socialist Camilo Torres, and Brazilian Bishop Antonio Fragoso, an advocate for small farmers in northeastern Brazil. Catholics had a responsibility to be part of a revolution that would bring justice to workers and farmers and others who struggle to survive in the current global economic and political system. Priests had as part of their mission a duty to serve the poor, and this included getting involved in radical politics and guerrilla movements if necessary.[24] Liberation theology gave Tin and other antiwar Vietnamese Catholics a model through which they could justify their willingness as Catholics to work for peace, even if that peace resulted in a communist takeover of a united Vietnam.

Not all of Tin's fellow Vietnamese Catholics espoused the tenets of liberation theology. Some still worried that communism was inherently anti-religion, and a communist government would curtail Catholics' freedom to worship. Advocating on behalf of the victims of the war was correct in their minds, but they were skeptical of communism's ability to bring justice for all. The archbishops of Saigon and Da Nang submitted a statement to the delegates at the Paris peace negotiations imploring them to ensure that political decisions aimed at peace also guaranteed civil liberties, including religious freedom. Peace without freedom was a "fake peace."[25]

As peace talks continued into the early 1970s, some Catholics sought to take a more forceful stand against communism. Fr. Nguyen Huy Chuong of the National Defense Movement represented Catholics who wanted to organize a protest against a cease-fire and the establishment of

[23] *Doi Dien*, Aug. 1969. Thu Vien Khoa Hoc Tong Hop (General Sciences Library), Ho Chi Minh City, Vietnam.
[24] *Doi Dien*, Jan. 1970. Thu Vien Khoa Hoc Tong Hop (General Sciences Library), Ho Chi Minh City, Vietnam.
[25] *Doi Dien*, Aug. 1969. Thu Vien Khoa Hoc Tong Hop (General Sciences Library), Ho Chi Minh City, Vietnam.

a cooperative government. Their demonstration would thank soldiers for doing their part and call upon all South Vietnamese to come together and fight communism for a true peace. Communism would make citizens slaves to the government, Fr. Chuong declared. So many soldiers and civilians had already lost their lives in the war that to quit would disrespect those who gave everything. The national reconciliation movement was a communist plot, Chuong argued. Catholics should unite with their military brethren and fight for peace.

Chan Tin would not have it. National reconciliation was the only way to achieve a lasting peace, the only way to prevent brothers from killing brothers. Vietnam had already suffered twenty-five years of war, he argued, and now the United States was finally willing to negotiate. For Tin, US involvement was the clear enemy, not an idea like communism or even North Vietnam. The United States had finally halted its bombing campaign and was beginning to withdraw its troops, and an antiwar movement was gaining traction in South Vietnam, so the best thing to do was to go with it, Tin maintained. The war was meaningless; they all knew that. Nothing about it was going to make Vietnamese lives better, Tin concluded.[26]

Americans sought to understand Tin's position and determine the degree to which it represented the attitudes of South Vietnamese Catholics more broadly. In May 1969, a US interfaith delegation traveled to Saigon to talk with Tin and other Catholics. The US group included Rep. John Conyers, Methodist minister James Armstrong, Rabbi Seymour Siegel, Navy Rear Admiral Arnold E. True, Rep. Robert F. Drinan, and peace activist and *National Catholic Reporter* correspondent Thomas Fox. At the office of *Doi Dien*, they met Tin, Fr. Tran Viet Tho, and writer Nguyen Huy Lich. Conyers opened the conversation with a frank question: What did the Vietnamese people want? Fr. Tho responded what Tin had been saying and writing: The Vietnamese people want peace. The real question was, what did Americans want? The US peace plan was not clear, Tho stated, and the Americans were the ones who had the power to end the fighting. Regardless of what the Vietnamese wanted, Americans had to be the ones to stop. If South Vietnamese citizens seemed fatalistic or fed up, it was because they were. Tho explained that while most Vietnamese understood that US support had sustained South Vietnam up to that point, many had come to resent and even hate the US presence. Americans were

[26] *Doi Dien*, Jan. 1970. Thu Vien Khoa Hoc Tong Hop (General Sciences Library), Ho Chi Minh City, Vietnam.

bossy and seemed to have little concern for the opinions and desires of the Vietnamese. More than that, Americans had corrupted Vietnamese society with their depravity. They lacked a moral compass when it came to women, Tho chided. Freewheeling American men used Vietnamese women for their bodies, and the war economy allowed women to make more money than men, upending familial gender conventions.[27]

Doi Dien reporter Nguyen Huy Lich joined the conversation and turned it from Americans' sins to Vietnamese Catholic ideas about peace. Americans and Europeans assumed that all Catholics were pro-war and pro-government while assuming that all Buddhists were for peace. It was not that simple, Lich explained. Many Vietnamese, whether Catholic or not, worried about what peace would actually look like for them under a communist government, should it come to that. They wanted peace, but they wanted religious freedom, too.[28]

Tin elaborated. Those Catholics who worry about a "fake peace" were thinking incorrectly. They assumed that peace would necessarily result in a communist government. If the war ended, though, it might allow southern people to come together and make the country better, even if the peace agreement was not perfect. In any case, the South Vietnamese were not free as it was because the United States was dominating the country. US intervention was the root of the problem. The Americans got involved in Vietnam's domestic disagreements, which only served to weaken the South because the United States took its sovereignty, Tin scolded. The only good thing Americans could do for Vietnam now was give the Vietnamese their sovereignty. Give the Vietnamese self-determination. Conyers wanted to know if the Thieu-Ky government represented the will of the majority of voters, but Tran Viet Tho replied that the American obsession with representation was not the most important thing for the Vietnamese at that time; peace was, so whatever leaders ensured peace represented the desires of the Vietnamese.[29]

It was on the subject of political prisoners that Chan Tin got the attention of American Embassy officers, policymakers, and antiwar activists beyond the interfaith fact-finding mission. Tin had founded an organization called the Committee to Reform the Prison System after talking with a student named Cao Thi Que Huong. She and her husband, who managed a youth hostel, were arrested and tortured in March 1970. Huong had been

---

[27] "Doi Dien voi phai doan Lien Ton My," *Doi Dien*, July 1969. Thu Vien Khoa Hoc Tong Hop (General Sciences Library), Ho Chi Minh City, Vietnam.

[28] Ibid.   [29] Ibid.

released, but her husband remained in jail and eventually died there. So she went to Chan Tin, the fifty-five-year-old leader of the Young Catholic Workers, and asked him for help. She hoped he would organize people to advocate on behalf of political prisoners in South Vietnam, and from that conversation, the Committee was born in Saigon.[30]

Tin arranged a meeting at the An Quang Pagoda of the Unified Buddhist Church and invited former inmates to testify to their experiences in prison. On November 15, 1970, the Committee was officially formed and held its first meeting. The Committee's mission was to tell Vietnam and the world what was happening in Thieu's prisons. The goals of the organization included ending arbitrary arrests and illegal detentions, the end of torture, no arrests of minors, pregnant women, the elderly, or the infirm, the establishment of boarding houses to help prisoners transition back into regular life, and the establishment of representative democracy. The group's manifesto demanded that police release prisoners who have served their sentence, pregnant women, elderly and sick inmates, and youth from jails. They also demanded an end to torture and to not classifying political dissidents as criminals. The group consisted of Catholic and Buddhist clergy including Chan Tin; lawyers and other professionals; representatives of students, workers, and women; writers; professors; current and former members of the National Assembly; and other government officials. On September 15, 1971, Tin, along with Catholic professor Nguyen Van Trung, lawyer and self-determination activist Nguyen Long, and two Buddhist bonzes met with Senator George McGovern. The following spring, the men were arrested for having held that meeting.[31]

In 1972, the Committee temporarily ceased activity because some members had been arrested and others went underground out of fear that they might be next. Chan Tin, despite his outspoken public advocacy for political justice and the global reach of the Committee, managed to avoid serving prison time even though he had been arrested and sentenced to five years and a $75,000 fine. In May 1972, security officers raided a boarding house the Committee ran for former prisoners recently released. Local government administrators shuttered the house without reason, and police arrested volunteers working there, including high school and

[30] "After the Signing of the Paris Agreements: Documents on South Vietnam's Political Prisoners," Vietnam Resource Center/*Thoi Bao Ga*, Cambridge, MA, June 1973, p. 3. Vietnam Archive, Texas Tech University.
[31] Ibid.

university students and three Buddhist nuns who cooked for the workers.
Police refused to explain why they had arrested the volunteers. It was the
latest in a series of arrests and imprisonments of members of a group
working to call attention to authoritarianism under Thieu.[32]

Earlier that year, officers had arrested Thieu Son, a writer in his
seventies; a thirty-eight-year-old music professor named Pham Trong
Cau; and Cau's parents. Tin, Nguyen Long's wife, and several monks
were summoned to court for contacting Senator McGovern. At the time
that police shut down operations at the boarding house, residents ranged
in age from late teens to late fifties, and most suffered from an illness or
physical problems related to torture while in prison. Con Son prison was
located on a collection of fourteen islands in the South China Sea, about
140 miles from Saigon. The French built it during the colonial period, and
the South Vietnamese government reopened it in 1957 due to an over-
flowing prison population on the mainland. The prison was known for its
tiger cages. In 1972, it held about 4,000 prisoners.[33]

In August 1972, *Doi Dien* published a statement, "Declaration of
Twelve Priests," signed by twelve Catholic priests in Saigon on July 4,
1972, accusing the South Vietnamese government of human rights violations due to its political repression. The repression had not silenced the
priests, who spoke out against the Thieu government and US intervention
even though Catholics had once been reliably pro-government. The priests
accused the Saigon government of a continuous pattern of terrorism with
arbitrary arrests and imprisonments, arrests that appear more like kidnappings, and the jailing of alleged criminals in unknown places for indeter-
minate lengths of time. State terrorism had increased recently, especially
targeting high school and university students. The state's policy of terrorism violated both South Vietnam's constitution and "the very basic
demands of human rights." It also contradicted the spirit of the Second
Vatican Council, the priests contended. "In any circumstances, even under
martial law or in a situation of tension, all rights of men and women must
always be respected." The priests took it upon themselves to be the
spokesmen of South Vietnamese citizens because state-sponsored terrorism had silenced them. They sought to capture the world's attention,
especially Christians. South Vietnam, as it was at that moment, the priests

---

[32] "A Cry of Alarm: New Revelations on Repression and Deportation in South Vietnam,"
1972, Committee to Reform the Prison System in South Vietnam. Vietnam Archive,
Texas Tech University.
[33] Ibid.

accused, was not part of the "free world," if Americans were actually talking about freedom when they coined that phrase.[34]

Five of the twelve signers had been invited to the International Assembly of Christians in Quebec, Canada, but the South Vietnamese government denied their visa applications. In response, the Redemptorist priest Fr. Nguyen Ngoc Lan, a philosophy professor at the University of Hue, sent a message to the Assembly. He wrote, "The fact that no Christian from Saigon can come to your Assembly, our total absence, points up the complete absurdity and hypocrisy of a situation which Nixon and the Pentagon continue to maintain at the price of ecocide and genocide which have been perpetrated for many years." In October 1972, a military court in Saigon sentenced Chan Tin to five years in solitary confinement and fined him $75,000 after convicting him of publishing "communist propaganda" that was "detrimental to the national security." Yet the courts did not force him to serve his sentence, and he continued to speak out on behalf of political dissidents.[35]

The Paris Peace Agreement stipulated that a National Council of National Reconciliation would be formed in the South and would include representatives from the government, the PRG, and "a third group representing those who support neither government." Activists such as Chan Tin, who cast themselves as members of the third force, argued that the establishment of a legitimate third group required the government to release political prisoners, as they most likely were part of the third way. The Indochina Resource Center accepted Tin's estimate of 200,000 political dissidents in South Vietnam's prisons. IRC activists argued that the establishment of a third force was required for true peace, but Thieu countered that there was no third force – that those claiming to be part of that group were actually pro-PRG.[36]

Prime among the points of contention between the Thieu government's American supporters and Tin was the number of political prisoners held in South Vietnam's jails. Tin came to the attention of US Embassy officials after he published a report alleging the South Vietnam's prisons contained 200,000 political dissidents. An American survey team tasked with the duty of determining how many political prisoners actually resided in

[34] "Voices of the Third Force," Indochina Resource Center, Nov. 6, 1972, Vietnam Archive, Texas Tech University.
[35] Ibid.
[36] "Voices of the Third Force," Indochina Resource Center, Nov. 6, 1972, p. 1. Vietnam Archive, Texas Tech University.

South Vietnam's jails met with Fr. Tin at his church in Saigon. When the Americans arrived, they found that Tin had also invited the family members of five prisoners. The relatives asserted that their imprisoned kin were victims of Thieu's political oppression, that their only crime was opposing the government, and even then, no judge or jury had actually convicted them of any wrongdoing. Members of the survey team argued that it was difficult to determine how many political prisoners were in jail in South Vietnam, but they did not believe Tin's claim. In a relatively small country, where would authorities put them, they wondered, and how would they feed them? They also wondered why, if there were so many political prisoners, Tin had only invited the relatives of five?[37]

US Embassy officials sought to counter Chan Tin's claim of more than 200,000 political prisoners in South Vietnam by conducting their own survey of the country's prisons. Embassy officials inspected forty prisons administered by the National Police and came up with the number 35,000 inmates. However, Chan Tin protested – and Americans admitted – that the Embassy's numbers did not include military prisons, interrogation centers, and district or other local jails. Amnesty International estimated the number of political prisoners in South Vietnam at 100,000. Tin said his figures came from official documents that he cross-checked with judges, prison officials, ex-prisoners, and witnesses. The primary area of dispute between Tin and the US Embassy officials was how to differentiate between political prisoners and other prisoners. Both sides argued that it was impossible to get accurate numbers because the Thieu government would not allow an independent study of the prisons, and at the local level, prisoners were often moved around from jail to jail. Tin himself was unique in his judicial status because he was a convicted national security risk but remained free. State Department officials wrote to J. William Fulbright about Tin but did not know why the courts had not enforced Tin's sentence. Another Catholic priest, Fr. Truong Ba Can, of the Young Catholic Workers, also had been arrested and charged but was not serving his sentence. In September 1972, Ngo Cong Duc, a Catholic deputy in the National Assembly's lower house, nephew of the Archbishop of Saigon, and an authority on the prison system in South Vietnam, affirmed Tin's statement that there were 200,000 political prisoners in South Vietnam's jails.

---

[37] "United States Aid to Indochina: Report of a Staff Survey Team to South Vietnam, Cambodia, and Laos, July 1974, Washington, DC: U.S. Government Printing Office, 1974, p. 9. Vietnam Archive, Texas Tech University.

Classifying Tin as an "anti-GVN Catholic activist," the US Mission survey of prisoners in South Vietnam insisted that the number of political prisoners was about 35,000. When Tin met with an Embassy representative, he gave the rep his two-volume bound report on political prisoners in South Vietnam. The issue came down to a question of definitions and a question of trust. Embassy officials questioned how Tin defined political prisoner, while Tin questioned the embassy survey's selection of prisons to study. From Tin's perspective, the US Embassy had an interest in underestimating Thieu's level of political repression. Embassy officials, in turn, viewed Tin skeptically given his open anti-government stance.[38]

The Americans were put off by Tin's stubborn piety. They could not quite decide if his determination to expose political injustices stemmed from his priesthood or from his Sorbonne education, which, according to Embassy officers, no doubt swayed him toward socialism. He viewed conflict and injustice through the lens of class struggle, the Americans asserted, and his empathy for human suffering prevented him from understanding the justice system and political repression in a rational way. It made sense, of course; as a priest, he probably listened to parishioners who had family members in the prison system. The embassy officers saw this in action. When one of them visited Tin at his office to discuss Tin's report, a teenaged girl arrived at his door seeking the whereabouts of a relative who was in prison. She had a note she wanted to deliver to him, but police had given her conflicting information about where he was. Tin stopped the meeting to listen to the young girl, and he promised her he would see to it that her relative received the letter. Tin's empathy clouded his view of the prison situation, and while it perhaps was a useful trait for a priest, it prevented him from objectively reporting prison statistics, the embassy officers asserted. The embassy reps did not believe there was enough evidence to say that Tin was a communist agent, but his prison report, along with his writings in *Doi Dien* and other publications, damaged government credibility, especially in the minds of those in Vietnam and in the world who already questioned the legitimacy of the Thieu government and of South Vietnam's nationhood.[39]

---

[38] U.S. Department of State Airgram-296, from: American Embassy Saigon, Subject: Father Chan Tin's View of "Political Prisoners": A Case Study of Militancy Overriding Objectivity, Dec. 26, 1973, p. 7. Vietnam Archive, Texas Tech University.

[39] U.S. Department of State Airgram-296, from: American Embassy Saigon, Subject: Father Chan Tin's View of "Political Prisoners": A Case Study of Militancy Overriding Objectivity, Dec. 26, 1973, p. 8. Vietnam Archive, Texas Tech University.

In the spring of 1973, it appeared that Pope Paul VI was on Chan Tin's side. On April 9, Nguyen Van Thieu met with the pontiff, and during the course of their meeting, the Pope asked Thieu to grant clemency to political prisoners. Thieu responded that there were no political prisoners in South Vietnam. Pope Paul had evidence to the contrary, courtesy of Chan Tin. He had organized a group of mothers, wives, and sisters of political prisoners, along with leaders of various activist groups in South Vietnam, including the Young Catholic Workers, to write letters to the pope offering their accounts of what they believed to be political repression in South Vietnam.[40]

Chan Tin's report from June 1973 was entitled "Political Prisoners in South Vietnam after the Signing of the Paris Agreement." In the report, Tin alleged that there were more than 200,000 political prisoners in South Vietnam and that police and prison guards mistreated them. The US Embassy identified political prisoners as "persons who have been imprisoned solely for their opposition to the government." Tin's definition was much broader, including all inmates held for political reasons. Tin included Viet Cong sympathizers, draft dodgers, and those guilty of destruction of property if such destruction was for political reasons. Analysts from the US General Accounting Office accused Tin of presenting arbitrary numbers, and Tin admitted that they were not exact. However, he argued that the number of political prisoners was not important. What was important was that political prisoners existed in South Vietnam at all, and as long as they did, there would not be peace. The GAO study found that some prisons were overcrowded and lacked adequate food.[41]

The Indochina Resource Center, a watchdog organization founded in 1971 to publicize information about the Vietnam War, particularly political repression and human rights abuses, published biographies of political prisoners as well as dissidents whose whereabouts were unknown. Among them in 1972 were student leaders Huynh Tan Mam and Nguyen Huu Thai. Mam, president of the General Association of Saigon Students, was an outspoken critic of the Saigon government and of U.S. intervention in Vietnam. As he was leaving a meeting with Saigon University

---

[40] "After the Signing of the Paris Agreements: Documents on South Vietnam's Political Prisoners," Vietnam Resource Center/Thoi Bao Ga, Cambridge, MA, June 1973, pp. 8–16. Vietnam Archive, Texas Tech University.

[41] United States General Accounting Office, Draft of Report to the Congress of the United States: Phaseout of U.S. Assistance to South Vietnam in Support of Police Organizations, Law Enforcement, and Public Safety Related Programs, February 1975, Vietnam Archive, Texas Tech University.

medical students one morning in May 1972, four plain clothes officers stopped Mam as he was about to ride away on a motorbike, handcuffed him, and pushed him into a military police jeep. Police took him to the National Police Headquarters in Saigon, where he was interrogated and allegedly tortured. Officers later transferred him to Chi Hoa prison.[42]

Nguyen Huu Thai was an ARVN captain at the time of his arrest in October 1972. The former architecture student at Saigon University and past president of the Saigon Student Union had known US Embassy officers who had sought information about student political attitudes in the mid-1960s. Authorities knew Thai was antiwar; he had written anti-war articles for Saigon newspapers while he was a student, and his reputation as a peace activist followed him even into the army. Military police arrested him in Saigon and questioned him about his antiwar activities and his associations with five friends from his student days who had recently been released from Con Son prison. One of those former prisoners had been charged with the murder of a Saigon politician. Sometime after the arrest, Thai disappeared from Saigon.[43]

In July 1973, staff of the Indochina Resource Center interviewed Chan Tin about the political prisoners issue. Tin declared that investigating the state prisons was not enough. Chi Hoa was Saigon's official prison, but police also held prisoners at police headquarters and interrogation centers. There were eleven police interrogation centers in Saigon alone, and it was unknown how many detainees were held there before being transferred. Accounting for these places was how Tin arrived at 200,000. At the time of the interview, there were only twenty members of the Committee because many of them had been imprisoned or went into hiding to avoid the police. Tin believed the reason he was not in jail was because of a Vietnamese respect for religion that made the government afraid to imprison him. The government was especially worried about the Catholic response because Catholics had been reliable friends of the state. Tin also believed his international support also protected him from jail. That would not have been in the government's interest.[44] Also in 1973, Jerry Tinker

---

[42] "Political Prisoners in South Vietnam," Amnesty International Publications, 1973, p. 33. Box 09, Folder 08, Douglas Pike Collection: Unit 11 – Monographs, The Vietnam Center and Archive, Texas Tech University.

[43] "Political Prisoners in South Vietnam," Amnesty International Publications, 1973, p. 34. Box 09, Folder 08, Douglas Pike Collection: Unit 11 – Monographs, The Vietnam Center and Archive, Texas Tech University.

[44] "Political Prisoners in South Viet Nam: Interview with Chan Tin," Indochina Resource Center, July 1973, Vietnam Archive, Texas Tech University.

from the office of Senator Edward Kennedy visited with Chan Tin to learn more about the fate of political prisoners in Saigon since the signing of the Paris agreement.[45]

New Jersey Representative Peter H. B. Frelinghuysen, a member of the House Committee on Foreign Affairs, led a special Congressional mission to South Vietnam in February 1974. During the visit, Frelinghuysen met with President Thieu and Vietnamese parliamentarians, visited the Mekong Delta, and met with ARVN personnel. Frelinghuysen came away from the trip convinced that the issue of political prisoners was the most damaging to Thieu's international reputation. The emphasis on political prisoners had been on the rise since the signing of the Paris peace agreement. Although he believed that much of the attention stemmed from communist efforts, he had met noncommunists who had sincere human rights concerns about political repression. That the humanitarian activists did not also condemn the human rights abuses of the Hanoi government or the NLF bothered Frelinghuysen, but international opinion also mostly ignored communist human rights abuses.[46]

Frelinghuysen's report specifically noted Chan Tin as a source of the allegations who, because of his status as a Catholic priest, enjoyed a certain legitimacy. Americans often pointed out that Chan Tin had remained free despite his repeated criticisms of the government, as if to illustrate the state's tolerance of free speech. Since June 1973, Tin had asserted that South Vietnam's prisons held more than 200,000 political dissidents. American and government reports attempted to refute Tin's statistics, arguing that South Vietnam's prisons did not have the capacity to keep that many inmates and that Tin did not make clear how he defined "political prisoner." Did he include ARVN deserters? People convicted of communist sympathy? The US Embassy flatly denied Tin's allegations. Ambassador Graham Martin defined political prisoner as "those imprisoned anywhere only because they are opposed by the regime which governs them." The report pointed out that noncommunist dissidents such as Chan Tin were free to live their lives and criticize the government. Only when speech turned to terrorism – "the throwing of a grenade or bomb" – did opposition become a crime. The report also

[45] May 1973, Newsletter, International Committee to Free South Vietnamese Political Prisoners from Detention, Torture and Death, Minneapolis, MN, p. 8. Vietnam Archive, Texas Tech University.
[46] "Vietnam – A Changing Crucible: Report of a Study Mission to South Vietnam," Washington, DC: U.S. Government Printing Office, May 1974, pp. 14–15.

asserted that because South Vietnam was in a state of war, the government had the right to suspend certain civil liberties, as the United States had done in past wartimes.[47]

The US Embassy paid much lip service to the notion that the Thieu government was trying to operate according to democratic principles. Embassy publications pointed to the political opposition as proof that Saigon was a politically open society. Although not "a model of American-style democracy," South Vietnamese people enjoyed more political freedom than most other countries in the developing world, embassy officers argued. Voters had elected opposition representatives to the National Assembly, and they were allowed to take their seats. Outspoken critics such as Chan Tin remained free. South Vietnam's politically active press included opposition newspapers and magazines, and the foreign press had reasonable access to government officials and their opponents. An embassy publication in 1974 highlighted a comment from a Polish member of the International Commission of Control and Supervision as vindication of the US point of view: "While South Vietnam has been open to journalists from all over the world, North Vietnam has granted visas chiefly to pro-Communist members of the press. Therefore, the news coverage has been distorted."[48] The quote illustrated a legitimate difference between the two regimes, but in the same publication, embassy officers appeared surprisingly naive by contrast. In response to the critique that the South Vietnamese government is not popular with the public, the fact sheet states that South Vietnam has an armed citizenry of 500,000 regular army men, half a million full-time local militiamen, and one million members of a people's self-defense force, which includes women, children, and older people. If the regime was unpopular, it would not "dare pass out so many guns which could easily be turned against it."[49]

Trying to determine whether Americans in Vietnam were naive or desperate is one of the most frustrating aspects of analyzing the Vietnam War. Americans were unwilling to take risks on politically minded Vietnamese they did not hand select, nor were they willing to risk criticizing publicly the leader they anointed. Even in the early seventies, as US troops came home and American citizens turned their attention away from

[47] Ibid.
[48] Fact sheet, Embassy of the Republic of Viet-Nam Information Office, Washington, D.C. May 31, 1974, p. 3. Folder 13, Box 16, Douglas Pike Collection: Unit 06 – Democratic Republic of Vietnam, The Vietnam Center and Archive, Texas Tech University.
[49] Ibid.

Vietnam, diplomats and politicians continued to emphasize the proto-
democratic nature of South Vietnam without working to facilitate the
further development of democratic political practices. Despite the admon-
itions of South Vietnamese intellectuals such as former Ambassador to the
United States Vu Van Thai, Americans failed to take a clear-eyed
approach to the political war in Vietnam and it as the seminal battle of
the war. In US publications such as *Foreign Affairs* and RAND studies,
Thai had proffered scenarios in which the US military and political efforts
in Vietnam could stabilize the government and offer a regional model for
other Southeast Asian nations. His suggestions assumed a certain amount
of political risk, and he acknowledged that a stable Saigon political
system might only be temporary. But the US-led efforts at maintaining
the status quo would not hold, either, he argued.

NGO CONG DUC: POLITICIAN, JOURNALIST, CATHOLIC, ANTI-THIEU

Ngo Cong Duc spent most afternoons at Givral's café in downtown
Saigon, drinking coffee and trading leads with other journalists and
rumors with other politicians. He himself was both a newsman and a
public servant, and in both capacities, he was on the wrong side of
Nguyen Van Thieu. The thirty-five-year-old Catholic was a lower house
deputy in South Vietnam's National Assembly and editor of the popular
Tin Sang (*Morning News*) newspaper. In neither position had he kept his
dissatisfaction with the government quiet. In response, the government
labeled him "pro-communist" and threw him in jail.[50] When Duc worked
in his newsroom, he kept a pistol within reach on his desk.[51] Hanging on
a wall in his office was a poster he had received from Representative
Augustus Hawkins of California. It compared the bombs dropped on
Vietnam by American planes to the smaller amount of bullets fired by
the communists. Its text read, "The bloodbath is now."[52] While Chan Tin
was an example of a Catholic clergyman on the frontlines of the anti-
Thieu movement, Ngo Cong Duc was a Catholic layman who challenged
the conventional wisdom that Vietnamese Catholics formed a pro-

[50] Peter Osnos, "Defeated Deputy Charges Rigging," *New York Times*, Aug. 30, 1971, Vietnam Archive, Texas Tech University.
[51] George Wald, "The South Vietnamese Catholics," *New York Times*, Jan. 11, 1972, http://jfk.hood.edu/Collection/White%20Materials/Indochina/Indochina%200353.pdf.
[52] A. J. Langguth, "1964: Exhilaration 1968: Frustration 1970: Hopelessness," *The New York Times Magazine*, Oct. 4, 1970, p. 27.

government monolith. NLF leader Truong Nhu Tang understood Duc to be a "true neutralist," someone who was not part of the NLF but who opposed the Thieu government. Other Catholics in this category included Fr. Tran Huu Thanh, leader of the People's Movement Against Corruption, and they worked with nationalist Buddhist bonzes such as Thich Tri Quang and Thich Thien Minh. George McGovern had invited Duc to come to the United States on an antiwar speaking tour in 1972 during the US presidential campaign.[53]

Ngo Cong Duc was a wealthy landowner from the Mekong Delta who had been elected to the National Assembly from Vinh Binh province after campaigning on an anti-Viet Cong platform. He was close with southern-born politicians and generals, including Duong Van Minh.[54] His uncle was Nguyen Van Binh, the Archbishop of Saigon, and Duc had been an assemblyman for four years. He got in trouble with the Thieu government after *Tin Sang* published articles describing the arrests and torture of members of the South Vietnamese Student Association, and also published editorials demanding a complete withdrawal of Americans from Vietnam. Duc asserted that from 1970 to 1972, government agents shut down publication of his newspaper nearly 300times. Attackers bombed Duc's house in October 1970. Unknown assailants firebombed his office twice before burning it down in March 1971. In 1971, he was jailed for five days, and then he went into exile, fleeing to France.[55]

About a year before the 1971 election, Thieu, through his press secretary, issued a warning to his opponents that they tone down their hostility or face legal action for treason. It was a general warning, but it was aimed at Duc, who had advocated for an immediate end to the war, the removal of all foreign intervention, and the establishment of a provisional government. The prosecution of another former lawmaker, Tran Ngoc Chau, led Thieu to limit his chasing of Duc, though. Chau was sentenced to ten years of hard labor for allegedly collaborating with communists, but the Chau case had resulted in negative publicity for Thieu, including frustration in the US Embassy. Americans were trying to democratize South Vietnam

[53] Truong Nhu Tang, *A Viet Cong Memoir: An Inside Account of the Vietnam War and Its Aftermath* (New York: Vintage Books, 1985), p. 216.

[54] "The Way to End the War: The Statement of Ngo Cong Duc," Nov. 5, 1970, *The New York Review of Books*, www.nybooks.com/articles/1970/11/05/the-way-to-end-the-war-the-statement-of-ngo-cong-d.

[55] "After the Signing of the Paris Agreements: Documents on South Vietnam's Political Prisoners," Vietnam Resource Center/Thoi Bao Ga, Cambridge, MA, June 1973, Vietnam Archive, Texas Tech University.

and prove to the world that it was happening. The opposition that Duc led in the Assembly called itself the New Society Bloc, and the members were mostly young legislators who were antiwar, anti-Thieu, and pro-Duong Van Minh. Duc visited Pope Paul VI on a recent visit to Rome. Duc had been represented Vinh Binh in the National Assembly since 1967, and in 1965, he had served in the province's Popular Forces. In his spare time, he headed the local table tennis and soccer associations.[56]

During the summer campaign season leading up to the 1971 election, members of the national elections committee told Duc he would not be allowed to run for a second term because he was too sympathetic to the communists. The government reserved the right to ban from candidacy draft dodgers, military deserters, communist sympathizers, and others the government considered unfit to serve. Duc was a test of how much restraint Thieu could show in order to prove he is open to some degree of political freedom.[57] Duc was popular in his home province of Vinh Binh, and when he lost reelection in 1971, he, and some American observers, argued that government agents had rigged the election. Duc brought poll watchers from Saigon to identify irregularities, but he argued that many of them had not been allowed to take their positions at the polls. He argued that government agents turned voters away from the polls, telling them that someone had already voted on their behalf. He said in other cases, government agents warned voters that if they cast their ballots for Duc, they would be accused of being communists and persecuted accordingly. In the fall of 1970, Duc had gone to Paris and held a press conference during which he offered a peace plan that, to Thieu, sounded like the communist plan. It was illegal, Thieu insisted, and Duc belonged in jail. Duc did go to jail, but not for the Paris press conference, at least not officially. He served time for punching a pro-government assemblyman in the nose during the campaign; the assemblyman had spit in his face first.[58]

Ngo Cong Duc was released from prison after ninety-one legislators from the lower house, including some who were pro-government, issued a statement demanding his release. The charge was attempted murder of the man he had punched in the nose. After Duc was freed, he flew back to Saigon on a helicopter Nguyen Cao Ky had sent for him, a move some

[56] Peter A. Jay, " War Critic Gets Thieu Ultimatum," *Washington Post*, Sep. 22, 1970, Vietnam Archive, Texas Tech University.
[57] Peter A. Jay, "Top Critic of Thieu Refused Candidacy," *Washington Post*, July 18, 1971, Vietnam Archive, Texas Tech University.
[58] Peter Osnos, "Defeated Deputy Charges Rigging," *New York Times*, Aug. 30, 1971, Vietnam Archive, Texas Tech University.

observers saw as an example of Ky's general challenge to Thieu. Some of Duc's friends apparently called him "the Fighting Cock" because of Tin Sang's unruly reputation and because he led the eighteen opposition deputies in the 133-member lower house of the Assembly. The incident that landed him in prison involved the president of the Vinh Binh provincial council, Dr. Pham Huu Gia. By Duc's account, they got into a fight at a Sunday evening dinner because Gia, who supported the Thieu government, threatened to take Duc's seat in the Assembly. Duc called Gia his "political enemy," and then Gia spat beer in his face. Duc punched him in the nose and chest, and the next day, police arrested Duc at his house.[59]

In February 1975, Duc traveled to Boston at the invitation of the American Friends Service Committee. He was thirty-nine years old at the time. Insurgents had killed his father, a district chief in Vinh Binh province, in 1954. As a legislator, he had been chairman of the anti-corruption and information committees of the lower house of the National Assembly. He was also the chairman of South Vietnam's Association of Newspaper Editors. He had been a political exile in Europe since 1972, after the election, which he lost. Time magazine had determined that if Duc, a popular candidate, lost reelection, it would call the entire 1972 election into question. In addition to being popular, he was one of the most outspoken anti-Thieu legislators in the Assembly. The campaign had gotten ugly – at one point, the pro-government candidate spit in the incumbent's face, and so Duc punched him and was thrown in jail for attempted murder. Duc accused the government of threatening to classify his districts as Communist, which would subject them to the removal of residents and demolition according to the pacification process. In early 1975, Duc was in the United States, lobbying Washington politicians to end the war, and the American Friends invited him to Boston to speak. Duc told them he was part of the "third force" – political activists who supported neither the Saigon government nor the PRG. He and like-minded people wanted reconciliation and neutrality. He opposed continued US aid to South Vietnam because he said democracy was only getting worse: "now they beat Congressmen, they beat Catholic priests," he said of the government. Not even Catholics have reason to be loyal anymore, he asserted.[60]

[59] Craig R. Whitney, "Opposition Deputy, Jailed in Delta, Now Back in Saigon," *New York Times*, June 6, 1971, Vietnam Archive, Texas Tech University.
[60] Seth M. Kupferberg, "Third Force Comes to Boston," *The Harvard Crimson*, Feb. 5, 1975, www.thecrimson.com/article/1975/2/5/third-force-comes-to-boston-pbnbgo.

In his final letter to President Richard Nixon as US Ambassador to South Vietnam, Ellsworth Bunker described the country's political climate and President Thieu's approach to his opposition. Bunker wrote that despite the presence of anti-Thieu activists, the president was in a good position because the "non-Communist opposition has been unable to find a formula for discrediting his leadership without exposing the country to a Communist takeover." The opposition had not identified a viable noncommunist alternative to Thieu, so their only choices were either stick with Thieu or risk a communist victory. It did not help the opposition that Thieu had recently cracked down on freedom of the press and the establishment of political parties, thereby restricting political activism. Infighting among the noncommunist opposition inadvertently strengthened Thieu's position, Bunker noted, but the communists could use that division to attract some anti-Thieu elements to their side. The letter's tone was one of cautious optimism.[61]

What it lacked was any condemnation of Thieu's antidemocratic behavior. This was consistent with US Embassy and policymaker approaches to the Thieu government and South Vietnam's political dynamism. Even in 1973, Americans were more comfortable with one man who was staunchly anticommunist and seemingly willing to remain close to the United States than with popular political movements that were independent and noncommunist. Americans' acceptance of Thieu's stifling of democratic processes was a typical characteristic of US nation-building efforts. Lost in this approach were opportunities to cultivate a stable, modern, democratic political structure in South Vietnam.

While American policymakers and political advisors excused Thieu's abuse of civil liberties, others in the United States established organizations committed to exposing the undemocratic nature of the Thieu government, particularly the plight of political prisoners. In the early 1970s in Cambridge, Massachusetts, a group of Vietnamese students published a monthly newsletter called *Thoi Bao Ga* that featured articles about political repression and the war's impact on South Vietnamese citizens. Ngo Vinh Long, a Vietnamese national from the Mekong Delta who graduated from Harvard in 1968 and continued on there for his Ph.D., was the founder of the newsletter and an outspoken critic of the Vietnam War. The October 1970 issue of *Thoi Bao Ga* published two pieces that drove home the central realities of the political situation in South Vietnam. One was a letter from the Saigon Student Association describing police abuse of students

---

[61] Telegram 96: May 5, 1973, *The Bunker Papers: Reports to the President from Vietnam, 1967–1973, Volume 3* (Berkeley: University of California Press, 1990), p. 859.

attending the fourth annual National Student Congress. The main topic of discussion at the meeting was the military training program that university students were required to complete. Students leaving the conference reported police using tear gas and clubbing students, including Huynh Tan Mam, a student leader who described his time in prison in Chan Tin's *Doi Dien*. The students ended their letter with rhetoric that would have resonated with Americans: "We are living in a democratic country with our freedoms guaranteed by the Constitution."[62] The other letter was from the Committee of Women's Action for the Right to Live on behalf of mothers whose children were serving time in South Vietnamese prisons for political reasons. Third force leader Ngo Ban Thanh had founded the organization, and she was one of the signers of the letter. The mothers wrote that police had arrested their children because they had advocated peace, and they had not been able to visit or contact their children.[63] The Indochina Resource Center also published articles in its newsletter about South Vietnam's political situation and focused on political repression. Such testimonies confirmed the critique of US intervention in Vietnam that US policy was not securing freedom for South Vietnamese citizens.

Political prisoners such as eighteen-year-old Nguyen Van Dan told their stories to watchdogs like the Indochina Resource Center and reached an international audience through their publications. Growing up in a working-class family in Saigon, Dan saw at a young age the corrupt practices of government authorities. Police officers knocked on doors demanding bribes in exchange for protection. He watched petty civil employees humiliate his father when they demanded money in exchange for signing government paperwork. As Dan got older, he joined student political movements, and in September 1972, he was arrested and sent to Chi Hoa prison.[64] In the same year, students wrote to UN Secretary-General Kurt Waldheim drawing attention to the Thieu government's oppressive tactics, including the imprisonment and torture of student activists such as Huynh Tan Mam.[65] The government's blatant

[62] "Open Letter to All Peace and Justice Loving Individuals and Organizations in the World," Saigon Student Union, *Thoi Bao Ga*, Oct. 1970, 7. Folder 05, Box 17, Douglas Pike Collection: Unit 06 – Democratic Republic of Vietnam, Vietnam Archive.
[63] "Voices of the Third Force," Indochina Resource Center, Nov. 6, 1972, p. 9. Vietnam Archive, Texas Tech University.
[64] Ibid., p. 3.
[65] "A Cry of Alarm: New Revelations on Repression and Deportation in South Vietnam," 1972, Committee to Reform the Prison System in South Vietnam, Vietnam Archive, Texas Tech University.

trampling upon of civil liberties in the name of order made it difficult for the Americans or anyone else to prove that South Vietnam was making inroads toward democracy.

Fr. Tin continued his efforts to bring attention to political prisoners in South Vietnam, and it became a significant issue in the years after most US troops left the country. Cao Thi Que Huong, the young widow who had sought Tin's help as she tried to secure her husband's release from prison before he died there, became one of the casualties. She had been working with Tin's Committee to Reform the Prison System when police arrested her in January 1973. Since then, Huong's whereabouts had been unknown. Another member of Fr. Tin's flock, Doan Khac Xuyen, also landed in prison for his activism. Xuyen was a student at the University of Saigon and a member of Young Catholic Workers, which Tin had founded. Police arrested Xuyen at the organization's headquarters in May 1972 and remained in prison for more than a year.[66] These were not the Catholics of the Diem era. They were tired of war, and they had the language of liberation theology to articulate their understanding of Catholic teachings as weapons in a political war. Fr. Tin continued to speak out against what he believed to be the injustice of Thieu's targeting of his opponents for arrest. Tin did not speak for all Catholics in South Vietnam, but through his journal, his connections with Ngo Ba Thanh and other outspoken anti-government activists, and his ability to reach Americans, he earned a reputation not as a holy man but as a dissident.

---

[66] "South Vietnamese Political Prisoners: An Action Guideline," June 25, 1973. Box 03, Folder 24, Social Movements Collection, The Vietnam Center and Archive, Texas Tech University.

8

Saigon in the Seventies

In the final weeks of 1974, Catholics and journalists in Saigon caused President Thieu to call in his riot police again. The alliance of church and press stemmed from a common desire to expose alleged corruption of Thieu and his family. Several Saigon newspapers had published Father Tran Huu Thanh's accusations of corruption against the president, including suppression of the press and rules making it difficult to form political parties so as to enshrine a one-party system and prevent the opposition from wresting control from Thieu. Thieu had the publishers of those papers arrested and placed on trial. Anti-government activists had planned a massive demonstration to take place on the first day of the trial, and when word of the protest reach Thieu, he warned citizens that 20,000 officers were preparing to put a damper on the march. When police and anti-Thieu protesters had clashed back in October, Fr. Thanh and some other Catholics gathered at Tan Sa Chau Church on the edge of Saigon and composed a statement in which they demanded that the president "return power to the people so that they can refashion the life of the country and reconstruct the independence of the nation." The two groups in trouble, Fr. Thanh's People's Anti-Corruption Movement and the Committee of Struggle for Freedom of the Press and Publications, did not want to tear down the Saigon government. They simply wanted Thieu gone. Fr. Thanh took abuse from all sides. Members of the Provisional Revolutionary Government called him an "American stooge." Thieu accused him of having the

support of both communists and colonialists.[1] In the midst of the chaos
and suspicion that marked Saigon in the seventies, it was difficult for
Fr. Thanh to prove that he was an anti-government, anticommunist,
anti-colonial nationalist.

Some mornings in the years when the US military began its slow retreat
from South Vietnam, a sort of quiet seemed to have settled on Saigon.
During that time, what Americans called Vietnamization, the city sometimes exuded a mellow vibe that contrasted sharply with the boisterous
energy of Saigon in the sixties. There was a sadness to the tranquility; bar
girls killed time in once crowded cafes as they watched their client base
dwindle. It got to where they were the ones offering to buy the first round
with the hope that a conversation might lead to love and a ticket out of
Vietnam. Even then, it was as though they knew that Southerners who
might be perceived to have collaborated with the Americans, such as the
women who sold "Saigon tea" and more to US servicemen in a trade that
allegedly had made them richer than some government officials, were on
the losing side. Others welcomed the decline of Saigon's vice trade and
saw the Vietnamization of the city as a return to what was right.[2] Saigon
in the seventies was experiencing what would turn out to be the calm
before the last vicious storm of the Vietnam War. In March 1972, as US
troops gradually left Vietnam due to President Richard Nixon's "Vietnamization" plan, the mayor of Saigon announced that all "hostess bars"
catering to Americans must move out of downtown Saigon. The mayor
ordered the clubs to the city's ninth precinct, across the Saigon River. The
only way to get there was by boat.[3]

In other ways, the spirit of the sixties lived on into the seventies, carried
by anti-government and peace activists emboldened by the Paris peace
talks. Ngo Ba Thanh's dramatic hunger strike and connections between
Vietnamese activists and international observers ensured that political
activism in Saigon remained on the minds of US Embassy officers and
State Department officials even as American military forces left the country. Fighting and terrorism continued in the provinces, bridging the
decades. Neither of the Vietnamese sides in the conflict could agree on

---

[1] Nayan Chanda, "Thieu Accepts the Challenge," *Far Eastern Economic Review*, Dec. 6,
  1974. Box 30, Folder 11, Douglas Pike Collection: Unit 01 – Assessment and Strategy, The
  Vietnam Center and Archive, Texas Tech University.
[2] Wesley Pruden, Jr., "Saigon Becomes Vietnamese," *The National Observer*, Feb. 9, 1970.
  NARA RG59, Box 1873, DEF 1-1-70, Folder 2.
[3] "Closing Time," *Time*, March 20, 1972, www.time.com/time/magazine/article/
  0,9171,942505,00.html.

the implementation of the Paris agreement, and political infighting within the International Commission of Control and Supervision between Eastern Bloc members and others limited the group's effectiveness in policing the cease-fire. Yet it was in the short period between the signing of the Paris Accords and the fall of Saigon that decisions about Vietnam's future were most fully in the hands of Vietnamese actors since the partition in 1954. Americans remained in South Vietnam, and Vietnam remained on the minds of US diplomats and policymakers, but absent the massive US military presence, the fate of Vietnam seemed finally to belong to the Vietnamese.

Although US troops had been moved out of Saigon and were departing the country by the start of the seventies, the more than 8,000 American civilian contractors and Defense Department employees still living and working in South Vietnam made some foreign correspondents and Vietnamese observers wonder if they were simply military advisors in civilian sheep's clothing. They were mostly men, although some women worked in Vietnam in the Defense Attache's Office long after most troops had left, and they haunted South Vietnamese military bases and the bars that had once catered to US soldiers. They raised the eyebrows and concerns of reporters and other observers because the Paris peace agreement prohibited US advisors, but it appeared as though the civilians in their casual, unmarked clothes could have been making informal conversation with Vietnamese military officers about strategy and tactics. Many of the US contractors had prior military experience, and although their purpose in Vietnam was to teach mechanical and electronic skills, rumors on the street in Saigon suggested that some of the contractors secretly maintained Vietnamese military aircraft and communications equipment.[4]

US State Department officials had been pressuring USOM and MACV since 1970 to continue moving Americans out of Saigon, especially the central city where they were most visible.[5] Yet the contractors did not want to leave. In addition to political pressure, South Vietnam's sluggish economy in the seventies required 1,000 American aircraft mechanics to be laid off. They were mad to have to leave "the tax-free world of good salaries, cheap booze, and Vietnamese girlfriends," and the bar girls, for

---

[4] Outgoing telegram, Department of State, April 1, 1973, Subject: American Presence in South Vietnam, NARA RG59, Box 1873-DEF 1-1-70, Folder 2.
[5] U.S. State Department memorandum, April 3, 1970, to the Under-Secretary, from William H. Sullivan, subject: American Presence in Vietnam – Action Memorandum, NARA RG59, Box 1873-DEF 1-1-70, Folder 2.

their part, would miss their money. They were the last connection to the days when thousands of American GIs swarmed Saigon and made the sex trade lucrative for Vietnamese women. A *Washington Post* reporter interviewed mechanics who said that the layoffs were shortsighted because Vietnamese mechanics needed additional training to be able to maintain their equipment. Some local mechanics failed to follow the aircraft maintenance and storage techniques the US contractors had taught them, one American said, and others sold hot parts and fuel on the black market. Some of the US mechanics condemned Congressional cuts to funding for South Vietnam, while others blamed Thieu for not fixing the economy and beating the communists. None were happy about returning to the United States. "The reason we came over here was to get away," one disgruntled, and recently laid off, US mechanic, complained.[6]

While American contractors fed their escapism in Saigon, the NLF made plans for taking the city. The NLF understood the importance of Saigon. In 1971, VC cadres in the Saigon area began making plans to launch a mass uprising in the capital city, believing it was key, more so than the villages, to the ultimate success of the communist movement. Saigon was a powerful cultural, political, and military symbol of South Vietnam, and with more than three million people concentrated in a fairly small area compared to two to three million rural dwellers spread throughout the Mekong Delta region, the political impact of a Saigon uprising would be greater. The VC speculated that the political engagement of Saigon's middle class would also be more significant given its location in the seat of the federal government, and so convincing this group to abandon their primarily neutral stance and join the communist front would constitute a major victory for the southern movement.[7] Such a victory could come through politics only, not another Tet Offensive–style military attack on the city. It would require a "hearts and minds" approach.

Though confident, the cadres in and around Saigon knew that gaining the support of the urban middle class was not a foregone conclusion. Pro-communist sympathies had never been the primary motivation of political unrest in the city. Opposition to the draft brought students into the streets, and austerity measures, including higher taxes, alienated small

[6] State Department telegram 239110, to all East Asian and Pacific Diplomatic Posts, Oct. 31, 1974, NARA RG 59 – Central Foreign Policy Files, National Archives Access to Archival Databases, Electronic Telegrams, 1974.

[7] VC Plan for Taking Over Saigon through a Large-Scale Mass Uprising, May 18, 1971, Folder 03, Box 16, Douglas Pike Collection: Unit 02 – Military Operations, The Vietnam Center and Archive, Texas Tech University (hereafter Vietnam Archive).

business owners and other members of the "petty bourgeoisie."[8] As frustration with President Nguyen Van Thieu spread to the political right, VC leadership in the cities, especially Saigon, instructed cadres to try and capitalize on anti-Thieu sentiment in order to control rightist groups that would not otherwise feel any connection to the communist cause. In order to do so, the VC would need to strengthen its leadership, build closer relationships with urban contacts, and convince the noncommunist anti-Thieu element to join the VC in demanding complete US withdrawal, not just troop withdrawal, from Vietnam.[9] To capture Saigon, the VC would have to appeal to groups that could be tough to reach.

SAIGON'S POLITICAL SCENE

On the political front, protests, hunger strikes, and general unrest marked Saigon and other cities and villages throughout South Vietnam. Ngo Ba Thanh commanded much of the US Embassy's attention in 1973 as she carried out a hunger strike to protest the Thieu government's imprisonment of political dissidents and its plan to turn over Thanh and other anti-government activists to the NLF. Thanh as well as former assemblyman Tran Ngoc Chau, lawyer and longtime political activist Nguyen Long, and student leader Huynh Tan Mam, as well as Thanh, were on Thieu's list for deportation to the communist side. She began her hunger strike in mid-April 1973, insisting that neither she nor her fellow activists were communists. They opposed the Thieu government and foreign involvement, but because they were not communists, they should be allowed to remain in Saigon.[10] The DRV national media caught wind of Thanh's hunger strike and used it as an opportunity to criticize the Saigon government and its holding and treatment of political prisoners.[11]

US Embassy officials monitored Thanh's situation closely, labeling her a "radical dissident." The conversation with government officials was that she would have the choice of either being turned over to the communists or given "freedom" if she wanted to remain under the jurisdiction

[8] Ibid.
[9] PRP C.C. Strategy for Political Struggle in Cities, Sep. 15, 1974, Folder 02, Box 34, Douglas Pike Collection: Unit 01 – Assessment and Strategy, Vietnam Archive.
[10] Telegram 08691 from AmEmbassy Saigon to Secretary of State, May 17, 1973. NARA RG 59 – Central Foreign Policy Files, National Archives Access to Archival Databases, Electronic Telegrams, 1973.
[11] Telegram 08466 from AmEmbassy Saigon to Secretary of State, May 14, 1973. NARA RG 59 – Central Foreign Policy Files, National Archives Access to Archival Databases, Electronic Telegrams, 1973.

of the South Vietnamese government. Saigon officials were unclear as to whether she would have to pledge allegiance to the Saigon government in order to receive freedom. The advantage of this route would be that she would avoid being branded a communist and not have to bear the hardship of traveling through the countryside to PLAF controlled areas. If choosing freedom meant that the Saigon government would not prosecute her further, should could continue various forms of anti-government activities while claiming that she clearly was not a communist since she did not choose to be released to the NLF. Would the government drop its charges against her? If government officials chose to turn her over to the NLF regardless of her choice, they risked major international outcry should something bad happen to Thanh given her poor health due to her hunger strike. US Embassy officials in conversation with Lt. Gen. Cao Hao Hon, chairman of the Interministerial Committee on Implementation of the Ceasefire emphasized that there was major international and US attention on Thanh's case. The attention was mainly supportive, and should something happen to her – should she die or suffer serious harm – that would cause much more damage to the government's reputation than detaining her further.[12]

Thanh's case had international appeal. She was an international citizen, and her activism on behalf of political prisoners spoke to global concerns about the war and the impact of US involvement in Vietnam. Born in Hanoi on September 25, 1931, Ngo Ba Thanh went with her father, Pham Van Huyen, to Paris in 1949. In 1950, she married South Vietnam's director of fisheries, but she also went on to earn several degrees, graduating from the University of Paris in 1957 and Columbia University in 1961, and receiving a Ph.D. from the University of Barcelona in 1962. Thanh returned to Saigon in 1963 and accepted a teaching position at the Saigon University of Law. Her articles in law journals and presentations at Vietnamese and international conferences earned her a high reputation in Vietnam and worldwide.[13]

As Thanh established her international reputation as a talented lawyer, she also embarked on what would be a long career as a political activist. She began participating in peace movements in Vietnam in 1963, and

[12] Telegram 10241 from AmEmbassy Saigon to Secretary of State, June 8, 1973. NARA RG 59 – Central Foreign Policy Files, National Archives Access to Archival Databases, Electronic Telegrams, 1973.
[13] Telegram 08980 from AmEmbassy Saigon to Secretary of State, May 23, 1973. NARA RG 59 – Central Foreign Policy Files, National Archives Access to Archival Databases, Electronic Telegrams, 1973.

police had arrested her multiple times since 1965. Around the time of her first arrest, South Vietnamese officials exiled her father and two other urban elite activists to North Vietnam. Pham Van Huyen eventually made his way to Paris, where he took up residence. In June 1966, she was arrested at a demonstration at Saigon University and remained in prison until 1968. From 1968 until her next arrest in 1971, she participated in various organizations of noncommunist leftist Saigon intellectuals. As part of this, she founded the Women's Movement for the Right to Live in 1970. Student unrest at the start of the decade was related in part to increased draft calls, and Thanh became closely involved with the Saigon Student Union and its president, Huynh Tan Mam, who was imprisoned in 1971. Thanh was also closely aligned with another lawyer, Nguyen Long, who was arrested multiple times, again in 1972.[14]

US Embassy officers who got to know Thanh over the years questioned the popularity of her political organizations. Her Women's Right to Live organization never attracted more than a few dozen members, and she failed to generate enough interest to establish chapters in the provinces. Yet foreign correspondents and activists loved her and sought her out for interviews and photo ops whenever they could. Thanh corresponded with foreign women's organizations and kept friendships with those she had met in the United States and Europe while in school. In April 1974, Thanh was elected the first woman member of the International Commission of Jurists. It was headquartered in Geneva and described itself as an "international nonpolitical organization of lawyers pledged to uphold the rule of law and human rights."[15] The relationships between elite activists across borders sustained Thanh's political work despite indifference from average Vietnamese citizens.[16]

A series of events led to Thanh's 1971 arrest and imprisonment without trial, beginning with a skirmish with a judge in Gia Dinh province. During a trial to determine occupancy rights in a Buddhist pagoda, Thanh argued with the judge and was arrested for contempt of court. She was released on bail about six weeks later, and charges eventually were dropped. Thanh was not free for long, though. On September 18, 1971,

[14] Ibid.
[15] Telegram 079735 from Secretary of State to AmEmbassy Saigon, April 19, 1974. NARA RG 59 – Central Foreign Policy Files, National Archives Access to Archival Databases, Electronic Telegrams, 1974.
[16] Telegram 08980 from AmEmbassy Saigon to Secretary of State, May 23, 1973. NARA RG 59 – Central Foreign Policy Files, National Archives Access to Archival Databases, Electronic Telegrams, 1973.

she was arrested for protesting in front of the lower house of the Assembly and remained in prison without a trial. She was brought before a military court only once, in March of 1972, but she was ill from asthma at that time, so the court postponed her hearing until her health improved. Thanh remained at Chi Hoa prison until December of 1972, when prison officials moved her to the prison hospital at Bien Hoa. US Embassy personnel admitted that her pretrial detention was much longer than the one-month limit allowed in military court cases. When embassy officials asked Chief Justice Tran Van Linh about it, he replied that a court committee was reviewing Thanh's case, and until the committee offers a recommendation, there was nothing he could do about it.[17]

Thanh went on a hunger strike on April 10, 1973, in protest against Thieu's statements made during a trip to the United States and Europe that there were no political prisoners in South Vietnam. On April 30, she added a thirst strike. As a result, she suffered from severe malnutrition, severe dehydration, and collapsed veins, and a US Embassy physician warned that a patient in her condition could weaken mortally with little warning. Journalists from Agence France Presse began reporting on her story, drawing international attention and making it a regular topic of conversation at South Vietnam government press briefings. *Washington Post* correspondent Thomas Lippman had been following Thanh's case, and he told embassy officers that political prisoners was the topic that the Saigon government was most sensitive about. Among his fellow foreign correspondents, those who had recently gotten in trouble with the government had written stories critical of the government's political repression and treatment of political prisoners.[18] Official responses illustrated the lack of a coordinated government position on Thanh's case. In one day alone, May 18, 1973, a government spokesman said she would be turned over to the communists, a general told embassy officers that Thieu had not yet decided what he would do with her, and a Ministry of the Interior official said her case was being debated. Even if the miscommunication was an anomaly, it confirmed opponents' accusations that the government was incompetent or worse.[19]

---

[17] Ibid.

[18] Telegram 09750 from AmEmbassy Saigon to Secretary of State, June 1, 1973. NARA RG 59 – Central Foreign Policy Files, National Archives Access to Archival Databases, Electronic Telegrams, 1973.

[19] Telegram 08980 from AmEmbassy Saigon to Secretary of State, May 23, 1973. NARA RG 59 – Central Foreign Policy Files, National Archives Access to Archival Databases, Electronic Telegrams, 1973.

An invitation to teach at Columbia University compounded the international interest in Thanh's case. In June 1973, Thanh had an offer from Columbia University's dean of the law school to teach law as a visiting scholar in the upcoming academic year. US Embassy officials argued that allowing her to leave the country to take the position, which she was willing to do even without the promise of being allowed back in to Vietnam, would be in the best interest of the Saigon government. The United States would help expedite the process, this route would avoid getting the PRG involved, and it would end the Ngo Ba Thanh saga that had been a distraction in Saigon.[20] Thanh had fans at other US universities, too. Nearly 1,000 Yale undergraduates and seventy-five faculty members had signed a petition asking that Yale confer an honorary degree on her and that she be allowed to travel to the United States to receive the degree. Yale administrators denied the requests.[21]

On September 21, 1973, Ngo Ba Thanh was released from prison after two years in confinement. A Saigon government liaison told US Embassy officers that the government likely would not follow through on the threat to turn her over to the Communists or ban her from leaving the country. Since her release, Thanh had entertained journalists and supporters at her Saigon home, and she continued to speak out against the government for its political repression and imprisonment of political dissidents.[22] She was part of a group of about seventy signers, including Father Chan Tin and other anti-government activists, of a petition demanding that "both South Vietnamese parties" – the government and the NLF – implement a ceasefire, protect civil liberties, and free third force dissidents imprisoned and send them to whatever place or side they chose. They also requested the immediate formation of a national council of reconciliation. Organizers sent the petition to the UN Secretary-General and representatives from the countries that had participated in the Paris international conference on Vietnam. The petition was also mimeographed and handed out throughout Saigon. It had made the news, but as far as the embassy knew, no

---

[20] Telegram 122699 from Secretary of State to AmEmbassy Saigon, June 22, 1973. NARA RG 59 – Central Foreign Policy Files, National Archives Access to Archival Databases, Electronic Telegrams, 1973.

[21] Telegram 090708 from Secretary of State to AmEmbassy Saigon, May 11, 1973. NARA RG 59 – Central Foreign Policy Files, National Archives Access to Archival Databases, Electronic Telegrams, 1973.

[22] Telegram 17097 from AmEmbassy Saigon to Secretary of State, Sep. 27, 1973. NARA RG 59 – Central Foreign Policy Files, National Archives Access to Archival Databases, Electronic Telegrams, 1973.

papers had published its full text. Saigon national radio accused the
petitioners of being "country sellers" and "crooked politicians" who
saw an opportunity in the US–North Vietnam meeting to gain power
for themselves. They were "parasites" and "cowards," the broadcast
accused, with "no real strength."[23]

Throughout 1974, Thanh joined with activist monks to launch peri-
odic protests against government crack downs on civil liberties and to
raise awareness of the plight of political prisoners. Thanh, Chan Tin, and
Buddhist nuns and monks joined journalists in protesting government
limits on press freedoms. They also marched to demand the release of
student leader Huynh Tan Mam, who had been in prison for anti-
government activism since 1972.[24] Anti-government demonstrations in
Saigon, Da Nang, Nha Trang, and other cities, demanding the release of
political prisoners continued into 1974 and united Buddhists, Catholic
priests, and other activists, including Ngo Ba Thanh and Chan Tin.[25]

On March 12, police raided the Long An Pagoda, long known for
harboring draft evaders. Some 300 monks went to Chi Hoa prison, and
they staged a hunger strike to protest their captivity, arguing that they
were conscientious objectors and had refused military induction based
on their religious beliefs. Thanh and a group of anti-government activists garnered attention from international media, which was her goal. US
Ambassador Graham Martin observed that the Vietnamese press in
Saigon paid little attention to the monks' hunger strike or Thanh's visit
to the prison, but Thanh knew that international attention was what
she needed, and it worked. Martin lamented that American antiwar
activists had picked up Thanh's story and used it to undermine support
for the Saigon government.[26] A monk from An Quang Pagoda and
Thanh tried to bring reporters to see the inmates who were striking.

[23] Telegram 21381 from AmEmbassy Saigon to Secretary of State, Dec. 22, 1973. NARA
RG 59 – Central Foreign Policy Files, National Archives Access to Archival Databases,
Electronic Telegrams, 1973.
[24] Telegram 13178 from AmEmbassy Saigon to Secretary of State, Oct. 11, 1974. Telegram
03501 from AmEmbassy Saigon to Secretary of State, March 16, 1974. NARA RG 59 –
Central Foreign Policy Files, National Archives Access to Archival Databases, Electronic
Telegrams, 1974.
[25] Telegram 12658 from AmEmbassy Saigon to Secretary of State, Sep. 30, 1974. NARA
RG 59 – Central Foreign Policy Files, National Archives Access to Archival Databases,
Electronic Telegrams, 1974.
[26] Telegram 05580 from AmEmbassy Saigon to Secretary of State, April 29, 1974. NARA
RG 59 – Central Foreign Policy Files, National Archives Access to Archival Databases,
Electronic Telegrams, 1974.

The prison head received the journalists and served them tea as he confiscated their tapes and film, saying that he was on orders from the national police. He dismissed the strikers as "merely young men trying to avoid the draft" and said they hid food in their rooms and were in quite good health. Reporter Phil McCombs of the *Washington Post* was with Thanh, who called the strikers political prisoners and threatened to report them to the ICCS. McCombs had learned that Thanh was followed by police, who tried to thwart her efforts to meet with large groups of reporters. It was clear to McCombs that the Saigon government was very sensitive on the prisoner issue because US congressmen, who held South Vietnam's financial fate in their hands, were paying close attention.[27]

Thanh organized and led marches with Buddhists in Saigon through the end of 1974. Her message in the marches was always about releasing political prisoners and allowing for a third force government to be implemented.[28] In October 1974, police had proactively cordoned off certain streets in Saigon to prevent demonstrations. Groups of Buddhist nuns had been repeatedly marching throughout the city demanding civil liberties and the release of political prisoners. One of the areas that police barricaded was the block on which Thanh lived, as well as the block where the pagoda of some of the militant nuns was located. Authorities also cordoned off the area near the National Assembly. One group of anti-government priests and monks protested the "massive police presence in downtown Saigon," the blocking of pagodas, and the constant police surveillance of suspected anti-government activists.[29]

In some cases, fairly small demonstrations grew larger spontaneously, as was the case when a protest of about 200 journalists demanding freedom of the press grew to include several thousand protesters demanding political reforms, according to American journalist McCombs. Thanh was involved, as well as about a dozen senators and deputies. Police were usually able to keep demonstrations fairly under control, but they seemed unable to

[27] Telegram 049497 from Secretary of State to AmEmbassy Saigon, March 12, 1974. NARA RG 59 – Central Foreign Policy Files, National Archives Access to Archival Databases, Electronic Telegrams, 1974.
[28] Telegram 094144 from Secretary of State to AmEmbassy Saigon, May 7, 1974. NARA RG 59 – Central Foreign Policy Files, National Archives Access to Archival Databases, Electronic Telegrams, 1974.
[29] Telegram 237697 from Secretary of State to All East Asian and Pacific Diplomatic Posts, Oct. 29, 1974. NARA RG 59 – Central Foreign Policy Files, National Archives Access to Archival Databases, Electronic Telegrams, 1974.

prevent spectators from joining in the "new air of fervor and spontaneity" Police carried no weapons and were under orders to not use violence. After police gave up trying to control the march, protesters roamed freely in front of the national assembly. Some Buddhist nuns later clashed with police, and a CBS reporter, Haney Howell, was karate kicked by a plainclothes police officer while filming the demonstration, landing Howell in the hospital.[30]

It became common to see crowds protesting in Lam Son Square, right in front of the National Assembly. The usual suspects included anti-Thieu politicians, Vietnamese journalists demanding freedom of the press, Madame Thanh along with various groupings of students and Buddhist nuns, and some Catholics, especially those associated with the People's Anti-Corruption Movement. Reverend Tran Huu Thanh, in his late fifties, was both anticommunist, which made him popular with Catholic migrants who had fled North Vietnam in the fifties, and anti-Thieu. Father Thanh had a history of political activism in Vietnam. Born in central Vietnam, Father Thanh organized anticommunist students in Hanoi, where he was ordained a priest, against the Viet Minh in 1943, and he fled the city in 1945. Later, he worked in the Diem administration and taught in the national military academy.[31] That he enjoyed a sizable following illustrated a decline in Catholic support for the president. With American news organizations having opened offices all around the square, the activity will mainly be seen by Americans, while Vietnamese will not notice because state news organizations won't show it. They don't want to show police beating up Western journalists or assemblymen shouting for Thieu's resignation. The photographs that get printed in newspapers give the illusion of widespread disorder, but the unrest could actually be confined to a small town ballpark. At the nearby Hotel Continental, however, service went on mostly uninterrupted, longtime waiters barely glancing up at shouts and booms. The Continental was the only open-air bar that did not put up screens during the old VC terrorist days, perhaps evidence that the bar's owner was paying taxes to both sides.[32] It all illustrated the unsettled nature of Saigon politics.

[30] Telegram 223906 from Secretary of State to All East Asian and Pacific Diplomatic Posts, Oct. 10, 1974. NARA RG 59 – Central Foreign Policy Files, National Archives Access to Archival Databases, Electronic Telegrams, 1974.

[31] Robert Shaplen, "Letter from Saigon," *New Yorker*, Jan. 6, 1975.

[32] Telegram 243999 from Secretary of State to All East Asian and Pacific Diplomatic Posts, Nov. 6, 1974. NARA RG 59 – Central Foreign Policy Files, National Archives Access to Archival Databases, Electronic Telegrams, 1974.

Thieu was reelected in 1971 and enacted emergency powers legislation in 1972. Senate elections were held in 1973. Opposition senators in the Assembly sought to undermine Thieu and assert themselves. Thieu generally tolerated the resistance, US diplomats noted, in part because none of the opposition groups appeared to pose any real threat to his authority. But it was worth watching. The war dragged on, South Vietnam's economic situation was precarious, and so conditions were ripe for an opposition party to gain steam. US Embassy observers argued that the unrest and political activism on display in Saigon were evidence of some semblance of democratic freedoms.[33]

Defending the position that the Saigon government was cultivating democracy was difficult because of ongoing processes of repression. Government agents confiscated twelve newspapers in a four-day period due to their publishing of articles that officials deemed detrimental to national security. This included coverage of the Catholic clergy-led anti-corruption movement. Editors of some of the shuttered newspapers had been involved in the press freedom movement, but according to American diplomatic reports, only a few were radical in any sense of the word. Some politically moderate publishers and members of the Vietnam Publishers Association tried to organize newsmen to propose working with the government toward press freedom.

The Catholic anti-corruption movement enjoyed broad support outside Saigon. On September 28, at a church in Cam Ranh, Fr. Tran Huu Thanh gave an anti-corruption sermon to an audience of some 500 faithful. The next day, he delivered his homily to a cathedral in Nha Trang, where more than 2,000 people listened. American observers noted that both events were nonviolent and did not involve crowds spilling out from the churches in protest. Meanwhile, as Fr. Thanh spoke in Nha Trang, a demonstration of about 100 Catholic priests, Buddhist monks, and opposition deputies marched in Saigon to the Central Market, denouncing Thieu. According to the US Embassy, this type of open criticism by a reliably pro-government Roman Catholic community was the first since 1954.[34] In October, Fr. Thanh traveled with a group of twenty, including Catholic assemblyman Le Chau Loc, throughout the

[33] Telegram 216729 from Secretary of State to AmEmbassy Saigon, Nov. 2, 1973. NARA RG 59 – Central Foreign Policy Files, National Archives Access to Archival Databases, Electronic Telegrams, 1973.
[34] Telegram 143032 from Secretary of State to AmEmbassy Saigon, July 2, 1974. NARA RG 59 – Central Foreign Policy Files, National Archives Access to Archival Databases, Electronic Telegrams, 1974.

Mekong Delta, visiting cities and towns to drum up support for the anti-corruption movement. According to US Embassy estimates, 3,000–4,000 spectators turned out to listen to Fr. Thanh and his associates. In Can Tho, Fr. Thanh led a march through the city's main streets, calling not for Thieu's resignation, but for him to work harder to eliminate government corruption.[35]

Archbishop Nguyen Van Binh was preparing to head to Rome for an international conference of clergy, and journalists speculated that he would meet with Hanoi's Bishop Trinh Van Can and perhaps would bring Can's seventy-three year-old mother. Bishop Can had not seen his mother since she fled North Vietnam as part of the Catholic exodus of 1954. More immediate on Archbishop Binh's mind, though, was tension among southern Catholics. He had heard that priests had established rival anti-corruption groups, some which allegedly supported Thieu's government, others that opposed the government. Before his trip, the archbishop met with priests and encouraged them to cooperate toward the goal of social progress and the elimination of corruption rather than succumb to fissures in Catholic cohesion.[36]

US Embassy officers learned that students were among the main supporters of the anti-corruption movement. PACM, along with the national reconciliation movement, had generated significant student interest. The students who spoke with embassy reps were fed up with government infiltration of student organizations and repression of civil liberties. The anti-corruption movement made sense to them, and national reconciliation sounded worlds better than continued warfare.[37] Yet despite the drumbeats of protest in Saigon and other cities, US diplomats were still unsure what the majority of South Vietnamese wanted in the confused climate of economic depression, continuing war, and apparent political apathy across large swaths of the population.[38]

[35] Telegram 13544 from AmEmbassy Saigon to Secretary of State, Oct. 23, 1974. NARA RG 59 – Central Foreign Policy Files, National Archives Access to Archival Databases, Electronic Telegrams, 1974.
[36] Telegram 13544 from AmEmbassy Saigon to Secretary of State, Oct. 23, 1974. NARA RG 59 – Central Foreign Policy Files, National Archives Access to Archival Databases, Electronic Telegrams, 1974.
[37] Telegram 12775 from AmEmbassy Saigon to Secretary of State, Oct. 2, 1974. NARA RG 59 – Central Foreign Policy Files, National Archives Access to Archival Databases, Electronic Telegrams, 1974.
[38] Telegram 014042 from Secretary of State to AmEmbassy Saigon, Jan. 22, 1974. NARA RG 59 – Central Foreign Policy Files, National Archives Access to Archival Databases, Electronic Telegrams, 1974.

On October 1, 1974, President Thieu addressed the nation for the first time since June. He denied allegations of corruption and explained that he was going to take steps to reform the government and democratize the country. Addressing accusations that he presided over a police state, Thieu announced that he would institute a rule banning soldiers and police from participating in politics and dismiss officers and government officials involved in corrupt practices. While Thieu said he was going to preserve national security and law and order "to the maximum," he also promised to move forward with amending laws that limited press freedom and political parties. The government needed multiple strong and healthy political parties, Thieu asserted, and he would order the government to institute processes to help parties develop. US Embassy officials saw this as evidence that Thieu intended to move South Vietnam toward representative politics. It was too soon to know if Thieu would actually back his words with action, but his speech appeared to be a move in the right direction.

Thieu also reached out to regional allies. At the 1974 Asian People's Anti-Communist League conference, held in Saigon in November, Thieu gave a keynote address in which he called for a ten-nation Southeast Asian conference to handle regional national security concerns. He called for the APACL to include North Vietnam, hoping that if Hanoi leaders agreed to participate, they would also consider ending aggression against South Vietnam. Thieu also restated his desire to resume talks with the communists without conditions aimed at establishing a National Council for National Reconciliation and Concord and internationally supervised elections. The Vietnamese communists rejected Thieu's overtures, calling his speech a "crafty maneuver" designed to "sabotage" the Paris agreement and "mislead the struggle movement of the urban compatriots."[39]

At every level, from the president down to the peasants, the South Vietnamese were worried. Thieu worried about his hold on the presidency, and he worried about communist infiltration of political organizations, especially student groups, so he instructed police officers to be vigilant, and plainclothes officers became infiltrators. Thieu approached his citizens with the attitude that anyone who is not vocally anticommunist is a communist. In his mind, the terms "neutrality" and "third force" were synonyms for communism. Some observers believed that it was

---

[39] Telegram 14785 from AmEmbassy Saigon to Secretary of State, Nov. 27, 1974. NARA RG 59 – Central Foreign Policy Files, National Archives Access to Archival Databases, Electronic Telegrams, 1974.

Thieu's way of justifying the captivity of political prisoners; others thought he actually believed what he preached. An officer in a South Vietnamese provincial reconnaissance unit told an American reporter that most dissidents who appeared to support or be willing to collaborate with communists were doing so not because they adhered to communist ideology but out of survival. If a coalition or communist government took control in Saigon, they wanted to appear on the right side, the safe side.[40] In this context, Thanh's work with Buddhists and militant lawyers to discuss options for a post-Thieu government made sense. Fr. Thanh shared his ideas with some 5,000 people in a Catholic village just south of Can Tho in December 1974.[41] Worry, not ideology, inspired their political allegiances.[42]

Young people's shifting alliances and the fickle nature of youth made students a prime target of government surveillance. Five of the nine children of Professor Ton That Duong Ky, one of three alleged dissidents the South Vietnamese government exiled to North Vietnam in 1965, had been arrested, some multiple times. Ky's eighteen-year-old son was beaten to death in prison, and a twenty-five-year-old daughter-in-law was arrested, beaten, and tortured in prison with electroshock over the course of five years. Fear of this type of treatment and worse drove anti-government students into communist arms. Former student leader Huynh Tan Mam, jailed in 1972, remained in prison because, during a prisoner exchange in March 1974, he refused to enter the Chieu Hoi program, arguing that doing so was tantamount to admitting he was a communist. Nguyen Long, an "aging antiwar lawyer who has defended many dissidents," was forced to the Viet Cong side despite his objections. Police use many tactics to prevent free assembly, including blocking roads and alleyways to the homes of known and suspected anti-government activists. Roman Catholic priests, journalists, students, and Assembly deputies were beaten in the streets of Saigon by police in 1974.[43]

[40] Telegram 183017 From Secretary of State to AmEmbassy Saigon, Aug. 20, 1974. NARA RG 59 – Central Foreign Policy Files, National Archives Access to Archival Databases, Electronic Telegrams, 1974.
[41] Telegram 15335 from AmEmbassy Saigon to Secretary of State, Dec. 11, 1974. NARA RG 59 – Central Foreign Policy Files, National Archives Access to Archival Databases, Electronic Telegrams, 1974.
[42] Telegram 183017 From Secretary of State to AmEmbassy Saigon, Aug. 20, 1974. NARA RG 59 – Central Foreign Policy Files, National Archives Access to Archival Databases, Electronic Telegrams, 1974.
[43] Ibid.

Catholic priests and young, energetic Catholic students in PACM continued their activism to the end of 1974. Fr. Thanh spoke to a group of 5,000–6,000 Catholics at Tan Mai Church in Bien Hoa. He charged corruption on the part of the government and denounced political repression and suppression of the press. Fr. Dinh Binh Dinh, another opposition priest, sent a letter to the prime minister telling him a demonstration was going to happen, originating from seven parishes throughout Saigon and converging in downtown Saigon before returning to points of origin. Dinh's letter said he would assume permission unless he heard otherwise. Prime Minister Khiem sent a brief letter back denying permission due to national security threats. The government began beefing up police presence downtown and implementing other anti-demonstration measures, including barricading some streets. The Catholic Students' Association announced the members of the Action Committee for Social Justice and held an inauguration ceremony on November 23. The eight members of the committee, who claimed to represent 20,000 Catholic students, pledged to work for social justice in the liberation tradition of Jesus. Bishop Tran Thanh Kham presided over the ceremony. The committee issued a declaration condemning NVA troops in South Vietnam and demanding that they return to the North. They also demanded that the Saigon government respect freedom and democracy, and that someone should resign for failing to meet the people's aspirations.[44] Meanwhile, Vietnamese students enrolled in American universities petitioned to stay overseas for fear that they would be imprisoned or otherwise persecuted by the South Vietnamese government because they participated in antiwar activities in the United States.[45]

A US Embassy investigation into PACM revealed that energetic, urban Catholic youth, especially in the Saigon suburbs of Gia Dinh and Bien Hoa, were its primary base of support. PACM was mainly located in III Corps, but pockets of support were scattered among Catholic communities that opposed the organization. Some priests declared that PACM was a ruse for American, specifically CIA, efforts to oust Thieu. Americans were manipulating Catholics to rile up political unrest that would eventually dethrone Thieu. Another belief was that Americans were responsible for

[44] Telegram 14785 from AmEmbassy Saigon to Secretary of State, Nov. 27, 1974. NARA RG 59 – Central Foreign Policy Files, National Archives Access to Archival Databases, Electronic Telegrams, 1974.
[45] Telegram 282843 from Secretary of State to AmEmbassy Saigon, Dec. 27, 1974. NARA RG 59 – Central Foreign Policy Files, National Archives Access to Archival Databases, Electronic Telegrams, 1974.

enabling PACM and other protest movements by abandoning South Vietnam. Clergy worried about the loss of much-needed government support if they or their congregations joined PACM. Other priests told their flocks that religion had no place in politics.[46] Like so much of South Vietnam's political culture, the divisions within groups made it difficult for any one movement to push a concrete agenda, and also posed a challenge to American diplomats, the CIA, and the Thieu government to identify bases of support for a noncommunist South Vietnam.

As Ngo Ba Thanh and other activists commanded international media attention and demanded an end to the war, the Saigon government along with intellectuals and artists worked to dispel the belief held among many foreign observers that South Vietnam lacked the materials necessary for nation building. Writing about Vietnam War for Yale University's alumni magazine in the fall of 1967, Howard Moffett argued that there was "no common culture, no common language, no common history, and no common national purpose" uniting the South Vietnamese.[47] Some South Vietnamese citizens hoped to prove otherwise. In the keynote address opening a three-day festival celebrating traditional Vietnamese music and theater in Saigon in 1972, the speaker warned the audience that preserving national traditions was crucial to preserving the nation. If Vietnamese did not invest in their classical music and plays, American culture would dominate once and for all. It had been creeping in since the 1950s, and the popularity of rock 'n' roll music and Western fashion was sure to only grow if Vietnamese people failed to embrace their own cultural contributions in defiance of Western encroachment. Laying claim to Vietnamese traditions was especially crucial for South Vietnam at that point, when the Paris peace negotiations threatened the struggling country's existence.[48]

For all of South Vietnam's brief life, there was a duality to it, especially in Saigon, where residents went about their days despite instances of urban terrorism and warfare so close to the edges of the city that people

---

[46] Telegram 15882 from AmEmbassy Saigon to Secretary of State Dec. 30, 1974. NARA RG 59 – Central Foreign Policy Files, National Archives Access to Archival Databases, Electronic Telegrams, 1974.

[47] Howard Moffett, "Reporting the Cool-Medium War," *Yale Alumni Magazine,* Oct. 1967, p. 30.

[48] Viet Nam Thong Tan Xa (VTX) So 7601 Chieu Thu Bay 8-1-1972 Dien Van Cua Ong QVK Dac Trach Van Hoa Doc Trong Dem Khai Mac Ba Buoi Hat Boi Tai Truong Quoc Gia Am Nhac Sai Gon, Ho so so 3615: Tap ban tin, bao cat cac bao trong nuoc ve cac hoat dong van hoa xa hoi trong Viet Nam Cong Hoa nam 1972. Trung Tam Luu Tru Quoc Gia II.

could sometimes see and hear it. Even as the war inched closer and closer to Saigon, festivals showcasing Vietnamese music and theater traditions suggested normalcy and nationhood. Historian Nu-Anh Tran has written about South Vietnamese nationalism and offers the concept "contested nationalism." The conventional wisdom says that noncommunist nationalism in South Vietnam was inauthentic or weak, whereas North Vietnam and the NLF represented true Vietnamese identity. Yet Tran argues that pro-government South Vietnamese combined anticommunism with Vietnamese cultural identity to craft a national character. By claiming to be the rightful descendant of Vietnam's cultural traditions, South Vietnam challenged the DRV's legitimacy, Tran contends.[49]

State media worked to promote knowledge of Vietnamese traditions and important figures in the South. The state wire service, VTX, introduced readers to patriotic South Vietnamese, including soldiers and military school cadets, in a series called "Nguoi Dan Muon Biet" ("The People Want to Know"). Efforts by cultural critics, directors of organizations, and professors to claim old Vietnamese cultural traditions aimed to position South Vietnam as the beneficiaries and the legacies of an older Vietnam. In 1972, a music festival in Saigon focused on the preservation of hát bội, traditional Vietnamese music influenced by Chinese opera. Its complex form and themes made it difficult for general audiences to understand. The festival's opening speaker called for making hát bội more accessible to the public to increase interest. The speaker warned that if Vietnamese fail to preserve their traditions, their children will have no identity. Other cultural critics called for the preservation of cải lương – "reformed theater" – plays adapted from classical theater to be more accessible to a wider audience. Cải lương originated in southern Vietnam in the early twentieth century and grew in popularity in 1930s among the Vietnamese middle class. Like preserving hat bội, the preservation of cải lương was a way to lay claim to Vietnamese culture, not "South Vietnamese" culture. Viet Nam Thong Tan Xa (VTX) – Vietnam News Agency – a government-run news agency in Saigon, suggested getting young, popular actors Hùng Cường and Bạch Tuyết to perform cai lương in order to draw more young people to it.[50] In order to spread Vietnamese history and

[49] Nu-Anh Tran, "Contested Nationalism: Ethnic Identity and State Power in the Republic of Vietnam, 1954–1963," ISSI Fellows Working Papers, Institute for the Study of Societal Issues, UC Berkeley, Jan. 3, 2012.
[50] VTX, so 7601, Chieu Thu Bay, 8-1-1972, Dien Van Cua Ong QVK Dac Reach Van Hoa Doc Trong Dem Khai Mac Ba Buoi Hat Boi Tai Truong Quoc Gia Am Nhac Sai Gon. Ho

culture internationally, the government sent eighty-four books on Vietnamese topics to Japan.[51]

In addition to exporting books on Vietnam, the government also
emphasized the importance of universities to national development. By
training the next generation of professionals and leaders, universities were
crucial to Vietnam's survival, Professor Nguyen Van Hao declared in an
interview with VTX. Universities in Saigon, Hue, Da Lat, and Can Tho
offered programs in medicine, pharmacy, economics, politics, and the
study of Southeast Asia, among other majors. Some universities also
established exchange programs with Japanese and South Korean universities in the 1970s.[52] Education in general was required if anticommunist
Vietnamese were to prevail over their red countrymen, argued Ngo Khac
Tran, South Vietnam's Director of the News Ministry. The war ultimately
was a war of ideas, and anticommunists had to be ready to debate against
communism, anywhere, anytime.[53]

One of the motivations of the government's efforts was to try and
prove that South Vietnam – not the communist North – was the rightful
heir to Vietnam's cultural roots. In an article about a memorial to Hung
Vuong, an ancient Vietnamese king, a writer argued that the Communist
Party was just another in a long line of invaders, going all the way back to
China. By following the Communist Party, North Vietnamese denied that
they were children of Hung Vuong, the writer contended. Those in Hanoi
had betrayed Vietnam, so it was up to anticommunist Southerners to save
the country like their heroes had.[54] Hung Vuong came up again in a
speech imploring southern Vietnamese to fight communism to save Vietnam. Enemies from the outside were easy to see, but the enemy from
within could hide. The country was divided, but Vietnamese should fight
for an anticommunist reunified country.[55]

so so: 3615, Tap ban tin, bao cat cac bao trong nuoc ve cac hoat dong van hoa, xa hoi
trong Viet Nam Cong Hoa nam 1972. Vietnam National Archives II.

[51] Viet Nam Cong Hoa Tang Thu Vien Quoc Hoi Nhat 84 Cuon Sach Ve Lich Su Van Hoa
Viet Nam. VTX 28-7-72. Ho so so 3615.

[52] Ho so so 3617: Tap Ban tin cua VTX, Bo Giao duc va thanh nien ve hoat dong cua cac
vien dai hoc nam 1969–1972. VTX So 7919 Chieu Thu Sau 24-11-72, GS Nguyen Van
Hao: Chanh Quyen Phai di Truoc dai hoc Trong viec phat trien Quoc Gia.

[53] VTX Feb.–March 1970.

[54] VTX so 7705 Chieu Thu Hai 24-4-72 Mai Tho Truyen Quoc Vu Khanh Dac trach van
hoa, "Dien Van Cua Quoc Vu Khanh Dac Trach Van Hoa Doc Trong Le Ky Niem Quoc
To Hung Vuong." Ho so so 3615.

[55] VTX So 7765, Chieu Thu Hai 24-4-72 Dien Van Cua Quoc Vu Khanh Dac Trach Van
Hoa Doc Trong Le Ky Niem Quoc To Hung Vuong. Ho so so 3615.

VTX also ran a regular feature called "Nguoi Dan Muon Biet" – "the People Want to Know." The series interviewed officials and groups linked to or supportive of the Saigon government and South Vietnam. Several install-ments of NDMB profiled servicemen and military school students, who explained their desires to serve and their commitment to the nation. They enjoyed the adventure and the danger, even, of military life, some students at the National Military Academy in Da Lat said. Vietnam had been at war for their entire lives, thy noted, and they wanted to do something to help the country. The Da Lat academy offered a good course of training, and the students especially enjoyed learning from their older peers.[56]

Another article profiled students enrolled in the Thu Duc Infantry School. They were students of privilege, and military officers had observed that soldiers from elite families lacked patience with rural villagers because they did not understand rural life. They were often impatient in their interactions with countryside folk, which was counterproductive to the goal of winning rural support for the government. To try and build empathy, the Thu Duc curriculum included education in the rural experience, as well as morality and physical exercise. If soldiers approached their rural country-men with compassion, the people will respect them, the article declared.[57]

Although government officials declared that political freedom was a hallmark separating the noncommunist South from the communist North, censorship, repression, and state control were central to South Vietnam's political scene. In an interview with a law enforcement official in the NDMB series, the officer sought to explain why Saigon had been under martial law since 1968. It was true that police gained more rights while martial law limited civilians' civil liberties. Security officers could inspect houses anytime, travel was restricted from eleven o'clock at night until six in the morning. The government could shut down newspapers whose content appeared to threaten national security. In a time of national emergency, the government had the right to seize property, monitor bank accounts, and funnel citizens in important professions – doctors, dentists, pharmacists, engineers, businessmen – into government service. This was not illegal repression, the officer contended; it was part of national preservation as South Vietnam remained under attack.[58]

[56] VTX So 7689 Sang Thu Bay 8-4-72, Nguoi Dan Muon Biet, Truong Vo Bi Quoc Gia Viet Nam. Ho so so 3615.
[57] VTX So 7815, San Thu Bay 12-8-72, Nguoi Dan Muon Biet, Phong Van Trung Tuong Chi Huy Truong Truong Bo Binh Thu Duc. Ho so so 3615.
[58] VTX so 7731 Chieu Thu Bay 20-5-72 "Nguoi Dan Muon Biet," Phong Van Tim Hieu ve Tinh trong thiet Quan Luat," Ho so so 3615.

NDMB features also included interviews with law professors talking about the importance of establishing a new national law code for South Vietnam not based on French legal code that still existed from the colonial era; an interview with the director of the National Library, who discussed the importance of studying the various newspapers and documents of South Vietnam in order to develop national culture; and museum preservationists who moved artifacts from the Citadel in Hue to a storage facility in Saigon out of fear that the fighting in I Corps would destroy the materials. In an interview on the nation's film industry, Vietnamese filmmakers explained how they contributed to the war effort by making upbeat movies to boost soldiers' morale and films that depicted the patriotic, anticommunist spirit of the Vietnamese people. They hoped that they eventually would be able to export their movies to foreign markets.[59]

The emphasis on traditional Vietnamese culture made sense because it was what Vietnamese young people liked. Ted Britton noticed it when he worked with youth voluntary societies in the sixties and heard students describe their longing for a connection to their heritage. Journalist A. J. Langguth also observed youth attraction to Vietnamese culture, which surprised him, as he had assumed that American entertainment, style, and food would have bulldozed its way into the hearts and minds of young Vietnamese. Yet he found that they preferred romantic, wistful ballads written and sung by Vietnamese musicians. Young women wear the *ao dai* more often than a miniskirt. American food did not suit their palettes, and they hated that *Playboy* was sold at local newsstands. Traditional Vietnamese values, not a commitment to any foreign ideology, whether Marxism or democracy, defined the nationalism of young Vietnamese.[60]

Government and officially sanctioned cultural products emphasized Vietnamese traditions, but younger Vietnamese expressed their views about the war, politics, and Vietnam's future through US-inspired rock 'n' roll. Popular music in South Vietnam revealed young people's ambivalence about the war, especially as the fighting dragged on with no end in sight. One of the most popular Vietnamese singer-songwriters was Trinh Cong Son, whose music expressed the sorrows of war and told stories of mothers grieving for their lost children, brothers killing brothers, and the absurdity of combat. The songs were his attempt to make sense of the war

---

[59] VTX So 7864 Sang Thu Bay 30-9-1972, Nguoi Dan Muon Biet, Phong Van Ve Dien Anh Viet Nam. Ho so so 3615.

[60] A. J. Langguth, "1964: Exhilaration 1968: Frustration 1970: Hopelessness," *New York Times*, Oct. 4, 1970, p. 220.

that devastated his country. A *New York Times* reporter called him "the most popular college singer and composer in Saigon." Legend has it Joan Baez called Son the Bob Dylan of Vietnam.[61]

By day, Son, who was born in Hue, supported his mother, two brothers, and five sisters writing love songs for Vietnamese television shows. As fighting in Vietnam intensified throughout the sixties, he decided to use his music to express his opposition to war, a sentiment he soon learned many young Vietnamese shared. By 1970, he had written 150 protest songs. "Wars, any wars, bring about death and destruction, and I am against war generally," he said. Son looked more like a poet than a rock star. He sported a wispy goatee and black glasses, and when he performed, he usually wore a white shirt, tight black pants, and pointy black shoes. He was quiet and unassuming when he took the stage at concerts, but as soon as he began to play and sing, the audience always joined him in loud choruses. In interviews, Son often named Dylan and Joan Baez as his main musical inspirations. Because of Son's antiwar stance, Thieu's government banned his music in 1969 and forbade him from performing protest songs. Officials confiscated sheet music and tape recordings that Son had sold in Saigon before and after his shows.[62]

Vietnamese youth comprised Trinh Cong Son's audience, but American military personnel stationed in South Vietnam made up another set of music fans, and they created a market for Vietnamese bands that could play rock and roll. The CBC Band became the most popular cover band during the war. The group was born in 1963 when a trio of Saigon siblings decided they wanted to play American music. An older brother noticed the talent of three of his younger siblings – nine-year-old Bich Loan as a singer, ten-year-old Tung Linh on guitar, and seven-year-old Tung Van on drums – and in 1963, he created a Vietnamese Partridge Family before the US version existed. They were the CBC Band, which stood for Con Ba Cu, "Mother's Children." It was a way to honor their mother for her unwavering support. At the time, Ngoc Lan, the band's manager, was also a drummer in South Vietnam's Navy band.[63]

The children were so small when they started the band that no one could see the youngest, the drummer, behind his drum set, even if he was

---

[61] Bernard Weintraub, "A Vietnamese Guitarist Sings of Sadness of War," *New York Times*, Jan. 1, 1968.

[62] Joseph B. Treaster, "Saigon Bans the Antiwar Songs of Vietnamese Singer-Composer," *New York Times*, Feb. 12, 1969.

[63] Author's telephone interview with Bich Loan, October 2017.

standing. They had started with songs such as "You Are My Sunshine" and Ray Charles' "What I Say," just for fun. None of the children spoke English, so Ngoc Lan wrote the lyrics down phonetically in Vietnamese so they could sing them even though they did not understand them. From 1963 to 1965, the CBC Band performed around Saigon in talent shows, but then US troops began arriving in Vietnam in earnest, and their presence turned a hobby into a career. The escalation of America's troop presence in Vietnam made the CBC Band famous.[64]

Ngoc Lan recognized a business opportunity in entertaining the large number of US troops in Vietnam in 1967. He reached out to local Vietnamese music promoters who contracted with the US Army's Special Services Agency to book acts for officers' and enlisted men's clubs on US bases. A sister had performed with another band in Vung Tau, where music acts were in high demand due the coastal city's status as an R&R spot for American servicemen. The CBC Band joined her there for several gigs, and she ended up joining the family band in 1969. By the early 1970s, the band was on the Army's approved entertainment list and made $325 per gig.[65]

The CBC Band traveled all over South Vietnam, wherever US troops were stationed. As the group played more gigs, they got tied in to the local rock and folk scene that included Khanh Ly, Trinh Cong Son, and Elvis Phuong. Every Sunday, they would jam together, playing music inspired by American rock 'n' roll, ballads, and folk songs. Word of the band spread through GI networks, and soon the demand for CBC Band shows grew so high that sometimes the band performed seven nights a week. Soldiers sought out Ngoc Lan and gave him tapes of rock 'n' roll songs they wanted the band to learn to play. Ray Charles and the Beatles were among the more popular requests.[66]

US troops showed their gratitude with money. The band members walked away from most gigs with more money in tips than what the clubs paid them. They gave all their earnings to their mother, and eventually, the CBC Band made enough money to allow her to quit her job on the naval base. It was war that brought the CBC Band success and financial security, but the siblings were too young to understand the complexities of the conflict. They wondered why Vietnamese were fighting each other, and why Americans had joined in, but that was the extent of their thoughts about it. Everyone seemed to come together and enjoy the show when the

[64] Ibid.   [65] Ibid.   [66] Ibid.

CBC Band played, so why did they go off and fight afterward? Couldn't rock 'n' roll music stop a war? Perhaps not, but it could raise money for Vietnamese soldiers and war widows. In 1970, the CBC Band helped Vietnam's first rock 'n' roll festival to raise money for military families. The Saigon government sanctioned the event, and Jo Marcel, a Vietnamese singer turned local nightclub owner and music producer whose given name was Vu Ngoc Tong, promoted it.[67] Even as the reporter A. J. Langguth described Saigon as hopeless in 1970, an entrepreneurial spirit, of which a certain type of hope is a central component, remained and shone in events like Saigon's rock 'n' roll fest for charity.

A cai luong revival or an outdoor rock concert would be an unremarkable event were it not in the midst of a war. That these types of entertainment occurred in Saigon during the war illustrates the duality of life in South Vietnam. Fighting continued despite the Paris Peace Agreement mandating a cease-fire, and yet life in Saigon continued on in ways that would be normal in a bustling capital city. Government officials claimed traditional cultural forms as South Vietnam's inheritance, and concert promoters brought what was increasingly a global musical style to a Saigon audience. Normal operations emanating from the capital included international relations, and President Thieu sent delegates out into the world to establish diplomatic ties with willing nations. International relations also involved the presence of the International Commission of Control and Supervision, which investigated alleged cease-fire violations. As South Vietnamese diplomats performed the seemingly normal acts of foreign affairs, ICCS representatives reminded locals that the country was still at war, which could shatter the illusion of normalcy at any time.

INTERNATIONAL RELATIONS

As representatives of North and South Vietnam argued over the meaning of the cease-fire and its terms, the governments of both countries sent delegates on international missions to build alliances and cultivate support. The Saigon government announced the establishment of a South Vietnamese embassy in Tehran and Thieu's planned visit to Thailand. Japan and North Vietnam agreed to open diplomatic relations, but tensions marred the relationship between the two countries because Japan had not recognized the PRG as the official government of South Vietnam. A North Vietnamese delegation made an eleven-day visit to Japan, and

[67] Ibid.

lead representative Hoang Quoc Viet struck his Japanese counterparts as rude in his demands that Japan recognize the PRG as the official southern government as a condition for the establishment of diplomatic relations and the mutual opening of embassies in Tokyo and Hanoi. He eventually backpedaled in the face of Japanese resistance.[68]

Former Senator Dang Van Sung, publisher of the prominent daily newspaper *Chinh Luan* and a roving goodwill envoy for South Vietnam's government, left Saigon on March 27, 1974, for a two-week tour of Africa, where he was scheduled to visit nine countries. It was part of South Vietnam's "diplomatic offensive" aimed to improve the government's image and counter the PRG's efforts to achieve recognition as a legitimate government from as many countries as possible and gain entry into international organizations.[69] Togo's President Eyadema accepted Sung's invitation to visit Vietnam. Meanwhile, Iran's ambassador to South Vietnam, Mohsan Sadigh Esfandiari, presented his credentials to Thieu on May 3, 1974. He was the first resident ambassador from Iran to South Vietnam, although Iran had sent diplomats to South Vietnam since 1963. South Vietnam's Minister of Veterans' Affairs Ho Van Cham and UN permanent observer Nguyen Huu Chi represented South Vietnam at the inauguration of Costa Rica's new president. US Embassy officers called these efforts examples of the government's "active diplomacy" to counter the PRG's diplomatic engagements. Sending delegates to Costa Rica also illustrated the government's interest in developing a diplomatic mission in the Caribbean, Americans in Saigon observed.[70]

The prisoner situation stymied South Vietnam's efforts. Keeping prisoners in places such as Con Son, known around the world for its poor conditions, endangered South Vietnam's reputation, its allies pointed out. Con Son made international news again in June 1974, when Hong Kong authorities deported more than 100 South Vietnamese citizens, most of them ethnic Chinese, back to South Vietnam. Hong Kong immigration officials caught them trying to enter illegally. Most were draft evaders or

---

[68] Telegram 19525 from AmEmbassy Saigon to Secretary of State, Nov. 15, 1973. NARA RG 59 – Central Foreign Policy Files, National Archives Access to Archival Databases, Electronic Telegrams, 1973.

[69] Telegram 04243 from AmEmbassy Saigon to Secretary of State, April 3, 1974. NARA RG 59 – Central Foreign Policy Files, National Archives Access to Archival Databases, Electronic Telegrams, 1974.

[70] Telegram 05966 from AmEmbassy Saigon to Secretary of State, May 8, 1974. NARA RG 59 – Central Foreign Policy Files, National Archives Access to Archival Databases, Electronic Telegrams, 1974.

army deserters, and US Embassy officers believed their escape was connected to a smuggling ring operating between South Vietnam and Hong Kong. Once back in South Vietnam, government officials decided to send them to Con Son because they worried about escape through bribery, a common problem in mainland jails. Officials from the British Embassy in Saigon worried about international reaction given Con Son's notoriety. It was another example of the government treating its citizens poorly beyond what was reasonable for the particular crimes the exiles had committed, British diplomats asserted.[71] The government's treatment of political prisoners haunted four South Vietnamese delegates who attended the Interparliamentary Union meeting in Bucharest in April 1974. They were already concerned about harassment in a communist country where a few hundred North Vietnamese students lived. The international attention that political oppression by Saigon authorities had garnered ensured that it would always hang as a dark cloud over South Vietnamese diplomatic efforts.[72]

As the fighting continued in South Vietnam, Americans paid attention to student unrest throughout Southeast Asia. Thai, Laotian, and Cambodian students staged demonstrations demanding government reforms and more freedoms, similar in tone to some of the student protests in South Vietnam. Thai students sought the implementation of a civilian government and an end to foreign involvement in Thailand's affairs, which was of particular interest to the United States due to American military bases in the country. The secretary general of the National Student Center said in an interview that Thailand would only be secure when it no longer relied on another country for its economic and military well-being, notably the United States.[73] Thai students also demanded a lowering of the voting age from twenty to eighteen and the parliamentary age from twenty-five to twenty-three.[74]

---

[71] Telegram 08835 from AmEmbassy Saigon to Secretary of State, July 3, 1974. NARA RG 59 – Central Foreign Policy Files, National Archives Access to Archival Databases, Electronic Telegrams, 1974.

[72] Telegram 03812 from AmEmbassy Saigon from Secretary of State, March 22, 1974. NARA RG 59 – Central Foreign Policy Files, National Archives Access to Archival Databases, Electronic Telegrams, 1974.

[73] Telegram 205835 from Secretary of State to AmEmbassy Saigon, Oct. 17, 1973. NARA RG 59 – Central Foreign Policy Files, National Archives Access to Archival Databases, Electronic Telegrams, 1973.

[74] Telegram 15209 from AmEmbassy Bangkok to Secretary of State, Sep. 21, 1974. NARA RG 59 – Central Foreign Policy Files, National Archives Access to Archival Databases, Electronic Telegrams, 1974.

Cambodian students also demanded an end to foreign interference and expressed their frustrations at Cambodia's economic problems and what they saw as general government incompetence. Student protests turned violent when students kidnapped and executed two government officials after holding them hostage in a school. The incident foreshadowed the brutality that would drench Cambodian society in blood by order of the Khmer Rouge. The students had been protesting the arrest of nine teachers on the charge of anti-government activism, and the demonstration spiraled out of control when some of the protesters took the Minister of Education and a staff member hostage and held them at a high school in Phnom Penh. Both officials, as well as several students, died in the ensuing violence.[75]

While Americans monitored regional unrest and violence, the International Commission of Control and Supervision investigated violations of the Paris Peace Accords in South Vietnam. Negotiators at Paris had stipulated that delegates from two communist countries, Poland and Hungary, and two noncommunist nations, Canada and Indonesia, would comprise the ICCS membership. In July 1973, Canada left the ICCS, and Iran took its place. In theory, equal representation between the communist and noncommunist spheres made the commission balanced and neutral, but in reality, political divisions hampered ICCS efficiency. This became clear when commissioners assessed a series of school attacks. On March 9, 1974, thirty-two children were killed and thirty-four wounded when a North Vietnamese mortar shell hit a school at Cai Lay, a village in the Mekong Delta. On May 5, seven children were killed and twenty-five wounded when North Vietnamese forces mortared a school at nearby Song Phu. On November 2, 1974, eighteen children and a militiaman were killed on a bus that hit a North Vietnamese mine in southern Quang Nam province. Thirty-three children were riding in the bus.[76]

On March 9, North Vietnamese troops fired an 82 MM round into an elementary schoolyard in Cai Lay in Mekong Delta province of Dinh Tuong. The missile round landed in the schoolyard just before three o'clock in the afternoon, when the yard was filled with children waiting

[75] Telegram 07610 from AmEmbassy Phnom Penh to Secretary of State, June 4, 1974. NARA RG 59 – Central Foreign Policy Files, National Archives Access to Archival Databases, Electronic Telegrams, 1974.
[76] Telegram 14482 from AmEmbassy Saigon to Secretary of State, Nov. 19, 1974. NARA RG 59 – Central Foreign Policy Files, National Archives Access to Archival Databases, Electronic Telegrams, 1974.

to come in for their afternoon classes. Children between the ages of six and fourteen were the victims at Cai Lay, as well as one teacher and two local residents who were wounded. It took three weeks for members of the ICCS to agree to investigate the attack. The Hungarian and Polish delegations initially refused to probe the case because they worried about security. ICCS rules required unanimous agreement of all members to act, so there was no official ICCS response immediately following the incident. Two Indonesian members of the ICCS team donated blood at the Song Be Health Service for wounded children in Cai Lay. Indonesian and Iranian delegations independently visited the site to collect evidence and interrogate witnesses, but this angered Hanoi officials, who accused the Saigon military of perpetrating the attack with US backing and decried the ICCS violation the provision of unanimity before action.[77] Given the unanimity provision, ICCS did not publish the Iranian and Indonesian reports on the attack.[78]

It took until the end of March for ICCS delegates to agree to investigate Cai Lay. On March 30, an ICCS team arrived in the morning by helicopter from the ICCS Region VI headquarters in My Tho. Delegates interviewed the Cai Lay district chief and police chief, the school principle, and a teacher. In mid-afternoon, the delegates finished their interviews and planned to return the next day to interview more people. A group of parents and relatives of murdered children had been waiting in a small classroom to present a petition to the ICCS team, but the delegates left without receiving it. The parents and relatives followed them out to the road, trying to give them the petition. Two mothers attempted to give it to the Hungarian delegate, who nervously tried to rush off. One mother grabbed a Hungarian by the arm. The Indonesian representative, Col. Isnoljano, head of the Indonesian delegation of Region VI, stayed behind to try and calm the situation and accept the petition. Four or five of the group members lay down in front of the cars trying to leave. As police tried to clear the situation, someone threw a rock at the car carrying the PRG representative. A car window shattered, and others began throwing rocks at the vehicle as it drove away. PRG Major Ha Can was in the car, and Cai Lay residents recognized him.

[77] Telegram 03276 from AmEmbassy Saigon to US Mission Geneva, March 12, 1974. NARA RG 59 – Central Foreign Policy Files, National Archives Access to Archival Databases, Electronic Telegrams, 1974.
[78] Telegram 06213 from AmEmbassy Saigon to Secretary of State, May 13, 1974. NARA RG 59 – Central Foreign Policy Files, National Archives Access to Archival Databases, Electronic Telegrams, 1974.

He had been well known years ago in Cai Lay for having ordered the executions of villagers.[79] The Hungarian and Polish delegates used the incident to argue that the ICCS safety was in danger, and they called for the suspension of the investigation. More than a month later, US Ambassador Graham Martin expressed pessimism about the chances of the investigation ever being completed.[80]

While ICCS delegates argued, local civilians responded quickly to the Cai Lay school incident. Students in Tay Ninh and Phuoc Tuy schools observed a moment of silence at schools before morning classes began on March 15. Students from thirty-two primary and secondary schools in Phuoc Long presented a petition to the Indonesian ICCS delegation condemning the atrocity. Street demonstrations by students and teachers took place in Long Khanh and Bien Hoa. Bien Hoa demonstrators marched to ICCS region V headquarters and met with ICCS representatives. A student spoke in Vietnamese with an ARVN officer translating into English. He argued that the ICCS should use its influence to stop Communist violations of the cease-fire and the South Vietnamese government must raise the Cai Lay massacre at the ongoing Paris meetings as an example of the North's violation of the Paris agreement. Where was the outcry from worldwide public opinion against Communist atrocities in South Vietnam, the student asked. It was up to the people of South Vietnam to support the national military to fight and defeat communism, he declared before handing the petition an Indonesian delegate. The Iranian delegation chief promised he would discuss the petition with his fellow Region V members before forwarding it to ICCS headquarters in Saigon. The Hungarian and Polish delegation chiefs declined to comment. The Indonesian delegation chief vaguely condemned all violence, especially violence against children. A Bien Hoa high school teacher asked all ICCS delegations to give blood for wounded children in Cai Lay.[81]

Two months after the Cai Lay school attack, Communists shelled a school in Song Phu village in the Delta province of Vinh Long province on

[79] Telegram 04169 from AmEmbassy Saigon to Secretary of State, April 1, 1974. NARA RG 59 – Central Foreign Policy Files, National Archives Access to Archival Databases, Electronic Telegrams, 1974.

[80] Telegram 06213 from AmEmbassy Saigon to Secretary of State, May 13, 1974. NARA RG 59 – Central Foreign Policy Files, National Archives Access to Archival Databases, Electronic Telegrams, 1974.

[81] Telegram 03541 from AmEmbassy Saigon to Secretary of State, March 18, 1974. NARA RG 59 – Central Foreign Policy Files, National Archives Access to Archival Databases, Electronic Telegrams, 1974.

May 4. Seven children were killed, and thirty-six were wounded. Indonesian and Iranian ICCS officers carried out an onsite investigation, but Polish and Hungarian members of the ICCS refused to visit the school.[82] In October, an NLF mine detonated near a school in Loc Khe hamlet of Hau Nghia province, killing five children and wounding seventeen others.[83] On November 2, a mine exploded on a commercial bus and killed nineteen passengers, all but one of whom were high school students.[84] In response to the bus attack, some 4,000 students gathered on November 14 at the Hoi An soccer field in the morning to protest the act. Also present were the province chief and the province council chairman, a representative of the Buddhist community, and several school principals. The demonstration lasted about an hour and a half and was without incident or violence. Students denounced the mining as an act of terrorism and called upon the ICCS to do the same.[85] Negotiations at Paris hadn't ended the war, as the residents of Cai Lay, Loc Khe, Hoi An, and other places understood. Cultural festivals and other attempts at normalcy in Saigon couldn't mask that reality, which encroached upon the city as 1974 gave way to 1975.

1975: THE LEAD-UP TO THE FALL

As 1974 wound to a close, and in the early months of 1975, Thieu gave speeches, citizens protested both government repression and communist advancement, and Americans considered whether South Vietnam was worth another financial investment. Thieu went on a speaking tour in January, and his lectures emphasized order in internal politics, resistance against communists, and self-reliance in economic matters and economic development. The president spoke on the theme of self-help at the Vietnamese Boy Scout National Jamboree on December 23 in Gia Dinh, a

---

[82] Telegram 05966 from AmEmbassy Saigon to Secretary of State, May 8, 1974. NARA RG 59 – Central Foreign Policy Files, National Archives Access to Archival Databases, Electronic Telegrams, 1974.

[83] Telegram 13544 from AmEmbassy Saigon to Secretary of State, Oct. 23, 1974. NARA RG 59 – Central Foreign Policy Files, National Archives Access to Archival Databases, Electronic Telegrams, 1974.

[84] Telegram 14503 from AmEmbassy Saigon to Secretary of State, Nov. 20, 1974. NARA RG 59 – Central Foreign Policy Files, National Archives Access to Archival Databases, Electronic Telegrams, 1974.

[85] Telegram 14472 from AmEmbassy Saigon to Secretary of State, Nov. 19, 1974. NARA RG 59 – Central Foreign Policy Files, National Archives Access to Archival Databases, Electronic Telegrams, 1974.

suburb of Saigon. Five days later, he was in Da Lat, addressing candidates and their families at the graduation ceremony of the National Military Academy. Again, Thieu stressed the need for order. South Vietnam would not be able to establish viable democratic institutions in the midst of disorder, he declared. On December 29, Thieu spoke to a public audience in Ninh Thuan province, and called upon every boy and girl in the community to serve in local People's Self-Defense Forces or Regional Forces/Popular Forces to resist communists. While Westerners celebrated New Years Day, 1975, 200 Vietnamese Catholic students joined with believers in others faiths and the People's Anti-Corruption Movement and held a rally at a suburban Saigon church. The demonstrators demanded the release of alleged political prisoners, the repeal of anti-democratic laws, and an end to military conscription of students. Fr. Tran Huu Thanh led the student marchers.[86]

Citizens protested the ongoing war, gathering in Danang City Stadium on January 19 to protest PAVN's seizure of Phuoc Long province near the Cambodian border. A group of older VNQDD stalwarts who had formed a new organization called the People's Anti-Communist Committee sponsored the rally. Vietnamese employees of the US Consulate in Danang, as well as officers in Danang's national police, reported that 30,000 people, mostly students, attended the demonstration. Youth and student groups presented petitions protesting the seizure of Phuoc Long province, Hanoi and PRG's violation of the cease-fire, and what the petitioners viewed as a lack of respect for human life on the part of the Communists.[87] A student demonstration of about 3,000 in Bien Hoa also protested the communist seizure of Phuoc Long. Several other demonstrations were held in surrounding provinces, ranging from hundreds to thousands of participants, mostly students.[88]

A bipartisan US congressional delegation arrived in South Vietnam on a fact-finding trip in late February to determine whether they would support President Ford's request for $300 million in aid to South

[86] Telegram 00041 from AmEmbassy Saigon to Secretary of State, Jan. 2, 1975. NARA RG 59 – Central Foreign Policy Files, National Archives Access to Archival Databases, Electronic Telegrams, 1975.
[87] Telegram 00381 from AmEmbassy Saigon to Secretary of State, Jan. 10, 1975. NARA RG 59 – Central Foreign Policy Files, National Archives Access to Archival Databases, Electronic Telegrams, 1975.
[88] Telegram 00406 from AmEmbassy Saigon to Secretary of State, Jan. 13, 1975. NARA RG 59 – Central Foreign Policy Files, National Archives Access to Archival Databases, Electronic Telegrams, 1975.

Vietnam. The group included Bella Abzug, Millicent Fenwick, Don Fraser, Pete McCloskey, and Dewey Bartlett, and members met with opposition leaders including Ngo Ba Thanh, anti-Thieu legislators such as Ly Quy Chung, antiwar Catholic priests Fr. Chan Tin, Fr. Nguyen Ngoc Lan, and Fr. Tran Huu Thanh, and other PACM leaders and opposition journalists. When McCloskey met with Chung, he asked about the whereabouts of Nguyen Huu Thai, a former student leader arrested in 1972 and released eight months ago. Stanford University had invited him to take a visiting professorship, and McCloskey had intervened on his behalf to try and obtain a visa for him, but no one had heard from him or had any information about him. Thai had been open about his neutral stance and opposition to the Thieu government, and he had worked as an opposition journalist after running an unsuccessful bid for a lower house assembly seat representing Da Nang in 1971.[89] Increased criticism of Thieu and government's emphasis on continued state of martial law. But also, some of the tougher draft laws revoked, allowing more young men to delay or suspend enlistment. Everything was falling apart.[90]

A lack of clarity as to the opposition's beliefs and the multilayered nature of who and what constituted the opposition made it difficult for Americans to know what to make of government opponents even though embassy authorities had been in contact with various opposition leaders and had been observing political activism in South Vietnam for more than a decade. Following the US congressional visit, Deputy Chief of Mission Wolfgang Lehmann and other diplomats met with various opposition leaders because they were confused about the anti-Thieu movement's ideology. Anticommunists, neutralists, and antiwar activists held meetings and protested together. Catholics and Buddhists showed up to the same demonstrations. Priests assisted students in their efforts to reach international audiences with stories of prison brutality against political dissidents. Archbishop Nguyen Van Binh told embassy officials that students believe the draft is inequitable, and they resent students who can get deferments, such as overseas students who have wealthy patrons

---

[89] Telegram 02764 from AmEmbassy Saigon to Secretary of State, March 12, 1975. NARA RG 59 – Central Foreign Policy Files, National Archives Access to Archival Databases, Electronic Telegrams, 1975.

[90] Telegram 04615 from AmEmbassy Saigon to Secretary of State, April 9, 1975. NARA RG 59 – Central Foreign Policy Files, National Archives Access to Archival Databases, Electronic Telegrams, 1975.

allowing them to stay out of the country.[91] Most confusing to some embassy officers were the dissidents who spoke out against Thieu while maintaining that South Vietnam still needed US aid. Diplomats wondered why some moderates aligned with radicals to publicly denounce further US aid to Thieu, even though they understood the importance of continued US aid to South Vietnam's survival.[92]

Ex-senator Dang Van Sung, publisher of *Chinh Luan*, told US Embassy officers that the opposition movement reminded him of the Viet Minh days when anticolonial activists felt pressured to tow one particular opposition line. Lower house opposition deputy Tran Van Tuyen offered a similar perspective, that the current opposition political situation reminded him of Communist meetings from back when he briefly worked with Ho Chi Minh. At a recent anti-Thieu meeting, people sang old revolutionary songs, and Ngo Ba Thanh gave an angry, passionate speech denouncing US intervention in Vietnam. When Deputy Nguyen Huu Thoi, an opposition deputy who was also staunchly anticommunist, took the podium and argued that the current economic crisis in South Vietnam was the fault of the communists because they had brought war to the country, radicals present wrestled the microphone from his hands. When embassy officers spoke with independent deputy Vo Long Trieu, publisher of radical daily, *Dai Dan Toc*, about why he had signed a letter signed by forty-seven opposition deputies of the lower house demanding an end to US aid to President Thieu, Trieu replied that he and some of the other supposed signatories did not actually sign. Someone had forged their signatures. He added that while he did not agree with the letter's message because he believed US aid was vital for South Vietnam's survival, he felt he could not defect from the ranks because it would give the public the impression that the opposition was splintered. He said in confidence that there actually was major splintering within the opposition. Radicals had been able to exploit that.[93]

Opposition statements focused on many different forms of discontent with Thieu's government. In March 1975, *Chinh Luan* published a statement from twenty-seven lower house assemblymen who had formed

[91] Telegram 03637 from AmEmbassy Saigon to Secretary of State, March 27, 1975. NARA RG 59 – Central Foreign Policy Files, National Archives Access to Archival Databases, Electronic Telegrams, 1975.

[92] Telegram 02974 from AmEmbassy Saigon to Secretary of State, March 17, 1975. NARA RG 59 – Central Foreign Policy Files, National Archives Access to Archival Databases, Electronic Telegrams, 1975.

[93] Ibid.

the "People's Society Bloc," another opposition party. The members accused the government of handing over the Central Highlands to PAVN and abandoning the civilians living there. This caused millions of Vietnamese to lose their lives and property and shocked the entire country, they argued in their statement. The group demanded that the government stop acting secretly and instead be transparent about its plans for the country so that citizens can prepare and not panic. Most importantly, bloc members asserted, the Thieu government and PRG leaders had finally agree on a path to peace and national reconciliation.[94]

As the communists advanced through South Vietnam, overseas students had problems of their own. Unsure of what kind of future they would have if they tried to go home, some petitioned their host countries to bring their parents and relatives to the country as refugees. Host governments such as New Zealand had to figure out how to balance these requests with establishing working relations with whatever new government took power in Vietnam.[95] Letters began pouring in to the US Embassy in Saigon and government offices in the United States, Australia, New Zealand, and elsewhere asking for help getting out of South Vietnam. On April 18, four Vietnamese students in Paris, claiming to represent anticommunist Vietnamese students in Europe, submitted an open letter to the US Embassy in Paris demanding that the US government continue aiding South Vietnam. They also staged a demonstration in front of the DRV Embassy. American diplomats had learned that the students originally planned to march in front of the US Embassy, but they moved their protest at the request of South Vietnam's diplomatic corps in Paris.[96]

A report out of Danang in mid-April after the communist takeover was grim. A Danang police officer who escaped the city on April 8 and arrived in Saigon four days later, told the story. Communists detained and disappeared Buddhist youths who had participated in the National Reconciliation and Concord Movement, arguing that the revolution belongs to the people, not any group in particular, and this group had not been

[94] Telegram 03321 from AmEmbassy Saigon to Secretary of State, March 22, 1975. NARA RG 59 – Central Foreign Policy Files, National Archives Access to Archival Databases, Electronic Telegrams, 1975.

[95] Telegram 01179 from AmEmbassy Wellington to Secretary of State, April 28, 1975. NARA RG 59 – Central Foreign Policy Files, National Archives Access to Archival Databases, Electronic Telegrams, 1975.

[96] Telegram 09984 from AmEmbassy Paris to Secretary of State, April 18, 1975. NARA RG 59 – Central Foreign Policy Files, National Archives Access to Archival Databases, Electronic Telegrams, 1975.

fighting nearly as long as others. Communist cadres appeared at the doors of pagodas to warn monks of reprisals if they demonstrate against new rules or leadership. Communists rounded up and executed about thirty people at Cho Con Market who were considered to be enemies of the revolution. They arrested and herded South Vietnamese troops, civil servants, and police officers into reeducation camps in the jungle. Only Hanoi, Beijing, and Liberation Radio were allowed, and movie theaters only showed communist films. In schools, students were demoted a grade level so as to relearn from a communist perspective. Cigarettes, meat, watches, radio, and scooters could bribe a communist cadre. Armed guards were posted at street corners for security.[97]

Ten years after his exile to North Vietnam, Pham Van Huyen, Ngo Ba Thanh's father, who by then was living in Paris, saw a path back to Saigon. On April 22, a Vietnamese-French citizen passed along a message to a US Embassy officer in Paris. Huyen had been in touch with PRG officials, and they allegedly agreed to accept him as a third force representative. With each passing day, it became clearer that the Saigon government would not hold, and some sort of changes were imminent. Huyen wanted the Americans to know that he was prepared to assist in whatever transitions were ahead. American responded by saying the Vietnamese would contact Huyen if they were interested in his services. The Americans had already washed their hands of South Vietnam; the diplomat told his associate in Paris that if South Vietnamese officials were interested in Huyen's services, they would contact him directly.

The departure of the US military brought a quiet, a melancholy, to Saigon, but political activism ensured that the city's electric character continued to buzz. At once weary of what seemed to be a war without end and emboldened by the peace agreements, various Saigon activists established movements for reform under the Thieu government, reached out to the NLF, and demanded that Thieu resign. The president sent diplomats abroad and pressed his American allies for financial assistance. State media attempted to cultivate a connection between citizens, the military, and traditional Vietnamese culture. South Vietnam remained a dangerous place, and for every quiet street scene in Saigon there was rocket fire in the villages. The US Embassy pointed to political protests as examples of democracy in action, but the cities swelled with

[97] Telegram 05316 from AmEmbassy Saigon to Secretary of State, 19, 1975. NARA RG 59 – Central Foreign Policy Files, National Archives Access to Archival Databases, Electronic Telegrams, 1975.

refugees who lived in squalor away from the city squares where students and elites aired their grievances and issued their demands. US Ambassador Graham Martin continued to insist that Saigon would stand, until embassy employees and military personnel found themselves rushing an evacuation of the city as NLF guerrillas and NVA regulars made their final advance.

Conclusion

When the members of the CBC Band embarked on an eighteen-month world tour in 1973, they did not realize it would be the last time they would ever see the Vietnam that they knew. The band, and the Phan siblings' lives in Vietnam, were casualties of war. Tung Linh, the guitarist, received his draft notice in 1973, and he entered boot camp for six months of training. But his mother, Hoang Thi Nga, in the role she had played his whole life, did what she could to help her son play music, which was what made him happy. She paid a handsome bribe to a high-ranking officer to secure her son's release from the army, arguing that she was old and needed him at home, and in any case, two older sons had already served in the navy.[1]

Normalcy proved elusive, as Tung Linh worried that he was constantly under police surveillance. When he drove his Honda to the market or around town and had to pass through security checkpoints, the guards always asked him why, given his young age, he was not in the army. Military officers began harassing Hoang Thi Nga because they suspected she had bought his release. Worried that the army might call for him again, his mother enlisted the help of some American and Canadian concert tour managers to organize a CBC Band world tour to get the band out of Vietnam. The promoters planned an eighteen-month tour, and the siblings figured they'd return home after it ended. Hoang Thi Nga cried when she said goodbye to her children.[2]

While the band was on the road, Saigon fell on April 30, 1975. Bich Loan and the other band members were asleep when it happened; when

---

[1] Author's interview with Bich Loan, Oct. 2017, Hattiesburg, MS.   [2] Ibid.

they woke up and heard the news, they cried. They took refuge in a Tibetan monastery and tried to figure out what to do. Their mother was still in Saigon. "We thought we'd just be on a world tour for a year or so," Bich Loan said. "We didn't think we'd never go back."[3]

They were afraid to go back. There was a picture of the band members in downtown Saigon wearing American clothing and T-shirts with the American flag emblazoned on them. The new government branded the band members criminals and placed them on a most wanted list because they had worked with Americans. The Phan siblings would later learn that their mother burned all their tapes and pictures of them with American troops, fearing retribution by the new government. They had been rock stars, but now they were refugees. In October 1975, the CBC Band entered the United States, thanks in part to a Vietnam veteran named Frank Ford, who worked in refugee resettlement after the fall of Saigon.[4]

Two or three years passed before band members could reach family still in Vietnam. In the meantime, the band had hooked up with American and Canadian concert promoters and booked some shows. After a concert in Montreal, a friend helped them call Vietnam. Over the next two decades, band members became US citizens, sponsored relatives, including their mother, to relocate to the United States, and returned to Vietnam to visit and perform. They could only do charity shows in Vietnam and donate all concert earnings to orphanages, nursing homes, and other places that serve the poor. Young Vietnamese, for whom "trước 1975" is a foreign world, are interested in the CBC Band and other singers and musicians from the era, Bich Loan said. It reflects a broader curiosity among the young about South Vietnam, especially the people and the stories that the government has erased from official histories.[5]

For as much attention historians have paid to the Vietnam War, they have written considerably little on the aftermath. Perhaps that is because it was no longer an American story, and interest in the American experience, US decision-making, and broader issues of US foreign interventions during the Cold War had motivated so much of the scholarship on the war. The Vietnamese were left to pick up the pieces of their lives, whether in Vietnam or as refugees. South Vietnamese experiences were complex and included desperate escapes, time served in reeducation camps, appointments to high government offices, and house arrest. Life went

---

[3] Ibid.   [4] Ibid.   [5] Ibid.

on after the proverbial last helicopter made its way to a US aircraft carrier in the Pacific.

For most Americans, and certainly in American popular memory, that is where the story of the Vietnam War ends. The iconic photograph of an Air America helicopter atop a Saigon apartment building (misremembered as the US Embassy) with a line of people desperate to board is burned into the public consciousness, but little is known about what happened in Saigon after that helicopter and others fled Vietnam. Those Vietnamese who were cleared to evacuate had family members who were not on the lists, and they faced tough choices amid the chaos of the final days. Tran Ngoc Ann, a US Embassy employee, placed her two young sons on a plane but stayed behind in hopes that she could leave later with her elderly parents who were still at home. Phong Xuan Nguyen, who had held a variety of posts in South Vietnam's government and had been part of the country's delegation to the Paris peace talks, was arrested in May and spent five years in a reeducation camp outside of Hanoi. Nguyen Van Phieu's crime was having been a policeman in support of the South Vietnamese government. A tribunal found him guilty of being an "officer of the old regime" and sentenced him to four years in a reeducation camp, where he met other political prisoners convicted of the "bloody crime" of siding with South Vietnam. Phieu's status limited his children's educational opportunities, and he struggled to provide for them after he was released from prison.[6] That Phieu was imprisoned rather than executed despite the fact that his having worked in law enforcement made him one of the lucky ones; others like him received death sentences.[7] Reeducation was a central part of the postwar transition to a unified Vietnam.

Jessica Nguyen was born in September of 1975 and was an infant when government officials ordered her mother and grandparents to leave their home in Da Nang and resettle in one of the New Economic Zones to farm government land. Her father, an ARVN officer, had been captured in May and sent to a reeducation camp. Her grandfather starved to death, and her mother and grandmother developed chronic health problems, although her mother persevered to take care of her four children under the age of seven. The family was relocated to the Central Highlands, and

---

[6] Orderly Departure Program (ODP) Application File for Nguyen Van Phieu – Nov. 17, 1995, Folder 20, Box 80, Families of Vietnamese Political Prisoners Association (FVPPA) Collection, The Vietnam Archive.

[7] Jacqueline Desbarats and Karl Jackson, "Political Violence: The Dark Side of Liberation," p. 8., no date, Folder 06, Box 03, Douglas Pike Collection: Other Manuscripts – Jackson-Desbarats Study, The Vietnam Archive.

then the Mekong Delta, before making a home in Ho Chi Minh City after Nguyen's father was released from prison in 1982. In 1990, the Nguyen family became eligible to emigrate to the United States via the Orderly Departure Program, and they eventually settled in Orange County, California's "Little Saigon."[8]

Even though Trinh Cong Son had been the most famous antiwar singer in Vietnam, he found himself on the wrong side of the new government. His songs called for peace, but that did not necessarily mean he supported Hanoi. After the war ended, Son spent time in a reeducation camp and on a government-owned farm. In 1978, police took him to a television station and told him to state a "self-criticism" for broadcast. Rather than obeying the command, "I sang a song about a woman going to market," Son said. Authorities then tried to make him write a self-critical article. The clever musician "did it in the form of a letter to an unknown person, in which I expressed my joy at the unification of the country."[9] Son held on to his rock-star spirit even when faced with prison or worse. Son was released from prison in 1980, and he settled into a quiet life of songwriting and painting in Ho Chi Minh City, the former Saigon, until his death in 2001.

Nguyen Huu Thai, the former Saigon student leader who met with US Embassy officers to try and explain students' desires for national independence and an end to war, was in the Presidential Palace on April 30, 1975, with NLF cadres. Over the radio airwaves at noon, Thai read the announcement that the war was over.[10] Foreign correspondents watched the events of April 1975 unfold with a mix of excitement, fear, and sadness. Some, like Tiziano Terzani, a correspondent for the German newspaper *Der Spiegel*, stayed on for months to observe the transfer of power. Representatives of the American Friends Service Committee were among the few Americans who remained in Vietnam after April 30. Claudia Krich and her husband, Keith Brinton, strolled through the streets of Saigon, mingling with ordinary Vietnamese who spoke in hopeful tones about government promises to end hunger and provide free health care. In Saigon, euphoria, fear, optimism, and disappointment marked the days and months after April 30, 1975.

[8] Author's e-mail correspondence with Jessica Nguyen, July 2013.
[9] Henry Kamm, "Vietnam Poet Sings a Song of Endurance," *New York Times*, April 4, 1993.
[10] "Nguyen Huu Thai: A Witness of April 30," April 29, 2015, https://vietnam.vnanet.vn/english/nguyen-huu-thai-a-witness-of-april-30/184004.html.

The new government rewarded some of the self-determination activists in the immediate aftermath of the conflict. Chan Tin, Huynh Tan Mam, and Ngo Ba Thanh all received political appointments and held positions in the new Vietnamese government. Chan Tin was cochair of the Central Committee of the Fatherland Front, a state-run umbrella organization of social movements. Huynh Tan Mam and Ngo Ba Thanh secured positions on the National Assembly, and Ngo Ba Thanh was on the committee that drafted Vietnam's new constitution.[11] Yet the new government authorities did not fully trust Madame Thanh, and she was subject to police surveillance.[12]

Yet even before the war ended, members of the NLF has begun to question whether Hanoi's Communist Party valued them. In 1970, Truong Nhu Tang, one of the founders of the NLF, and other NLF and PRG representatives, traveled to Cambodia to meet with Ba Cap, a Party delegate from Hanoi. The southerners were taken aback when Ba Cap received them coldly. Ba Cap was a Marxist true believer, and he made no effort to hide his disdain for the wealthy, educated elites who stood before him.[13] Party representatives continued to treat their southern allies with contempt, which eventually took the form of reeducation. In 1971, Party leadership ordered Tang and others to spend three months attending "seminars" on Marxism-Leninism. The southerners may have been revolutionaries, but they were still "bourgeoisie." Discussions during the seminars pitted Party devotees and their emphasis on the primacy of international class struggle against southern nationalists who sought independence and democracy. Marxism was not necessary for achieving national liberation and independence, Tang argued. Conversations devolved into shouting matches between doctrinaire Party members and educated southerners, many of whom had been trained in the West and had learned the art of debate in French schools.[14] The Party considered the southern revolutionaries to be its agents, not independent nationalists.

---

[11] Statement of Don Luce, Codirector, Clergy and Laity Concerned, June 21, 1977. Folder 01, Box 22, Douglas Pike Collection: Unit 06 – Democratic Republic of Vietnam, Vietnam Archive.

[12] "Situation in South Vietnam According to Refugees," Nov. 1975. Folder 11, Box 25, Douglas Pike Collection: Unit 06 – Democratic Republic of Vietnam, The Vietnam Center and Archive, Texas Tech University.

[13] Truong Nhu Tang, *A Viet Cong Memoir: An Inside Account of the Vietnam War and Its Aftermath* (New York: Vintage Books, 1986), p. 187.

[14] Ibid., p. 196.

In 1990, police arrested Chan Tin and Huynh Tan Mam and placed them under house arrest. Huynh Tan Mam's crime was writing a letter to Nguyen Van Linh, general secretary of Vietnam's Communist Party and a supporter of the doi moi reforms, calling for an expansion of democracy. Chan Tin had preached a sermon on the subject of repentance that the Party interpreted as a critique of its human rights and religious freedom record. Neither Huynh Tan Mam nor Chan Tin was brought to trial, but authorities ruled that they had violated article 82 of the criminal code, which forbade the dissemination of "anti-socialist propaganda." Chan Tin was also guilty of defying article 81, which prohibited actions or speech that caused "divisions between the religious and non-religious and separating religious followers from the people's government and social organizations." From house arrest, Chan Tin wrote to friends that he "always struggled for the people under the old regime, and it was always on their behalf that I asked the State and the Party to repent their ways."[15] Loyalty to a government or political party had never been Chan Tin's reason for speaking out against injustice, and the suppression of civil liberties did not end on April 30, 1975.

News of reeducation camps, executions, seizures of property, and other human rights violations gradually made its way out of Vietnam not long after the fall of Saigon. This posed a dilemma to US antiwar activists and those on the political left who believed the communist movement were the true nationalists and had the moral high ground in a conflict that embodied the arrogance and misguidedness of US Cold War foreign relations. On May 30, 1979, Joan Baez and eighty other signers wrote an "Open Letter to the Socialist Republic of Vietnam," which the *New York Times*, *Washington Post*, *Los Angeles Times*, and other newspapers published as a full-page ad. The letter expressed concerns about reeducation camps, the disappearances of alleged enemies of the state, and the forcing of average citizens to clear mine fields without proper training or equipment. Disappointed, the letter writers noted that "with tragic irony, the cruelty, violence, and oppression practiced by foreign powers in your country for more than a century continue today under the present regime."[16]

---

[15] General Office Files – Correspondence, Incoming – *Asia Watch*, June 11, 1991. Folder 018, Box 118, Families of Vietnamese Political Prisoners Association (FVPPA) Collection, Vietnam Archive.

[16] "A Reply to Joan Baez," no date. Folder 20, Box 01, John Donnell Collection, Vietnam Archive.

The Southeast Asia Resource Center, formerly the Indochina Resource Center, one of the organizations that had exposed Thieu-era human rights abuses, challenged the letter. Members questioned the credibility of the Vietnamese refugees and others who had described conditions in socialist Vietnam and argued that it was inaccurate to compare what the Vietnamese government was doing to its people to the destructive policies of the United States, France, and Japan.[17] In October 1975, longtime peace activist and editor of *Fellowship* magazine, Jim Forest, published an article about human rights abuses in Vietnam, and fellow antiwar activists accused him of being a CIA agent, a covert anticommunist, and a "white bourgeois American." A member of the American Friends Service Committee warned Forest that publishing the article would ruin his standing in the peace movement.[18] Disagreements within the American left over the political situation in postwar Vietnam would not be resolved quickly. For some who fought in the streets, in the press, and in international antiwar coalitions against US intervention in Vietnam, it was difficult to accept that the revolutions they supported included members who were just as brutal as the ones they had opposed. Humans are complicated like that.

From the perspective of those who had known the political repression of the Republic of Vietnam and now acknowledged the Socialist Republic of Vietnam's human rights abuses, it looked as though Vietnam had simply traded one undemocratic government for another. This was an especially sad observation because of the democratic potential of South Vietnam's vibrant, if chaotic, urban political culture. It was difficult to categorize activists such as Ngo Ba Thanh, Huynh Tan Mam, and Chan Tin, and Americans failed to see their movements as viable alternatives to the repressive military governments and the Thieu regime. Although Vietnamese agency defined the fate of Vietnam during the war years, the US presence and influence was significant in directing South Vietnamese politics. Americans lacked the will or the foresight to imagine a Vietnam forged through self-determination, even if it featured some type of communist or socialist government.

In Vietnam, it is difficult to find the remains of South Vietnam. The archival documents that remain from the government of the Republic of Vietnam are housed in an unassuming building on Le Duan Street,

---

[17] Ibid.
[18] Jim Forest, "After the War Was Over: Seeing What You'd Rather Not See," Oct. 10, 2011, http://jimandnancyforest.com/2011/10/after-the-war.

named for the Communist Party official who called for the taking of South Vietnam by force. The building sits next to a Sofitel. The official history, told in textbooks and in museums, on billboards, and through monuments, is a story of Vietnamese freedom fighters against American imperialists. There is truth in that portrayal, in the image of Vietnamese soldiers and citizens taking up arms against an impatient superpower that was eager to impose its idea of political order and control on the decolonizing world. American men, money, and materiel were major components of the war and certainly prolonged it. The United States made bad policy decisions, and the Vietnam War remains an example of the hubris and short-sightedness that has guided US foreign policy at various points since 1945.

Missing from the narrative are all the southern Vietnamese who fought for South Vietnam. South Vietnamese veterans and their families, Saigon civil servants, anticommunists, and antiwar activists are not part of Vietnam's national narrative of the war. They were on the losing side, some would say the wrong side, of the war. These perspectives live on beyond the one-dimensional official narrative. They come out in conversations with Vietnamese in the United States and in Vietnam. At a Tet festival at Mary Queen of Vietnam Catholic Church in New Orleans, James Mac-Nguyen reflected on his youth in Saigon, and he remembered becoming aware of the NLF as a teenager in the early 1970s. He wondered why NLF leaders thought he needed to be "liberated." He did not believe in their way of life, and he wondered why they were disturbing his country?[19]

As it would turn out, some of those who fought hardest to "liberate" the South would never enjoy the benefits of liberation themselves. In Ho Chi Minh City, restaurant owner Nickie Tran's family was divided over the war. Her father fought with the Viet Minh against the French, and after the First Indochina War, Hanoi authorities brought him and other southerners to the North to prepare for another war. He returned to the South to fight with the NLF. Some of Tran's uncles joined the ARVN and then fled to the United States after Saigon fell, while her parents went to universities in the Soviet Union. Now, though, this once-divided family comes together over a shared dislike of the Vietnamese government. It had promised to support NLF fighters once they won the war, but southerners are still waiting on the spoils, they argue, while Party officials and their relatives drive Bentleys and send their children

---

[19] Oral history interview with James Mac-Nguyen, Feb. 24, 2018, New Orleans, LA. West Point-Southern Miss Joint Oral History Project.

to US universities.[20] The divide between the very wealthy elites and the rest of the population remains.

The losing side is visible in a few communities in the United States in cities such as New Orleans, Houston, and Los Angeles. On some residential blocks in New Orleans East, homes fly the flag of South Vietnam, and a bakery called Dong Phuong, owned by Vietnam War refugees, sells king cakes during Mardi Gras season. When I asked a Vietnamese friend in Vietnam where to get the best pho bo, she said California. The meat is better quality, she said, but the recipes are tried-and-true Vietnamese, brought by refugees and migrants. The entertainment company Thuy Nga, headquartered in Orange County, California, produces DVDs, CDs, and the variety show, *Paris By Night*, all featuring Vietnamese music and entertainment, including "nhac truoc nam 1975" – music from before 1975. Nguyen Cao Ky's daughter, Nguyen Cao Ky Duyen, hosts the show. April 30 is a day of mourning in some of these communities, especially for the generation that fled Vietnam.

When I taught in Vietnam, my students were curious when they learned that I was researching about Viet Nam Cong Hoa – the Republic of Vietnam. They knew very little about that chapter in their national history, and they were surprised to learn that an American was studying it. After a talk I gave, a student approached me and asked about my research. He said his family had been in the NLF, but he wanted to know more about the other side. No one ever talked about it, he said. At a spa in Ho Chi Minh City, a woman who was about my age told me that he father had served in ARVN, and the family's position on the losing side still shaped their lives. She said that her family was ineligible for certain government benefits, and the government forbade her from getting a job in a state-owned industry, which was why she worked in the private sector. In the 1990s, a group of unemployed ARVN veterans in the Central Highlands city of Dalat established a motorbike tour company called Dalat Easy Riders. They capitalized on a growing tourism industry in Vietnam and their English and French language skills they honed during the war years. The losing side remains in Vietnam, part of the body politic even though excluded from official accounts of the conflict.

That the stories of South Vietnamese who supported the Saigon government, served in the RVN military, or opposed the establishment of

[20] Author's conversations with Nickie Tran, Ho Chi Minh City, Vietnam, 2013–2014.

communism as Vietnam's political and economic structure remain on the margins of, if not absent from, US and Vietnamese narratives of the war illustrates how deeply politicized the war's historiography is. The telling of the history of the conflict has been a zero-sum game in which the Vietnam War was a case study amplifying a broader critique of US foreign policy and intervention in the world. This orthodox view of the war emphasizes the actions of American policymakers, military authorities, and troops. Vietnamese actors appear fairly one-dimensional, as corrupt puppets controlled by the US State Department, romanticized revolutionaries, or a faceless mass of peasants caught in the crossfire. The orthodoxy pays little attention to Vietnamese agency, strategy, or worldview, and it does not account for the diversity of opinions in North Vietnam and South Vietnam about what an independent Vietnam should look like. Historians who are working with Vietnamese sources are leading us to a reckoning of the complexity of Vietnamese attitudes about their country's future, the politics involved, the impact of international opinion on how the conflict played out, and the nature of the violence perpetrated against Vietnamese civilians. The question of who had the right to determine Vietnam's future was a fundamental part of the broader conflict that involved the governments in Saigon and Hanoi, the NLF, and Vietnamese and foreign citizens across the political spectrum.

After the *New York Times* published an article I wrote about NLF terrorism, an angry reader e-mailed me asking why I would write about that topic. The scale of violence and destruction the United States perpetrated in Vietnam was so much larger, the reader argued, that there is no point in examining NLF atrocities. As a historian who is interested in how human motivations and choices have driven history, I found this question at once unbelievable and typical. Why would we *not* want to try and fully understand the multitude of perspectives involved in this complicated event in global history? For all the ink that writers have spilled explaining the mindsets and decision-making processes of US political and military leaders and the various reactions of American citizens to US intervention in Vietnam, scholars have spent considerably less time trying to understand Vietnamese agency and outlook. Making the Vietnam War only or primarily an American issue through selective coverage is as much an act of hubris as US policymaking regarding Vietnam was.

Yet the reader's comment was unsurprising because it very clearly reflected the orthodox approach to Vietnam War history. In addition to the argument that the immorality of US intervention in Vietnam precludes any criticism of Vietnamese-inflicted violence, another line of thinking in the orthodox school asserts that there was never enough citizen support for the Saigon government, so incorporating NLF atrocities or anticommunist voices will not add anything to the story. But alternative perspectives do enhance the narrative. They illustrate that there was not a consensus among Vietnamese about how their nation should look. They highlight Americans' inability or unwillingness to trust their Vietnamese allies, and they force us to ask additional questions about why. They remind us how messy and difficult it is to implement democracy, and that in democracy's dynamic chaos, attitudes and allegiances can change, making it challenging for outsiders to assign monolithic political perspectives to particular groups.

The Vietnam War remains the touchstone to which policy analysts look when trying to understand twenty-first-century US interventions in Afghanistan and Iraq, and so it is not enough to rehash the same narrative without broadening it to include more South Vietnamese as legitimate actors in the conflict. It is not enough simply to ask whether the United States should have been in Vietnam. The United States went there and embarked on a long, costly, and devastating war, that much we know. To fully understand the consequences of US intervention, we must also ask what Americans understood about Vietnam, especially their allies, why US Embassy officers and others on the ground in Vietnam perceived and interacted with South Vietnamese in certain ways, what various political perspectives existed in South Vietnam throughout the course of the war, and what influenced regional and international public opinion on the Vietnam question. It is in the search for answers to these questions that we may achieve a deeper understanding of why US-led nation building stalls and fails.

Select Bibliography

ARCHIVES

Vietnam

- National Archives II, Ho Chi Minh City, Vietnam (Trung Tâm Lưu Trữ Quốc Gia II)
- General Sciences Library (formerly the National Library of the Republic of Vietnam), Ho Chi Minh City, Vietnam (Thư Viện Khoa Học Tổng Hợp)

United States

- National Archives and Records Administration, College Park, Maryland
- The Vietnam Center and Archive, Texas Tech University, Lubbock, Texas

PUBLISHED SOURCES

Appy, Christian. *American Reckoning: The Vietnam War and Our National Identity*. New York: Penguin Books, 2016.

Asselin, Pierre. *A Bitter Peace: Washington, Hanoi, and the Making of the Paris Agreement*. Chapel Hill: University of North Carolina Press, 2002.

Hanoi's Road to the Vietnam War, 1954–1965. Berkeley: University of California Press, 2015.

Vietnam's American War: A History. New York: Cambridge University Press, 2018.

Bartimus, Tad. *War Torn: Stories of War from the Women Reporters Who Covered Vietnam*. New York: Random House, 2002.

Blackburn, Robert M. *Mercenaries and Lyndon Johnson's "More Flags": The Hiring of Korean, Filipino, and Thai Soldiers in the Vietnam War*. Jefferson, NC: McFarland, 1994.

Bradley, Mark Philip. *Vietnam at War*. New York: Oxford University Press, 2009.

Brigham, Robert K. *Guerrilla Diplomacy: The NLF's Foreign Relations and the Viet Nam War*. Ithaca, NY: Cornell University Press, 1999.

ARVN: Life and Death in the South Vietnamese Army. Lawrence: University Press of Kansas, 2006.

Brown, Timothy Scott. "The Sixties in the City: Avant-Gardes and Urban Rebels in New York, London, and West Berlin," *Journal of Social History*, Vol. 46, No. 4 (Summer 2013) 817–842.

Catton, Philip. *Diem's Final Failure: Prelude to America's War in Vietnam*. Lawrence: University Press of Kansas, 2003.

Celis, Leila. "The Legacy of Liberation Theology in Colombia: The Defense of Life and Territory," *Latin American Perspectives*, Vol. 43, No. 3 (May 2016) 69–84.

Chapman, Jessica. *Cauldron of Resistance: Ngo Dinh Diem, the United States, and 1950s Southern Vietnam*. Ithaca, NY: Cornell University Press, 2013.

Chavez, Joaquin M. "Catholic Action, the Second Vatican Council, and the Emergence of the New Left in El Salvador, 1950–1975," *The Americas*, Vol. 70, No. 3 (Jan. 2014) 459–487.

Davis, Belinda. "What's Left? Popular Political Participation in Postwar Europe," *American Historical Review*, Vol. 113, No. 2 (April 2008) 363–390.

DeBenedetti, Charles. *An American Ordeal: The Antiwar Movement of the Vietnam Era*. Syracuse, NY: Syracuse University Press, 1990.

Duiker, William J. *Vietnam: Revolution in Transition*. Boulder, CO: Westview Press, 1995.

The Communist Road to Power in Vietnam. Boulder, CO: Westview Press, 1996.

Dunn, Christopher. "Desbunde and Its Discontents: Counterculture and Authoritarian Modernization in Brazil, 1968–1974," *The Americas*, Vol. 70, No. 3 (Jan. 2014) 429–458.

Elliott, Duong Van Mai. *The Sacred Willow: Four Generations in the Life of a Vietnamese Family*. New York: Oxford University Press, 1999.

RAND in Southeast Asia: A History of the Vietnam War Era. Santa Monica, CA: RAND Corporation, 2010.

Ellis, Sylvia. *Britain, America, and the Vietnam War*. Westport, CT: Praeger, 2004.

Fitzgerald, Francis. *Fire in the Lake: The Vietnamese and the Americans in Vietnam*. Boston: Back Bay Books, 2002.

Foley, Michael Stewart. *Confronting the War Machine: Draft Resistance during the Vietnam War*. Chapel Hill: University of North Carolina Press, 2003.

French, Jan Hoffman. "A Tale of Two Priests and Two Struggles: Liberation Theology from Dictatorship to Democracy in the Brazilian Northeast," *The Americas*, Vol. 63, No. 3 (Jan. 2007) 409–443.

Geary, Daniel. "'Becoming International Again': C. Wright Mills and the Emergence of a Global New Left, 1956–1962," *The Journal of American History*, Vol. 95, No. 3 (Dec. 2008) 710–736.

Gettig, Eric. "'Trouble Ahead in Afro-Asia': The United States, the Second Bandung Conference, and the Struggle for the Third World, 1964–1965," *Diplomatic History*, Vol. 39, No. 1 (Jan. 2015) 126–156.

Ginat, Rami. *Egypt's Incomplete Revolution: Lutfi al-Khuli and Nasser's Socialism in the 1960s*. London: Frank Cass & Co. Ltd., 1997.

Gould, Jeffrey L. "Solidarity under Siege: The Latin American Left, 1968," *American Historical Review*, Vol. 114, No. 2 (April 2009) 348–375.

Halberstam, David. *The Best and the Brightest*. New York: Ballantine Books, 1993.

Hansen, Peter. "Bac Di Cu: Catholic Refugees from the North of Vietnam, and Their Role in the Southern Republic, 1954–1959," *Journal of Vietnamese Studies*, Vol. 4, No. 3 (Fall 2009) 173–211.

Herring, George C. *America's Longest War: The United States and Vietnam, 1950–1975*. New York: McGraw-Hill, 2001.

Hue Tam Ho Tai, *Radicalism and the Origins of the Vietnamese Revolution*. Cambridge, MA: Harvard University Press, 1992.

Hunt, David. *Vietnam's Southern Revolution: From Peasant Insurrection to Total War*. Amherst: University of Massachusetts Press, 2008.

Hunt, Michael. *Lyndon Johnson's War: America's Cold War Crusade in Vietnam, 1945–1968*. New York: Hill and Wang, 1997.

Jacobs, Seth. *America's Miracle Man in Vietnam: Ngo Dinh Diem, Religion, Race, and U.S. Intervention in Southeast Asia, 1950–1957*. Durham, NC: Duke University Press, 2005.

Jamieson, Neil. *Understanding Vietnam*. Berkeley: University of California Press, 1995.

Kaiser, David. *American Tragedy: Kennedy, Johnson, and the Origins of the Vietnam War*. Cambridge, MA: Belknap Press, 2002.

Karnow, Stanley. *Vietnam: A History*. New York: Penguin Books, 1997.

Kolko, Gabriel. *Anatomy of a War: Vietnam, the United States, and the Modern Historical Experience*. New York: The New Press, 1994.

Lam Quang Thi. *The Twenty-Five Year Century: A South Vietnamese General Remembers the Indochina War to the Fall of Saigon*. Denton, TX: University of North Texas Press, 2001.

Lawrence, Mark Atwood. *The Vietnam War: A Concise International History*. New York: Oxford University Press, 2010.

Lessard, Micheline. "More than Half the Sky: Vietnamese Women and Anti-French Political Activism, 1858–1945," *Vietnam and the West: New Approaches*, Wynn Wilcox, ed. Ithaca, NY: Cornell University Press, 2010.

Lewy, Guenter. *America in Vietnam*. New York: Oxford University Press, 1978.

Logevall, Fredrik. *Choosing War: The Lost Chance for Peace and the Escalation of the War in Vietnam*. Berkeley: University of California Press, 2001.

Lucks, Daniel S. *Selma to Saigon: The Civil Rights Movement and the Vietnam War*. Lexington: University Press of Kentucky, 2016.

Mackin, Robert Sean. "Liberation Theology: The Radicalization of Social Catholic Movements," *Politics, Religion & Ideology*, Vol. 13, No. 3 (Sep. 2012) 333–351.

Manzano, Valeria. "'Rock Nacional' and Revolutionary Politics: The Making of a Youth Culture of Contestation in Argentina, 1966–1976," *The Americas*, Vol. 70, No. 3 (Jan. 2014) 393–427.

Maraniss, David. *They Marched into Sunlight: War and Peace, Vietnam and America, October 1967*. New York: Simon & Schuster, 2004.

Marr, David G. *Vietnamese Anticolonialism, 1885–1925*. Berkeley: University of California Press, 1971.

    Vietnamese Tradition on Trial, 1920–1945. Berkeley: University of California Press, 1984.

    Vietnam 1945: The Quest for Power. Berkeley: University of California Press, 1997.

    Vietnam: State, War, and Revolution, 1945–1946. Berkeley: University of California Press, 2013.

Markarian, Vania. "To the Beat of 'the Walrus': Uruguayan Communists and Youth Culture in the Global Sixties," *The Americas*, Vol. 70, No. 3 (Jan. 2014) 363–392.

Masur, Matthew. "Exhibiting Signs of Resistance: South Vietnam's Struggle for Legitimacy, 1954–1960," *Diplomatic History*, Vol. 33, No. 2 (April 2009) 293–313.

McMaster, H. R. *Dereliction of Duty: Johnson, McNamara, the Joint Chiefs of Staff, and the Lies That Led to Vietnam*. New York: Harper Perennial, 1998.

Miller, Edward. "Vision, Power, and Agency: The Ascent of Ngo Dinh Diem, 1945–1954," *Making Sense of the Vietnam Wars: Local, National, and Transnational Perspectives*, Mark Philip Bradley and Marilyn B. Young, eds. New York: Oxford University Press, 2008.

    Misalliance: Ngo Dinh Diem, the United States, and the Fate of South Vietnam. Cambridge, MA: Harvard University Press, 2013.

Ngo Vinh Long. "Legacies Foretold: Excavating the Roots of Postwar Viet Nam," *Four Decades On: Vietnam, the United States, and the Legacies of the Second Indochina War*, Scott Laderman and Edwin A. Martini, eds. Durham, NC: Duke University Press, 2013.

Nguyen, Lien-Hang T. "Cold War Contradictions: Toward an International History of the Second Indochina War, 1969–1973, *Making Sense of the Vietnam Wars: Local, National, and Transnational Perspectives*, Mark Philip Bradley and Marilyn B. Young, eds. New York: Oxford University Press, 2008.

Nguyen, Nathalie Huynh Chau. *South Vietnamese Soldiers: Memories of the Vietnam War and After*. Santa Barbara, CA: Praeger, 2016.

Nguyen-Marshall, Van. "Tools of Empire? Vietnamese Catholics in South Vietnam," *The Journal of the Canadian Historical Association*, Vol. 20, No. 2 (2009) 138–159.

    "Student Activism in Time of War Youth in the Republic of Vietnam, 1960s–1970s," *Journal of Vietnamese Studies*, Vol. 10, No. 2 (Spring 2015) 43–81.

Nguyen-Marshall, Van, Lisa B. Welch Drummond, and Danièle Bélanger eds., *The Reinvention of Distinction: Modernity and the Middle Class in Urban Vietnam*. Singapore: Springer-Singapore National University Press, 2012.

Ott, Marvin. "Malaysia: The Search for Solidarity and Security," *Asian Survey*, Vol. 8, No. 2 (Feb. 1968) 127–132.

Pike, Douglas. *War, Peace, and the Viet Cong*. Cambridge, MA: MIT Press, 1969.

Quinn-Judge, Sophie. "The Search for a Third Force in Vietnam: From the Quiet American to the Paris Peace Agreement," *Vietnam and the West: New Approaches*, Wynn Wilcox, ed. Ithaca, NY: Cornell University Press, 2010.

  The Third Force in the Vietnam War: The Elusive Search for Peace, 1954–1975. London: I. B. Taurus, 2017.

Rakove, Robert B. *Kennedy, Johnson, and the Non-Aligned World*. New York, Cambridge University Press: 2012.

Roberts, Philip. "Passive Revolution in Brazil: Struggles over Hegemony, Religion, and Development, 1964–2007," *Third World Quarterly*, Vol. 36, No. 9 (2015) 1663–1681.

Rottman, Gordon L. *Army of the Republic of Vietnam, 1955–1975*. Oxford: Osprey Publishing, 2010.

Schneider, Gregory L. *Cadres for Conservatism: Young Americans for Freedom and the Rise of the Contemporary Right*. New York: New York University Press, 1999.

Sheehan, Neil. *A Bright Shining Lie: John Paul Vann and America in Vietnam*. New York: Vintage, 1989.

Sodhy, Pamela. "The Malaysian Connection in the Vietnam War," *Contemporary Southeast Asia*, Vol. 9, No. 1 (June 1987) 38–53.

  "Malaysian-American Relations during Indonesia's Confrontation against Malaysia, 1963–66," *Journal of Southeast Asian Studies*, Vol. 19, No. 1 (March 1988) 111–136.

Steinman, Ron. *Women in Vietnam: The Oral History*. New York: TV Books, 2000.

Stewart, Geoffrey C. *Vietnam's Lost Revolution: Ngo Dinh Diem's Failure to Build an Independent Nation, 1955–1963*. New York: Cambridge University Press, 2016.

Stoler, Ann Laura. "Intimidations of Empire: Predicaments of the Tactile and Unseen," *Haunted by Empire: Geographies of Intimacy in North American History*, Ann Laura Stoler, ed. Durham, NC: Duke University Press, 2006.

Stur, Heather Marie. *Beyond Combat: Women and Gender in the Vietnam War Era*. New York: Cambridge University Press, 2011.

Suri, Jeremi. *Power and Protest: Global Revolution and the Rise of Détente*. Cambridge, MA: Harvard University Press, 2005.

Topmiller, Robert J. *The Lotus Unleashed: The Buddhist Peace Movement in South Vietnam, 1964–1966*. Lexington: University Press of Kentucky, 2002.

Tran, Nu-Anh. "South Vietnamese Identity, American Intervention and the Newspaper *Chính Luận* [Political Discussion], 1965–1969." *Journal of Vietnamese Studies*, Vol. 1, No. 1–2 (Feb./Aug. 2006) 169–209.

  "Contested Identities: Nationalism in the Republic of Vietnam, 1954–1963," Ph.D. diss., University of California, Berkeley, 2013.

Truong Nhu Tang. *A Viet Cong Memoir: An Inside Account of the Vietnam War and Its Aftermath*. New York: Vintage Books, 1986.

Varon, Jeremy. *Bringing the War Home: The Weather Underground, the Red Army Faction, and Revolutionary Violence in the Sixties and Seventies.* Berkeley: University of California Press, 2004.

Wiest, Andrew. *Vietnam's Forgotten Army: Heroism and Betrayal in the ARVN.* New York: New York University Press, 2007.

Williams, Marion L. *My Tour in Vietnam: A Burlesque Shocker.* New York: Vantage Press, 1970.

Young, Marilyn. *The Vietnam Wars, 1945–1990.* New York: HarperCollins, 1991.

Index